A STRANGER IN THE VILLAGE

A STRANGER IN THE VILLAGE

Two Centuries of African-American Travel Writing

Edited by Farah J. Griffin
and Cheryl J. Fish

Beacon Press

Boston

B E A C O N   P R E S S
Boston, Massachusetts
www.beacon.org

Beacon Press books
are published under the auspices of
the Unitarian Universalist Association of Congregations.

22 21 20 19   8 7 6 5 4 3

This book is printed on recycled acid-free paper that contains at least 20
percent postconsumer waste and meets the uncoated paper ANSI/NISO
specifications for performance as revised in 1992.

Text design by Margaret M. Wagner

Library of Congress Cataloging-in-Publication Data

A stranger in the village: two centuries of African-American travel
writing / edited by Farah J. Griffin and Cheryl J. Fish.
p.   cm.
Includes bibliographical references.
ISBN 0-8070-7120-X (cloth)
ISBN 0-8070-7121-8 (paper)
1. United States—Description and travel.   2. Afro-Americans—
Travel—History—Sources.   3. Travelers' writings, American—Afro-
American authors.   I. Griffin. Farah Jasmine.   II. Fish, Cheryl J.
E161.5.S77   1998
910'.8996073—dc21   98-5265

No road whatever will lead Americans back to the simplicity of this European village where white men still have the luxury of looking on me as a stranger. . . . This world is white no longer, and it will never be white again.

— J A M E S   B A L D W I N

"A Stranger in the Village," 1955

CONTENTS

CONTENTS

PART II

3. Africa

CONTENTS

PART III

6. TRUTH SEEKERS: STATESMEN, SCHOLARS AND JOURNALISTS (FROM 1930 TO THE CIVIL RIGHTS ERA)

7. VISITORS, TOURISTS, AND "OTHERS"

INTRODUCTION

James Baldwin's astute utterance that "this world is white no longer, and it will never be white again," proves to have been prophetic, for as the selections included in this book demonstrate, there are few places where African Americans have not ventured. Although Baldwin has a well-earned reputation as a prophet, here he is also a historian: For over two centuries black travelers have journeyed to the seven continents and beyond. And, as is the case with Baldwin's classic essay, from which the title of this collection is taken, the African-American traveler has often found herself to be a "stranger in the village." This is true even when the inhabitants of the village share skin color and ancestral lineage with the African-American visitor.

Much of the black experience in the new world is characterized by migration, mobility, and travel, and much attention has been paid to acts of forced migration, such as the Middle Passage and the international slave trade. In the United States, significant black migrations took place in post–Civil War wanderings by freedmen in search of kinfolk, employment, and the exodus to Kansas and Oklahoma; in the first half of the twentieth century, many blacks relocated from the South to urban centers in the North, Midwest, and West.

Although the slave experience is central to the literature of the African diaspora, this book takes as its focus narratives of journeys by African Americans who wrote about their experiences as tourists, emigrants, expatriates, sailors, educators, missionaries, philanthropists, artists, and leaders of political or nationalistic movements.

African-American mobility is often connected to the impulse for increased opportunities and the desire to find a home or homeland as well as for the purpose of pilgrimage, exile, and pleasure; thus, it is both unique and typical of the urge that many people have had throughout history in the quest for improvement and the claim for new dwelling places.

As a tradition, then, African-American travel must be looked at in the context of the genre of travel writing and the particular occasions and historical time frame that led each writer to take a journey and record his or her experience of it. The narratives included here present only a partial scope of primary accounts written by African Americans that include both black Atlantic traditions (the Americas, Africa, and Europe) and others from outside this tradition. We have selected some writings by well-known African-American artists, intellectuals, and political activists as well as entries by less well known (but not necessarily less important) travelers. The genres included in our definition of "travel narrative" include autobiographical materials and selections from books, pamphlets, personal letters, notes, diaries, dispatches, travel guides, official reports, lectures, and ethnographies. The genre of travel writing is blessed with a hybridity that incorporates and employs many other sources, including polemics, manifestos, oratory, anthropology, poetry, letter writing, maps, and fiction. The selections included here vary greatly in style, length, and purpose. The specific contexts are briefly explained in introductions to each geographical or thematic section and in each author's biographical note.

This book is intended to make us rethink old or limited definitions of African-American agency and narrative voice. The literature of the journeys of mobile African Americans and others within the African diaspora is only beginning to receive significant attention by scholars. The recent publication of the *Norton Anthology of African American Literature* and of *Call and Response: The Riverside Anthology of the African American Literary Tradition* is a landmark in terms of the widespread institutionalization of African-American literature; yet, because of its hybridity, the travel narrative tends to fall between the cracks or get classified as autobiography, which may fail to account for the significance of mobility and its relationship to subjectivity. Furthermore, in the growing body of primary and secondary texts on the literature of travel, very little attention has been given specifically to African-American or black travelers.[1] There has been a tradi-

---

[1] Notable exceptions include Mary G. Mason, "Travel as Metaphor and Reality in Afro-American Women's Autobiography, 1850–1972," *Black American Literature Forum* 24, no. 2 (summer 1990): 337–55; John C. Gruesser, "Afro-American Travel Literature and Africanist Discourse," *Black American Literature Forum* 24, no. 1 (Spring 1990): 5–20; selections from Carla L. Peterson, *"Doers of the Word": African American Women Speakers and Writers of the North, 1830–1880* (New York: Oxford University Press, 1995); Cheryl Fish, "Voices of Restless (Dis)Continuity: The Significance of Travel for Free Black Women in the Antebellum Americas," *Women's Studies* 26, no. 5 (summer 1997): 475–95; Paul Gilroy, *The Black Atlantic: Modernity and Double Consciousness* (Cambridge: Harvard University Press, 1993); Michael Cohn and Michael K. Platzer,

tion of direct and indirect discourse on this topic: For example, in 1842, Charles Lenox Remond, a leading orator and abolitionist, spoke before legislators on "The Rights of Colored Citizens in Traveling," explaining that "the treatment to which colored Americans are exposed in their own country finds a counterpart in no other; and I am free to declare that in the course of nineteen months' traveling in England, Ireland, and Scotland, I was received, treated and recognized . . . without any regard to my complexion" (quoted in Woodson, 126). We hope this book creates a space for much more work to be done in this promising field. The narratives included here will reveal to readers a complex range of racial and national identities, unfixing and relocating narrow or set notions of black subjectivity.

Our intention is for readers to discover commonalities (as well as differences) in the journeys represented here and to realize that blacks drew on resources from a number of communities, sometimes crossing racial and national boundaries to accomplish goals at home and abroad.

To help facilitate this discovery, we have organized selections into four major groupings: Adventurers and Missionaries; specific destinations where African Americans have historically traveled because of their reputation amongst blacks as a place where they will be free of racial limitations; Truthseekers: Statesmen, Scholars, and Journalists; and Visitors, Tourists, and "Others." Within these sections, readers will encounter travelers, especially those in the nineteenth century, who link travel with benevolent and missionary work. The antebellum narratives encourage us to redefine notions of freedom and slavery: Some of the travelers are free persons going to slave territory and, as such, endangering their free status; others are former or fugitive slaves traveling to free countries. In the pre–Civil War period, black travelers constantly call attention to the hypocrisy of American democracy and seek alternative homelands where justice and "redemption" of the African race can be found.

During and immediately following Reconstruction, when lynching and other backlash policies made advancement difficult, the quest for alternative homelands once again seemed like a significant survival tactic. Many of the women travelers in this collection link travel with freedom from

Black Men of the Sea (New York: Dodd, Mead, 1978). Jeffrey Bolster, *Black Jacks: African American Seamen in the Age of Sail* (Cambridge: Harvard University Press, 1997). William W. Stowe examines William Wells Brown and David F. Dorr in chapter 4 of *Going Abroad: European Travel in Nineteenth Century American Culture* (Princeton, N.J.: Princeton University Press, 1994).

narrow definitions of womanhood; they achieve this sense of liberation through religious and educational outreach and artistic self-expression.

We also hope to show the relationship between traveling African Americans and specific cities or countries over time. In the nineteenth and twentieth centuries, Russia remained a fascinating destination for a few exceptional American blacks who saw it as a society without color-based prejudice and one that provided a close-up look at the notion of class, whether one noted the stark difference between tsars and serfs or celebrated or questioned the ideals of the classless communist state. France has long been a favored destination of African-American tourists and expatriates since the nineteenth century as well. It was often embraced by blacks as a welcoming place; nevertheless, for many black travelers, France was also the place where they encountered others from the African diaspora, where they gained a sense of themselves in relation to blacks in Africa and the Caribbean. African countries, especially Ghana, are places where African-American travelers have ventured in search of a home place or in hopes of engaging in the project of nation building.

These regional sections also reveal the impact of gender and sexuality on experiences of travel. Although the Russians of Audre Lorde's *Notes from a Trip to Russia* have encountered black male travelers, performers, and students, they were not as familiar with black women.

Although much has changed in the twentieth century, African Americans are still able to highlight contradictions in America's claims of equality and democracy from abroad. Nonetheless, these travelers often find that in spite of their critiques of the land of their birth, they are made to feel their sense of being American on foreign soil. With classical educations and a fairly elite status within African-American communities, many of the travelers/observers included here tend to reproduce at least some values of Western superiority despite a desire to challenge white supremacy and classist, nationalist, or gendered barriers. This contradiction reminds us that when African-American travelers enter into the "contact zone" and confront otherness, they take their values and sense of being American with them wherever they go. As Eddy L. Harris writes, illustrating his sense of what W. E. B. Du Bois called "double consciousness": "I am American. And I am black. I live and travel with two cultural passports, the one very much stamped with European culture and sensibilities . . . the other was issued from the uniquely black experience . . . we are an American people, products of a new culture and defined by it" (*Native Stranger*, 28–29).

For others, travel, especially to Africa, causes them to overcome ambivalence and become lifelong advocates of the land of their ancestry. For instance, Sylvia Boone, in *West African Travels*, seeks to counter negative perceptions of African history, cultures, and peoples. Thus, travel today, as in the past, has the power to cleanse, reinforce, enlighten, and transform the lives of many who venture beyond home.

Most of the travelers included in this collection are exceptional human beings who often overcame obstacles that were based on racial discrimination; in addition, they may have faced class, gender, and institutional barriers to advancement. Perhaps it is not surprising, then, that many of the writers included here either knew each other or shared similar mentors, communities, and experiences. For instance, Paul Cuffe and Alexander Crummell were both influenced by the Reverend Peter Williams, who spoke at Cuffe's funeral and influenced young Crummell; Martin Delany visited Crummell when he stopped in Liberia en route to Nigeria; William Wells Brown visited Crummell in Cambridge, England, when the latter studied there; Harry Dean studied with Fanny Jackson Coppin at the Institute of Colored Youth in Philadelphia; and Delany visited the young Dean's home when he was a major in the Civil War. Of course, Du Bois and Booker T. Washington were contemporaries and adversaries. The former was also a close colleague of Jessie Fauset, who befriended younger artists Langston Hughes and Gwendolyn Bennett. In short, if these individuals were strangers in the lands they visited, they certainly were not to each other. With this volume they also fulfill Baldwin's prophecy: Indeed, "the world will never be white again."

CJF and FJG
New York and Philadelphia, 1998

A note on the text: In most cases, we have retained each author's original style and spelling; editors' footnotes are numbered while authors' footnotes are indicated by symbols.

PART I

1

ADVENTURERS

Historically, the "heroic" adventurer has always assigned a positive value to travel; the risks and uncertainties of such endeavors were thought to be worth it for the territorial gains and social mobility. In addition, there was the cleansing effect or psychic growth that one experienced after surviving danger. "The association of mobility with autonomy, of departure with freedom . . . has become a constituent element of modern Western culture" (Leed, 49). In narratives that focus on heroic adventure, exploration, and life on the Western frontier of the United States, we see increased emphasis on the sensational. By the nineteenth century, first-person accounts as well as fiction concerning shipwrecks, mutinies, captivities, and life among exotic natives at home and on foreign shores had become popular with the reading public, which benefitted from the growth of mass print culture (Pratt, 86). The narrators included in this section are likely to emphasize how they became the heroic survivors of their own adventure and to emphasize their race in a double-edged manner as both a barrier to success and a force that motivated it.

The African-American contribution to the settlement of the American West is one that has largely been erased by popular culture — "in westerns or novels, the settlers, cowboys and cavalrymen . . . always looked something like Gary Cooper or John Wayne" (Katz, i) — but that significant history is being recuperated. James Beckwourth and Nat Love, black cowboys who rode the Western range, wrote narratives of their lives that distinguish them from the many African Americans who did not leave written accounts of their contributions. Both men weave colorful tales of frontier life, of heroic survival in multiple confrontations and gunfights with Native Americans and periods of captivity with tribes. Beckwourth minimalizes his racial heritage while Love proudly proclaims it. Thomas Detter, a frontier businessman, gold miner, early civil rights leader, and writer, points out the racial discrimination in Idaho territory while acknowledging the broader range of treatment he received during his travels through northwestern territories: ". . . wherever I have met gentlemen, they have always treated me as a man, and not as a thing." For many African Americans, the West offered more freedom and a chance for increased prosperity; blacks comprised an estimated one percent of gold rush prospectors, but in 1855 African Americans in California reportedly had property worth more than $3.6 million (Foster, introduction to Detter, ix).

As a female adventurer who traveled alone to the Panamanian frontier during the height of California gold rush fever and later established herself as a proprietor and doctress at the Crimean War front, Mary Seacole offers a different model from her male counterparts. She constantly justifies her love of adventure and brilliantly uses irony to mediate the pleasures and the pathos of war and empire in an effort to, in her words, "become a Crimean heroine" (Fish, *Going Mobile*, 100). Seacole must distinguish herself from the "camp followers" and prostitutes in both locations and feels a need to emphasize that it is not vanity or a lack of femininity that draws her there; rather, "mother" Seacole explains how she loves to serve others in need. Today's reader can marvel at how she successfully negotiates a narrative strategy that would not threaten her English readers yet displays her pleasure at surviving and thriving in the face of many obstacles. Unfortunately, many of the African American women whose names we might add to this list of explorers and adventurers did not leave any written documentation of their travels. Among these are women such as Biddy Mason, who, after migrating to California in 1848 during the California Gold Rush, would later become a wealthy philanthropist, Stagecoach Mary, who delivered the U.S. mail throughout the West, and Bessie Coleman, the first African American woman to receive a pilot's license. We have paid homage to all these women explorers and adventurers by placing Coleman's photograph on the cover of this collection.

Life aboard ship provided African-American men with many opportunities and economic privileges unavailable on land. Sailing "conveyed a distinctive identity separate from common laborers. Seamen boasted to provincial acquaintances of their worldly travels and exotic encounters . . . they valued pugilism and pluck . . ." (Bolster, "Every Inch a Man," 154).

Thus, Harry Dean's narrative of life aboard *The Pedro Gorino* takes him "to the ends of the world," where he meets unforgettable characters, such as the Texas cowboy in Cape Town during the Boer War.

Taking exploration to the world's frontier of ice and mystery, Matthew Henson was one of the party of Robert Peary's 1909 expedition to the North Pole. He expressed his joy and patriotism when the American flag was planted in the ice of the pole; he contextualized it as a moment in African-American history linked to other landmarks, such as the building of the pyramids and the discovery of the New World. "Another world's accomplishment was done . . . and as in the past, from the beginning of history, wherever the world's work was done by a white man, he had been accompanied by a colored man . . ."

JAMES P. BECKWOURTH

James P. Beckwourth was born in Virginia around 1789 to a slave mother and a white Revolutionary War officer, although he fails to mention his mother or to refer to an African-American identity in his narrative *The Life and Adventures of James P. Beckwourth, Mountaineer, Scout and Pioneer and Chief of the Crow Nation of Indians*, written from dictation by T. D. Bonner and published in 1856. Beckwourth and his family went to St. Louis, Missouri, where as a young man he was a blacksmith's apprentice but was soon overcome by a desire to travel. He went first to New Orleans, then signed on as a scout or servant with the Rocky Mountain Fur Company, during which time he first encountered hostile Native American tribes and forbidding mountain passes in the Rocky Mountains.

In 1825 Beckwourth was adopted as a long-lost son by the Crows, a migratory tribe with excellent riding skills. In his narrative he tells how he became celebrated as a fearless warrior who led slaughters against the Crows' enemy tribes: the Blackfeet and the Cheyenne. His ability to communicate in English and to trade with whites was also important to the Crow. He earned the names "Bloody Arm" (red with the blood of his foe) and "Enemy of Horses" (for prowess in stealing horses), both of which bestowed honor. Beckwourth was eventually made a chief and had many Native American wives, according to the narrative.

Beckwourth's narrative is thought to be part truth, part myth, like many of the early Western travel and exploration accounts; but it is one of the rare texts of the Western frontier by an African American.

After leaving the Crow, Beckwourth served as an army scout during the third Seminole war in Florida and had a ranch near Marysville, California. In 1850 he discovered a passage through the Sierra Nevada Mountains in California that is now known as Beckwourth's Pass.

f r o m
The Life and Adventures of James P. Beckwourth, Mountaineer, Scout and Pioneer and Chief of the Crow Nation of Indians (1856)

Bidding adieu to all my friends, I proceeded to the boat and went on board. The object for which the boat was dispatched up the Fever River was to make a treaty with the Sac Indians, to gain their consent to our working the mines, at that time in their possession. The expedition was strictly of a pacific character, and was led by Colonel R. M. Johnson. A brother of the colonel's accompanied us, and several other gentlemen went in the boat as passengers.

The expedition consisted of from six to eight boats, carrying probably about one hundred men. The party in our boat numbered some eight or ten men, among whom were Colonel Johnson, his son Darwin Johnson, Messrs. January, Simmes, Kennerley, and others, whose names have escaped me. I engaged in the capacity of hunter to the party.

We pushed off, and after a slow and tedious trip of about twenty days, arrived at our place of destination (Galena of the present day). We found Indians in great numbers awaiting our disembarkation, who were already acquainted with the object of our expedition. The two tribes, Sacs and Foxes, received us peaceably, but, being all armed, they presented a very formidable appearance. There was a considerable force of United States troops quartered in that region, under the command of Colonel Morgan, stationed in detachments at Prairie du Chien, Rock Island, St. Peter's, and Des Moines.

After nine days' parleying, a treaty was effected with them, and ratified by the signatures of the contracting parties. On the part of the Indians, it was signed by Black Thunder, Yellow, Bank, and Keokuk (father to the Keokuk who figures in the Black Hawk war). On the part of the United States, Colonels Morgan and Johnson attached their signatures. This negotiation concluded, the mines were then first opened for civilized enterprise.

During the settlement of the preliminaries of the treaty, there was great difficulty with the Indians, and it was necessary for each man of our party to be on his guard against any hostile attempts of the former, who were all armed to the teeth. On the distribution of presents, which followed the conclusion of the treaty, consisting of casks of whisky, guns, gunpowder, knives, blankets, &c., there was a general time of rejoicing. Pow-wows, drinking, and dancing diversified the time, and a few fights were indulged in as a sequel to the entertainment.

The Indians soon became very friendly to me, and I was indebted to them for showing me their choicest hunting-grounds. There was abundance of game, including deer, bears, wild turkey, raccoons, and numerous other wild animals. Frequently they would accompany me on my excursions (which always proved eminently successful), thus affording me an opportunity of increasing my personal knowledge of the Indian character. I have lived among Indians in the Eastern and Western States, on the Rocky Mountains, and in California; I find their habits of living, and their religious belief, substantially uniform through all the unmingled races. All believe in the same Great Spirit; all have their prophets, their medicine men, and their soothsayers, and are alike influenced by the appearance of omens; thus leading to the belief that the original tribes throughout the entire continent, from Florida to the most northern coast, have sprung from one stock, and still retain in some degree of purity the social constitution of their primitive founders.

I remained in that region for a space of eighteen months, occupying my leisure time by working in the mines. During this time I accumulated seven hundred dollars in cash, and, feeling myself to be quite a wealthy personage, I determined upon a return home.

My visit paid, I felt a disposition to roam farther, and took passage in the steam-boat Calhoun, Captain Glover, about to descend the river to New Orleans. My stay in New Orleans lasted ten days, during which time I was sick with the yellow fever, which I contracted on the way from Natchez to New Orleans. It was midsummer, and I sought to return home, heartily regretting I had ever visited this unwholesome place. As my sickness abated, I lost no time in making my way back, and remained under my father's roof until I had in some measure recruited my forces.

Being possessed with a strong desire to see the celebrated Rocky Mountains, and the great Western wilderness so much talked about, I engaged in General Ashley's Rocky Mountain Fur Company. The company consisted of twenty-nine men, who were employed by the Fur Company as hunters and trappers.

We started on the 11th of October with horses and pack-mules. Nothing of interest occurred until we approached the Kansas village, situated on the Kansas River, when we came to a halt and encamped.

Here it was found that the company was in need of horses, and General Ashley wished for two men to volunteer to proceed to the Republican Pawnees, distant three hundred miles, where he declared we could obtain a supply. There was in our party an old and experienced mountaineer, named Moses Harris, in whom the general reposed the strictest confidence for his knowledge of the country and his familiarity with Indian life. This Harris was reputed to be a man of "great leg," and capable, from his long sojourning in the mountains, of enduring extreme privation and fatigue.

There seemed to be a great reluctance on the part of the men to undertake in such company so hazardous a journey (for it was now winter). It was also whispered in the camp that whoever gave out in an expedition with Harris received no succor from him, but was abandoned to his fate in the wilderness.

Our leader, seeing this general unwillingness, desired me to perform the journey with Harris. Being young, and feeling ambitious to distinguish myself in some important trust, I asked leave to have a word with Harris before I decided.

Harris being called, the following colloquy took place:

"Harris, I think of accompanying you on this trip."

"Very well, Jim," he replied, scrutinizing me closely, "do you think you can stand it?"

"I don't know," I answered, "but I am going to try. But I wish you to bear one thing in mind: if I should give out on the road, and you offer to leave me to perish, as you have the name of doing, if I have strength to raise and cock my rifle, I shall certainly bring you to a halt."

Harris looked me full in the eye while he replied, "Jim, you may precede me the entire way, and take your own job. If I direct the path, and give you the lead, it will be your own fault if you tire out."

"That satisfies me," I replied: "we will be off in the morning."

The following morning we prepared for departure. Each man loading himself with twenty-five pounds of provisions, besides a blanket, rifle, and ammunition each, we started on our journey. After a march of about thirty miles, I in advance, my companion bringing up the rear, Harris complained of fatigue. We halted, and Harris sat down, while I built a large, cheering fire, for the atmosphere was quite cold. We made coffee, and partook of a hearty supper, lightening our packs, as we supposed, for the following day. But while I was bringing in wood to build up the fire, I saw Harris seize his rifle in great haste, and the next moment bring down a fat turkey from a tree a few rods from the camp. Immediately reloading (for old mountaineers never suffer their guns to remain empty for one moment), while I was yet rebuilding the fire, crack went his rifle again, and down came a second turkey, so large and fat that he burst in striking the ground. We were thus secure for our next morning's meal. After we had refreshed ourselves with a hearty supper, my companion proposed that we should kill each a turkey to take with us for our next day's provision. This we both succeeded in doing, and then, having dressed the four turkeys, we folded ourselves in our blankets, and enjoyed a sound night's rest.

The following morning we breakfasted off the choicest portions of two of the turkeys, and abandoned the remainder to the wolves, who had been all night prowling round the camp for prey. We started forward as early as possible, and advanced that day about forty miles. My companion again complained of fatigue, and rested while I made a fire, procured water, and performed all the culinary work. The selected portions of last evening's turkeys, with the addition of bread and coffee, supplied us with supper and breakfast.

After a travel of ten days we arrived at the Republican Pawnee villages, when what was our consternation and dismay to find the place entirely deserted! They had removed to their winter quarters. We were entirely out of provisions, having expected to find abundance at the lodges, We searched diligently for their *caches* (places where provisions are secured), but failed in discovering any. Our only alternative was to look for game, which, so near to an Indian settlement, we were satisfied must be scarce. . . .

The same evening Captain Bridger and myself started out with our traps, intending to be gone three or four days. We followed up a small stream until it forked, when Bridger proposed that I should take one fork and he the other, and the one who had set his traps first should cross the hill which separated the two streams and rejoin the other. Thus we parted, expecting to meet again in a few hours. I continued my course up the stream in pursuit of beaver villages until I found myself among an innumerable drove of horses, and I could plainly see they were not wild ones.

The horses were guarded by several of their Indian owners, or horse-guards, as they term them, who had discovered me long before I saw them.

I could hear their signals to each other, and in a few moments I was surrounded by them, and escape was impossible. I resigned myself to my fate: if they were enemies, I knew they could kill me but once, and to attempt to defend myself would entail inevitable death. I took the chances between death and mercy; I surrendered my gun, traps, and what else I had, and was marched to camp under a strong escort of horse-guards. I felt very sure that my guards were Crows, therefore I did not feel greatly alarmed at my situation. On arriving at their village, I was ushered into the chief's lodge, where there were several old men and women, whom I conceived to be members of the family. My capture was known throughout the village in five minutes, and hundreds gathered around the lodge to get a sight of the prisoner. In the crowd were some who had talked to Greenwood a few weeks before. They at once exclaimed, "That is the lost Crow, the great brave who has killed so many of our enemies. He is our brother."

This threw the whole village into commotion; old and young were impatient to obtain a sight of the "great brave." Orders were immediately given to summon all the old women taken by the Shi-ans at the time of their captivity so many winters past, who had suffered the loss of a son at that time. The lodge was cleared for the *examining committee,* and the old women, breathless with excitement, their eyes wild and protruding, and their nostrils dilated, arrived in squads, until the lodge was filled to overflowing. I believe never was mortal gazed at with such intense and sustained interest as I was on that occasion. Arms and legs were critically scrutinized. My face next passed the ordeal; then my neck, back, breast, and all parts of my body, even down to my feet, which did not escape the examination of these anxious matrons, in their endeavors to discover some mark or peculiarity whereby to recognize their brave son.

At length one old woman, after having scanned my visage with the utmost intentness, came forward and said, "If this is my son, he has a mole over one of his eyes."

My eyelids were immediately pulled down to the utmost stretch of their elasticity, when, sure enough, she discovered a mole just over my left eye!

"Then, and oh then!" such shouts of joy as were uttered by that honest-hearted woman were seldom before heard, while all in the crowd took part in her rejoicing. It was uncultivated joy, but not the less heartfelt and intense. It was a joy which a mother can only experience when she recovers a son whom she had supposed dead in his earliest days. She has mourned him silently through weary nights and busy days for the long space of twenty years; suddenly he presents himself before her in robust manhood, and graced with the highest name an Indian can appreciate. It is but nature, either in the savage breast or civilized, that hails such a return with overwhelming joy, and feels the mother's undying affection awakened beyond all control.

All the other claimants resigning their pretensions, I was fairly carried along by the excited crowd to the lodge of the "Big Bowl," who was my father. The news of my having proved to be the son of Mrs. Big Bowl flew through the village with the speed of lightning, and, on my arrival at the paternal lodge, I found it filled with all degrees of my newly-discovered relatives, who welcomed me nearly to death. They seized me in their arms and hugged me, and my face positively burned with the enraptured kisses of my numerous fair sisters, with a long host of cousins, aunts, and other more remote kindred. All these welcoming ladies as firmly believed in my identity with the lost one as they believed in the existence of the Great Spirit.

My father knew me to be his son; told all the Crows that the dead was alive again, and the lost one was found. He knew it was fact; Greenwood had said so, and the words of Greenwood were true; his tongue was not crooked—he would not lie. He also had told him that his son was a great brave among the white men; that his arm was strong; that the Black Feet quailed before his rifle and battle-axe; that his lodge was full of their scalps which his knife had taken; that they must rally around me to support and protect me; and that his long-lost son would be a strong breastwork to their nation, and he would teach them how to defeat their enemies.

They all promised that they would do as his words had indicated.

My unmarried sisters were four in number, very pretty, intelligent young women. They, as soon as the departure of the crowd would admit, took off my old leggins, and moccasins, and other garments, and supplied their place with new ones, most beautifully ornamented according to their very last fashion. My sisters were very ingenious in such work, and they well nigh quarreled among themselves for the privilege of dressing me. When my toilet was finished to their satisfaction, I could compare in elegance with the most popular warrior of the tribe when in full costume. They also prepared me a bed, not so high as Haman's gallows certainly, but just as high as the lodge would admit. This was also a token of their esteem and sisterly affection.

While conversing to the extent of my ability with my father in the evening, and affording him full information respecting the white people, their great cities, their numbers, their power, their opulence, he suddenly demanded of me if I wanted a wife; thinking, no doubt, that, if he got me married, I should lose all discontent, and forego any wish of returning to the whites.

I assented, of course.

"Very well," said he, "you shall have a pretty wife and a good one."

Away he strode to the lodge of one of the greatest braves, and asked one of his daughters of him to bestow upon his son, who the chief must have heard was also a great brave. The consent of the parent was readily given. The name of my prospective father-in-law was Black-lodge. He had three very pretty daughters, whose names were Still-water, Black-fish, and Three-roads.

Even the untutored daughters of the wild woods need a little time to prepare for such an important event, but long and tedious courtships are unknown among them.

The ensuing day the three daughters were brought to my father's lodge by their father, and I was requested to take my choice. "Still-water" was the eldest, and I liked her name; if it was emblematic of her disposition, she was the woman I should prefer. "Still-water," accordingly, was my choice. They were all superbly attired in garments which must have cost them months of labor, which garments the young women ever keep in readiness against such an interesting occasion as the present.

The acceptance of my wife was the completion of the ceremony, and I was again a married man, as sacredly in their eyes as if the Holy Christian Church had fastened the irrevocable knot upon us.

Among the Indians, the daughter receives no patrimony on her wedding-day, and her mother and father never pass a word with the son-in-law after—a custom religiously observed among them, though for what reason I never learned. The other relatives are under no such restraint.

My brothers made me a present of twenty as fine horses as any in the nation—all trained war-horses. I was also presented with all the arms and instruments requisite for an Indian campaign.

My wife's deportment coincided with her name; she would have reflected honor upon many as civilized household. She was affectionate, obedient, gentle, cheerful, and, apparently, quite happy. No domestic thunder-storms, no curtain-lectures ever disturbed the serenity of our connubial lodge. I speedily formed acquaintance with all my immediate neighbors, and the Morning Star (which was the name conferred upon me on my recognition as the lost son) was soon a companion to all the young warriors in the village. No power on earth could have shaken their faith in my positive identity with the lost son. Nature seemed to prompt the old woman to recognize me as her missing child, and all my new relatives placed implicit faith in the genuineness of her discovery. Greenwood had spoken it, "and his tongue was not crooked." What could I do under the circumstances? Even if I should deny my Crow origin, they would not believe me. How could I dash with an unwelcome and incredible explanation all the joy that had been manifested on my return—the cordial welcome, the rapturous embraces of those who hailed me as a son and a brother, the exuberant joy of the whole nation for the return of a long-lost Crow, who, stolen when a child, had returned in the strength of maturity, graced with the name of a great brave, and the generous strife I had occasioned in their endeavors to accord me the warmest welcome? I could not find it in my heart to undeceive these unsuspecting people and tear myself away from their untutored caresses.

Thus I commenced my Indian life with the Crows. I said to myself, "I can trap in their streams unmolested, and derive more profit under their protection than if among my own men, exposed incessantly to assassination and alarm." I therefore resolved to abide with them, to guard my secret, to do my best in their company, and in assisting them to subdue their enemies.

MARY SEACOLE

Mary Seacole was born Mary Jane Grant in Kingston, Jamaica, in 1805. Her father was a Scottish army officer, and her mother, a free black woman, ran a successful boarding house, Blundell Hall, which was patronized by army and naval officers. Seacole's mother was a notable doctress who was familiar with Afro-Jamaican healing practices and the treatment of tropical diseases. In her youth Mary developed a desire to travel, and after the death of her husband, about whom very little is known, she decided to join her brother Edward in Panama. He had established a hotel amid the frontier for travelers going by boat to and from the California gold rush. In Panama Seacole established her own British hotel and was known as the "yellow doctress" by the natives and travelers who needed her attention; she was called on during a cholera epidemic, and in the excerpt here she details her mixed reaction to the local customs and her desire to become more knowledgeable as a medical practitioner. She adopts a female version of the picaro, or rogue narrator, often addressing her reader directly and explaining her rationale for participating in settings that were considered inappropriate for women. Seacole skillfully uses parody and back talk to paint her unflattering portraits of Americans, whom she finds racist and nationalistic; she admits to having an anti-American bias, largely because of the institution of slavery.

Seacole's book-length narrative *Wonderful Adventures of Mrs. Seacole in Many Lands*, published in 1857, details her adventures in Jamaica and Panama, but the central focus is her service at the Crimean War front. Seacole was excited by the event of the Crimean War, and she applied to serve officially as a nurse but was turned down by Florence Nightingale's people, most likely because of race and age. When she was rejected, she devised a scheme to "trespass" and travel there at her own expense to set up a store in partnership with Mr. Thomas Day, a distant connection of the late Mr. Seacole. Seacole ran the British Hotel, a combination restaurant/cantine/social gathering spot for British officers, while she also tended to the wounded. Her narrative includes many testimonies by the Englishmen she healed to justify her presence at the front and to valorize her healing skills at a time when curing and caring were being split by gender into the separate spheres of doctoring and nursing (Ehrenreich and English, 40). Mary Seacole is a fascinating narrator who becomes a "mother" to her English soldier-sons while simultaneously valorizing her Afro-Jamaican healing skills, her entrepreneurial prowess, and her desire to re-create the notion of home and family. She was briefly celebrated in London after the war and later worked as a masseuse for the Princess of Wales. She died in 1881, leaving a small fortune to her sister and other friends and relatives (Alexander and Dewjee, 36; Fryer, 252).

f r o m
WonderfUl AdvenTURes of
Mrs. Seacole iN MaNy LaNds (1857)

After a few weeks, the first force of the cholera was spent, and although it lingered with us, as though loath to leave so fine a resting-place, for some months, it no longer gave us much alarm; and before long, life went on as briskly and selfishly as ever with the Cruces survivors, and the terrible past was conveniently forgotten. Perhaps it is so everywhere; but the haste with which the Cruces people buried their memory seemed indecent. Old houses found new masters; the mules new drivers; the great Spaniard chose another pretty woman, and had a grand, poor, dirty wedding, and was married by the same lazy black priest who had buried his wife, dead a few months back; and very likely would all have hastened as quickly to forget their doctress, had circumstances permitted them; but every now and then one of them sickened and died of the old complaint; and the reputation I had established founded for me a considerable practice. The Americans in the place gladly retained me as their medical attendant, and in one way or other gave me plenty to do; but, in addition to this, I determined to follow my original scheme of keeping a hotel in Cruces.

Right opposite my brother's Independent Hotel there was a place to let which it was considered I could adapt to my purpose. It was a mere tumble-down hut, with wattled sides, and a rotten thatched roof, containing two rooms, one small enough to serve as a bedroom. For this charming residence—very openly situated, and well ventilated—twenty pounds a month was considered a fair and by no means exorbitant rent. And yet I was glad to take possession of it; and in a few days had hung its rude walls with calico of gayest colour in stripes, with an exuberance of fringes, frills, and bows (the Americans love show dearly), and prepared it to accommodate fifty dinner guests. I had determined that it should be simply a *table d'hôte*, and that I would receive no lodgers. Once, and once only, I relaxed this rule in favour of two American women, who sent me to sleep by a lengthy quarrel of words, woke me in the night to witness its crisis in a fisticuff *duello*, and left in the morning, after having taken a fancy to some of my moveables which were most easily removeable. I had on my staff my black servant Mac, the little girl I have before alluded to, and a native cook. I had had many opportunities of seeing how my brother conducted his business; and adopted his tariff of charges. For an ordinary dinner my charge was four shillings; eggs and chickens were, as I have before said, distinct luxuries, and fetched high prices.

Four crowds generally passed through Cruces every month. In these were to be found passengers to and from Chili, Peru, and Lima, as well as California and America. The distance from Cruces to Panama was not great—only twenty miles, in fact; but the journey, from the want of roads and the roughness of the country, was a most fatiguing one. In some parts—as I found when I made the journey, in company with my brother—it was almost impassable; and, for more than half the distance, three miles an hour was considered splendid progress. The great majority of the travellers were rough, rude men, of dirty, quarrelsome habits; the others were more civilised and more dangerous. And it was not long before I grew very tired of life in Cruces, although I made money rapidly, and pressed my brother to return to Kingston. Poor fellow! it would have been well for him had he done so; for he stayed only to find a grave on the Isthmus of Panama.

The company at my *table d'hôte* was not over select; and it was often more difficult for an unprotected female to manage them, although I always did my best to put them in good humour. Among other comforts, I used to hire a black barber, for the rather large consideration of two pounds, to shave my male guests. You can scarcely conceive the pleasure and comfort an American feels in a clean chin; and I believe my barber attracted considerable custom to the British Hotel at Cruces. I had a little outhouse erected for his especial convenience; and there, well provided with towels, and armed with plenty of razors, a brush of extraordinary size, and a foaming sea of lather, José shaved the new-comers. The rivalry to get within reach of his huge brush was very great; and the threats used by the neglected, when the grinning black was considered guilty of any interested partiality, were of the fiercest description.

This duty over, they and their coarser female companions—many of them well known to us, for they travelled backwards and forwards across the Isthmus, hanging on to the foolish gold-finders—attacked the dinner, very often with great lack of decency. It was of no use giving them carving-knives and forks, for very often they laid their own down to insert a dirty hairy hand into a full dish; while the floor soon bore evidence of the great national American habit of expectoration. Very often quarrels would arise during the progress of dinner; and more than once I thought the knives, which they nearly swallowed at every mouthful, would have been turned against one another. It was, I always thought, extremely fortunate that the reckless men rarely stimulated their excitable passions with strong drink. Tea and coffee were the common beverages of the Americans; Englishmen, and men of other nations, being generally distinguishable by their demand for wine and spirits. But the Yankee's capacity for swilling tea and coffee was prodigious. I saw one man drink ten cups of coffee; and finding his appetite still unsatisfied, I ran across to my brother, for advice. There was a merry twinkle in his eyes as he whispered, "I always put in a good spoonful of salt after the sixth cup. It chokes them off admirably."

It was no easy thing to avoid being robbed and cheated by the less scrupulous travellers; although I think it was only the 'cutest Yankee who stood any fair chance of outwitting me. I remember an instance of the biter bit, which I will narrate, hoping it will make my reader laugh as heartily as its recollection makes me. He was a tall, thin Yankee, with a furtive glance of the eyes, and an amazing appetite, which he seemed nothing loath to indulge: his appetite for eggs especially seemed unbounded. Now, I have more than once said how expensive eggs were; and this day they happened to be eightpence apiece. Our plan was to charge every diner according to the number of shells found upon his plate. Now, I noticed how eagerly my thin guest attacked my eggs, and marvelled somewhat at the scanty pile of shells before him. My suspicions once excited, I soon fathomed my Yankee friend's dodge. As soon as he had devoured the eggs, he conveyed furtively the shells beneath the table, and distributed them impartially at the feet of his companions. I gave my little black maid a piece of chalk, and instructions; and creeping under the table, she counted the scattered shells, and chalked the number on the tail of his coat. And when he came up to pay his score, he gave up his number of eggs in a loud voice; and when I contradicted him, and referred to the coat-*tale* in corroboration of *my* score, there was a general laugh against him. But there was a nasty expression in his cat-like eyes, and an unpleasant allusion to mine, which were not agreeable, and dissuaded me from playing any more practical jokes upon the Yankees.

I followed my brother's example closely, and forbade all gambling in my hotel. But I got some idea of its fruits from the cases brought to me for surgical treatment from the faro and monte-tables. Gambling at Cruces, and on the Isthmus generally, was a business by which money was wormed out of the gold-seekers and gold-finders. No attempt was made to render it attractive, as I have seen done elsewhere. The gambling-house was often plainer than our hotels; and but for the green tables, with their piles of money and gold-dust, watched over by a well-armed determined banker, and eager gamblers around, you would not know you were in the vicinity of a spot which the English at home designate by a very decided and extreme name. A Dr. Casey— everybody familiar with the Americans knows their fondness for titles—owned the most favoured table in Cruces; and this, although he was known to be a reckless and unscrupulous villain. Most of them knew that he had been hunted out of San Francisco; and at that time—years before the Vigilance Committee commenced their labours of purification—a man too bad for that city must have been a prodigy of crime; and yet, and although he was violent-tempered, and had a knack of referring the slightest dispute to his revolver, his table was always crowded; probably because—the greatest rogues have some good qualities—he was honest in his way, and played fairly. . . .

Whenever an American was arrested by the New Granada authorities, justice had a hard struggle for the mastery, and rarely obtained it. Once I was present at the court-house, when an American was brought in heavily ironed, charged with having committed a highway robbery—if I may use the term where there were no roads—on some travellers from Chili. Around the frightened soldiers swelled an angry crowd of brother Americans, abusing and threatening the authorities in no measured terms, all of them indignant that a nigger should presume to judge one of their countrymen. At last their violence so roused the sleepy alcalde, that he positively threw himself from his hammock, laid down his cigarito, and gave such very determined orders to his soldiers that he succeeded in checking the riot. Then, with an air of decision that puzzled everybody, he addressed the crowd, declaring angrily,

that since the Americans came the country had known no peace, that rob-
beries and crimes of every sort had increased, and ending by expressing his
determination to make strangers respect the laws of the Republic, and to
retain the prisoner; and if found guilty, punish him as he deserved. The
Americans seemed too astonished at the audacity of the black man, who
dared thus to beard them, to offer any resistance; but I believe that the prisoner was allowed ultimately to escape.

I once had a narrow escape from the thieves of Cruces. I had been down
to Chagres for some stores, and returning, late in the evening, too tired to put
away my packages, had retired to rest at once. My little maid, who was not so
fatigued as I was, and slept more lightly, woke me in the night to listen to a
noise in the thatch, at the further end of the store; but I was so accustomed
to hear the half-starved mules of Cruces munching my thatch, that I listened
lazily for a few minutes, and then went unsuspiciously into another heavy
sleep. I do not know how long it was before I was again awoke by the child's
loud screams and cries of "Hombro—landro!" and sure enough by the light
of the dying fire, I saw a fellow stealing away with my dress, in the pocket of
which was my purse. I was about to rush forward, when the fire gleamed on
a villainous-looking knife in his hand; so I stood still, and screamed loudly,
hoping to arouse my brother over the way. For a moment the thief seemed
inclined to silence me, and had taken a few steps forward, when I took up an
old rusty horse-pistol which my brother had given me that I might look determined, and snatching down the can of ground coffee, proceeded to prime it,
still screaming as loudly as my strong lungs would permit, until the rascal
turned tail and stole away through the roof. The thieves usually buried their
spoil like dogs, as they were; but this fellow had only time to hide it behind
a bush, where it was found on the following morning, and claimed by me.

I remained at Cruces until the rainy months came to an end, and the river
grew too shallow to be navigable by the boats higher up than Gorgona; and
then we all made preparations for a flitting to that place. But before starting,
it appeared to be the custom for the store and hotel keepers to exchange
parting visits, and to many of these parties I, in virtue of my recent services
to the community, received invitations. The most important social meeting
took place on the anniversary of the declaration of American independence,
at my brother's hotel, where a score of zealous Americans dined most
heartily—as they never fail to do; and as it was an especial occasion, drank
champagne liberally at twelve shillings a bottle. And, after the usual patri-

otic toasts had been duly honoured, they proposed "the ladies," with an especial reference to myself, in a speech which I thought worth noting down at the time. The spokesman was a thin, sallow-looking American, with a pompous and yet rapid delivery, and a habit of turning over his words with his quid* before delivering them, and clearing his mouth after each sentence, perhaps to make room for the next. I shall beg the reader to consider that the blanks express the time expended on this operation. He dashed into his work at once, rolling up and getting rid of his sentences as he went on:—

"Well, gentlemen, I expect you'll all support me in a drinking of this toast that I du ———. Aunty Seacole, gentlemen; I give you, Aunty Seacole ———. We can't du less for her, after what she's done for us ———, when the cholera was among us, gentlemen ———, not many months ago ———. So, I say, God bless the best yaller woman He ever made ———, from Jamaica, gentlemen ———, from the Isle of Springs. Well, gentlemen, I expect there are only tu things we're vexed for ———; and the first is, that she ain't one of us ———, a citizen of the Great United States ———; and the other thing is, gentlemen ———, that Providence made her a yaller woman. I calculate, gentlemen, you're all as vexed as I am that she's not wholly white ———, but I du reckon on your rejoicing with me that she's so many shades removed from being entirely black ———; and I guess, if we could bleach her by any means we would ———, and thus make her acceptable in any company as she deserves to be ———. Gentlemen, I give you Aunty Seacole!"

And so the orator sat down amidst much applause. It may be supposed that I did not need much persuasion to return thanks, burning, as I was, to tell them my mind on the subject of my colour. Indeed, if my brother had not checked me, I should have given them my thoughts somewhat too freely. As it was, I said:—

"Gentlemen,—I return you my best thanks for your kindness in drinking my health. As for what I have done in Cruces, Providence evidently made me to be useful, and I can't help it. But I must say that I don't altogether appreciate your friend's kind wishes with respect to my complexion. If it had been as dark as any nigger's, I should have been just as happy and as useful, and as much respected by those whose respect I value; and as to his offer of bleaching me, I should, even if it were practicable, decline it without any thanks. As to the society which the process might gain me

*Lump of chewing tobacco.

2 1

admission into, all I can say is, that, judging from the specimens I have met with here and elsewhere, I don't think that I shall lose much by being excluded from it. So, gentlemen, I drink to you and the general reformation of American manners."

I do not think that they altogether admired my speech, but I was a somewhat privileged person, and they laughed at it good-naturedly enough. Perhaps (for I was not in the best humour myself) I should have been better pleased if they had been angry.

Rightly, I ought to have gone down to Gorgona a few weeks before Cruces was deserted, and secured an hotel; but I did not give up all hope of persuading my brother to leave the Isthmus until the very last moment, and then, of course, a suitable house was not to be hired in Gorgona for love or money. Seeing his fixed determination to stay, I consented to remain with him, for he was young and often ill, and set hard to work to settle myself somewhere. With the aid of an old Jamaica friend, who had settled at Gorgona, I at last found a miserable little hut for sale, and bought it for a hundred dollars. It consisted of one room only, and was, in its then condition, utterly unfit for my purpose; but I determined to set to work and build on to it—by no means the hazardous speculation in Gorgona, where bricks and mortar are unknown, that it is in England. The alcalde's permission to make use of the adjacent ground was obtained for a moderate consideration, and plenty of material was procurable from the opposite bank of the river. An American, whom I had cured of the cholera at Cruces, lent me his boat, and I hired two or three natives to cut down and shape the posts and bamboo poles. Directly these were raised, Mac and my little maid set to work and filled up the spaces between them with split bamboo canes and reeds, and before long my new hotel was ready to be roofed. The building process was simple enough, and I soon found myself in possession of a capital dining-room some thirty feet in length, which was gaily hung with coloured calico, concealing all defects of construction, and lighted with large oil lamps; a store-room, bar, and a small private apartment for ladies. Altogether, although I had to pay my labourers four shillings a day, the whole building did not cost me more than my brother paid for three months' rent of his hotel. I gave the travelling world to understand that I intended to devote my establishment principally to the entertainment of ladies, and the care of those who might fall ill on the route, and I found the scheme answer admirably. And yet, although the speculation paid well, I soon grew as weary of my life in Gorgona as I had been at Cruces; and when I found my brother proof against all persuasion to quit the Isthmus, I began to entertain serious thoughts of leaving him.

NAT LOVE

Nat Love was born a slave in Tennessee in 1854. After emancipation, he realized that "there was so much more of the world than what I had seen, the desire to go grew on me from day to day." At age fifteen he headed West for Kansas, where he landed a thirty-dollar-a-month job as a cowpuncher and was nicknamed "Red River Dick." For many years he took part in cattle drives and delivered herds of horses and cattle to ranch owners all over Texas, Wyoming, and the Dakotas.

Love conveys tales of courage and miraculous survival as part of his cowboy life; at one point he remarks, "I carry the marks of fourteen bullet wounds on different parts of my body, most any one of which would be sufficient to kill an ordinary man, but I am not even crippled." Love does not mention racial discrimination. In fact, in an excerpt here he relays how he entered the rodeo at Deadwood City, Dakota Territory, and won both roping and shooting competitions, earning bragging rights and the name "Deadwood Dick." Also included here is an excerpt describing Love's proximity to the Little Big Horn massacre in June 1876: "we were only two days behind them . . . we did not know that at the time or we would have gone to Custer's assistance."

Love left the range in 1890, at which time the frontier appeared to be closing. He got married and took a job on the Denver and Rio Grande Railroad as a pullman porter, the only type of position open to blacks at the time (Katz, iv). In 1907 he published his memoir, *The Life and Adventures of Nat Love, Better Known in Cattle Country as "Deadwood Dick."*

f r o m
The Life and Adventures of Nat Love (1907)

It was on the tenth day of February, 1869, that I left the old home, near
Nashville, Tennessee. I was at that time about fifteen years old, and though
while young in years the hard work and farm life had made me strong and
hearty, much beyond my years, and I had full confidence in myself as
being able to take care of myself and making my way.

I at once struck out for Kansas of which I had heard something. And
believing it was a good place in which to seek employment. It was in the
west, and it was the great west I wanted to see, and so by walking and occasional lifts from farmers going my way and taking advantage of every thing
that promised to assist me on my way, I eventually brought up at Dodge
City, Kansas, which at that time was a typical frontier city, with a great
many saloons, dance halls, and gambling houses, and very little of anything
else. When I arrived the town was full of cow boys from the surrounding
ranches, and from Texas and other parts of the west. As Kansas was a great
cattle center and market, the wild cow boy, prancing horses of which I was
very fond, and the wild life generally, all had their attractions for me, and
I decided to try for a place with them. Although it seemed to me I had met
with a bad outfit, at least some of them, going around among them I
watched my chances to get to speak with them, as I wanted to find some
one whom I thought would give me a civil answer to the questions I wanted
to ask, but they all seemed too wild around town, so the next day I went out
where they were in camp.

Approaching a party who were eating their breakfast, I got to speak with
them. They asked me to have some breakfast with them, which invitation
I gladly accepted. During the meal I got a chance to ask them many questions. They proved to be a Texas outfit, who had just come up with a herd
of cattle and having delivered them they were preparing to return. There
were several colored cow boys among them, and good ones too. After
breakfast I asked the camp boss for a job as cow boy. He asked me if I could
ride a wild horse. I said "yes sir." He said if you can I will give you a job.
So he spoke to one of the colored cow boys called Bronko Jim, and told
him to go out and rope old Good Eye, saddle him and put me on his back.
Bronko Jim gave me a few pointers and told me to look out for the horse

was especially bad on pitching. I told Jim I was a good rider and not afraid of him. I thought I had rode pitching horses before, but from the time I mounted old Good Eye I knew I had not learned what pitching was. This proved the worst horse to ride I had ever mounted in my life, but I stayed with him and the cow boys were the most surprised outfit you ever saw, as they had taken me for a tenderfoot, pure and simple. After the horse got tired and I dismounted the boss said he would give me a job and pay me $30.00 per month and more later on. He asked what my name was and I answered Nat Love, he said to the boys we will call him Red River Dick. I went by this name for a long time.

The boss took me to the city and got my outfit, which consisted of a new saddle, bridle and spurs, chaps, a pair of blankets and a fine 45 Colt revolver. Now that the business which brought them to Dodge City was concluded, preparations were made to start out for the Pan Handle country in Texas to the home ranch. The outfit of which I was now a member was called the Duval outfit, and their brand was known as the Pig Pen brand. I worked with this outfit for over three years. On this trip there were only about fifteen of us riders, all excepting myself were hardy, experienced men, always ready for anything that might turn up, but they were as jolly a set of fellows as one could find in a long journey. There now being nothing to keep us longer in Dodge City, ever prepared for the return journey, and left the next day over the old Dodge and Sun City lonesome trail, on a journey which was to prove the most eventful of my life up to now.

A few miles out we encountered some of the hardest hail storms I ever saw, causing discomfort to man and beast, but I had no notion of getting discouraged but I resolved to be always ready for any call that might be made on me, of whatever nature it might be, and those with whom I have lived and worked will tell you I have kept that resolve. Not far from Dodge City on our way home we encountered a band of the old Victoria tribe of Indians and had a sharp fight.

These Indians were nearly always harassing travelers and traders and the stock men of that part of the country, and were very troublesome. In this band we encountered there were about a hundred painted bucks all well mounted. When we saw the Indians they were coming after us yelling like demons. As we were not expecting Indians at this particular time, we were taken somewhat by surprise.

We only had fifteen men in our outfit, but nothing daunted we stood our ground and fought the Indians to a stand. One of the boys was shot off his horse and killed near me. The Indians got his horse, bridle and saddle. During this fight we lost all but six of our horses, our entire packing outfit and our extra saddle horses, which the Indians stampeded, then rounded them up after the fight and drove them off. And as we only had six horses left us, we were unable to follow them, although we had the satisfaction of knowing we had made several good Indians out of bad ones.

This was my first Indian fight and likewise the first Indians I had ever seen. When I saw them coming after us and heard their blood curdling yell, I lost all courage and thought my time had come to die. I was too badly scared to run, some of the boys told me to use my gun and shoot for all I was worth. Now I had just got my outfit and had never shot off a gun in my life, but their words brought me back to earth and seeing they were all using their guns in a way that showed they were used to it, I unlimbered my artillery and after the first shot I lost all fear and fought like a veteran.

We soon routed the Indians and they left, taking with them nearly all we had, and we were powerless to pursue them. We were compelled to finish our journey home almost on foot, as there were only six horses left to fourteen of us. Our friend and companion who was shot in the fight, we buried on the plains, wrapped in his blanket with stones piled over his grave. After this engagement with the Indians I seemed to lose all sense as to what fear was and thereafter during my whole life on the range I never experienced the least feeling of fear, no matter how trying the ordeal or how desperate my position.

The home ranch was located on the Palo Duro river in the western part of the Pan Handle, Texas, which we reached in the latter part of May, it taking us considerably over a month to make the return journey home from Dodge City. I remained in the employ of the Duval outfit for three years, making regular trips to Dodge City every season and to many other places in the surrounding states with herds of horses and cattle for market and to be delivered to other ranch owners all over Texas, Wyoming and the Dakotas. By strict attention to business, born of a genuine love of the free and wild life of the range, and absolute fearlessness, I became known through the country as a good all around cow boy and a splendid hand in a stampede.

After returning from one of our trips north with a bunch of cattle in the fall of 1872, I received and accepted a better position with the Pete

Gallinger company, whose immense range was located on the Gila River in southern Arizona. So after drawing the balance of my pay from the Duval company and bidding good bye to the true and tried companions of the past three years, who had learned me the business and been with me in many a trying situation, it was with genuine regret that I left them for my new position, one that meant more to me in pay and experience. I stayed with Pete Gallinger company for several years and soon became one of their most trusted men, taking an important part in all the big round-ups and cuttings throughout western Texas, Arizona and other states where the company had interests to be looked after, sometimes riding eighty miles a day for days at a time over the trails of Texas and the surrounding country and naturally I soon became well known among the cowboys rangers, scouts and guides it was my pleasure to meet in my wanderings over the country, in the wake of immense herds of the long horned Texas cattle and large bands of range horses. Many of these men who were my companions on the trail and in camp, have since become famous in story and history, and a braver, truer set of men never lived than these wild sons of the plains whose home was in the saddle and their couch, mother earth, with the sky for a covering. They were always ready to share their blanket and their last ration with a less fortunate fellow companion and always assisted each other in the many trying situations that were continually coming up in a cowboy's life.

When we were not on the trail taking large herds of cattle or horses to market or to be delivered to other ranches we were engaged in range riding, moving large numbers of cattle from one grazing range to another, keeping them together, and hunting up strays which, despite the most earnest efforts of the range riders would get away from the main herd and wander for miles over the plains before they could be found, overtaken and returned to the main herd.

Then the Indians and the white outlaws who infested the country gave us no end of trouble, as they lost no opportunity to cut out and run off the choicest part of a herd of long horns, or the best of a band of horses, causing the cowboys a ride of many a long mile over the dusty plains in pursuit, and many are the fierce engagements we had, when after a long chase of perhaps hundreds of miles over the ranges we overtook the thieves. It then became a case of "to the victor belongs the spoils," as there was no law respected in this wild country, except the law of might and the persuasive qualities of the 45 Colt pistol.

Accordingly it became absolutely necessary for a cowboy to understand his gun and know how to place its contents where it would do the most good, therefore I in common with my other companions never lost an opportunity to practice with my 45 Colts and the opportunities were not lacking by any means and so in time I became fairly proficient and able in most cases to hit a barn door providing the door was not too far away, and was steadily improving in this as I was in experience and knowledge of the other branches of the business which I had chosen as my life's work and which I had begun to like so well, because while the life was hard and in some ways enacting, yet it was free and wild and contained the elements of danger which my nature craved and which began to manifest itself when I was a pugnacious youngster on the old plantation in our rock battles and the breaking of the wild horses. I gloried in the danger, and the wild and free life of the plains, the new country I was continually traversing, and the many new scenes and incidents continually arising in the life of a rough rider. . . .

It was my pleasure to meet Buffalo Bill often in the early 70s, and he was as fine a man as one could wish to meet, kind, generous, true and brave.

Buffalo Bill got his name from the fact that in the early days he was engaged in hunting buffalo for their hides and furnishing U. P. Railroad graders with meat, hence the name Buffalo Bill. Buffalo Bill, Yellowstone Kelley, with many others were at this time serving under Gen. C. C. Miles.

The name of Deadwood Dick was given to me by the people of Deadwood, South Dakota, July 4, 1876, after I had proven myself worthy to carry it, and after I had defeated all comers in riding, roping, and shooting, and I have always carried the name with honor since that time.

We arrived at the home ranch again on our return from the trip to Deadwood about the middle of September, it taking us a little over two months to make the return journey, as we stopped in Cheyenne for several days and at other places, where we always found a hearty welcome, especially so on this trip, as the news had preceded us, and I received enough attention to have given me the big head, but my head had constantly refused to get enlarged again ever since the time I sampled the demijohn in the sweet corn patch at home.

Arriving at home, we received a send off from our boss and our comrades of the home ranch, every man of whom on hearing the news turned loose his voice and his artillery in a grand demonstration in my honor.

But they said it was no surprise to them, as they had long known of my ability with the rope, rifle and 45 Colt, but just the same it was gratifying to know I had defeated the best men of the West, and brought the record home to the home ranch in Arizona. After a good rest we proceeded to ride the range again, getting our herds in good condition for the winter now at hand. . . .

With the march of progress came the railroad and no longer were we called upon to follow the long horned steers or mustangs on the trail, while the immense cattle ranges, stretching away in the distance as far as the eye could see, now began to be dotted with cities and towns and the cattle industry which once held a monopoly in the west, now had to give way to the industry of the farm and the mill. To us wild cowboys of the range, used to the wild and unrestricted life of the boundless plains, the new order of things did not appeal, and many of us became disgusted and quit the wild life for the pursuits of our more civilized brother. I was among that number and in 1890 I bid farewell to the life which I had followed for over twenty years.

It was with genuine regret that I left the long horn Texas cattle and the wild mustangs of the range, but the life had in a great measure lost its attractions and so I decided to quit it and try something else for a while. During my life so far I had no chance to secure an education, except the education of the plains and the cattle business. In this I recognize no superior being. Gifted with a splendid memory and quick observation I learned and remembered things that others passed by and forgot, and I have yet to meet the man who can give me instruction in the phases of a life in which I spent so long. After quitting the cowboy life I struck out for Denver. Here I met and married the present Mrs. Love, my second love. We were married August 22, 1889, and she is with me now a true and faithful partner, and says she is not one bit jealous of my first love, who lies buried in the city of Old Mexico.

One year later, in 1890, I accepted a position in the Pullman service on the Denver and Rio Grande Railroad, running between Denver and Salida, Colorado. The Pullman service was then in its infancy, so to speak, as there was as much difference between the Pullman sleeping cars of those days and the present as there is between the ox team and the automobile.

Thomas Detter

Thomas Detter was born to a free black family in Maryland or Washington, D.C., around 1826. His father was a stonemason, who, on his death, decreed that Thomas be apprenticed as a shoemaker until he turned twenty-one. In 1852 Detter migrated to California, being attracted the by the prospect of gold. Within three years he was elected a Sacramento County delegate to the first Colored Citizens of the State of California Convention. He traveled extensively through the Idaho and Washington Territories, living in mining camps and writing newspaper accounts describing the beauty and economic opportunities there, in an effort to attract and develop African-American communities. In 1871 he published *Nellie Brown, or The Jealous Wife with Other Sketches*, which contains a novella, "one of the earliest examples of American divorce fiction" (Foster, Introduction, xv) as well as fictional "sketches" and essays set in the antebellum South and in Cuba, Idaho, and California. Detter lived in Elko and Eureka, Nevada, where he continued to advocate for black participation and scrutiny of the American political system. The excerpt here, written about Boise City, describes both the prejudice and the promise he finds in the towns of the northwestern frontier.

from
Nellie Brown, or The Jealous Wife with Other Sketches (1871)

We shall not attempt to give a graphic description of the place. It is a neat little burg, situated in a beautiful and fertile valley, and is the capital of Idaho Territory. It contains many permanent buildings, including neat and handsome cottages. It being a central point, it has many advantages over its sister towns. It contains a population ranging from nine to twelve hundred inhabitants. Many of its citizens are afflicted with the terrible disease of Negrophobia. The very air seems to be pregnated with this disease. A respectable colored man can scarcely get accommodations at any of the hotels or restaurants. I was compelled, on my way from Idaho City to Silver City, to lay over from five P.M. until two A.M. the following morning. A few moments before the stage started for Silver City, I was invited by a swarthy, but generous-looking Spaniard, to take a cigar. We started down the street. The most of the saloons at this unseasonable hour being closed, my companion saw a light in a saloon kept by Mr. J. Old. We entered and called for what we wanted. The polite and accommodating Mr. Old bent over the counter and said, in a low tone of voice: "Detter, I cannot accommodate you." I regarded it as a polite insult, and walked out. He was the last man I expected that would treat me thus. Had I approached him with my hat in my hand, trembling like a quarry slave, I have no doubt this proud Saxon would have accommodated me. I have seen many like Mr. Old come to naught, and who would gladly accept a favor, though extended by a Negro. I have lived in mountain towns where the lowest and basest females, white and colored, could be served with meals. If a respectable colored man desired a meal, the landlord would politely invite him to be seated in the kitchen. I ever have and ever will take issue against any such treatment. In my travels wherever I have met gentlemen, they have always treated me as a man, and not as a thing. The rough usages and insults that colored men receive, invariably come from that class of whites who have little to recommend them outside of a white skin. Were I to say that there are no good feeling men in Boise City, I would be doing an injustice, to many. I appreciate my friends. I never can condescend to lick the hand that smites me, nor respect the man that insults me.

HARRY DEAN

The Pedro Gorino was published simultaneously in 1929 in Boston, London, and New York by Houghton Mifflin. At times it appears like a work of fiction in the picaresque tradition. However, although Harry Dean might exaggerate for storytelling purposes, most of his story is true. Dean was born in Philadelphia, where he grew up in a household frequented by black intellectuals and activists such as Martin Delany. He was a descendant of Paul Cuffe, and he was taught by Fanny Jackson Coppin. From 1876 to 1879 he traveled around the world with an uncle. As such he joins a tradition of black men of the sea who have been recently documented (e.g., Bolster, *Black Jacks: African American Seamen in the Age of Sail*). After spending seven years in South Africa, Dean went to Liberia, where he tried to convince the government to develop a merchant fleet. In 1921 he met with officials of the Garvey movement, although he does not seem to have ever met Marcus Garvey. Dean founded and chartered the Dean Nautical College of Almeda, California, in an effort to train African Americans in seafaring and science, but the school was short-lived. In the 1930s Dean relocated to Chicago, where he organized a group of young African Americans with whom he discussed black history. He died there in 1935.

The Pedro Gorino is edited by Sterling North, a writer for the *Chicago Daily News*. In 1989 it was republished by Pluto Press of London. The selections here are taken from descriptions of Dean's childhood and education in Philadelphia, his first sea trips to California and Mexico, and finally his years and adventures in South Africa. Throughout, Dean is fiercely proud of his African ancestry and is clearly an early pan-Africanist.

f r o m
THE PEDRO GORINO (1929)

I GO TO SEA

There were eighteen children in my family, seven boys and eleven girls. I was the youngest boy. Of that family only three of us are now alive, Alice, Mayme, and I.

I am an African and proud of it. There is not a drop of white blood in my veins. My ancestors have been sea captains and merchants and I have spent my life on the sea.

My father was a tall, proud, not very religious, but kindly sort of man. My mother was a fine singer and a cultured and idealistic woman. I hope I have proved worthy of them.

While I was still a boy I was given copies of Horace, Homer, Virgil, Petrarch, Shakespeare, Coleridge's "Ancient Mariner," a translation of "The Arabian Chronicles," "Arabian Nights," Colonel George Williams's "History of the Negro," a hand-illumined "Spirit of the Laws," and many others. Mother delighted in training us, and when I was old enough she put me under the tutelage of Fannie Jackson, the great "negro" woman educator, at the Institute for Colored Youth in Philadelphia. Here I was taught grammar, arithmetic, and a foundation in the five natural sciences. Everything theoretical, nothing practical.

I lived such a sheltered life that I became idealistic. I was entirely unaware of the race problem. I knew nothing of the hardships and treacheries of life. We had all the money we needed and I knew nothing of poverty. Since that time I have experienced all the hardships known to man.

Often we had visitors. Major Martin R. Delaney, major in the Union Army during the Civil War; United States Senator Revels, and General Belaski, an escaped rebel officer from Cuba, were among the most frequent. I remember General Belaski in particular. He was as black as pitch and as far across as he was tall. He told me stories of the Cuban Rebellion in his mild voice. "I come from salt water, Sonny, land alive! Should see them islands and the sea a-swishin' on the shore. Should see them black boys, Sonny, creepin' on their bellies through the brush. Guns no good, clothes all ragged, but filled with the spirit and not afraid o' the Devil himself." It was music to my young ears. I could have listened forever.

Besides these few celebrities there were many fine neighbors, particularly the Mintons, Wares, Fortunes, and Dutrelles, a strange class of people whose history has never been written. They were for the most part of maritime ancestors and had become enmeshed in the devastating American environment only after generations of protest. We kept in close contact with these people, for they were the few who could understand our aims and ideals.

The summer I was twelve we went as usual to our cottage at Atlantic City. I swam in the sea and played on the beaches in the sunshine. Some days my father would let me ride in the little twenty-ton schooners whose business it was to carry any who chose to the horizon and back for twenty-five cents. Suddenly I was crazy to go to sea. The salty tang in the air, the rough sailors, the glamour about boats, the stories of adventure I had heard all through my childhood, filled me with a tremendous urge. I thought of the sea night and day.

On returning to Philadelphia we found my Uncle Silas, an honest-to-goodness sea captain come to stay with us for a few days. He was preparing to make a three-year voyage around the world, aboard his ship Traveler the Second. He was, therefore, a hero. He was a man of splendid physique, rapid in his movements and a true sea captain. He had a terrible stare. I was never sure when he looked at me whether he was angry or not. If he had not been my uncle I should have been afraid of him. But his stories were as rich and fabulous as those of Sinbad the Sailor.

One evening as we sat at supper he said to my father: "John, I can tell by the cut of his jib the boy would make a good sailor. He'd reef and furl in no time and I'd have him boxing the compass and shooting the sun before we got around the Horn. Why not let me take him along?"

It seemed as if whole minutes passed before my father answered and when he did I hung one very word.

"Would you take good care of him, Silas?"

"Bring him back shipshape or my name's not Dean," my uncle answered.

"The sea's a rough place for a boy."

"There's nothing like the sea to test what's in a boy. It would make a man of him, John."

"I'll have to think it out," my father said. "Give me till morning." He seemed worried that evening. Mother cried a little. But with all the thoughtlessness of youth I was hardly aware of their sorrow. It was more miraculous than my Arabian Nights. They must let me go, I knew they would. But why did I have to wait until morning to be sure? My brain was whirling with excitement and emotion.

Morning came at last. I could go. Ah, Christophe, Toussaint l'Ouverture, strong men of my race, were you as exultant in your power as I in mine upon that happy morning! In my imagination I already ruled the seas. I had a fleet of ships, their white sails filled with the wind. But little did I realize the hardships of the sea or the hard life that awaited me. And little did I realize the impotence of a child of twelve.

My uncle and I took a train from Philadelphia and landed at Jersey City late at night. We went from the station to the ferry landing and for the first time I saw the lights of New York. The way they were reflected on the dark waters of the Hudson stays with me all these years. Then aboard the ferry boat. Everywhere there was the bustle of boats, horns blowing, and men calling over the water. Having lived in the quiet city of Philadelphia all my life, I had never seen anything like this wild, tumultuous life. We landed at wooden docks that thronged with rough dirty barefoot boys selling newspapers, sleeping in out-of-the-way corners, fighting for no apparent reason. It was an Irish part of town crowded with sailors and toughs. Uncle Silas pushed and crowded, pulling me along by the hand. We passed along narrow streets and between high brick buildings until we came to Manetta Lane, squalid enough to-day but respectable then. Here we put up for the night with an aunt who made a great fuss over me. "Honey-chile let me give yo' one mo' cake."

The next morning we went down to the harbor and for the first time I saw my uncle's ship, Traveler the Second. I liked the smell of Stockholm tar. The way the sailing vessels floated and bobbed on the water was a mystery. The lines and the rigging of the ship impressed me and set me wondering. I remember the Traveler was a barkentine with both square rig and fore-and-aft rig, a mixture of the two types of rigging. She carried studding booms for studding sails that bellied balloon-like on each side so that to those on board and to those who saw her pass, she gave the impression of a sea-gull on the wing. She was very fast under full sail.

There on the docks at New York were sailors from every country. Some of them were dressed in flannel shirts as red as fire. Their great bulging muscles showed through their clothing. Where their sleeves were rolled up their strong brown arms rippled like the surface of water in a breeze. The proportions of these men and their hoarse voices impressed me and made me wish I were as big and strong as they.

Where will you find such men now? Gone are the sailing vessels and gone the men who sailed them. They were a singing, laughing, bunch in port, but let their ship get into rough weather rounding the Horn or off the Cape of Storms, up in the Gulf of Alaska or wherever they were, let the decks get icy and the gale go whistling and moaning through the shrouds, and see if they weren't as true as steel. No grumbling or growling when the bos'n called "All hands ahoy!" They're gone now, but there they were on the dock at New York and aboard the Traveler when I went to sea as a boy.

Sometimes chanties came clearly over the water, one sailor singing a line, the crew answering:

> Haul the bowline, the good ship's a rolling.
> Haul the bowline, the bowline haul.

Then before I could catch more, a dozen voices on the dock laughing and shouting would drown out the singing. "Give a hand there, man."

"An' if the mate ain't seven kinds of Devil I ain't never been in Cork."

"Shet your mouth, Folley. Give a heave on that puncheon."

"Where's Mr. Watson? Oh, Mr. Watson."

It was our men making the racket. They were loading the cargo of hardware, notions, bright cloth, beads and trade goods of all kinds into puncheons, great barrel-like containers as tall as a man. They had been at the work for over a week. The Traveler had made her departure from Boston some two weeks before, dropped anchor at New York and prepared to receive cargo. Uncle Silas had come to Philadelphia to get me, leaving the loading of the vessel in charge of the first mate. We had arrived in New York in time to see the last of that work.

My uncle was talking to the first mate. "We'll muster the men this evening, Mr. Watson. See that they're aboard early. We'll up anchor at dawn." My uncle and I went aboard late that afternoon and made ourselves comfortable in his spacious cabin. What a great man I thought him, with his charts, and sextants, and compasses, his wealth of sea knowledge, and his exciting stories. Aboard ship, however, he had little time to play. His stern expression seldom relaxed into a smile. And although I admired and respected him as did his sailors, I was a little in awe of this dark brown giant whose word was law to so many men. And he was a man to inspire awe, courageous, as every sea captain must be. I found in the days that followed that he was perfectly fearless and would never shorten sail until the docks were at an angle of forty degrees.

At dawn we made our departure form Red Bank. We might have been a phantom ship we moved so gently over the ocean. The pale early morning light flooded the decks of the ship where men moving at their work seemed scarcely men of this world. But as the breeze stiffened and the sun rose higher and the last mist of sleep cleared from before my eyes, I realized that we had put to sea and that my life of adventure had begun. Because of my experiences on the small pleasure schooners I felt myself quite a sailor. The commodious barkentine seemed perfectly safe in my young eyes. Everything was expectation. I wanted to see pirates and buried treasure. I wanted to lead a wild and gallant life. I did not realize how helpless I was or how unprepared for the sea and the hardships of sailors.

The crew was a mixed one. More than half of the men were "negroes." As they worked they sang,

> For seven long years I courted Sally,
> Weigh, roll and go.
> The sweetest flower in all the valley;
> Spend my money on Sally Brown.

How many times I was to hear that and similar songs, filled with the wailing rhythm of the African race. What is it you have lost, what have you left behind, what are you looking for, you unhappy hostages of an alien race?

At Charleston, South Carolina, a colored pilot came out in a small sailing vessel and took us into port. That was the only colored pilot I ever saw in American waters. I remember my uncle had a lot of trouble in Charleston. There was an argument with a port official of which I caught but little and understood less.

"Ain't no nigguh goin' run this po't," the official shouted.

And my uncle in his quiet cold voice, "I merely asked for clearance papers and the usual civility shown a ship's officer."

Whatever the trouble was, my uncle thought it necessary to admonish the crew not to leave the ship. He told them that the boat was to up anchor the minute the clearance papers were ready. Other crews swarmed all along the water-front, but ours remained aboard the ship sullen and angry. Each man felt that the indignity done the ship was a personal affront.

My uncle and I went ashore, however. I accompanied him everywhere, particularly to the custom house. We were in Charleston over one Sunday. We went to church. The colored people were nice to us, but their dialect was so strange that I could scarcely understand them at times.

At last we got our clearance papers and made our departure. We were no sooner out of the harbor than we ran into severe rain and hail storms. The ship was fighting adverse winds and currents and the hail set up a great tattoo on the deck. I was too young to realize our danger. The excitement was more or less pleasurable to me. That night was an anxious one for the crew and for my uncle.

I could not understand the serious demeanor of the men. None of them would talk or laugh with me. Each hurried about the deck doing his appointed task. Some clambered up the ratlines to reef sails, some pulled and hauled on halyards. The mate's orders and the crew's "Aye, aye, sir!" were carried far out over the water by the storm. I heard their voices as if they had come from a great distance.

Most of the crew were on deck all night. And although my uncle told me to go to my bunk in the cabin and get some sleep I was unable to close my eyes. I was not afraid. But I was aware of a sinister foreboding. It was as if the sailors could sense something terrible and strange, something within the darkness which I could not see or hear or feel with my unaccustomed senses. Of course the weather was dark and stormy with black clouds hurrying across the flattened dome of heaven, but that alone was not enough to account for their actions. Their silence was more expressive than all the rough weather.

Later in the night the rain and hail let up and I got out of my bunk to see how things were going on deck. At the door of the galley sat Johnson, a fine old man who was our cook and steward. He liked me a great deal and always carried on an engaging conversation. Even he was still. He had been sitting there at the door of his galley all night. His pipe had long since gone out. When I spoke to him he would only answer in monosyllables.

The sea was running high and white caps were breaking. The salt spray stung my face. And although I did not realize that we were on a lee shore with a shifting wind and in great danger, I did know that I was lonesome and lost and very homesick. . . .

STAVANGER AND THE PEDRO GORINO

I spent the rest of my youth in securing an education in the arts and sciences of the sea. My quest for knowledge and adventure took me to the ends of the world. It was a strenuous, tragic, and terrible part of my life; often I was at the mercy of heartless men. But through travail and toil I still retained in the back of my mind the story of the Full Moon and her sorry cargo. And I determined some day to start a campaign based upon the eternal truth that a race without ships is like a man stricken and blind. I would instigate a movement to rehabilitate Africa and found such an Ethiopian Empire as the world has never seen. It would be greater than the empire in Haiti, for while that island kingdom with its Toussaint l'Ouvertures and Christophes produced great palaces, and forts, and armies—battalions strong enough to whip the best soldiery of France—yet the island itself is a mere pin-point on the earth's surface compared to the great continent of Africa where I planned to build my empire. It would be greater than the empires of Africa's past—such powerful nations as those who raised their enormous stone structures at Zimbabwe and elsewhere—for although these kingdoms must have numbered their subjects by the hundreds of thousands, their store of knowledge was limited. I dreamed of an empire infinitely more cultured. Africa could again lift up her head. Her fleets would sail upon the sea. Her resources would once more enrich her own children. I dreamed of downfall for the imperialists, those wolves from the Zuider Zee and the slums of White Chapel.

Fortunately for my project I met Captain Forbes early in life. He became my patron and sponsor just as Clarkson and Wilberforce had been Paul Cuffee's. To him I attribute what I possess of the higher reaches of nautical science. He it was who taught me the theory and technique of international maritime practice.

Captain Forbes looked something like Sir John Fisher. He was slender and dark skinned with a Norman profile. He was quick and accurate in conversation, devastating in debate. We became great friends as our views were all in harmony. He was a humanitarian and a universalist with the good of the whole world at heart. I was no less a humanitarian, but my particular object was the betterment of the Ethiopian race.

Before I could even begin to help my people it was necessary to secure a ship. One day Captain Forbes came to me with the news that Count Thesen of Norway, one of his very good friends, had just such a ship as I had been seeking. It lay at anchor at Stavanger, Norway, and it was necessary for us to journey there if we wished to make arrangements for its purchase. We took passage on a steamer bound for Norway.

There were three of us who went up to Stavanger, Captain Forbes, Sydney Wilson, and I. I had found Sydney Wilson sitting on a park bench in Leicester Square, London. He was a rawboned Basian, shiny black and as strong as a bull. I could tell by the cut of his jib that he was as true as steel. He had run away from his ship after having been badly treated. He told me about his troubles in his deep, musical, West Indian brogue. "Been sailin' since I was pickaninny. Seen some billows. Never seen mate like de mate on dat ship. Dat buck of a man tink I'm a fool. He whip me. I knock him down and run away from ship." I determined then and there to take him with me if I found a boat. Before many weeks had passed I was to find that he was a fearless sailor and an excellent cook.

As we three traveled northward aboard the steamer we watched the northern lights which until this time I had never seen in such brilliance. As we approached the coast of Norway we sat transfixed at the magnificent scenery. Neither Sydney Wilson nor I in all our travels had seen these fjords and cliffs and snow-capped mountains. The water was blue and clear. The land seemed clean and unlittered. On the hilly meadows cattle grazed. Here and there dark forests came down to the sea. But more miraculous than all else were the mountains that were not mountains at all, phantom hills and cliffs through which the eye could penetrate to valleys and green pastures beyond.

Before we realized it our journey was over and we were at Stavanger, Norway. We found the little city quite as clean as the hilly meadows along the coast. The fishermen's cottages with their quaint gardens were bright and colorful. I was impressed with the gentility, refinement, and quiet culture of these people. They seemed positive but just, deliberate but intelligent; people who could understand the realities of life yet with men among them who could dream as well as any.

The day after our arrival we went to the offices of Thesen and Company. The count himself was in South Africa, but his agent made us welcome and told us about the boat. We all went down to the dock together. The water was crowded with fishing boats and small craft of every kind. One among them seemed as proud as a swan in a flock of wild geese. She was the ship we hoped to buy. I have sailed aboard many boats in my life, but not one was as graceful as this. She was a freak topsail schooner rigged to carry a great mass of canvas. She was some seventy feet long with the lines of a grayhound. She had what is known as a "pink" stern, a stern almost as high and pointed as the prow, giving the boat an unusual symmetry. And although her two masts were bare I could picture them with white canvas bellying in the wind.

We took a skiff and went aboard. We examined her from stem to stern. She was the worthy product of the sons of the Vikings and as strong as the day she was launched. Her strakes and wales were of oak, staunch enough for a man-of-war. When I went into the hold I found the keelson of enormous strength as were the garboard strakes. The way things were shored and braced would have delighted any sailor. Every point in the whole boat where there was any stress was made of oak. She had been given such good care she was really better than new. She was a seasoned boat. We found no defects in the stays or shrouds, clamps or yards. And although we searched for rot with our pocket knives we could find none. Above all she was beautifully and newly copper-sheathed. I realized from our examination that she would hold herself to a course and carry sail without lying on her side.

The name on the prow was almost obliterated by the weather so we hunted up her log. The name was the "Pellar Guri," and beneath the name was a page of illuminated script which Captain Forbes translated. It ran something like this:

In the early part of the fifteenth century, Norway was under the sway of independent robber barons. There was one tyrant who became so cruel and greedy that the people drove him from the land. He escaped to Scotland where he bribed a Scottish chief named Sinclair to assist him in conquering Norway. Together these schemers gathered a huge army and descended upon the unsuspecting Norwegians. There was a peasant girl named Pellar Guri living in one of the valleys. With great courage and spirit she rallied all the peasants of Norway and drove the robber and his hirelings from the land. From this united effort rose the Kingdom of Norway.

The boat had been named for this heroic girl, and the figurehead was a fine representation of her strength and beauty. Sydney Wilson, who was a West Indian and who had been under Spanish influence all his life, misunderstood the name, however. He thought we had said the Pedro Gorino.

He was a clever man with the brush as most sailors are, and several days later he took it upon himself to paint the name on the prow. He led me proudly to the dock to show me his handiwork.

"But that isn't her name," I protested, "her name is the Pellar Guri."

"Pellar Guri no name for black man's ship," he replied. And he looked so dejected when I suggested changing it that I said no more about it. And Pedro Gorino she was from that day forth.

I attribute to Captain Forbes all my success in this deal for the Pedro Gorino. He arranged such liberal terms with Thesen's agent that I took a new lease on life. Before the week was out he had solved another of our problems. The ship was without sails and he had found an extraordinary bargain. We went up to see the sail-makers in their loft. There were a dozen old salts sewing away on canvas for all they were worth. The light fell upon them from little windows opening out over the sea. Ah, there was a scene for a great master, the light falling upon those old men and the character in their faces.

Captain Forbes could talk Norwegian and most of the men could talk good English so we understood each other very nicely. When they heard my story and found that I was going out to South Africa they informed us of an extraordinary coincidence. They had in another loft connected with their organization sixteen young men who for several months had been preparing to go to South Africa to seek their fortune. They were all young sailors and it came to my mind that they might be willing to man the ship and sail her out to Cape Town for their passage. We met the young sail-makers later that afternoon and they were eager to accept our terms. Consequently we drew up a contract with these people purchasing the gear and sails and arranging for the exchange of the services of these young men for their passage to South Africa.

The next day we opened ship and commenced to take in stores. There was practically no repair work necessary, but we gave the boat a thorough inspection and overhauling. Within the scheduled time the sails were aboard and the crew was ready for the journey. They were as fine and clean cut a bunch of boys as I have known. There were fifteen Norwegians, one Scotchman, Sydney Wilson cook par excellence, Captain Forbes, and I. One of the Norwegians, Captain Carlson, was a very experienced mariner so I made him my first mate. We took aboard the last of our hundred tons of cargo and luggage and prepared to up anchor.

The next morning we made our departure and plotted a great circle for England. The North Sea was choppy and we hit rather rough weather during the first part of our trip. It was cold and rainy with leaden-colored skies overhead. The Pedro Gorino responded to our every touch, and proved herself a fine, seaworthy little ship. In several days we sighted the lights eighty miles northeast of London and were soon in the channel. We shaped our course due west by south with a favorable breeze and finally dropped anchor at Southampton.

I was very sorry to have to leave Captain Forbes, but our parting at Southampton was inevitable as his business held him in England. While we were at anchor he gave me literally tons of useful cargo and dozens of nautical instruments. Among his gifts were sextants, books, charts and maps, three fine solar chronometers, two sidereal chronometers, a four-inch telescope, and a muzzle-loading salute cannon. The cannon proved to be not the least serviceable of these, and on one occasion saved us from a real catastrophe. The captain went with us as far as the Lizards, the point where ships leaving England make their departure. We had a sorrowful parting and he promised to come to South Africa within the year. When he could accompany us no farther he hailed a pilot boat and stepped aboard, leaving me to the great task we had planned together.

We plotted our course in a great circle from the Lizards to Funchal, and went bowling along piling up knot after knot. Far out on the wild Atlantic we had no thought of the Biscayan tides, but were surrounded by porpoises even before we came to cloudless Madeira and the pearl Teneriffe set as they were in a sea of glass.

The Scotchman aboard our ship was a great story-teller as were one or two of the Norwegians. The weather was fine and there was little work and much time for games and stories. I remember one story the Scotchman told the name of which was, *All About Jonah and His Voyage in the Belly of the Whale*. It is a raw story and one to which religious people might take exception, so for the sake of discretion *I* had better not relate it.

The Scotchman, however, had no such scruples. He would say, "Hoot mon, that's nae story. Listen to this one." Whereupon we would receive another deluge of his racy narration. He knew most of Bobby Burns by heart; and his favorite poem was,

> Ye flowery banks o' bonnie Doon,
> How can ye blume sae fair?
> How can ye chant, ye little birds,
> And I sae fu' o' care?

Finally we made landfall at Madeira and dropped anchor at Funchal. Here we took on water and provisions and I invested the rest of my money in Madeira lace and carved furniture of rare woods which I knew I could sell at a profit at Cape Town. Soon we made our departure, and putting up every bit of rag we could carry, sailed day after day ahead of a light but favorable breeze. We passed the peaks of Teneriffe off the coast of Rio de Oro and after uneventful sailing sighted St. Vincent in the Cape Verde Islands.

So far we had encountered good weather, but one morning the sun arose red-yellow and we knew we were in for a storm. We shaped our course due south under full sail trying to miss its path and sail out of danger, but by noon the wind had slackened until the ship scarcely moved through the water. By mid-afternoon there was not a breath of air save for an occasional puff from every quarter which only served to make the sails flap idly where they hung. A haze began to spread over the ocean. This and the peculiar color of the sky told us more plainly than words what to expect. We put things in shipshape and waited. We must have lain becalmed over an hour laboring for breath in the hot sultry air, the ship rolling quietly on the glassy water. Suddenly we noticed a disturbance in the haze several hundred yards off our starboard. Then out of the ocean arose a great waterspout drawn higher and higher by a powerful wind which whirled like a corkscrew. The great column of water a hundred feet high was headed for the ship and came down upon us at an enormous rate of speed. But the wind that brought it did not fill our sails and we lay helpless, directly in the path of the oncoming disaster. I had once been aboard a ship when a small waterspout passed near throwing tons of water over the midship and taking several men from their feet. I remembered how the ship had staggered under the impact, and in the second I had for thought I realized that this great column of water rushing down upon us might easily send us to the bottom. Then in the nick of time I remembered the advice of my old Uncle Silas. "If a spout comes at you shoot it with a gun. It'll fall same as any living thing." Our salute cannon mounted on the bow was always filled with shot and powder. I rushed to this and, aiming it at the oncoming pillar of water, fired. The waterspout broke at less than fifty yards from the ship and poured back into the sea like a waterfall. We were very thankful for our deliverance. Within a few hours a breeze sprang up from the port quarter and we got a splendid run all the evening.

We sighted St. Paul on our port some days later and continued to sail day after day through an untroubled sea. We plotted our course southeast and piled up knot after knot of southern latitude. As we approached St. Helena the weather grew squally but we would not shorten sail. We passed outside the island, only sighting her hills. The menacing sky kept us on the alert, but the splendid stiffness of our lady Pedro Gorino held to her course and would not give an inch, but instead gained to windward and mounted the waves like a Guinea goose.

At last we sighted Table Mountain and the Lion's Rump without mishap or accident, having made our reckoning to the second of a degree. Thus we came to Cape Town from Stavanger, Norway, in seventy-one days on the good ship the Pedro Gorino.

MATTHEW A. HENSON

Matthew Henson was born in Charles County, Maryland, in 1866. Following the death of his parents, Henson went to Baltimore, where he hired himself out as a cabin boy; he was twelve at the time. In 1886, he became Lieutenant Robert E. Peary's personal servant on a survey expedition and for the next ten years worked closely with Peary on several expeditions, the most famous being their attempts to reach the North Pole. After five aborted attempts, Peary, Henson, and their four Eskimo guides were the first people ever to reach the North Pole.

Henson was largely ignored by white America until the years just before his death, when he finally was recognized by the Pentagon, the White House, and the Geographical Society of Chicago. He died in 1955.

f r o m
A Negro Explorer at the North Pole (1908)

July 6, 1908: We're off! For a year and a half I have waited for this order, and now we have cast off. The shouting and the tumult ceases, the din of whistles, bells, and throats dies out, and once again the long, slow surge of the ocean hits the good ship that we have embarked in. It was at one-thirty P.M. to-day that I saw the last hawse-line cast adrift, and felt the throb of the engines of our own ship. Chief Wardwell is on the job, and from now on it is due north.

Oyster Bay, Long Island Sound: We are expecting President Roosevelt. The ship has been named in his honor and has already made one voyage towards the North Pole, farther north than any ship has ever made.

July 7: At anchor, the soft wooded hills of Long Island give me a curious impression. I am waiting for the command to attack the savage ice- and rock-bound fortress of the North, and here instead we are at anchor in the neighborhood of sheep grazing in green fields.

Sydney, N.S., July 17, 1908: All of the expedition are aboard and those going home have gone. Mrs. Peary and the children, Mr. Borup's father, and Mr. Harry Whitney, and some other guests were the last to leave the *Roosevelt*, and have given us a last good-by from the tug, which came alongside to take them off.

Good-by all. Every one is sending back a word to some one he has left behind, but I have said my good-bys a long time ago, and as I waved my hand in parting salutation to the little group on the deck of the tug, my thoughts were with my wife, and I hoped when she next heard of me it would be with feelings of joy and happiness, and that she would be glad she had permitted me to leave her for an absence that might never end. . . .

All of the rest of the members of the expedition are the same as were on the first trip of the *Roosevelt*:—Commander Peary, Captain Bartlett, Professor Marvin, Chief Engineer Wardwell, Charley Percy the steward, and myself. The crew has been selected by Captain Bartlett, and are mostly strangers to me.

Commander Peary is too well known for me to describe him at length; thick reddish hair turning gray; heavy, bushy eyebrows shading his "sharpshooter's eyes" of steel gray, and long mustache. His hair grows rapidly and, when on the march, a thick heavy beard quickly appears. He is six feet tall, very graceful, and well built, especially about the chest and shoulders; long arms, and legs slightly bowed. Since losing his toes, he walks with a peculiar slide-like stride. He has a voice clear and loud, and words never fail him.

Captain Bartlett is about my height and weight. He has short, curly, light-brown hair and red cheeks; is slightly round-shouldered, due to the large shoulder-muscles caused by pulling the oars, and is as quick in his actions as a cat. His manner and conduct indicate that he has always been the leader of his crowd from boyhood up, and there is no man on this ship that he would be afraid to tackle. He is a young man (thirty-three years old) for a ship captain, but he knows his job.

Professor Marvin is a quiet, earnest person, and has had plenty of practical experience besides his splendid education. He is rapidly growing bald; his face is rather thin, and his neck is long. He has taken great interest in me and, being a teacher, has tried to teach me. Although I hope to perfect myself in navigation, my knowledge so far consists only of knot and splice seamanship, and I need to master the mathematical end.

The Chief Engineer, Mr. Wardwell, is a fine-looking, ruddy-complexioned giant, with the most honest eyes I have ever looked into. His hair is thinning and is almost pure white, and I should judge him to be about forty-five years old. He has the greatest patience, and I have never seen him lose his temper or get rattled.

Charley Percy is Commander Peary's oldest hand, next to me. He is our steward, and sees to it that we are properly fed while aboard ship, and he certainly does see to it with credit to himself.

From Sydney to Hawks Harbor, where we met the *Erik*, has been uneventful except for the odor of the *Erik*, which is loaded with whale-meat and can be smelled for miles. We passed St. Paul's Island and Cape St. George early in the day and through the Straits of Belle Isle to Hawks Harbor, where there is a whale-factory. From here we leave for Turnavik.

We have been racing with the *Erik* all day, and have beaten her to this place. Captain Bartlett's father owns it, and we loaded a lot of boots and skins, which the Captain's father had ready for us. From here we sail to the Esquimo country of North Greenland, without a stop if possible, as the Commander has no intention of visiting any of the Danish settlements in South Greenland.

Cape York is our next point, and the ship is sailing free. Aside from the excitement of the start, and the honor of receiving the personal visit of the President, and his words of encouragement and cheer, the trip so far has been uneventful; and I have busied myself in putting my cabin in order, and making myself useful in overhauling and stowing provisions in the afterhold.

July 24: Still northward-bound, with the sea rolling and washing over the ship; and the *Erik* in the distance seems to be getting her share of the wash. She is loaded heavily with fresh whale-meat, and is purposely keeping in leeward of us to spare us the discomfort of the odor.

July 25 and 26: Busy with my carpenter's kit in the Commander's cabin and elsewhere. There has been heavy rain and seas, and we have dropped the *Erik* completely. The *Roosevelt* is going fine. We can see the Greenland coast plainly and to-day, the 29th, we raised and passed Disco Island. Icebergs on all sides. The light at midnight is almost as bright as early evening twilight in New York on the Fourth of July and the ice-blink of the interior ice-cap is quite plain. We have gone through Baffin's Bay with a rush and raised Duck Island about ten A.M. and passed and dropped it by two P.M.

I was ashore on Duck Island in 1891, on my first voyage north, and I remember distinctly the cairn the party built and the money they deposited in it. I wonder if it is still there? There is little use for money up here, and the place is seldom visited except by men from the whalers, when their ships are locked in by ice.

From here it is two hundred miles due north to Cape York.

August 1: Arrived at Cape York Bay and went ashore with the party to communicate with the Esquimos of whom there were three families. They remembered us and were dancing up and down the shore, and waving to us in welcome, and as soon as the bow of the boat had grazed the little beach, willing hands helped to run her up on shore. These people are hospitable and helpful, and always willing, sometimes too willing. As an example, I will tell how, at a settlement farther north, we were going ashore in one of the whale-boats. Captain Bartlett was forward, astraddle of the bow with the boat-hook in his hands to fend off the blocks of ice, and knew perfectly well where he wanted to land, but the group of excited Esquimos were in his way and though he ordered them back, they continued running about and getting in his way. In a very short while the Captain lost patience and commenced to talk loudly and with excitement; immediately Sipsoo took up his language and parrot-like started to repeat the Captain's exact words: "Get back there, get back—how in ———— do you expect me to make a landing?" And thus does the innocent lamb of the North acquire a civilized tongue.

It is amusing to hear Kudlooktoo in the most charming manner give Charley a cussing that from any one else would cause Charley to break his head open.

For the last week I have been busy, with "Matt! The Commander wants you," "Matt do this," and "Matt do that," and with going ashore and trading for skins, dogs, lines, and other things; and also walrus-hunting. I have been up to my neck in work, and have had small opportunity to keep my diary up to date. We have all put on heavy clothing; not the regular fur clothes for the winter, but our thickest civilized clothing, that we would wear in midwinter in the States. In the middle of the day, if the sun shines, the heat is felt; but if foggy or cloudy, the heavy clothing is comfortable.

All of the Esquimos want to come aboard and stay aboard. Some we want and will take along, but there are others we will not have or take along on a bet, and the pleasant duty of telling them so and putting them ashore falls to me. It is not a pleasant job to disappoint these people, but they would be a burden to us and in our way. Besides, we have left them a plentiful supply of needfuls, and our trading with them has been fair and generous.

The "Crow's-Nest" has been rigged upon the mainmast, and this morning, after breakfast, Mr. Whitney, three Esquimos, and myself started in Mr. Whitney's motor-boat to hunt walrus. The motor gave out very shortly after the start, and the oars had to be used. We were fortunate in getting two walrus, which I shot, and then we returned to the ship for the whale-boat. We left the ship with three more Esquimos in the whale-boat, and got four more walrus. . . .

THE POLE!

Captain Bartlett and his two boys had commenced their return journey, and the main column, depleted to its final strength, started northward. We were six: Peary, the commander, the Esquimos, Ootah, Egingwah, Seegloo and Ooqueah, and myself.

Day and night were the same. My thoughts were on the going and getting forward, and on nothing else. The wind was from the southeast, and seemed to push us on, and the sun was at our backs, a ball of livid fire, rolling his way above the horizon in never-ending day.

The Captain had gone, Commander Peary and I were alone (save for the four Esquimos), the same as we had been so often in the past years, and as we looked at each other we realized our position and we knew without speaking that the time had come for us to demonstrate that we were the men who, it had been ordained, should unlock the door which held the mystery of the Arctic. Without an instant's hesitation, the order to push on was given, and we started off in the trail made by the Captain to cover the Farthest North he had made and to push on over one hundred and thirty miles to our final destination.

The Captain had had rough going, but, owing to the fact that his trail was our track for a short time, and that we came to good going shortly after leaving his turning point, we made excellent distance without any trouble, and only stopped when we came to a lead barely frozen over, a full twenty-five miles beyond. We camped and waited for the strong southeast wind to force the sides of the lead together. The Esquimos had eaten a meal of stewed dog, cooked over a fire of wood from a discarded sledge, and, owing to their wonderful powers of recuperation, were in good condition; Commander Peary and myself, rested and invigorated by our thirty hours in the last camp, waiting for the return and departure of Captain Bartlett, were also in fine fettle, and accordingly the accomplishment of twenty-five miles of northward progress was not exceptional. With my proven ability in gauging distances, Commander Peary was ready to take the reckoning as I made it and he did not resort to solar observations until we were within a hand's grasp of the Pole.

The memory of those last five marches, from the Farthest North of Captain Bartlett to the arrival of our party at the Pole, is a memory of toil, fatigue, and exhaustion, but we were urged on and encouraged by our relentless commander, who was himself being scourged by the final lashings of the dominating influence that had controlled his life. From the land to 87° 48′ north, Commander Peary had had the best of the going, for he had brought up the rear and had utilized the trail made by the preceding parties, and thus he had kept himself in the best of condition for the time when he made the spurt that brought him to the end of the race. From 87° 48′ north, he kept in the lead and did his work in such a way as to convince me that he was still as good a man as he had ever been. We marched and marched, falling down in our tracks repeatedly, until it was impossible to go on. We were forced to camp, in spite of the impatience of the Commander, who found himself unable to rest, and who only waited long enough for us to relax into sound sleep, when he would wake us up and start us off again. I do not believe that he slept for one hour from April 2 until after he had loaded us up and ordered us to go back over our old trail, and I often think that from the instant when the order to return was given until the land was again sighted, he was in a continual daze.

Onward we forced our weary way. Commander Peary took his sights from the time our chronometer-watches gave, and I, knowing that we had kept on going in practically a straight line, was sure that we had more than covered the necessary distance to insure our arrival at the top of the earth.

It was during the march of the 3d of April that I endured an instant of hideous horror. We were crossing a lane of moving ice. Commander Peary was in the lead setting the pace, and a half hour later the four boys and myself followed in single file. They had all gone before, and I was standing and pushing at the upstanders of my sledge, when the block of ice I was using as a support slipped from underneath my feet, and before I knew it the sledge was out of my grasp, and I was floundering in the water of the lead. I did the best I could. I tore my hood from off my head and struggled frantically. My hands were gloved and I could not take hold of the ice, but before I could give the "Grand Hailing Sigh of Distress," faithful old Ootah had grabbed me by the nape of the neck, the same as he would have grabbed a dog, and with one hand he pulled me out of the water, and with the other hurried the team across.

He had saved my life, but I did not tell him so, for such occurrences are taken as part of the day's work, and the sledge he safeguarded was of much more importance, for it held, as part of its load, the Commander's sextant, the mercury, and the coils of piano-wire that were the essential portion of the scientific part of the expedition. My kamiks (boots of sealskin) were stripped off, and the congealed water was beaten out of my bearskin trousers, and with a dry pair of kamiks, we hurried on to overtake the column. When we caught up, we found the boys gathered around the Commander, doing their best to relieve him of his discomfort, for he had fallen into the water also, and while he was not complaining, I was sure that his bath had not been any more voluntary than mine had been.

When we halted on April 6, 1909, and started to build the igloos, the dogs and sledges having been secured, I noticed Commander Peary at work unloading his sledge and unpacking several bundles of equipment. He pulled out from under his *kooletah* (thick, fur outer-garment) a small folded package and unfolded it. I recognized his old silk flag, and realized that this was to be a camp of importance. Our different camps had been known as Camp Number One, Number Two, etc., but after the turning back of Captain Bartlett, the camps had been given names such as Camp Nansen, Camp Cagni, etc., and I asked what the name of this camp was to be — "Camp Peary"? "This, my boy, is to be Camp Morris K. Jesup, the last and most northerly camp on the earth." He fastened the flag to a staff and planted it firmly on the top of his igloo. For a few minutes it hung limp and lifeless in the dead calm of the haze, and then a slight breeze, increasing in strength, caused the folds to straighten out, and soon it was ripping out in sparkling color. The stars and stripes were "nailed to the Pole."

A thrill of patriotism ran through me and I raised my voice to cheer the starry emblem of my native land. The Esquimos gathered around and, taking the time from Commander Peary, three hearty cheers rang out on the still, frosty air, our dumb dogs looking on in puzzled surprise. As prospects for getting a sight of the sun were not good, we turned in and slept, leaving the flag proudly floating above us.

This was a thin silk flag that Commander Peary had carried on all of his

Arctic journeys, and he had always flown it at his last camps. It was as glorious and as inspiring a banner as any battle-scarred, blood-stained standard of the world—and this badge of honor and courage was also blood-stained and battle-scarred, for at several places there were blank squares marking the spots where pieces had been cut out at each of the "Farthests" of its brave bearer, and left with the records in the cairns, as mute but eloquent witnesses of his achievements. At the North Pole a diagonal strip running from the upper left to the lower right corner was cut and this precious strip, together with a brief record, was placed in an empty tin, sealed up and buried in the ice, as a record for all time.

Commander Peary also had another American flag, sewn on a white ground, and it was the emblem of the "Daughters of the Revolution Peace Society"; he also had and flew the emblem of the Navy League, and the emblems of a couple of college fraternities of which he was a member.

It was about ten or ten-thirty A.M., on the 7th of April, 1909, that the Commander gave the order to build a snow-shield to protect him from the flying drift of the surface-snow. I knew that he was about to take an observation, and while we worked I was nervously apprehensive, for I felt that the end of our journey had come. When we handed him the pan of mercury the hour was within a very few minutes of noon. Laying flat on his stomach, he took the elevation and made the notes on a piece of tissue-paper at his head. With sun-blinded eyes, he snapped shut the *vernier* (a graduated scale that subdivides the smallest divisions on the sector of the circular scale of the sextant) and with the resolute squaring of his jaws, I was sure that he was satisfied, and I was confident that the journey had ended. Feeling that the time had come, I ungloved my right hand and went forward to congratulate him on the success of our eighteen years of effort, but a gust of wind blew something into his eye, or else the burning pain caused by his prolonged look at the reflection of the limb of the sun forced him to turn aside; and with both hands covering his eyes, he gave us orders to not let him sleep for more than four hours, for six hours later he purposed to take another sight about four miles beyond, and that he wanted at least two hours to make the trip and get everything in readiness.

I unloaded a sledge, and reloaded it with a couple of skins, the instruments, and a cooker with enough alcohol and food for one meal for three, and then I turned in to the igloo where my boys were already sound asleep. The thermometer registered 29° below zero. I fell into a dreamless sleep and slept for about a minute, so I thought, when I was awakened by the clatter and noise made by the return of Peary and his boys.

The Commander gave the word, "We will plant the stars and stripes—*at the North Pole!*" and it was done; on the peak of a huge paleocrystic floeberg the glorious banner was unfurled to the breeze, and as it snapped and crackled with the wind, I felt a savage joy and exultation. Another world's accomplishment was done and finished, and as in the past, from the beginning of history, wherever the world's work was done by a white man, he had been accompanied by a colored man. From the building of the pyramids and the journey to the Cross, to the discovery of the new world and the discovery of the North Pole, the Negro had been the faithful and constant companion of the Caucasian, and I felt all that it was possible for me to feel, that it was I, a lowly member of my race, who had been chosen by fate to represent it, at this, almost the last of the world's great *work*.

2

MISSIONARIES AND ACTIVISTS OF THE NINETEENTH CENTURY

*I*n the nineteenth century the rise of interest in missions at home and abroad reflected the expansionist agenda of Christianity, which encouraged its followers to seek converts from other faiths. The increase in missionary activity by whites and blacks also reflected nationalistic and imperialistic ideologies based on the notion that the United States and other Western nations were more "civilized" and thus needed to spread enlightened Christianity to other cultures. Narratives in this section include descriptions of missionary and other benevolent work in Haiti, Jamaica, England, India, and Africa. Sometimes the work of religious uplift was intertwined with the desire to evaluate possible sites for African-American emigration (see the introduction on pan-Africanism and African colonization in the Africa section).

In relation to Africa many American blacks felt that it was their special duty to "redeem" the natives of that continent. Daniel H. Peterson expressed that sentiment in his narrative *The Looking Glass:* "I have visited Liberia without fee or reward ... trusting only in the promises of my blessed Lord, for the benefit of my beloved and afflicted brethren, and the promotion of the Gospel" (99). According to Walter L. Williams, between 1877 and 1900 at least 113 black American missionaries served in Africa; although they were from every region of the United States, most were from middle-class families (85).

Although many missionaries were men, most of the writers included in this section are women. Missionary work was one of the few acceptable examples of useful "women's work" in the early nineteenth century, but that generally meant serving as a missionary wife. In fact, the black women included here were traveling without male companions, with the exception of Coppin. Often these women were bucking husbands, male church authorities, or both in leaving home to preach or teach the gospel. For example, Amanda Berry Smith served as an "independent" missionary in England, Ireland, Scotland, India, and Africa from 1878 to 1890 after being limited by the African Methodist Episcopal Church; Nancy Prince was recruited by American Baptists but appeared to travel independently in Jamaica; Zilpha Elaw pursued her calling without the sanction or support of the American Board of Commissioners for Foreign Missions (Andrews, *Sisters of the Spirit*, 2). Thus, for black women evangelists and missionaries, traveling abroad to find meaningful work and an authoritative voice beyond the narrow confines of "women's sphere" can be read as an example of feminist activism in a Christian context. Generally, women missionaries were active in helping women and children in the areas they served; in their narratives, they were likely to note the conditions of life for girls and women.

THOMAS PAUL, SR.

Thomas Paul, Sr., was born in Exeter, New Hampshire, in 1773. He became a prominent minister of the African Baptist Church on Belknap Street in Boston, an institution that served as a center of education and activism for the black community. He was also a chaplain of the Masonic African Grand Lodge No. 459 and an abolitionist. In 1808 Paul's fame as a charismatic preacher spread, and he lectured in white Baptist churches in New York City, where in 1809 he helped blacks found the Abyssian Baptist Church, which became the largest black church in America.

In 1823 Paul traveled to Haiti as a missionary; he followed David George, Daniel Coker, and Lott Carey as among the earliest African-American missionaries. He returned to New England, where he died in 1831.

LETTER TO THE EDITOR

The following letter from Thomas Paul, a Minister of the Baptist Society in Boston, is taken from the "Columbian Sentinel" of July 3, 1824.

●

MR. EDITOR,

In compliance with the request of several very respectable gentlemen of this city, and the solicitations of persons of my own colour, I am induced to publish the following statement in relation to the country and government of Hayti. I the more cheerfully comply with these requests, in hopes that those free people of colour especially, who are disposed to seek an asylum for the enjoyment of liberty, and the common rights of man in a foreign clime, may be benefitted by this publication.

Having been a resident for some months in the Island of Hayti, I am fully persuaded that it is the best and most suitable place of residence which Providence has hitherto offered to emancipated people of colour, for the enjoyment of liberty and quality with their attendant blessings. At an interview which I had with President Boyer, some months ago, he was pleased to make a verbal statement of the same offers to me, as an organ of communication to the free people of colour in the United States, which he has recently made to the Colonization Society, in answer to several inquiries made by the Rev. Mr. Dewey.

After having made known to his Excellency the object of my visit, and having received permission from him to preach, and discharge the duties of a missionary of the gospel in the Island, I never received the least molestation from any person; but on the contrary, was always treated with the greatest respect by all the officers of the government, and by all classes of the people.

The Island is delightfully situated, abounding with all the necessaries and even the luxuries of life. It presents to the eye the most romantic and beautiful scenery; and while its verdant mountains recall to our minds what we have read of ancient Gilboa, Tabor, Lebanon, Carmel, and Sion, its fertile valleys present us with the rich luxuriance of the valleys of the Israelitish Canaan.

The staple productions are coffee, rice, tobacco, indigo, and Indian corn. The forests abound with the best of mahogany, log-wood, and fustic; and the pastures are literally covered with flocks and herds.

A yoke of well made oxen, measuring six feet six inches, may be purchased for 17 or $18; a handsome cow and calf, for $7; and swine and poultry at the same rate. The markets are supplied with a plenty of fresh and salt water fish—oysters, lobsters, and turtles. A turtle weighing 80 or 90 lbs. may be purchased for $2. Through the months of June, July, August, and September, I resided upon the Island, and during this time, which is considered the hottest part of years, and the most unhealthy to strangers, I enjoyed as good health as at any period of my life.

The Haytiens have made great progress in the mechanical arts, which receive liberal encouragement. Goldsmiths, silversmiths, blacksmiths, tailors, bootmakers, painters, cabinetmakers, coopers, tanners, curriers, house-carpenters, ship-carpenters, turners, wheel-wrights, tin-workers, sugar-manufacturers, and distillers would find constant and profitable employment.

A country, the local situation of which is favourable to trade and commercial enterprise, possessing a free and well regulated government, which encourages the useful and liberal arts, a country possessing an enterprising population of several hundred thousands of active and brave men, who are determined to live free or die gloriously in the defense of freedom, must possess advantages highly inviting to men who are sighing for the enjoyment of the common rights and liberties of mankind. The time, I trust, is not far distant, when all wise and good men will use their influence to place the Free Coloured People of the United States upon the delightful Island of Hayti.

Thomas Paul

Zilpha Elaw

Zilpha Elaw was born to free parents in the Philadelphia area in 1790. Her mother died when she was twelve years old, so her father put her to service in a Quaker family, with whom she lived until age eighteen. She began to have mystical visions in her midteens; in her narrative, she describes seeing Jesus while she was milking a cow (Elaw, 6–7). She converted to Methodism in 1808, married John Elaw in 1810, and gave birth to a daughter in 1811. In 1817 Elaw attended her first camp meeting, where she became convinced that her soul was sanctified by God. She began to pursue an itinerant ministry in 1819, but when her husband died in 1823 Elaw worked as a domestic; later she opened a school for black children in Burlington, New Jersey, where she resided. After two years, she closed the school, put her daughter in the care of a relative, and began preaching again.

In the spring of 1828 Elaw felt the call to travel to slaveholding states, regardless of the danger of being kidnapped or sold as a slave. She preached to blacks and whites in Baltimore and Annapolis, Maryland; Washington, D.C.; and Alexandria, Virginia. She returned to preach in the mid-Atlantic and northern states until 1840, when she booked passage to London, convinced that God had prepared some great work for her there. The passages included here show the recurrent opposition that Elaw faced from those who felt that women's preaching was unscriptural. Elaw estimates that she preached more than a thousand sermons in England. *Memoirs of the Life, Religious Experience, Ministerial Travels and Labours of Mrs. Zilpha Elaw,* from which this excerpt is taken, was published by the author in London in 1846.

f r o m
MEMOIRS OF THE LIFE, RELIGIOUS EXPERIENCE, MINISTERIAL TRAVELS AND LABOURS OF MRS. ZILPHA ELAW (1846)

. . . I left home again in July, 1835, and was absent fifteen months: the Lord graciously prepared the minds of the people everywhere for my ministry; and many received the word with gladness and singleness of heart. I was in Boston when Mr. George Thompson[1] was lecturing there on the abominations of slavery; great crowds were attracted to his lectures, and much light was diffused by his zealous exertions in the cause of emancipation. From Boston I went to Lynn to attend the Conference. I was there introduced to Bishop Heading, and spent an afternoon in his company. He requested a sight of my testimonials and letters of recommendation, which I handed him; and he expressed his entire satisfaction with them, but inquired if it should be found that my ministry was calculated to excite contention, many persons being strongly averse to the ministry of females, whether I would be willing to relinquish it. To which, I replied, that no ambition of mine, but the special appointment of God, had put me into the ministry; and, therefore, I had no option in the matter; and as to such Christians as take up ignorant and prejudiced objections against my labours; men whose whims are law, who walk after the imagination of their own hearts, and to whom the cause of God is a toy; I could not for a moment study their gratification at the sacrifice of duty. It is an easy matter to adopt a string of notions on religion, and make a great ado about them; but the weight of religious obligation, and the principle of conscientious obedience to God are quite another matter. I enjoyed the good bishop's company, and heard him with pleasure avow that he should be sorry in any way to discourage me.

From Lynn I itinerated from city to city, and from village to village, preaching the gospel of the kingdom in the fear of the Lord; and great was the number those who believed and were baptised. . . .

[1]George Thompson was a well-known British abolitionist who was on a lecture tour in the United States.

I remained at home this time for the space of three years, with the exception of an occasional short journey, and visit of a few weeks; and throughout this period, my mind was often burdened with the weight of a voyage to England. I often argued the matter before the Lord pleading my ignorance, my sex, my colour and my inability to minister the gospel in a country so polished and enlightened, so furnished with Bibles, so blessed with ministers, so studded with temples; but the Lord said, "say not, I cannot speak; for thou shalt go to all to whom I send thee, and what I command thee, thou shalt speak."

In 1837, when on a visit to some religious friends, one morning, I saw a remarkable vision; I appeared to be in a strange place, and conversing with a stranger when three enormous balls of fire came perpendicularly over my head, and each of them exploded and burst at the same moment: I instantly appeared to fall to the ground; but was caught up by an unseen hand, and placed upon an animal, which darted with me through the regions of the air, with the velocity of lightning, and deposited me inside the window of an upper chamber. I there heard the voice of the almighty, saying, "I have a message for her to go with upon the high seas, and she will go." This occurrence took place just three years prior to my departure from America.

In 1839, the Lord was pleased to send me again into the Southern states; and as I travelled from city to city, I felt the impression that the time was near when I must leave the land of my nativity for a foreign shore. . . . From Providence I visited New York, Philadelphia and Baltimore and wherever I went, the inquiry was continually made, if I was not about shortly to embark for England accompanied by observations that my ministry was ultimately destined for a different arena than was furnished by America . . . and I could not but remark, how the Lord everywhere moved the minds of my friends to make it a topic of conversation; thereby keeping it always before me, and increasing the stimulus of my mind towards it; and without any solicitation of mine, they presented me their cheerful contributions; yea both white and coloured brethren, voluntarily came forward with their free-will offerings, to enable me to undertake the voyage, and bade me go and preach to strangers in a strange land, in the name of the Lord. Many were the proofs besides those related this work, that the Lord gave me of His purpose that I should come to England; and being now many hundreds of miles distant from my daughter, and feeling that the Lord's time had arrived, I wrote to apprise her thereof, and shortly after returned homewards as far as New York, where I attended the anniversary of the abolition society: Many of the speakers on that occasion came over to England to attend the great anti-slavery meeting in Exeter Hall. I then returned home; and was very affectionately received by my dear daughter; and made all possible dispatch in preparations for my departure.

The parting moment was painful in the extreme; for my daughter, and her two dear little boys, were entwined in the strongest affections of my heart; but I durst not disobey Him who had said unto me, as he had said unto Abraham, "Get thee out from thy country, and from thy kindred, and from thy father's house, unto a land that I will show thee." . . .

On the 23rd day of July, we were cheered with the sight of land; and on the 24th, we came to anchor off Falmouth, where most of the cabin passengers left us. On the evening of the 25th, we came safely into the London Docks: this was on a Saturday; and on the morning of the Lord's-day, I first set my foot on British ground . . . I became acquainted also with Mrs. T.— a true sister in the Lord, who has since fallen asleep in Jesus: and was introduced to a gentleman who interested himself greatly on my behalf very considerably enlarged the circle of my acquaintance, and even ushered me before the committees of the peace and anti-slavery societies. I found my situation rather awkward in reference to the latter body. I was first received by a deputation of three gentlemen, and afterwards admitted before the board. It was really an august assembly; their dignity appeared so redundant, that they scarcely knew what to do with it all. Had I attended there on a matter of life and death, I think I could scarcely have been more closely interrogated or more rigidly examined; from the reception I met with, my impression was, that they imagined I wanted some pecuniary or other help from them; for they treated me as the proud do the needy. In this however, they were mistaken. Among many other questions, they demanded to be informed, whether I had any new doctrine to advance, that the English Christians are not in possession of? To which I replied, no; but I was sent to preach Christ . . . they also wished to be informed, how it came about that God should send me? to which I replied, that I could not tell; but I knew that God required me to come hither, and that I came in obedience to His sovereign will; but that the Almighty's design therein was best known to Himself; but behold! said I, "I am here." Pride and arrogancy are among the master sins of rational beings; an high look, a stately bearing, and a proud heart, are abominations in the sight of God, and insure a woeful reverse in a future life. Infidels will indulge in pomposity and arrogance; but Christians are and must be humble and lowly. As a servant of Jesus, I am required to bear testimony in his name, who was meek and lowly, against the lofty looks of man, and the assumptions of such lordly authority and self-importance. Ere this work meets the eye of the public, I shall have sojourned in England five years and I am justified in saying that my God hath made my ministry a blessing to hundreds persons; and many who were living in sin and darkness before they saw my coloured face, have risen up to praise the Lord, for having sent me to preach His Gospel on the shores of Britain; numbers who had been reared to maturity, and were resident in localities plentifully furnished with places of worship and ministers of the gospel, and had scarcely heard a sermon in their lives were attracted to hear the coloured female preacher were inclosed in the gospel net, and are now walking in the commandments and ordinances of the Lord. I have travelled in several parts of England, and I thank God He has given me some spiritual children in every place wherein I have laboured. . . .

Having written to the family in Liverpool who had so pressingly invited me to visit them, to apprise them of my coming, on the 2nd of August, I took leave of sister W. and the kind friends at Wirksworth, and travelled thither by way of Manchester, and arrived in Liverpool about six o'clock in the evening. On going to the residence of the parties who had invited me, I found that the lady and her daughter were absent from home; and the gentleman's memory was so reluctant, that he very distantly recognised me. I was greatly fatigued with my journey, and somewhat disappointed after such a journey, to find my reception so different from the invitation. I soon took my leave of one whom I found not at all careful to entertain strangers, or practice the Christian duty of hospitality, and went in search of lodgings, which I had great difficulty in procuring: but after wandering from place to place, and making fruitless applications, I at length succeeded. It was of the Lord's goodness that I was at that inauspicious time possessed of sufficient money for my exigencies. My visit to this town was replete with discouragements I attended several meetings of the association, who were holding their annual conference there at that time I also made inquiries for the Wesleyans, and attended at Brunswick Chapel; and afterwards called upon the Rev. Mr. H., who received me with kindness, and referred me to Mr. D. the Wesleyan superintendent minister at that station. On my visit to Mr. D., he left directly on my introduction, to attend a funeral; but Mrs. D. entered into conversation with me, and assuming the theologian, reprobated female preaching as unscriptual; adding, that Mr. D. was greatly opposed to it, and always put it down if possible: she further said, that Paul ordained that a woman should not be suffered to speak in the church: but to sit in silence, and ask information of her husband at home. I was, however, too blind to discern, that for a female to warn sinners to flee from the wrath to come; to preach Christ to them, invite them to come to Him, and exhort them to be saved, was equally disorderly and improper with the interruptions of a church in its meetings and services, by the inquisitive questions of the females present; nor could I possibly understand how my ministry, which is directed to bring sinners to repentance, and employed in humble and affectionate attempts to stir up the pure minds of the saints, by way of remembrance and exhortation, involved any dictation or assumption of authority over the male sex. The apostle directed that a woman, when praying or prophecying, have her head covered; from which it may be inferred, that the praying and prophecying of a woman is allowable, but Mrs. D. was differently minded, and thought that a preaching female ought to depart from the Methodist body, and unite with the Quakers; but the Lord, who raised up Deborah to be a prophetess, and to judge His people, and inspired Hulda to deliver the counsels of God, sent me forth not as a Quakeress, but as a Methodist, and chiefly employed me to labour amongst the Methodists. I mentioned to her, some of the methods, by which the Lord made known to me His will, that I should go and preach the gospel; and these she met, by supposing, that it was possible I might have been misled. By this time, Mr. D. returned, and his Christian charity seemed put to some little expense on finding that I had not decamped; I presented him my testimonials and certificates; as he returned them, he said, "But do you not know we do not allow women to preach and that there is nothing in the Scriptures that will allow of it at all?" Addressing me with much assumed authority and severity. "We do not allow," sounded very uncouthly in my ears in a matter in which the commission of the Almighty is assumed. I again related some of the manifestations made to me by the Holy Ghost in reference to this matter; to which he replied, that he could not see how God could, consistently with Himself, give me such directions . . . I then departed from this iron-hearted abode, somewhat distressed and grounded in spirit and at a loss what step I should take next.

But thanks be unto God; He knoweth how to deliver the godly out of temptations, and will not suffer us to be tempted above what we are able to bear. On the following morning I awoke, with these words passing through my mind,

> Angels are now hovering round us;
> Unperceived, they mix the throng;

> Wondering at the love which crowned us;
> Glad to join the holy song.
>   Hallelujah!
> Love and praise to Christ belong.

I then felt the assurance of the Holy Spirit that the dark cloud which had so thickly and heavily pressed upon me was breaking; and a way soon after opened for me to visit Manchester, which in a few days after I did; and took lodgings on Chetham-hill, of Mrs. H—— who conducted me to Mr. R——'s, a local preacher, at whose house I was invited to spend the day: in the evening the class met there, and I assisted to lead it; the people were in a healthy, spiritual condition; and are enjoyed a sweet fellowship of the Spirit and communion with each other. . . .

I returned to Huddersfield on the 11th of July, where I remained a few weeks; it is delightfully situated; being entirely surrounded with majestic hills, with several streams of water running through it, which conduces much to the property of its manufacturing enterprise. There are in this town four places of worship belonging to the Episcopalians; two very large Wesleyan chapels, and two others occupied by the Primitive Methodists. The houses are neat, and chiefly built of stone; there are several bridges, watering places, and baths. It has a large market; and appears to be situated in a fruitful soil, abounding with fruit trees; the gardens are extensive and many of them tastefully laid out; and the approches to it are by railway and good height roads. On the 29th, I again visited Hull, when I preached morning and evening to immense congregations; and afterwards we held a prayer-meeting; and the Lord blessed the word that day; many were comforted, and many others inquired "what must we do to be saved."

On the 2nd of August, I embarked on board a steamer for London: there were a great many passengers on board; several of whom were from very widely distant parts of the earth. Some of the passengers requested me to preach to them, and the captain having given permission, we ascended the poop, and there held our meeting, which many persons seemed much interested. One gentleman afterwards came and inquired my name, saying that he was about to write to his wife, and wished to give her an account of a meeting so interesting and so novel to the crew of a steamship. . . .

I have felt much gratitude to the Lord for enkindling so great a friendship for me in the bosoms of many persons in England; many of my En-

Z i l p H a   E l a w

glish acquaintances possess a large share of my affections; and an imperishable image in my memory; but I know by experience the heart of a
stranger; many and deep and raging have been the billows of affliction
which have rolled over my soul since I crossed the Atlantic Ocean. My
reader may perceive that I have not been an idle spectator in my Heavenly
Master's cause. During my sojourn in England, I have preached considerably more than a thousand sermons. I have expended all my means in
travels of no little extent and duration; devoted my time, employed the
energies of my spirit, spent my strength and exhausted my constitution in
the cause of Jesus; and received of pecuniary supplies and temporal remu-
nerations in comparison with my time and labours a mere pittance, altogether inadequate to shield me from a thousand privations, hardships,
target-fires, vexatious anxieties and deep afflictions, to which my previous
life was an utter stranger.

NANCY PRINCE

Nancy Gardner Prince was born to free black parents in Newburyport, Massachusetts, on September 15, 1799. Her maternal grandfather, Tobias Wornton, or Backus, had been a slave of Winthrop Sargent of the influential New England Sargent family. In her narrative Prince proudly mentions that although a slave, her grandfather had fought in the battle of Bunker Hill. Her father, Thomas Gardner of Nantucket, had parents of African descent, and he died when Nancy was three months old. Her mother remarried twice and bore many children. At age eight, Nancy was forced to leave home, and all through her youth she worked as a servant. Out of necessity, she became responsible for finding work and lodging for her brothers and sisters, and by the age of fourteen, she traveled by herself from Gloucester to Salem to find a higher-paying domestic position. At seventeen, Nancy traveled to Boston to remove her sister from a brothel. In the first and most personal section of her narrative, Nancy describes with admiration how her stepfather, Money Vose, succeeded in making an escape from slavery by jumping ship and landing in a free state.

These early travels and scenes of youth in A *Narrative of the Life and Travels of Mrs. Nancy Prince* (Boston, 1850) set the tone for the use of mobility as a form of resistance, struggle, and freedom. Prince writes briefly of her involvement in the abolition movement in New England after she returned from nine years in Russia. However, she left Boston for Jamaica just when the debates over women's participation in the abolition movement were heating up. "These meetings I attended with much pleasure until a contention broke out among themselves ..." (*Narrative*, 42). In Jamaica between 1840 and 1842, Prince's political passions were stirred, but she was in a less secure institutional position as she traveled there. This section of her narrative is significant for containing warnings to African American readers about emigration schemes, which were advertised in newspapers such as Garrison's *Liberator*, promising African-Americans a better life and ample money if they emigrated to Jamaica. Prince expresses admiration for the newly emancipated natives and points to their industriousness and desire to work and acquire property. This example can also serve as an important example for her white abolitionist readers to keep up the struggle to end American slavery.

The final excerpt included here is of a perilous journey home from Jamaica, as Prince was forced to abandon raising funds for a proposed manual labor school because of political unrest in Kingston. Prince's discussion of treachery at sea emphasizes racial different and the tenuous relationship between slavery and the unofficial criminal status of free blackness. She resists discrimination and cruelty by speaking and acting even as her mobility is restricted; her empowered voice intervenes from the troubled ship and creates a powerful voice in her narrative (Fish, "Voices of Restless (Dis)Continuity," 485–86).

f r o m

A Narrative of the Life and Travels of Mrs. Nancy Prince (2d ed., 1853)

My mind, after the emancipation in the West Indies, was bent upon going to Jamaica. A field of usefulness seemed spread out before me. While I was thinking about it, the Rev. Mr. Ingraham, who had spent seven years there, arrived in the city. He lectured in the city at the Marlboro Chapel, on the results arising from the emancipation at the British Islands. He knew much about them, he had a station at a mountain near Kingston, and was very desirous to have persons go there to labor. He wished some one to go with him to his station. He called on me with the Rev. Mr. William Collier, to persuade me to go. I told him it was my intention to go if I could make myself useful, but that I was sensible that I was very limited in education. He told me that the moral condition of the people was very bad, and needed labor aside from any thing else.

I left America, November 16th, 1840, in the ship Scion, Captain Mansfield, bound for Jamaica, freighted with ice and machinery for the silk factory.

There were on board a number of handicraftsmen and other passengers. We sailed on Monday afternoon, from Charlestown, Massachusetts. It rained continually until Saturday. Sunday, the 23d, was a fine day. Mr. De Grass, a young colored clergyman, was invited to perform divine service, which he did with much propriety. He spoke of the dangers we had escaped and the importance of being prepared to meet our God, (he died of fever about three weeks after arriving at Jamaica) some who were able to attend came on deck, and listened to him with respect, while others seemed to look on in derision; these spent the afternoon and evening in cardplaying. About twelve at night a storm commenced; on Monday were in great peril; the storm continued until Friday, the 27th. On that day a sail was seen at some distance making towards us, the captain judging her to be a piratical vessel, ordered the women and children below, and the men to prepare for action. The pirates were not inclined to hazard an engagement; when they saw the deck filled with armed men they left us. Thus were we preserved from the storm and from the enemy . . . Monday, and we mortals are still alive. Tuesday, thus far the Lord has led us on. Wednesday, thus far his power prolongs our days. Thursday, December 3d, today made Turks Island. Friday, this day had a view of Hayti, its lofty mountains presented a sublime prospect. Saturday, we had a glance at Cuba. Sunday, December 6th, at six o'clock in the evening, dropped anchor at St. Ann Harbor, Jamaica. We blessed the Lord for his goodness in sparing us to see the place of our destination; and here I will mention my object in visiting Jamaica. I hoped that I might aid, in some small degree, to raise up and encourage the emancipated inhabitants, and teach the young children to read and work, to fear god, and put their trust in the Savior. . . .

I then called on the American Consul, he told me he was very glad to see me for such a purpose as I had in view in visiting Jamaica, but he said it was a folly for the Americans to come to the island to better their condition; he said they come to him every day praying him to send them home.

He likewise mentioned to me the great mortality among the emigrants. The same day I saw the Rev. J. S. Beadslee, one of our missionaries, who wished me to accompany him forty miles into the interior of the country. . . . I called, on my return, at the market, and counted the different stalls. For vegetables and poultry 196, all numbered and under cover; beside 70 on the ground; these are all attended by colored women. The market is conveniently arranged, as they can close the gates and leave all safe. There are nineteen stalls for fresh fish, eighteen for pork, thirty for beef, eighteen for turtle. These are all regular built markets, and are kept by colored men and women. These are all in one place.

Others also may be found, as with us, all over the city. Thus it may be hoped they are not the stupid set of beings they have been called; here surely we see industry; they are enterprising and quick in their perceptions, determined to possess themselves, and to possess property besides, and quite able to take care of themselves. They wished to know why I was so inquisitive about them. I told them we had heard in America that you are lazy, and that emancipation has been of no benefit to you; I wish to inform myself of the truth respecting you, and give a true account on my return. Am I right? More than two hundred people were around me listening to what I said.

They thanked me heartily. I gave them some tracts, and told them if it so pleased God I would come back to them and bring them some more books, and try what could be done with some of the poor children to make them better. I then left them, and went to the East Market, where there are many of all nations. The Jews and Spanish looked at me very black. The colored people gathered around me. I gave them little books and tracts, and told them I hoped to see them again.

There are in this street upwards of a thousand young women and children, living in sin of every kind. From thence I went to the jail, where there were seventeen men, but no women. There were in the House of Correction three hundred culprits; they are taken from there, to work on plantations. I went to the Admiral's house, where the emigrants find a shelter until they can find employment, then they work and pay for their passage. Many leave their homes and come to Jamaica under the impression that they are to have their passage free, and on reaching the island are to be found, until they can provide for themselves.

How the mistake originated, I am not able to say, but on arriving here, strangers poor and unacclimated, find the debt for passage money hard and unexpected. It is remarkable that whether fresh from Africa, or from other islands, from the South or from New England, they all feel deceived on this point. I called on many Americans and found them poor and discontented—rueing the day they left their country, where, notwithstanding many obstacles, their parents lived and died—a country they helped to conquer with their toil and blood; now shall their children stray abroad and starve in foreign lands. . . .

Most of the people of Jamaica are emancipated slaves, many of them are old, worn out and degraded. Those who are able to work, have yet many obstacles to contend with, and very little to encourage them; every advantage is taken of their ignorance; the same spirit of cruelty is opposed to them that held them for centuries in bondage; even religious teaching is bartered for their hard earnings, while they are allowed but thirty-three cents a day, and are told if they will not work for that they shall not work at all; an extraordinary price is asked of them for every thing they may wish to purchase, even the Bibles are sold to them at a large advance on the first purchase. Where are their apologists, if they are found wanting in the strict morals that Christians ought to practice? Who kindly says, forgive them when they err. "Forgive them, this is the bitter fruit of slavery." Who has integrity sufficient to hold the balance when these poor people are to be weighed? Yet their present state is blissful, compared with slavery.

Many of the farmers bring their produce twenty or thirty miles. Some have horses or ponys, but most of them bring their burdens on their head. As I returned from St. Andrews Mountain, where I had been sent for by a Mr. Rose, I was overtaken by a respectable looking man on horseback; we rode about ten miles in company. The story he told me of the wrongs he and his wife had endured while in slavery, are too horrible to narrate. My heart sickens when I think of it. He asked me many questions, such as where I came from? why I came to that Isle? where had I lived, &c. I told him I was sent for by one of the missionaries to help him in his school. Indeed, said he, our color need the instruction. I asked him why the colored people did not hire for themselves? We would be very glad to, he replied, but our money is taken from us so fast we cannot . . . The Macroon hunters take all—this is a nickname they give the missionaries and the class-leaders—a cutting sarcasm this! . . .[1]

After leaving Jamaica, the vessel was tacked to a south-west course. I asked the Captain what this meant. He said he must take the current as there was no wind. Without any ceremony, I told him it was not the case, and told the passengers that he had deceived us. There were two English men that were born on the island, that had never been on the water. Before the third day passed, they asked the Captain why they had not seen Hayti. He told them they passed when they were asleep. I told them it was not true, he was steering south south-west. The passengers in the steerage got alarmed, and every one was asking the Captain what this meant. The ninth day we made land. "By ———," said the Captain, "this is Key West; come, passengers, let us have a vote to run over the neck, and I will go ashore and

---

[1]Prince is pointing to the pun, combining Mack, the name of a coin, and Maroon, the fugitives who were part of the population she encountered.

bring aboard fruit and turtle." They all agreed but myself. He soon dropped anchor. The officers from the shore came on board and congratulated him on keeping his appointment, thus proving that my suspicions were well founded. The Captain went ashore with these men, and soon came back, called for the passengers, and asked for their vote for him to remain until the next day, saying that he could by this delay, make five or six hundred dollars, as there had been a vessel wrecked there lately. They all agreed but myself. The vessel was soon at the side of the wharf. In an hour there were twenty slaves at work to unload her; every inducement was made to persuade me to go ashore, or set my feet on the wharf. A law had just been passed there that every free colored person coming there, should be put in custody on their going ashore; there were five colored persons on board; none dared to go ashore, however uncomfortable we might be in the vessel, or however we might desire to refresh ourselves by a change of scene. We remained at Key West four days.

September 3d, we set sail for New York, at 3 o'clock in the afternoon. At 10 o'clock a gale took us, that continued thirty-six hours; my state-room was filled with water, and my baggage all upset; a woman, with her little boy, and myself, were seated on a trunk thirty-six hours, with our feet pressed against a barrel to prevent falling; the water pouring over us at every breaker. Wednesday, the 9th, the sun shone out so that the Captain could take an observation. He found himself in great peril, near the coast of Texas. All hands were employed in pumping and bailing. On the eleventh, the New Orleans steamer came to our assistance; as we passed up the river, I was made to forget my own condition, as I looked with pity on the poor slaves, who were laboring and toiling, on either side, as far as could be seen with a glass. We soon reached the dock, and we were there on the old wreck a spectacle for observation; the whites went on shore and made themselves comfortable, while we poor blacks were obliged to remain on that broken, wet vessel. The people were very busy about me; one man asked me who I belonged to, and many other rude questions; he asked me where I was born; I told him Newburyport. "What were your parents' names?" I told him my father's names was Thomas Gardner; his countenance changed; said he, "I knew him well;" and he proved friendly to me. He appeared very kind, and offered to arrange my affairs so that I might return to New York through the States. I thought it best to decline his proposal, knowing my spirit would not suffer me to pass on, and see my fellow-creatures suffering without a rebuke. We remained four days on the wreck; the boxes that contained the sugar were taken out; the two bottom tiers were washed out clean. There were a great many people that came to see the vessel; they were astonished that she did not sink; they watched me very closely. I asked them what they wished. In the mean time, there came along a drove of colored people, fettered together in pairs by the wrist; some had weights, with long chains at their ankles, men and women, young and old. I asked them what that meant. They were all ready to answer. Said they, "these negroes have been imprudent, and have stolen; some of them are free negroes from the northern ships;" "and what," I asked "are they there for?" "For being on shore, some of them at night." I asked them who made them Lord over God's inheritance. They told me I was very foolish; they should think I had suffered enough to think of myself. I looked pretty bad, it is true; I was seated on a box, but poorly dressed; the mate had taken my clothes to a washerwoman; why he took this care, he was afraid to send the cook or steward on shore, as they were colored people. I kept still; but the other woman seemed to be in perfect despair, running up and down the deck, wringing her hands and crying, at the thought of all her clothes being destroyed; then her mind dwelt upon other things, and she seemed as if she were deranged; she took their attention for a few minutes, as she was white. Soon the washer-woman came with my clothes; they spoke to her as if she had been a dog. I looked at them with as much astonishment as if I had never heard of such a thing. I asked them if they believed there was a God. "Of course we do," they replied. "Then why not obey him?" "We do." "You do not; permit me to say there is a God, and a just one, that will bring you all to account." "For what?" "For suffering these men that have just come in to be taken out of these vessels, and that awful sight I see in the streets." "O that is nothing; I should think you would be concerned about yourself." "I am sure," I replied, "the Lord will take care of me; you cannot harm me." "No; we do not wish to; we do not want you here." Every ship that comes in, the colored men are dragged to prison. I found it necessary to be stern with them; they were very rude; if I had not been so, I know not what would have been the consequences. They went off for that day; the next day some of them came again. "Good morning," said they, "we shall watch you like the d—— until you go away; you must not say anything to these negroes whilst you are here." "Why, then, do you talk to me, if you do not want me to say any thing to you? If you will let me alone, I will you." "Let me see your protection," they replied, "they say it is under the Russian government." I pointed them to the 18th chapter of Revelations and 15th verse: "The merchants of these things which were made rich by her, shall stand afar off, for the fear of her torment, weeping and wailing. For strong is the Lord God who judgeth her." They made no answer, but asked the Captain how soon he should get away.

On the 17th, the Captain put eight of us on board the bark H.W. Tyler, for New York; we had about a mile to walk; the Captain was in honor bound to return us our passage money, which we had paid him at Jamaica; he came without it to see if we were there, and went away saying he would soon return with it; but we saw no more of him or our money! Our bark, and a vessel loaded with slaves, were towed down the river by the same steamer; we dropped anchor at the bottom of the bay, as a storm was rising. The 18th, on Sabbath, it rained all day. Capt. Tyler knocked at my door, wishing me to come out; it rained hard; the bulwark of the bark was so high I could not look over it; he placed something for me to stand on, that I might see the awful sight, which was the vessel of slaves laying at the side of our ship! The deck was full of young men, girls, and children, bound to Texas for sale! Monday, the 19th, Capt. Tyler demanded of us to pay him for our passage. I had but ten dollars, and was determined not to give it; he was very severe with all. I told him there were articles enough to pay him belonging to me. Those who had nothing, were obliged to go back in the steamer. Tuesday, the 20th, we set sail; the storm was not over. The 22d the gale took us; we were dismasted, and to save sinking, sixty casks of molasses were stove in, and holes cut in the bulwarks to let it off. All the fowls, pigs, and fresh provisions were lost. We were carried seventy-five miles up the bay of Mexico. The Captain was determined not to pay the steamer for carrying him back to New Orleans, and made his way the best he could.

The 3d of October we arrived again at Key West. The Captain got the bark repaired, and took on board a number of turtles, and a plenty of brandy. Friday, the 7th, set sail for New York; the Captain asked me why I did not go ashore when there in the Comet; "had you," said he, "they intended to beat you. John and Lucy Davenport, of Salem, laid down the first ten dollars toward a hundred for that person who should get you there." The Florida laws are about the same as those at New Orleans. He was very talkative: wished to know if I saw anything of the Creole's crew while at Jamaica. I told him they were all safe, a fine set of young men and women; one dear little girl that was taken from her mother in Virginia, I should have taken with me, if I had had the money. He said his brother owned the Creole, and some of the slaves were his. "I never owned any; I have followed the sea all my life, and can tell every port and town in your State."

October 19th, 1842, arrived at New York, and thankful was I to set my feet on land, almost famished for the want of food; we lost all of our provisions; nothing was left but sailors' beef, and that was tainted before it was salted. . . .

I waited in New York until the last of July, when I started for Boston. August 1st, 1843, arrived, poor in health, and poor in purse, having sacrificed both, hoping to benefit my fellow creatures. I trust it was acceptable to God, who in his providence preserved me in perils by land, and perils by sea.

AMANdA BERRy SMiTH

Amanda Berry Smith was born to slaves located near Long Green, Maryland, in 1837. Her father bought the family's freedom, and they moved to York County, Pennsylvania, where his farm became a stop on the Underground Railroad. Smith wrote that "three months of schooling was all I ever had . . . at a school for whites . . . my brother and I walked five and a half miles each day . . ." (iv).

In 1854 Smith married Calvin M. Devine, and they had two children; one died in infancy, and her daughter Mazie lived into her twenties. Smith had a religious conversion in 1856 and was widowed when her husband was killed fighting for the Union army in 1863. She married James Smith of Philadelphia, a coachman and an African Methodist Episcopal (AME) clergyman, and gave birth to three more children, but none survived childhood. Smith worked as washerwoman and servant until she had a second conversion experience in 1868 and felt a call to preach. When James Smith died, she began to speak in black churches throughout New York City and northern New Jersey. Despite meeting some resistance from AME pastors, she became a full-time "independent" evangelist in 1870 and was a familiar figure at camp meetings from Tennessee to Maine, attracting the attention of both blacks and whites. In two months alone in 1871 she was credited with 156 conversions (Dodson, xxix).

Because of some resistance by the black AME Church to her preaching and a controversy over the inclusion of women as clergy, Smith formed a relationship with missionaries of the white Methodist Episcopal church and in 1878 traveled to London to begin the international phase of her preaching ministry. She did missionary work in England, India, Liberia, and Sierre Leone before returning to the United States in 1890. In 1892, while living in the temperance community of Harvey, a Chicago suburb, she wrote her memoirs, from which this excerpt on her travels to India and Burma is taken. In her last two decades Smith operated orphanages for African-American children.

f r o m
An Autobiography: The Story of the Lord's Dealings with Mrs. Amanda Smith

Containing an account of her safe work of faith and her travels in America, England, Ireland, Scotland, India and Africa, as an independent missionary (1893)

●

... Naini Tal, India, Wednesday, September 15, 1880. The morning is beautiful. Miss Fannie Sparks and I take our men and go up to what is called the snow seat. It is about two miles, I suppose, right up hill. The men who carry you in the dandies, when they get to a certain point on the hill, turn you round, and carry you up backwards. I don't know why they do this, but I think they have an idea that you are not so heavy carried that way. Miss Sparks had four men and I had four. When we got up to the top of the hill we found it very broad, a kind of tableland. You can look for miles away, and the hills are covered with snow.

When they put us down, and we stepped out of our chairs and turned round, we looked right on the great mountain ridge of snow, beautifully white, and the sun shining on it like silver. Oh! I thought I never saw anything so beautiful. I wanted to shout right out, and wave my hat.

But then one has to be so careful, because the natives watch you, and they think that it means you are worshiping the snow or the great mountains. So I had to restrain myself from shouting and dancing.

Oh! the sight was glorious to behold! Miss Sparks and I walked about, and then we sat down and had a nice little Bible reading together, and then we knelt down and had such a blessed prayer meeting. I shall never forget that morning.

That night, Wednesday night, was our prayer meeting. We were not very spiritual, still we had a good meeting.

Thursday, September 16th. The day the great flood began. It rained all day Thursday. Sometimes it would lighten up, and seem as though it was going to clear off; then a heavy cloud and fog would set in, and the rain would pour. All day Thursday, all night Thursday night, all day Friday, and all night Friday night.

By that time we began to get serious; we wondered; for the water ran in torrents; great trenches would give way in the ground: banks were falling in; and we did not know but danger was coming to us. . . .

This was a blessed time. We should like to have stayed a few days longer; but previous engagements being made, we had to pass on with praise in our hearts to God that He gave us the privilege of sowing, if only a little, for Him, and with prayers and tears to be watered, and in due time the harvest will be reaped. May the Lord help us to believe as we pray.

Miss Anstea came to Bangalore to attend the meetings. She came, she said, for a definite object, and that was for a renewed baptism of the Spirit; and, after waiting several days, the Lord helped her, among others, to claim by faith what she had asked for; and she returned to her home and work, filled; and when I got there and saw the work, I said in my heart, "If ever there was need of such an anointing and empowering, dear Miss Anstea needed it."

Three hundred helpless souls God had committed to her care; and they leaned upon her as they would upon a mother. You have no idea of the care and anxiety and responsibility of such a position unless you were there to see it.

In connection with the orphanage there are two farms: Nazareth and Bethany. Miss Anstea is the head of all this work: and while she was so anxious that they should know all that would help them on in life, temporally, she had the greatest concern in the salvation of every soul; for this she labored and prayed daily; and, according to her faith, so it was unto her.

I am more and more convinced that to succeed in God's work everywhere, one needs to be filled with the Spirit and mightiness of God, and especially so in India and Africa.

Superstition and idolatry, and infidelity, are so rampant it seems the very air one breathes is impregnated with them. Oh, how the dear workers all over, need constantly the fresh anointing of the Holy Ghost, which can and does reveal the almightiness of Jesus to save from all unrighteousness.

Sunday was their Communion Sunday. It was a beautiful sight to see so many remembering the Lord's death, till He come again. It was very solemn and impressive. A sight like this means more in India than it would in England; these are poor orphans redeemed from heathenism. I expect to laud and wonder at His grace through all eternity. Amen.

Miss Anstea had invited me to come to Colar and visit her mission. So, on my way from Bombay, I stopped at Colar for a week. Colar was a large, native town, and Miss Anstea's mission covered a large area, in which she had a chapel, and a very nice, comodious mission house, large, comfortable houses for missionaries, all nicely situated and well furnished.

I held meetings in the little chapel every night. Our morning prayer was similar to a service; at the ringing of the bell the boys and girls would file in and take their seats, and we would have prayers before they went to work.

The Lord gave us great blessings during the week's services. At night the church would be crowded; large numbers of the heathen for the outside came in; many of them seemed to be deeply interested. The Lord wonderfully helped me to speak to them every night; and several of the children professed to be converted.

One Sabbath morning as we were at prayers at the Mission House, a poor woman came and sat on the veranda, outside, with a beautiful baby in her arms, about three or four months old. When prayers were over, she was asked what she wanted. She said she wished to see Miss Sob. That is what the unmarried ladies are called in India by the natives; a married lady is called Mame Sob.

Miss Anstea had several helpers, English persons, a man and his wife, and two unmarried ladies. Always after the prayers with the boys in the chapel in the morning, they had their family prayer at the Mission House.

So, when Miss Anstea went to this woman and asked her what she wanted, she said that she had had nothing to eat for two days, and she was starving, and she wanted her to take her baby; she had come a very long way from a native town; she said she had three other children, and had nothing for them to eat; and if she would give her fifty cents and keep the baby, she would go and get something for the other children; but she could not bear to see the baby starve to death before her eyes.

It was a beautiful little child, a little girl. By that time we were all around her. Miss Anstea questioned her in every possible way to find out if her story was true.

She told her she was afraid she had taken somebody's baby and wanted to pass it off for her own; but at this the poor woman wept bitterly and declared the baby was her own, but that they were starving, and it was her last resort to save her baby, to bring it to the Mission; the others, she said, were older, and somebody might help them; but nobody wanted the baby.

Miss Anstea told her there was no one there who knew anything about taking care of so young a baby, and that she herself knew but very little how to manage a young baby.

As we stood around looking and listening, my mother heart ached, and I would have gladly taken it myself, but I had no where only as the Lord gave me friends who would invite me to their homes for awhile, as Miss Anstea did. But we prevailed on Miss Anstea to take the baby.

One of Miss Anstea's Christian girls said she would look after it. I think Miss Anstea offered to pay her a small sum; or some of the rest suggested that; another said they would milk the goat so the baby would have milk. I said, "I will give the woman the fifty cents"; but I gave her a little more than fifty cents.

She laid the baby down on the mat. Of course, they have no clothes on them; they were perfectly naked. She put her hand on her heart and sighed. And then ran away out of the compound. When she got to the gate she turned and looked back; poor thing! She was so thin, and looked just like what she had said, that she was starving to death; you could see she was weak; but, oh, that look when she got to the gate! I shall never forget it; it was full of mother's love and tenderness for her baby. My heart ached for her; and to save my life I could not keep back the tears.

How often the missionary in different foreign fields comes up against heart rending scenes, before which they often stand helpless. All they could do was to weep with them that weep, and pray with them that don't know how to pray for themselves.

We took the baby in, and Miss Anstea adopted it, and we named it "Amanda Smith."

I left on Friday. Up to that time the baby had got on very well, but cried a good deal, nights; there were plenty to look after it in the daytime, but at night everybody wanted to sleep, but the baby. Dear, little Amanda Smith.

I went from Colar to Bangalore, then to Madras. I never heard whether the poor, little thing pulled through or not; if she did, I know it was hard, after the novelty had worn off with the children.

Miss Anstea was a grand woman, and did a noble work in that province. How they have missed her since she has returned to England. She spent many years in India, and established and ran the missions mostly at her own personal expense. . . .

Saturday, 22d. Arrived at Banglore late in the afternoon . . . Oh, Lord, revive Thy work. A blessed time at family prayers. I go with Brother Carter and make some pastoral calls among the people. At night we have a good meeting, a crowded church.

But the good Plymouth brethren were much disturbed, because I was a woman, and Paul had said, "Let your women keep silence in the churches." So they had nice articles in the daily papers; then they wrote me kind letters, and bombarded me with Scriptural texts against women preaching; pointed out some they wished me to preach from. I never argue with anybody—just say my say and go on. But one night I said I would speak on this subject as I understood it. Oh, what a stir it made. The church was packed and crowded. After I had sung, I read out my text: "Let your 'men' keep silence in the church," quoting the chapter and verse (1 Cor., 14:28) where Paul was giving directions so as not to have confusion—one to speak at a time, while the others listened. And then one was to interpret, and if there was no interpreter, they should keep silence in the church. So I went on with my version of it. We had an excellent meeting, and the newspaper articles stopped, and the letters stopped, and I went on till I got through. . . .

Rangoon, British Burmah, April 4, 1881. "Praise God, from Whom all blessings flow." This has been a precious day . . .

One of the first things I was struck with was the pagoda, or Burmese temple. You can see its dome for two miles away, as you look off, before you get into harbor. The streets of Rangoon are wide and rectangular, like those in Philadelphia, and the shade trees over the city are very graceful.

After being in Burmah a few days I wanted to visit this great temple. So I started, in company with some friends, and after walking some distance from Brother Robinson's house, we came to what I suppose would be called the park. There was an ascent of about seventy-five feet up a series of steps into the pagoda; a gentle ascent, not tiresome. On either side of the way were devotees at prayers, or beggars waiting for their rice; or booths where you could buy false pearls, imitation diamonds, beads, packages of gold leaf, flowers and cakes. The trinkets and flowers are given as offerings to Buddha; The gold leaf was sold for acts of piety.

Oh, how horrid this all seemed to me. I looked at the sad expression on the faces of the poor women devotees, and then I thought that they would go on, and live and die, and never know that Jesus died that they might live and have life and happiness in Him.

Inside of this park where the pagoda stands, are thousands of gods, of all sizes. I thought I would count them, and when I got up to a hundred of those that were not broken, I quit. And then to think of the many, many years that the religion of Buddha and Brahma has gone on, and holds such sway yet. To me this is among the incomprehensibles.

The Burmese ladies walk about in the street; their dress is very pretty; a very handsome figured cloth, almost always silk, and just wrapped about the waist and tucked in at the side. They do not fasten them with pins and hooks and buttons, as we do, and yet they look very neat.

You never see a Burmese woman with her hair uncombed; but they use no hairpins; how they put it up I don't know; but it is as straight, every hair, as it can be. It is done like the Chinese women do their hair.

They are very shrewd business women. I saw them unloading wood and marketing, just like men; and in any kind of business you will see Burmese women sharp and active.

I was so amused to see the Chinese and Burmese carpenters. I watched them one day as they were building a house, and there would be a half-dozen men, and they would be sitting down using their planes, holding the board with their toes. They have some very large and fine buildings there.

Their funerals are something like the Hindoos'. A big man had died; I heard a great sound of music, such as they have there; I can't describe it; it couldn't be described by music that we hear here; tin-pans and tambourines, and something like the noise that a stove pipe, or something of that kind would make. Oh, it was a jingle. Mrs. Robinson called me to look out at it; it was on the main street of the town, and it was a large funeral. Dozens of men would go before the hearse and lay down cloth; the hearse would drive over this cloth; and so they went on, the music following this procession.

When a poor coolie man dies they carry him around til he becomes so offensive that I was told sometimes the authorities have to interfere. They give them all the chance they can to come to. But poor things! They are dead, three times dead; plucked up by the roots. . . .

I had wished that my own daughter would have such a desire to do something for her fellowmen. I have prayed and asked the Lord to thus incline her heart, if He would have her. I have educated her, and done all I could, as fast I was able, to prepare her for a useful life; and now I leave it with her and her God. He knows my heart. I long to have her do what I know she could do if she was only fully consecrated to God. I would not have her come to this country without a full and entire consecration. And in her own land I fear she will do but little without it, like so many others.

When I think of what God has done for me, and how he has led me since I gave myself fully to Him, I am encouraged to praise Him for all that has passed, and trust Him to guide my child that she may work for Him. Amen.

At eight o'clock one night I held a meeting in the methodist Church for colored men especially, as there are a number in Burmah, and Rev. Mr. Robinson, who is pastor of the Methodist Church, was very much interested in these men. Several of them had families; and he had tried to get them to come to church.

Being an American, he seemed to sympathize with them, and to know how they felt in that country where customs are so different from what they are in the United States. So he said while I was there he thought it would be nice to call them together and have me talk to them, which I was very glad to do.

There was a nice company of these men gathered; some were from the West Indies, some from the west coast of Africa, and some from Boston, Philadelphia, and Baltimore. One man from the West Indies had been in Burmah for twenty years.

They were all men of average intelligence, clean, well-dressed, and sober; there were but three men in the company who acted a little as though they were under the influence of strong drink; one of these was from Boston, and his name was John Gibbs. He had been in Burmah for sixteen years; another was a Mr. Jordan, a man of good position, a stevedore; he had been here for sixteen years, also; and another, a fine looking young man from Baltimore, by the name of Jenkins.

There was about twenty of these men in all. They sang, just like colored people can sing. I spoke to them from the fifty-fifth chapter of Isaiah. I dwelt mostly on these words, "Let the wicked forsake his ways, and the unrighteous man his thoughts." The Lord helped me, and His Spirit was present.

I asked before I began who amongst them was converted. Only one man answered; he was a grand, old man. He walked in the light of full salvation, and followed the sea, for fifteen years.

After I got through speaking I asked him to pray; he did; and how the Lord helped him! He said he had been in Burmah twenty-five years. His son was with him; a nice young lad; may God save him! When the prayer was over, I said, "Is there anything you would like to sing?"

"Yes," said one young man, from the west coast of Africa, and who had been here for only three days, "Sing such a number."

I found it; it was, "Stand up for Jesus, Christians, stand." As soon as it was announced they all seemed to know it, and they sang it well. After they were seated I talked to them for a while. I said, "Now, who of you would like us to pray for you? Hold up your hand."

And six or seven said, "Pray for me." Then Brother Robinson, the pastor of the church, spoke to them. Then after another season of prayer, I said, "What shall we sing to close?" when young Gibbs, from Boston, said, "Please sing 'God our help in ages past.' "

He started it, and they sang it as if they knew how. Oh, it was good. How I have prayed that God would get glory out of this meeting to Himself, and save those men. Amen.

In talking I told them I believed that God meant they should live in a heathen land as Christians, and as colored men they should show the heathen with whom they came in contact that their God, whom they are taught to believe, is able to save them out here, as well as home.

We arranged to have them come together on Wednesday evening for a little tea meeting. May God help us. Would to God that He would anoint some one who would work his way to this land, rather than not to come at all, and see after the flock here that stray and wonder and have no shepherd. I saw this need in Liverpool, England; and also in Bombay and Calcutta.

These were colored men; my own people. Some of them had left good, Christian homes, and started out Christians themselves. But they get into these ports, and there are no colored churches or missions to go to, and often give up all hope in Christ.

How my heart has ached for them. How I wished that my people in America might feel that they had a mission in this, looking after these poor men that brave the stormy sea. I wish they could think and feel about it, and put their thoughts and feelings in action, as the white people do; for in every port there is work done among white sailors; and if any men deserve to be looked after, and comforted, and helped, and cheered, it is these brave men, white and black.

I hardly ever hear the wind blow at night that my heart does not breathe a prayer to God for sailors. How many young men, and old ones, too, leave their homes converted, and many times get through the voyage all right; but they have no place to go to but these sailors' boarding houses, and they are thrown in with all sorts of sin and wickedness, and they finally drop into those ways.

How my heart has ached for them in London and Liverpool; they would go to church and be better treated there than at white churches at home; but the old feeling of prejudice follows them, and they seldom venture to church. If there were a church or place of worship where they knew their own people were assembled, they would feel free to go, I think. That is why I think our ministers at home should take this into consideration.

A good many of our men, when they get to England, or India, or Burmah, or any other country, if they stay, feel they must get a wife, of whatever place they are in; if in England, an English wife; if in Burmah, a Burmese wife, and so on; and, in so many of these instances, when these sailors do marry, whether it is a white woman in England, or whether in Burmah, or anywhere else, it is generally somebody that likes whisky; and that is the sad part of it.

In Burmah it seemed that these men were better off than the most that one meets on foreign shores; some of them were engineers on railways, some conductors, some in government service, and they all had good positions, and made money. Some of them had nice families of children; but their wives didn't go to church, and their children didn't go to Sabbath School; so they generally were a hindrance to their husbands, instead of a help, in that respect.

FANNY JACKSON COPPIN

During the last year of her life, Fanny Jackson Coppin (1837–1913) wrote *Reminiscences of School Life, and Hints on Teaching*, from which this excerpt on her travels to South Africa is taken. *Reminiscences* is a hybrid text that chronicles important aspects of her youth, education, and career and incorporates advice from her experiences in the classroom. Included are narratives of two of her journeys abroad.

Fanny Jackson was born a slave in Washington, D.C. Her freedom was eventually purchased by an aunt who worked as a domestic. She was sent to New Bedford, Massachusetts, where she worked and managed to go to school part time. When she moved to Newport, Rhode Island, and secured a better position with the Calvert family, she was able to hire tutors and briefly attend the segregated black public schools and then the Normal School in Bristol. She attended Oberlin College with the financial assistance of her aunt Sarah Orr Clark and a scholarship from Daniel Payne of the AME Church. She was the second African-American woman to receive a bachelor of arts degree from Oberlin, where she studied the classics rather than the traditional "ladies course." After her graduation in 1865 Jackson was appointed to the Institute for Colored Youth (ICY) in Philadelphia, a classical high school founded by the Society of Friends in 1837. She taught there for more than thirty years and was the school's principal.

In 1881 Jackson married AME minister Levi Jenkins Coppin, some fifteen years her junior. She kept her position as principal at ICY while her husband held a pastorate in Baltimore. In 1888 she traveled to London as a delegate to the Centenary of Missions, and in 1902, after retiring from ICY, she accompanied Bishop Coppin to Capetown, South Africa. As Shelley P. Haley points out, Fanny Coppin Jackson was a foremother and pioneer for many black women, foreshadowing the work, feminism, and activism of Ida B. Wells, Mary Church Terrell, Anna Julia Cooper, and Nannie Helen Burroughs (Haley, xv).

f r o m
Reminiscences of School Life, and Hints on Teaching (1913)

MY VISIT TO SOUTH AFRICA

To go to Africa, the original home of our people, see them in their native life and habits, and to contribute, even in a small degree, toward the development, civil and religious, that is going on among them, is a privilege that anyone might be glad to enjoy.

After having spent thirty-seven years in the school room, laboring to give a correct start in life to the youth that came under my influence, it was indeed, to me, a fortunate incident to finish my active work right in Africa, the home of the ancestors of those whose lives I had endeavored to direct.

All this came about thru my marriage in 1881 to Rev. L. J. Coppin who, in 1900, was elected one of the Bishops of the African Methodist Episcopal Church, and assigned to South Africa.

It may not be of special interest to the reader to hear all about the trip across the Atlantic to Liverpool on the steamship Umbria, of the Cunard Line, nor of the voyage from London, down the river Thames to Southampton, on the steamship German, and thence down the coast via Teneriffe Island.

The objective point was Cape Town, South Africa, and when on Sunday morning, November 30, 1902, we came to anchor in Table Bay, a new world seemed to rise before me, and a new vision.

Our new residence was at Cape Town, where rooms had been prepared on the second floor of a building, which constituted our headquarters when not traveling over the work.

Cape Town is, in a sense, a modern city. It has been occupied a long time by the English, and such sanitary conditions obtain as might be expected of a city under English rule.

The historic Table Mountain affords a natural reservoir, and supplies the town with drinking water of a superior quality. The markets are not large, and much of the food is imported, and the "high cost of living" is a familiar topic. Being situated right on the Bay, fishing is one of the daily vocations, and we have fish in abundance. But then, even missionaries will tire of fish if they are the daily food, for surely man can no more live on fish alone than on bread alone.

We were made as comfortable in our quarters as missionaries have reason to expect, and the one absorbing thought was, how shall we accomplish the work for which we left our homes.

In uniting with the A. M. E. Church after my marriage, I asked my husband what particular work I would be required or expected to do, and was told that a certain portion of missionary work was given by the Church to its women. Now, here was the field, for, with all the outward show of civilization at this English seaport, the needs of the native and "coloured" people were everywhere plain to be seen.

The colored people are the mixed bloods, a condition that obtains wherever a strong people force their way into a country and take possession.

In many cases, the children of the dominant race were cared for by being given, at least, a primary education, and such employment as enabled them to have a fair proportion of the necessities of life. But the much larger portion of "Cape coloured" people were left to live their lives as best they might, and rear their children in or out of wedlock.

It was not an unusual sight to see my husband marry couples and at the same time baptise both their children and their grandchildren, and that within a very short distance of Cape Town.

The homes in which many of them lived in those nearby places might well be called huts, and very poor ones at that.

The Dutch farmers who gave them employment were largely engaged in grape farming, and the manufacture of wine, the poorest brands of which would be given to those miserable dependents as part wages.

In Cape Town itself, saloons were plentiful. Sometimes one on every corner of street after street, and occasionally one between.

It surely cannot be difficult to imagine how easily a people so neglected in the higher ideals of life would turn to the drink habit as a mere pastime.

The native people — those of unmixed African blood — who came down from the country beyond, and found employment principally as loaders and unloaders of ships, and the heavier work along the railroads, would be quartered in "Locations" a mile or two beyond the city limits. The cabins, or huts, provided for them by the government at Cape Town, are very inferior for comfort to those built by the natives in their rural habitat before being brought into contact with our so-called civilization. The Cape Town Location was on a tract of land that would be fairly flooded with water during the rainy season, and many who came down hale and hearty would return consumptives—a disease practically unknown to the "heathen"—or never return at all.

The drink habit would soon be learned by those raw natives, and their last state would become worse than the first.

We were often asked why we made our headquarters at Cape Town instead of going and remaining far away into the interior, doing work entirely among the uncivilized. But it was hard indeed for us to turn away entirely from the conditions that met us upon the very entrance into the country. It is true the bulk of our work was far away from Cape Town, and among people in primitive life; but it was a good thing to have a base at this seaport town, where occasionally we could ourselves return to modern life, and where we could also work among those who needed us quite as much as those who had not been introduced into the blessedness (?) of a civilization that places the acquisition of wealth far above the redemption of souls.

Well, here my "special" work began. My husband, who preceded me on the field, had purchased a building and turned it into a school and mission house—Bethel Institute—and here I called the women together, the women who had risen above their environments, really noble, faithful, Christian women, and began my temperance work.

We organized after the model of our work at home. A local society was started, not only at Cape Town, but at many nearby places where we had mission stations, and, drawing from their membership, a Conference Branch was organized for the Cape Colony Conference.

At our first Annual Session of the Conference, which met at Port Elizabeth, the sight of native and colored women in a missionary session was one of the features of the Conference; and a glorious and inspiring sight it was. Gathered about me on the platform, and around the altar, were women who never before had appeared in public for Christian work, at least, never before to take a leading part in it. They had been lately organized, and now they were called upon to do the work of officers, and to speak to the public gathering for themselves: some in Dutch—their mother tongue—some in broken English, and some in their own God-given native language.

In my travels over the work with my husband I went as far as Bulawayo, 1360 miles from Cape Town. The journey was long, tiresome and trying.

At the meeting held there in our mission house, I had a new and not pleasant experience, for, after endeavoring to forget the fatigue caused by the journey, I made my accustomed address by the aid of an interpreter, and was seized with a fainting spell. I had for years been accustomed to hard work, and often deprivations, but had never before fallen at my post.

I was tenderly carried by the loving hands of native women out into the open, while Mr. Coppin went on with the meeting.

The small child of one of the native women was much disturbed when the mother left it in the care of others while she waited on me. The little one was not yet old enough to take in the situation, and so, openly revolted against such neglect, caused by a stranger who had been speaking in an unknown tongue.

At this particular meeting we afterwards learned that the government had spies on hand, native spies, to observe all that was said, and report to the authorities. The fear seemed to be that the instruction likely to be given to the natives would cause them to become dissatisfied with their lot, and as some said, "bring on a native problem as they had had a Boer problem." The spirit of suspicion was everywhere prevalent, and did much, for a time, to retard our work. I think, however, the authorities finally came to understand that we were missionaries pure and simple, and not politicians, and if there was any cause for alarm it must grow out of the fact that enlightenment does indeed enable people to see their true condition, and that they do sometimes become dissatisfied when convinced that injustice, and a general lack of the Christian spirit of brotherhood, is responsible for much of their misery.

The route to Bulawayo is upon the road constructed by that great empire builder, John Cecil Rhodes, with the view of carrying out his scheme, "from Cape to Cairo." It goes thru a large portion of country that is governed entirely by native chiefs, with, of course, the English oversight that is now given to all of South Africa, for there is no portion of the country that is absolutely in the hands of native rulers, such as obtained previous to the coming of the white man. But, in those native colonies like Basutoland, for instance, the land is occupied by the people of a given tribe, or "nation," as they like to call themselves, with a chief—paramount chief—in authority. The chief is the ruler and judge in all matters, not including capital punishment, or the leasing of lands to foreigners. They live their shepherd life and pay but little attention to agriculture. Having learned the value of money as an exchange, they go to the mining camps and work for periods of time, six months, a year, or even more, according to contract; take their money, return home, buy cattle, and, if they wish, add more wives to their household.

Many of them have never been away from their desert homes, and when the trains pass periodically thru their country, they come out to the Halts, where water is taken on and telegraphic connections made. Those Halts, or stations, are in the care of English officials. Perhaps a man, his wife and their children are the only occupants of that home, away out into the desert, far removed from civilization, in the midst of native people, called heathen, who are counted by multiplied thousands, but they have no fear and suffer no harm.

These innocent children of the forest come out to meet the trains. They come in great numbers and in native garb, which cannot be called clothing, but merely a sheep skin, or strings of beads about their loins. They seem amazed as they gaze at the trains, filled with people so unlike themselves in appearance. They chatter away among themselves. Just what they are thinking and saying, their distinguished guests have no means of knowing.

But when we, as missionaries, turn aside and go among them with our interpreters, we have an opportunity to come in possession of their thoughts and find out what manner of people they are.

That which always seems to be the prevailing desire among them is to acquire a knowledge of the new conditions which they see, but cannot understand.

They soon learn what is meant by school, and immediately express a desire to have their children taught. In my experience among them, I have never found them entirely satisfied with mere abstract teaching of religion. They have religious views before we teach them. Cruder, of course: unenlightened, uncertain, speculative, false, just as all people hold who have not been given the true word of God. When those who come to them win their confidence, they readily modify their religious views, regarding their teachers as their superiors in matters religious. But there is nothing like a superstitious worshipping of their benefactors, nor of the new doctrines which they bring. With an incredible clearness of vision, they look forward to and expect some practical and really tangible benefits to grow out of their new relation.

They already have, as it were, an intuitive sense of right and wrong, hence they do no harm to the stranger in their midst. Indeed, our religious teaching is, in a sense, but an explanation of their own religious impulses.

In their own moral and religious ethics they teach thou shalt, and thou shalt not, without being able to give philosophical reasons for it. Now when light is thrown into their benighted minds, and reasons are given for certain ways of life required of them, and their own creeds revised, taken from and added to, imagine their surprise when they see their teachers, disregarding in their lives, their own teaching. With child-like credulity they turn from the old to the new, and when disappointed in those who bring them the light they are not prepared at first to conclude, by a process of reasoning that there is chaff among the wheat, dross with the gold, but, rather, they feel that they have been deceived, and this accounts for some of the lapses of which we hear so much.

Our interpreters are native men who have come in contact with civilization by being trained at mission schools. Some of them have been to England and America and studied. But many of them have never been out of Africa, and yet they speak fluently English, Dutch and several of the tribal languages, and read the Bible in those languages. We are dependent upon the interpreter, and greatly indebted to the forerunners in the mission fields who made such indispensible aid possible.

On our way from Bulawayo we stopped at Mafeking and spent some time. There was a public reception given to us at the Masonic temple. Mafeking became famous during the Anglo-Boer war on account of the siege, and the gallant defense by General Baden-Powell.

John Cecil Rhodes was there during the siege, and when they brought him butter he refused to eat it, and sent it to the sick soldiers. Some of our societies were called the Cecil Rhodes Bands of Mercy.

Living at Mafeking are a large number of Malay people who are Mohammedans. The leading spirit among them is a merchant, Hadje Ben Hassen. Ben Hassen is his name, and he is a Hadje by virtue of having made a pilgrimage to Mecca. One of the moving spirits in the reception which was tendered was this Hadje. He headed a delegation of his countrymen and fellow religionists to the hall, and himself occupied a seat on the platform among the speakers. In his address he said that it was not customary for Christians and Mohammedans to thus come together, but, as there was a Negro Bishop in their midst, he felt that the religious idea should be set aside, and that all should come out to do honor to a distinguished member of the race.

Some of the Mohammedan people sent their children to our school at Cape Town, and even provided them with Bibles that they might take part in the opening services of the school.

Perhaps one of the things that has caused Mohammedans to step over the religious barriers that have kept the dark races apart in Africa, is the fact that, when the lines of proscription are drawn—and this is becoming more and more so—the Malay, the Indian—East Indian—the native and the "coloured" are all treated alike in matters social. Some of the Malays and Indians are very wealthy, and the renewal of license has been refused to some of the Indian merchants because it was said that English merchants could not compete with them. This happened at Port Elizabeth during the time that we were there in conference sessions.

Much wisdom and patience will be required on the part of our ministers and teachers lest they should add to the spirit of unrest that comes of injustice and proscription. Wisdom dictates that by all means a conflict between the races should be avoided. The Europeans, armed and drilled, would have the advantage of all others, and there could be but one result. The Kingdom of God does not proceed in its conquests by the employment of carnal weapons, and right can afford to be patient because it is bound to win in the end.

The native people have had enough of war. Their vocation in the ages past was to war among themselves, and it would not be difficult to impress them that that is not the way to right their wrongs. But the new life which we offer them is the life of peace and good will, and they cannot believe in God and our holy religion without believing that He is able to carry out His purposes, tho He be long-suffering.

My stay in Africa was pleasant, for I did not count the deprivations, and sometimes hardships. We were graciously kept from disease, even the bubonic plague that came to our very door. I was permitted to go with my husband thru the greater portion of his work, and mingle with and talk to the women upon the subjects of righteousness, temperance and the judgment to come. If some seed was sown that took root, and will never be entirely uprooted, the visit to Africa was not in vain. In selecting names for our local auxiliary societies, we chose the names of some of the women at home who labored during their lifetime in home missions, besides helping the foreign work. And so we have the Mary A. Campbell Society at one place, the Florida Grant at another, and other names of worthy ones which will be handed down to posterity, and be a means of inspiring those who will be told of their work and worth.

PART II

3

AFRICA

Pan-Africanism and Colonization

Pan-Africanism as an ideology and as a social and political movement is based on the assertion that a unified Africa is in the best interest of all members of the African diaspora. The ideology emerged in the Western Hemisphere as early as the late eighteenth century, immediately following the Haitian Revolution. Encouraged by the success of the revolt, Africans and their descendants throughout the Americas attempted to initiate similar rebellions. Other forms of political action included the free African societies of the Northeast, which were among the earliest organized efforts to articulate an identification with Africa. However, the most overt and sustained of the early expressions of pan-Africanism can be found in the various colonization plans.

In the early nineteenth century a number of African American leaders of the North became proponents of colonization plans to relocate African Americans to Africa. Recognizing the harsh reality of slavery as well as living with discrimination, unequal rights to citizenship, and threats of mob violence, some blacks sought an alternative homeland where they imagined economic opportunity and lack of color-based prejudice would prevail. Colonization, however, remained controversial in the African-American community, mainly because of its association with the American Colonization Society (ACS). Founded in 1816, the ACS included prominent white politicians, clergy, and professional men, including Southern slaveholders, and had as its goal the resettlement of free blacks and emancipated slaves in Africa. Some ACS members believed negative stereotypes about blacks and doubted that blacks could become useful citizens of the United States.

Furthermore, slaveholders wanted emancipated slaves removed lest they take action that could lead to the overthrow of slavery. Many African Americans and abolitionists opposed colonization on the grounds that leaving the United States meant abandoning the antislavery struggle. They also thought it better for blacks to stay and fight for rights in the nation they helped to build and defend.

After the Fugitive Slave Law was passed in 1850, many black Americans did look outside the borders of the U.S. for freedom and uplift, and Africa offered great promise and personal history. Nineteenth-century African Americans who supported African colonization expressed early forms of what could be called pan-Africanism—seeing Africa as a homeland for all blacks in the diaspora—and in most cases these men were connected to the Christian Church. Inseparable from their ideology was a desire to spread Christianity in Africa and to provide land and economic opportunity and self-reliance for African Americans. The theology of the black church regarding the return to Africa was heavily influenced by the books of Exodus and Psalms 68:31: "Ethiopia shall soon stretch forth her hands unto God." African-American Christians interpreted this verse around the themes of "the African race," "the redemption of Africa," and "the mission of the darker races" (Raboteau, 42). The claim of a noble and glorious past was part of a refutation of charges of inferiority against African Americans, and the idea behind the "redemption" of Africa was to find God's greater purpose in permitting slavery: Through suffering, God was purifying Ethiopia's sons in America to make them a chosen people who would return to Africa and rekindle the flame of religion and civilization (Raboteau, 46–47).

Paul Cuffe was one of the earliest and best-known African Americans who advocated the repatriation of black Americans to Africa. He turned his attention to the British colony of Sierra Leone and transported thirty-eight African Americans there in 1815.

Martin Delany, on the other hand, was first opposed to colonization in Africa, because of associations with Liberia, sponsored by the ACS in 1847. Delany believed that Central and South America or the West Indies were the best choices for colonization, but eventually he led an exploring party to Nigeria to sign a treaty with chiefs for land for black emigrants. Delany's belief was that the descendants of Africa were the only ones fit to carry out the redemption of the "fatherland"; the continent had superior potential for cotton production and the sugar and palm oil industries but would require the skills of America's free blacks to be realized.

Alexander Crummell was the chief American advocate in the later nineteenth century for the evangelization of Africa; he admired many native Africans but felt that the "civilizing" influence of the West was necessary. Edward Blyden argued that God had singled out black people as his chosen instrument to redeem Africa by enslaving them and then directing them back. Blyden, however, saw the importance of Islam and argued for an independent black church. He believed that Africa would develop a superior civilization with strong moral development. In either case, all these westerners revealed a certain ambivalence about Africa that reflected a dream, a nightmare, or both, internalizing Western biases and often setting up binary oppositions (Gruesser, 7). Pan-Africanism and emigration movements in the nineteenth century combined aspects of nationalism and racial pride while taking stock of historical successes and abuses in colonial relations. The desire for economic and social sovereignty is blended with (mostly) Christian religious traditions, but each traveler presented here had a slightly different approach or attitude. It is worth noting that the women who traveled as missionaries to Africa and elsewhere (more information is given in their respective geographical and biographical sections) also embraced Western religion and culture, which portrayed Africa as a "Dark Continent" in need of "Christian enlightenment" (Jacobs, 18), but they did not participate as major players in the colonization movement.

One of Crummell's most well known associates and protégés was Dr. W. E. B. Du Bois, who, although opposing early pan-Africanist efforts by Marcus Garvey, later became a proponent of a pan-Africanist vision. By the 1950s Du Bois was a revered elder to a new generation of pan-Africanists, led by Kwame Nkrumah, Nnamdi Azikewe, and Jomo Kenyatta. Nkrumah, who led the Gold Coast into independent Ghana, maintained strong ties with blacks in the United States, and at his encouragement many of them moved to Ghana and set up a community of expatriates that included Max Bond, Shirley Graham Du Bois, Maya Angelou, and Tom Feelings. Many of these expatriates returned to the United States during the most heated times of the Civil Rights and Black Power movements; however, they all continued to nurture and maintain a pan-Africanist vision among a new generation of artists, activists, and intellectuals.

Paul Cuffe

Paul Cuffe (1759–1817), born on Cuttyhunk Island, Massachusetts, was the youngest of ten children of Cuffe Slocum, a former slave, and Ruth Moses, a Wampanoag Indian. By the age of sixteen Cuffe had begun his illustrious seafaring career, and he soon became known in New England and beyond as a successful mariner, shipbuilder, and trader who possessed his own fleet. In 1808 he converted to the Quaker faith and developed many business contacts through this association. Cuffe grew increasingly interested in his African heritage and the "redemption" of Africa; he believed that Western technology and Christianity would free Africans from a dependence on profits from the slave trade. He hoped to be instrumental in setting up some new type of triangular trade between Africa, the United States, and Europe. Cuffe visited Sierra Leone and England, where he orchestrated a plan to bring some African Americans to the African nation, but the War of 1812 interrupted. He also caused quite a sensation in England with his crew, which consisted entirely of blacks and Native Americans. The newspapers were filled with information on this impressive and successful African American, and Cuffe found himself dining and meeting with the elite. In 1815 he sailed from Boston with supplies and thirty-eight African Americans planning to settle in Sierra Leone—Cuffe paid the expenses of many of the passengers. He also helped set up the Friendly Society at Sierra Leone, a black-run cooperative trading organization sponsored by one of the colony's Methodist congregations (S. Harris, 55). Cuffe died in 1817 before he was able to see his colonization project fully realize its potential and is considered one of the earliest forefathers of pan-Africanism. This excerpt, from the pamphlet *A Brief Account of the Settlement and Present Situation of the Colony of Sierra Leone*, contains information that Cuffe disseminated as he spoke to groups of free Negroes on the favorable conditions of the colony.

f r o m

A Brief Account of the Settlement and Present Situation of the Colony of Sierra Leone, in Africa (1812)

[as communicated by Paul Cuffe
(A Man of Colour to his friend in New York . . .)]

●

Having been informed that there was a settlement of people of colour at Sierra Leone under the immediate guardianship of civilized power, I have for these many years past felt a lively interest in their behalf, wishing that the inhabitants of the colony might become established in the truth, and thereby be instrumental in its promotion amongst our African brethren. It was these sentiments that first influenced me to visit my friends in this colony, and instead of repenting, I have cause to rejoice in having found many who are inclined to listen and attend to the precepts of our holy religion. Nevertheless, I am convinced that further help will be requisite to establish them in the true and vital spirit of devotion; for although there are many who are very particular in their attendance of public worship, yet I am apprehensive that the true substance is too much overlooked; and by thus mistaking the form for the substance, that their religious exercise is rendered rather a burden than a pleasure. . . . I merely wish to convey a brief account of the situation of the colony as I found it, hoping the information may prove serviceable and interesting to some of my friends in the United States.

Sierra Leone is a country on the west coast of Africa. Its situation is inviting, and its soil generally very productive. A river of the same names passes through the country, and the land for a great extent on each side is peculiarly fertile, and with the climate well calculated for the cultivation of West India and other tropical productions. In the year 1791 an act passed the British parliament incorporating a company called the Sierra Leone Company, whose object was to settle and cultivate these lands, and open a trade with other countries in the products of the soil. The first settlers amounted to about 200 white persons, and a number of free blacks or people of colour from North America; and their experiments in sugar, cotton, & c. soon convinced them that they would be abundantly rewarded for their labour. The promising appearance of the settlement soon attracted the attention of the neighboring chiefs, who with their subjects generally, became very friendly. The colony is now considerably increased, and continues to be in a flourishing situation. The population at present as taken by order of Governor Columbine in the 4th mo. 1811, is as follows:

Europeans	22	4	2
Nova Scotians	188	295	499
Maroons	165	195	447
Africans	20	43	37
	395	537	985

making together 1917

Besides which there are 601 Crue Men, so called from their being natives of a part called Crue Country,[1] from which they have emigrated since the establishment of this colony.

These people have not yet been enrolled in the list of citizens, but are generally hired by the inhabitants as labourers. The disposition prevails amongst them either for the purpose of cultivating the land, or engaging in commercial enterprise. A petition, of which the following is an outline, was lately presented to his excellency governor Columbine, and signed by several of the most respectable inhabitants, viz.

1st. That encouragement may be given to all our brethren, who may come from the British colonies or from America, in order to become farmers, or to assist us in the cultivation of our land.

2d. That encouragement may be given to our foreign brethren who have vessels for the purpose, to establish commerce in Sierra Leone.

3rd. That those who may undertake to establish the whale fishery in the colony may be encouraged to persevere in that useful and laudable enterprise.

[1]The Kru were tribesmen whose home was in an area that is now part of the Liberian coast; as they had difficulty making a living in their own country, they came to Freetown in search of jobs (S. Harris, 83, n.7). They came to be known as watermen, or marines, who make contact with a vessel and handle many of the duties required (Delany, 145). The Nova Scotians who emigrated to Sierra Leone were blacks who had been refugees from the American Revolution as well as Jamaican Maroons who came by way of Nova Scotia (S. Harris, 45).

There are at this time 7 or 8 schools established throughout the colony. One of these is for the instruction of grown persons, and the others contain together about 230 children, who are instructed in all the necessary branches of education.

The inhabitants have likewise six places of worship, which are generally well attended. . . . An institution was formed . . . for the relief of the poor and disabled. . . . Everyone can judge of the happy effect of such institutions as these in improving the dispositions and softening the manners of our native brethren.

The colonists have instituted 5 courts, consisting first, of the Court of Quarter Sessions . . . the governor always presides as judge, and is attended by a justice of the peace, sheriff's clerk, messengers of the bailiff and constables. The petit jury consists of 12 men selected from Europeans, Nova-Scotians, and Maroons. . . .

The inhabitants are governed entirely by the British law, and are generally peaceable and willing to abide by the decisions of their civil magistrates. Governor Columbine lately issued a proclamation in which he offers the protection of these laws to any slave who may arrive in the colony with the consent of his or her owners, and leaves them at liberty to remain or go elsewhere, as they may think proper.

On the 18th of the 3rd month, I travelled in amongst the natives of Africa. The first tribe I met was called the Bullone Tribe. Their king, whose name is George, appeared to be very friendly. He could speak but very little English himself, but had a young man with him by the name of Peter Wilson, who had received his education in England, and appeared to be a man of very good information. This tribe, from what I could gather, have adopted the mode of circumcision, and seem to acknowledge by words the existence of a Deity. So accustomed are they to wars and slavery that I apprehend it would be a difficult task to convince them of the impropriety of these pernicious practices. I gave the king a testament and several other books, and let him know by the interpreter the useful records contained in those books, and the great fountain they pointed unto.

The Mendingo Tribe professes Mahometanism. I became acquainted with two men of this tribe who were apparently men of considerable learning: indeed this tribe generally appeared to be a people of some education. Their learning appeared to be the Arabic. They do not allow spiritous liquors to be made use of in this tribe. They have declined the practice of selling their own tribe, but notwithstanding this, they continue to sell those of other tribes, and thought it hard that the traffic in slaves should be abolished, as they were made poor in consequence thereof. I endeavoured to hold this out as a light to convince them of their error. But the prejudice of education had taken too firm hold of their minds to admit of much effect from reason on this subject.

ADDRESS

To my scattered brethren and fellow countrymen at Sierra Leone.

Grace be unto you and peace be multiplied from God our Father and from the Lord Jesus Christ, who hath begotten a lively hope in remembrance of you, and for which I desire ever to be humbled, world without end. Amen. . . .

ADVICE

First. That sobriety and steadfastness, with all faithfulness, be recommended, that so professors may be good examples in all things; doing justly, loving mercy, and walking humbly.

Secondly. That early care be extended towards the youth, whilst their minds are young and tender, that so they may be redeemed from the corruptions of the world—such as nature is prone to—not swearing, following bad company and drinking of spiritous liquors. That they may be kept out of idleness, and encouraged to be industrious, for this is good to cultivate the mind, and may you be good examples therein yourselves.

Thirdly. May servants be encouraged to discharge their duty with faithfulness; may they be brought up to industy; may their minds be cultivated for the reception of the good seed, which is promised to all that will seek after it. I want that we should be faithful in all things, that so we may become a people, giving satisfaction to those, who have borne the heat and burden of the day, in liberating us from a state of slavery. I must leave you in the hands of him who is able to preserve you through time, and to crown you with that blessing that is prepared for all those who are faithful unto death.

Farewell,
Paul Cuffe.

MARTIN R. DELANY

Martin R. Delany was born in 1812 in Charles Town, Virginia, to a freeborn mother and slave father who traced his ancestry to African chieftains. Delany began his career as a doctor, abolitionist, and editor, publishing *The Mystery*, the first African-American newspaper west of the Alleghenies, and in 1847 co-edited the Rochester *North Star* with Frederick Douglass.

Delany criticized the American Colonization Society and its plans to send free blacks to Liberia as a way of ridding the United States of black Americans who had helped to build the nation. Eventually, many free blacks did look outside U.S. borders for economic opportunities, especially with the passing in 1850 of the Fugitive Slave Law, which enabled slaveholders to recover runaway slaves in free states. There was support among a number of black leaders for colonization to places like Canada, the West Indies, Central America, and Africa. Delany became a strong supporter of black separatism and pan-Africanism. In 1852 he published the first book-length analysis of African-American life, *The Condition, Elevation, Emigration, and Destiny of the Colored People of the United States, Politically Considered*, in which he laid out plans for colonization in Africa.

Delany recruited an exploring party to go to Nigeria that included Robert Campbell, a science educator from the Institute for Colored Youth in Philadelphia. Both men published separate accounts of their journeys.

Delany stopped first in Liberia, where he met with Alexander Crummell, and in the excerpt here on Liberia he reveals his support of the colony that had been developed there. He joined Campbell in Abeokuta, where they signed a treaty with the Alake.

As Delany and Campbell began to explore Egbaland and Yorubaland, a border dispute broke out, prompting the two men to split up for a time. Delany's narrative focuses less on the logistics of the journey and more on his mission for blacks to develop a nation for blacks, promoting the idea of regeneration of Africa. Although Delany and Campbell gave presentations in England and the United States on their plans for a colony, within a few months of their return the tribal wars spread, and the African chiefs reneged on the treaty (Bell, 20). Delany began to turn his attention to the American Civil War, but he never gave up his dedication to Africa and African nationalism.

f r o m
Official Report of The Niger Valley Exploring Party (1861)

I sailed from New York May 24th, in the fine *barque Mendi*—Captain M'Intyre—vessel and cargo owned by Johnson, Turpin and Dunbar, three enterprising colored gentlemen of Monrovia, Liberia, all formerly of New York, U.S. In the name of the General Board of Commissioners for the promotion of the political and other interest of the colored people of the United States and the Canadas, by self-exertion, I thank them. . . .

My explorations in Liberia extended to every civilized settlement in the Republic except Careysburg, and much beyond these limits up the Kavalla River. There is much improvement recently up the St. Paul River, by the opening up of fine, and in some cases, extensive farms of coffee and sugar; also producing rice, ginger, arrow-root, and pepper, many of which have erected upon them handsome and well-constructed dwellings; also sugar mills and machinery for the manufacture of sugar and molasses, which articles manufactured, compare favorably with the best produced in other countries. There has, as yet, been no improvement introduced in the hulling and drying of coffee, there being probably not enough produced to induce the introduction of machinery. I am informed that there have also been commenced several good farms on the Junk River, which district, farther than the settlement at the mouth, I did not visit. The people are willing and anxious for improvement, and on introducing to many of the farmers the utility of cutting off the centre of each young coffee-tree so soon as it grew above the reach of a man or ordinary height, I had the satisfaction of seeing them immediately commence the execution of the work. . . .

The schools are generally good, every settlement being amply accommodated with them; and in Monrovia and at Cape Palmas the classics are being rigidly prosecuted.

Churches are many and commodious, of every Christian denomination—except, I believe, the Roman Catholic. The Missionaries seem to be doing a good work, there being many earnest and faithful laborers among them of both sexes, black and white, and many native catechists and teachers, as well as some few preachers.

The principal business carried on in Liberia is that of trading in native and foreign produce, the greater part being at the Capital. The greater part of merchants here are Liberians; but there are also three white houses—two German and one American. And along the coast there are a number of native trading-posts, the proprietors of which are white foreigners, with black agents. Many of the Liberian Clergy of all denominations are well educated gentlemen; and the Medical Profession is well represented by highly accomplished Physicians; but of all the professions, the Law is the most poorly represented—there being, as I learnt when there, but one young gentlemen at the bar who had been bred to the profession; and not a Judge on the bench who was learned in the law. This I do not mention in disparagement of the gentlemen who fill those honorable positions of presiding over the legal investigations of their country, as many—indeed, I believe the majority of them—are clergymen, who from necessity have accepted those positions, and fill their own legitimate callings with credit. I sincerely hope that the day is not far distant when Liberia will have her learned counsellors and jurists—dispensing law, disseminating legal opinions, and framing digests as well as other countries, for the benefit of nations. . . .

One word as a suggestion in political economy to the young politician of Liberia: Always bear in mind, that the fundamental principle of every nation is *self-reliance*, with the *ability to create their own ways and means*: without this, there is no capacity for *self-government*. In this short review of public affairs, it is done neither to disparage nor under-rate the gentlemen of Liberia with whom, from the acquaintance I have made with them in the great stride for black nationality, I can make common cause, and hesitate not to regard them, in unison with ourselves, a noble band of brothers. . . .

A word about slavery. It is simply preposterous to talk about slavery, as that term is understood, either being legalized or existing in this part of

Africa. It is nonsense. The system is a patriarchal one, there being no actual difference, socially, between the slave (called by their protector *son* or *daughter*) and the children of the person with whom they live. Such persons intermarry, and frequently become the heads of state: indeed, generally so, as I do not remember at present a king or chief with whom I became acquainted whose entire members of the household, from the lowest domestic to the highest official, did not sustain this relation to him, they calling him *baba* or "father," and he treating them as children. And where this is not the case, it either arises from some innovation among them or those exceptional cases of despotism to be found in every country. Indeed, the term "slave" is unknown to them, only as it has been introduced among them by whites from Europe and America. So far from abject slavery, not even the old feudal system, as known to exist until comparatively recent in enlightened and Christian Europe, exists in this part of Africa.

Criminals and prisoners of war are *legally sold* into slavery among themselves, just as was the custom in almost every civilized country in the world till very lately, when nothing but advanced intelligence and progressive Christianity among the people put a stop to it. There is no place, however, but Illorin, a *bona fide* Mohammedan kingdom, where we ever witnessed any exhibition of these facts.

Slaves are abducted by marauding, kidnapping, depraved natives, who, like the organized bands and gangs of robbers in Europe and America, go through the country thieving and stealing helpless women and children, and men who may be overpowered by numbers. Whole villages in this way sometimes fall victims to these human monsters, especially when the strong young men are out in the fields at work, the old of both sexes in such cases being put to death, whilst the young are hurried through some private way down to the slave factories usually kept by Europeans (generally Portuguese and Spaniards) and Americans, on some secluded part of the coast. And in no instances are the parents and relatives known to sell their own children or people into slavery, except, indeed, in cases of base depravity, and except such miserable despots as the kings of Dahomi and Ashantee; neither are the heads of countries known to sell their own people; but like the marauding kidnapper, obtain them by war on others. . . .

Lagos, at the mouth of the Ogun river in the Bight of Benin, Gulf of Guinea, 6 deg. 31 min. west coast of Africa, 120 miles north-west of the Nun (one of the mouths of the great river Niger) is the place of our location. This was once the greatest slave-trading post on the west coast of

Africa, and in possession of the Portuguese—the slavers entering Ako Bay, at the mouth of the Ogun river, lying quite inland, covered behind the island till a favorable opportunity ensued to escape with their cargoes of human beings for America. Wydah, the great slave-port of Dahomi, is but 70 or 80 miles west of Lagos. This city is most favorably located at the mouth of a river which during eight months in the year is a great thoroughfare for native produce, which is now brought down and carried up by native canoes and boats, and quite navigable up to Aro the port of Abbeokuta, a distance of eighty or a hundred miles, for light-draught steamers, such as at no distant day we shall have there. Ako Bay is an arm of the gulf, extending quite inland for three and a half miles, where it spreads out into a great sea, extending north ten to fifteen miles, taking a curve east and south, passing on in a narrow strip for two or three hundred miles, till it joins the Niger at the mouth of the Nun. It is the real harbor of Lagos, and navigable for light-draught vessels, as the Baltimore clippers and all other such slavers, formerly put into it; and Her Majesty's war-steamer Medusa has been in, and H. M.'s cruiser Brun lies continually in the bay opposite the Consulate. . . .

As to the possibility of putting a stop to the slave-trade, I have only to say, that we do not leave America and go to Africa to be passive spectators of such a policy as traffic in the flesh and blood of our kindred, nor any other species of the human race—more we might say—that we will not live there and permit it. "Self-preservation is the first law of nature," and we go to Africa to be *self-sustaining*; otherwise we have no business there, or anywhere else, in my opinion. We will bide our time; but *the Slave-trade shall not continue!*

Another important point of attention: that is, the slave-trade ceases in Africa, wherever enlightened Christian civilization gains an influence. And as to the strength and power necessary, we have only to add, that Liberia, with a coast frontier of seven hundred miles, and a sparse population, which at the present only numbers fifteen thousand settlers, has been effective in putting a stop to that infamous traffic along her entire coast. And I here record with pleasure, and state what I know to be the fact, and but simple justice to as noble-hearted antagonists to slavery as live, that the Liberians are uncompromising in their opposition to oppression and the enslavement of their race, or any other part of the human family. I speak of them as a nation or people and ignore entirely their Iscariots, if any there be. What they have accomplished with less means, we, by the help of Providence, may reasonably expect to effect with more—what they did with little, we may do with much. And I speak with confidence when I assert, that if we in this new position but do and act as we are fondly looked to and expected—as I most fondly hope and pray God that, by a prudent, discretionate and well-directed course, dependent upon Him, we may, nay, I am certain we will do—I am sure that there is nothing that may be required to aid in the prosecution and accomplishment of this important and long-desired end, that may not be obtained from the greatest and most potent Christian people and nation that ever graced the world. There is no aid that might be wanted, which may not be obtained through a responsible, just, and equitable negotiation. . . .

Robert Campbell

Robert Campbell was born in Jamaica in 1829 and had experience as a printer, teacher, and traveler to Central America. He was head of the Science Department of the Institute for Colored Youth in Philadelphia when he agreed to take part in Martin Delany's topographical and geographical examination of the valley of the River Niger.

Although a fervent nationalist, Campbell disagreed with Delany over the source of funding for the expedition to Nigeria. Campbell arrived in England in May 1859 and accepted funds from white-led organizations to underwrite the journey to Africa. Delany and Campbell hoped to sign a treaty with the Alake of Abekouta for land in the Niger Valley that would be used by African-American emigrants.

Campbell's narrative includes detailed descriptions of various tribal practices and an analysis of African slavery and its difference from the kind practiced in the United States and elsewhere. He also describes some of the tribal disputes that were taking place and his own confrontation and negotiations with Ibadan soldiers. Amidst his descriptions of customs both impressive and "uncivilized," we are reminded of modernity and the presence of the tourist/explorer even in 1859, when Campbell reports the difficulty of transporting luggage in the tropics and of securing reputable carriers to help him move from one place to another.

f r o m
A PilgRimAqe to My MotHeRlANd
(1859)

. . . Acting-Consul Lieut. Lodder had furnished me with a letter of introduction to his Majesty Okukenu, Alake of Abbeokuta, which I was anxious
to present. The Reverend Henry Townsend of the Church Missionary Society kindly accompanied me.[1] My reception by the King was very cordial. I
explained to him the object of my visit to the country, which he was
pleased to hear. He observed that for people coming with such purposes,
and for missionaries, he had great "sympathy," and would afford every
encouragement; but that some of the people (emigrants from the Brazils,
Cuba, and Sierra Leone) who were now coming into his dominion, especially traders, gave him much trouble. His body above the loins was nude;
otherwise his attire consisted of a handsome velvet cap trimmed with gold,
a costly necklace of coral, and a double strand of the same ornament about
his loins, with a velvet cloth thrown gracefully about the rest of his person,
under which he wore his shocoto, a sort of loose trowsers reaching only to
the knees. One of his wives (he has more than a hundred) was seated on
the same mat fanning him. He fondled on his knees an infant, and eight or
ten of his other little children, all about the same age, were gamboling
around him. On his right were seated several very old men dressed in white
cloths, elders of the Ogboni council. . . . He offered me the only chair
in his establishment. The Reverend Mr. Townsend, being an intimate
acquaintance, sat on an end of his mat. A few slaves, by the by, his chief
administrative officers, also sat near him. He presented me on my departure a head of cowries, worth nearly fifty cents.[2] During the next few days
I visited the principal chiefs, to explain the object of my visit and to make

[1]Townsend was an English missionary who was largely responsible for the introduction of
one sovereign chief in Abeokuta, the Alake, preferring to deal with him rather than a multi-
plicity of chiefs (Crowder, 129). Townsend did not support the treaty Delany and Campbell
signed with the Alake.
[2]Cowries are shells of mollusks used as currency; they have also been used in Yoruba divination systems.

to each a small present. Though humble, these presents were well received and in every instance a return present of cola nuts, (*cola sterculia acuminata,*) or of cowries was given. The natives generally at first regarded me as a white man, until I informed them of my connection with the Negro.[3] This announcement always gained me a warmer reception.

The reader here will permit me to digress to explain a matter respecting which there has hitherto been some misconception. It has been asserted that the native African does not manifest under any circumstance the same deference for colored men, as he does for white men; and so fully is this believed, particularly in the United States, that both my colleague Dr. Delany and myself were frequently cautioned respecting the danger to which we should be exposed in consequence of our complexion. It is indeed true that more respect has been accorded to white men, on account of their superior learning and intelligence, than to the generality of semi-civilized black men from the Brazils and other places, who now live in the Aku country; but it is a great mistake to think that the same is withheld from colored men similarly endowed with their white brethren. Let any disinterested person visiting Abbeokuta, place himself in a position to notice the manner which such a person, for instance, as the Reverend Samuel Crowther,[4] or even his son of the same name, each a pure Negro, is treated, and he would soon perceive the profound respect with which Africans treat those of their own race worthy of it. The white man who supposes himself respected in Africa, merely because he is white, is grievously mistaken. I have had opportunities to know, that if he should, presuming on his complexion, disregard propriety in his bearing towards the authorities, he would receive as severe rebuke as a similar offense would bring him in England. One of the chiefs of Abbeokuta, Atambala, was with us one day when a young missionary entered, and passed him with only a casual nod of the head. As soon as he was seated the haughty old chief arose and said, in his own tongue: "Young man, whenever any of my people, even the aged, approaches me, he prostrates himself with his face to the ground. I do not expect the same from you, or from civilized men, (*oyibo*), nevertheless remember always that I shall demand all the respect due to a chief

[3]Campbell had a light complexion.
[4]Crowther was a well-known native African minister who was later named the first bishop of Nigeria by the Church of England. Crowther assisted Campbell and Martin Delany in negotiating their treaty and in traveling in Nigeria (Ullman, 231).

of Abbeokuta." A sufficient apology was given, and the matter ended, not without, it is hoped, teaching a salutary lesson.

The king of Abbeokuta, whose person is considered too sacred for the popular gaze, is never permitted to leave the palace except on special occasions, and then he only goes into the open space without the palace-gates, one of his wives being in attendance to screen his face with a large fan. So with the king of Oyo, who once or twice only in the year exhibits himself to the public, decorated in his best robes and wearing a crown of coral. At these times any one can stare at his majesty with impunity. In Ilorin the king may not be seen, except as a mark of special favor, even by those to whom he affords the privilege of an audience.

If the reader will permit the expression, Abbeokuta might be said to be in for an irregular circle. The circumference of its outer wall, for in some parts of the city there are three walls, is about twenty-three miles. It was originally formed of over one hundred townships, each independent and governed by its own chief. The people are of the Egba tribe of the Akus, sometimes incorrectly called Yorubas. About fifty years ago, wars with the surrounding tribes, particularly with the Yorubas, had disorganized their nation, the greatest number of their people being enslaved, and sent to the Brazils, Cuba, and other places; many of them were also recaptured by British cruisers and taken to Sierra Leone. A few flying before their relentless enemy, and wandering from place to place at length found refuge beneath a shelf of rock now called "Olumo"; this hiding-place is said to have been before the den of a band of robbers. Advantage was taken of the security thus afforded, by others of the Egba tribe, and their number continued to increase until they felt strong enough to form a town and build a wall. In a short time that town, as before stated, contained the remnants of over one hundred townships, and became too powerful to be successfully assaulted by their enemies. The walls now include a number of huge hills of superior building granite, the quarrying of which will doubtless yield large profit to its inhabitants at no remote day.

They called the town very appropriately, "Abbeokuta," which means under a rock. It is now estimated to contain more than one hundred thousand inhabitants, and its population is fast increasing by accessions, not only from the surrounding tribes, who find in it greater security for life and property, but also from many of those, and their descendants, who were sold away as slaves.

Although the people have increased, one is at a loss to divine what has become of the chiefs of so many townships. One after another they have fallen off, and their successors have either never been appointed or are too insignificant to command attention. The treaty we concluded with the authorities of the place was signed by only seven chiefs, the king's signature not included. To them we were sent specially by the king, an act which seemed to indicate, either that they alone were of sufficient consequence to take part in such a matter, or that they, by common consent, were deemed the representatives of the rest. . . .

Viewed as to its power of enforcing order, and affording security for life and property, the government of Abbeokuta is as efficient as a civilized government can be, and it accomplishes these ends with the greatest ease and simplicity. Punishment is always summary and certain; notwithstanding, nobody complains of injustice. The penalty for theft is extreme, being either decapitation or foreign slavery. Before the advent of missionaries and civilized people adultery was sometimes also a capital offense; now it is modified to heavy fines, the amount of which is always proportioned to the position and wealth of the offender. Cases of adultery often occur, and must be expected until they are taught to abandon the disgusting system of polygamy.

The tenure of property is as it is among civilized people, except as to land, which is deemed common property; every individual enjoys the right of taking unoccupied land, *as much as he can use*, wherever and whenever he pleases. It is deemed his property as long as he keeps it in use; after that, it is again common property. This custom is observed by all other Akus.

The surviving relatives of one buried on any lot of ground, have a right to that ground which nothing can tempt them to relinquish, and from respect to the sentiment, no one would invade, on any pretext, particularly when the deceased was a mother or father. Mr. S. Crowther, Jr., has long desired to possess a strip of land contiguous to his place of business but no offer of money can induce the owner to part with it, although he is very poor; because his father lies buried there. . . .

Wives are commonly engaged at an early age, frequently before six or seven years old. This is done by paying to the parents a stipulated sum, and occasionally making presents both to them and the betrothed. When the engagement is concluded, a bracelet is placed about the wrist to signify the new relation she sustains. She remains with the parents until of proper age to be taken home to her husband. If she comes with honor, two or three days after, adorned with costly cloths and jewels, and with music, she marches with a large company of maidens through the city, to receive the congratulations and presents of her friends, which are generally on such an occasion very liberally bestowed. Otherwise, the parents are made to refund the whole amount advanced in engaging her, and the guilty partner to her infidelity, if known, is prosecuted for adultery. If the intended husband is a youth, never before married, his mother, or less frequently his father, makes the engagement for him; and the parties are respectively kept in ignorance of each other until they are both of suitable age to live together.

A less troublesome way of procuring a wife, with many, is to resort to the slave-marts of Ilorin at once, money in hand, and make their choice. The latter, of course, are slaves, as well as their children, between whom, however, and other slaves, there is some distinction. Wives procured according to the first of these methods, although not regarded as slaves, are practically as much so as the others, for like them, at the death of their lord they become nominally, and often really, the wives of his eldest son, except, of course, his own mother. They have, however, the privilege of choosing the next elder son, or of observing ever after a state of celibacy, which but women would choose, as it is regarded reproachfully.

According to their means of procuring them, men possess from a single wife to two or three hundred. Except the chiefs there are few, however, who have more than twenty. The Yoruba king at Oyo, Adelu, who is reputed the wealthiest man of the Akus, maintains about three hundred wives.* They are never suffered to leave the palace-yard, except on certain days, when they march in procession through the town in charge of eunuchs, of whom the king has a large number. Men are not suffered to approach them in these excursions. The King of Ilorin and other great personages of his court also keep their wives always confined. In this case, however, they are supported. In Abbeokuta, where even the wives of the king must support themselves, they are permitted to go abroad, and are generally among the most industrious traders of the place. . . .

After polygamy it may be appropriate to make a few remarks respecting its sister evil, slavery, which exists all through this section of Africa. Although the term "slavery" is the only word by which the institution can be properly designated, it is certainly not of the same character as the American institution, there being but little disparity between the condition of the master and that of his slave, since the one possesses almost every advantage

---

*Including the surviving wives of his father, who as already mentioned, are all nominally his, he is said to have about one thousand.

accessible to the other. Slaves are often found filling the most exalted positions: thus at Abbeokuta all the king's chief officers are his slaves, and they are among his most confidential advisers. On certain state occasions, one or other of these slaves is often permitted to assume in public the position of the king, and command and receive in his own person the homage and respect due to his master. So in Ilorin, Dungari, the prime minister of the king, daily sits in the market-place to receive the homage of the populace intended for the king, and yet Dungari, really the most important personage of the kingdom, and in rank even above the king's own sons, is a slave. Instances of this kind might be afforded almost indefinitely.

Slaves are procured chiefly by conquest, sometimes in warfare as justifiable and even more so than the wars waged among civilized nations; at other times predatory, and undertaken solely for their capture. Not a few incur slavery as a penalty for crime. Some are sold to defray either their own debts, or it may be the debts of others for which they have become liable; and frequently children are kidnapped and sold away into distant parts.

Although but a few years since every heathen town in this region abounded with slave-markets, there is now, doubtless through the influence of Christian civilization, nothing of the kind seen; and although it would be unsafe to say that slaves are not sometimes sold, yet if so, it is done secretly. The first and only marts we met for "this description of property," were at Ilorin, a Mohammedan kingdom. There was there, besides several small numbers exposed in different places throughout the town, a large market, the Gambari, almost exclusively devoted to their sale, and in which there were certainly not less than from five to six hundred. Christian America and Mohammedan Ilorin do with complacency what the heathens of Yoruba and Egba feel it a disgrace to practice.

At Ilorin we sojourned with Nasamo, the king's sheriff, in whose company only we were permitted to walk about the city. On arriving at the Gambari market in one of our excursions, he pointed to the slaves and jocularly asked whether I wished to purchase. I embraced the opportunity to show him the wrong of making slaves of our fellows, and the great injury which it inflicted not only upon those who suffer, but also on those who practice it. Nasamo fills a high position in the state, and is the master of a large number of slaves; nevertheless he is himself a slave, and doubtless thought of his youthful home and dear parents from whom he was stolen. He admitted all I said, and observed that he wished there was no such thing; but while it existed it was better that they be exposed in the markets than that they should be sold privately, "for then bad men would seize the defenseless and our children, and we would not know where to find them."

The Mohammedans do not sell their co-religionists into slavery: they sometimes hold them as slaves, but only when they were bought as heathens and converted after coming into their possession; but these are never after sold. Here is a vast difference from that class of Christians, so called, who buy and sell the members of their own church, the partakers of the same communion with themselves. How much better are such than the heathens, or even these benighted Mussulmans?

Although, as I have before shown, slavery in Africa is not like slavery in America, or even as it is in Cuba, yet it is still a fact which must not be disregarded, that, more or less, it is slavery—such, it is true, as the teachings and example of good men might quietly but certainly in time overthrow, but which might also by an obverse course assume most of the abhorrent phases of the American institution. My own opposition to slavery does not arise simply from the suffering and ill-treatment which the bondman endures, for in that case I would have to acquit perhaps the majority of American masters. I oppose it because a human being is by it reduced to the condition of a thing, a mere chattel, to be bought or sold at the option of his fellow-man, whose only right to do so is the accidental circumstance of superior power—a power which the good should use to protect rather than oppress the weak. I oppose it because I feel the common instinct that man has an inalienable right to "life, liberty and the pursuit of happiness." Hence I do not regard a slave-owner, even when he makes his slave as comfortable and happy as a slave can be—in all other respects, it may be, as well off as himself—I do not, I say, regard such a person as therefore less guilty: indeed, if there is one class of them whom I detest more heartily than another, it is that class whose course is to render the slave, if possible, contented with his condition.

From this view, therefore, I place my opposition to African slavery on the same ground as to American slavery, and God helping me, shall labor as earnestly for the overthrow of one as for the other. . . .

We continued at Ijaye for a fortnight spending the time in visiting the objects of interest in the neighborhood, taking photographic views, and otherwise making ourselves as comfortable as possible. On account of threatened hostilities between Ijaye and Oyo, the next town, we were unable to procure carriers when ready to resume our journey, and our interpreter, participating in the fears of the natives, would do little to help us in procuring them. We were finally obliged to go to seek them ourselves, in which we succeeded by lending each carrier a shirt, for so great is the respect entertained for the civilized, that even the assumption of the garb affords protection and the liberty of passing unmolested through a hostile country. . . .

It was necessary to send a messenger the day before, to announce to Fufu, the king's lieutenant, our intended visit to his majesty, as, because we were strangers he would only receive us in state, and required due notice to effect the necessary preparations. He was seated under an *acabi*, one of the turret-like arrangements already mentioned, surrounded by his wives, his head reclining on one, his feet resting on another; one fanned him, another wiped the perspiration from his face; one held an umbrella of many colors over his head, and another a small vessel carefully covered up, in which his majesty occasionally deposited his salivary secretions,* which accumulated fast in consequence of the quantity of snuff he takes in the mouth, in common with all the native adults, and often even the children of the region. His dress consisted of a costly tobe and shocoto of the same pattern, both nicely embroidered, a cap of red silk-velvet, and Moham-medan sandals. On his wrists he wore massive silver rings, and a strand of large corals about his neck.

In front of the acabi, on both side of a passage left by which to approach his majesty, were several of his slaves, the principal officers of his household, several men with long trumpets, on which they blew loud blast, applauding those points of the conversation deemed wise of witty, and several eunuchs.

As usual, we explained the object of our visit to Africa, with which he was as much pleased as any of the other native authorities with whom we had before treated. We made him a small present, and received according to custom a return present of a fine sheep and three heads of cowries. Our interview was an exceedingly pleasant one, and every day we continued at Oyo after that the health of the king's relatives, as he ever after called us. . . .

We left Isehin about eleven A.M., and reached Awaye, the next town, the same evening. The road was quiet and deserted, the people every where fearing to leave home on account of the unsettled condition of affairs.

*They have a superstition that their enemies can hurt them by procuring their spittle and subjecting it to certain manipulations.

There was the body of a man near the road, a mile from the town, where it had lain for more than a week. A few of a straggling party of Ijaye soldiers lurking in the neighborhood, having unsuccessfully pursued some farmers, were returning to their companions, who fired on them, mistaking them for the fugitives, and unfortunately killed one. The chief ordered that his body, which of course his companions had no time either to take away or bury, should remain, as a lesson to similar marauding parties.

Not more than half an hour after our arrival, the chief waited on me in person to salute me and welcome me to his town. He is the youngest chief in the Aku country, but certainly one of the most intelligent, to judge by his conversation. He sent me a large bowl of milk for supper, and the next morning a fine pig, although he knew I was not in a position to make him a return present. He was very anxious that some civilized person should come to live in his town. It is strange that while, including teachers and catechists, a place like Abbeokuta should have ten or twelve missionaries, besides an indefinite number of native readers or visitors, there should be only an ignorant visitor, whose sole qualification is his ability to read, allowed to a town of from sixteen to twenty thousand people. . . .

A woman with her son and daughter besought me to permit them to go under our protection to Abbeokuta. I told her she was welcome to all the protection I could afford, and we left together the next morning early. At about eleven o'clock, when halfway on our journey to Bi-olorun-pellu, we suddenly met about two hundred Ibadan soldiers. My servants, who were before me, attempted to pass by the foremost of them, but were very roughly arrested. Myself and the rest of the party soon came up and were all immediately surrounded. They kept us, while discussing the fate of my people, for nearly two hours. At length they demanded a present as the condition on which they would allow us to proceed. I had nothing to give, having left Oyo with only two suits of clothes, one on my back, the other in a small bundle. My other things consisted only of a gutta-percha sheet and some cooking utensils. I told the man who carried them to open the things and allow them to take whatever they desired: seeing we had nothing they informed my interpreter, after a little consideration among themselves, that we could depart peaceably, but they must keep as their captives the woman and her two children. It was too distressing to see three human beings about to be deprived of their liberty. The old woman wept bitterly, but the tears were apparently unheeded. I told them that it was impossible for me to leave these people; they had placed themselves under my protection, therefore I could not permit them to be taken away, except with myself also; that they could take my horse, my watch, my money, all I had, in short; but I would not permit them to take these people. They hesitated, I saw they were moved, and I kept up my entreaties. At length the balagun or captain, to whom I addressed myself, and who remained silent all the time I spoke, with almost a tear in his eye, exclaimed "*Oto, oto, oyibo, molo!*" "Enough, enough, white man, go on." When one of his party attempted to take away a tin cup my interpreter carried, he drew his sword, declaring that it was at the peril of any one to touch us. Some of his people seemed much disappointed. We hurried away, and four hours after were climbing an immense rock, rising like an island from the surrounding plain, on the summit of which is situated "Bi-olorun-pellu," "*If the Lord wills.*". . .

There is always trouble travelling in Africa with luggage, but it is far less in the interior than among the semi-civilized, neither Christian nor heathen, natives of the coast, who acquiring all the vices of the white man, know little and practice still less of his virtues.

I never experienced real hardship until in this little journey between Abbeokuta and the coast. No sooner had we fairly started than it began to rain heavily, and it continued raining more or less until we reached Lagos, so that, sleeping and waking, I was wet the whole time, forty-eight hours; but I warded off the efforts by helping the canoe-man with a paddle the entire way, by which means we also arrived at Lagos earlier. One more unpleasant incident, and I shall relieve the reader. It seemed that the canoe in which we travelled was purchased down the river, the canoe-man stopped at a small market-village, not expecting to meet there his creditor, but did unfortunately. Some altercation ensued, when the Ijebu began to take things out of the boat, in order to repossess himself of his property. I remained quiet until he attempted to remove my things, when I interposed. He turned from me, and began to talk very angrily with the canoe-man. Both became more and more excited. At this time another canoe with several men and women came up and all these took part in the row, which grew more fierce every instant. I saw some of the crowd running away, who in a few moments returned, and with them about thirty men, all armed with knives, their chief at their head. They rushed at the poor man, and the chief seizing the resistless creature was about to slay him, when a woman heroically threw herself in the way of the weapon, and saved him. The row continued fully an hour longer, and terminated at last only from the sheer exhaustion of all concerned. Without an interpreter, and my own knowledge of the language being very limited, I was unable except by conjecture and an expression understood here and there, to learn the details of the dispute.

We arrived at Lagos on the evening of the 7th of April. Dr. Delany accomplished his overland journey in the same time, so that we met crossing the bay, and landed together. The next day, Sunday — Easter Sunday — we attended divine service, and heard a sermon from our venerable friend the Rev. Samuel Crowther, who was now spending a short time with his family, and expecting to return to his labors up the Niger in a few days. Let me here, as well for my colleague as myself, record my acknowledgements and thanks to him, his family, and to the many kind friends we met with in our travels, not omitting our friend Capt. Davis, who kindly furnished us a passage in his boat to the steamer, free of expense.

On the morning of the 10th of April we bade adieu to Lagos, and after an unusually fine passage across the bar, embarked on board the Royal Mail S. S. "Athenian," Capt. Laurie, for Liverpool. The steamer, as in the outward voyage, stopped at the intermediate places on the coast, and at Teneriffe and Madeira. She had on board a large number of Kru men, returning from different points of the coast, where they had been serving either on board men-of-war or trading vessels. These men are of incalculable advantage, as without them it would be impossible to work the ships, European sailors being unfit to labor in such warm latitudes, and not understanding so well the management of boats in heavy surfs. No where, I believe, can people be found so at home in the water. At Cape Palmas and other places on the Liberian coast, the steamer stops to allow them to land, which they do in very small canoes, bought off from the beach by their countrymen in which no other human beings would venture. They make fearful noise as they are departing and preparing to do so, and if not hurried off by the officers, would detain the vessel much longer than necessary. Sometimes the steamer starts before they have all left, and then without the slightest hesitation they throw into the water such of their property as will float, taking the rest in their hands, and jumping overboard swim with the greatest ease to their canoes. . . .

At Freetown, Sierra Leone, we saw a large slaver brought in a few days before by H. M. S. S. "Triton." Her officers and crew, consisting of over thirty persons, were there set at liberty, to be disposed of by the Spanish Consul as distressed seamen. They were as such forwarded in the same ship with us to Teneriffe. No wonder that the slave-trade should be so difficult to suppress, when no punishment awaits such wretches as these. What scamp would fear to embark in such an enterprise, if only assured that there was no personal risk — that he has only to destroy the ship's flag and papers on the approach of a cruiser, not only to shield himself and his crew from the consequence of his crime, but to receive the consideration rightly accorded distressed honest men. These villains of course return to Havana or the United States, procure a new ship, and again pursue the wicked purpose which their previous experience enables them to accomplish with all the more impunity.

The incidents of a voyage to England under every variety to circumstance, have been so often described, that I shall both save myself the trouble of writing, and you, dear reader, the tedium of perusing them.

Alexander Crummell

Alexander Crummell was born in 1819, the son of Boston Crummell, whose stories of his kidnapping from the Timmanee tribe in West Africa greatly affected young Alexander and created a resolve to go to Africa. The Crummells were Episcopalian, and Alexander came under early influence of the Reverend Peter Williams, a supporter of back-to-Africa movements and a close friend of Paul Cuffe. The first black newspaper, *Freedom's Journal,* was founded in the Crummell household.

After being ordained as an Episcopal priest in 1842, Crummell sailed for England to raise funds for his planned church in New York City. While in England, he studied at Cambridge University; he already had a strong pan-African identity, referring to himself and other black people as Africans. He believed, like other pan-Africanists of the period, that enslaved African Americans had as their destiny been chosen to return to the motherland to enlighten the African natives for the benefit of regenerating the race and creating a holy nation.

Crummell spent sixteen years, between 1853 and 1872, in Liberia as an Episcopal missionary, educator, farmer, and orator. He appreciated native Africans, praising them for natural modesty and generosity of nature, and he believed they were superior to the immoral English and Americans yet thought the African was in need of the civilizing effects of Western Christianity. The excerpt from his letter "The Relations and Duties of Free Colored Men" reveals his appeal to talented blacks with "high souls and lofty reserves" to consider emigration to Liberia as a duty, a good business opportunity, and to help prevent the corruption of African potential. Crummell's ideas became widely known throughout this letter, which was published in the *African Repository,* a publication of the American Colonization Society.

Crummell eventually returned to the United States after being dismissed from his post at Liberia College in a power struggle with a group of mulattos. Crummell felt that mulattos and westerners in Liberia "will prevent that republic from becoming the great nation it can be" (Rigsby, 120). He died in 1898 and was a great influence on W. E. B. Du Bois and Marcus Garvey, among others.

f r o m
"The Relations and Duties of Free Colored Men in America to Africa" Addressed to Mr. Charles B. Dunbar, formerly of New York City, now a citizen of Liberia. (1860)

HIGH SCHOOL, MT. VAUGHAN, CAPE PALMAS, LIBERIA, 1ST SEPT., 1860

My Dear Sir: It is now many months since I received a letter from you, just as you were about sailing from our shores for your home. In that note you requested me to address you a letter setting forth my views concerning Liberia, suggesting, at the same time, that such a letter might prove interesting to many of our old friends and schoolmates in New York. I have not forgotten your request, although I have not heretofore complied with it. Though convinced of the need and possible usefulness of such a letter as you asked from me, I have shrunk from a compliance with your request. Not to mention other grounds of reluctance, let me say here that I have felt it a venturesome thing to address four hundred thousand men; albeit it be indirectly through you. Neither my name, position, nor any personal qualities give me authority thus to do. The only excuse I have is the depth and solemnity of all questions connected with Africa. I see that no one else of our race has done it; perhaps I may be pardoned for assuming so great a task.

I may add here that I address the "Free Colored Men of America," because I am identified with them; and not because I feel that *they*, especially, and above all the other sons of Africa, in distant lands, are called upon for zeal and interest in her behalf. It is the exaggeration of the relation of *American* black men to Africa, which has turned the hearts of many of her own children from her. Your duties, in this respect, are no greater than those of our West Indian, Haytian, and eventually our Brazilian brethren. Whatever in this letter applies to our brethren in the United States, applies in an equal degree to them. But I am not the man to address them. I fear I *presume* even in writing this letter to American black men, and have only just now concluded to do so by the encouragement I have received in two pleasant interviews with Mr. Campbell and Dr. Delany.

And even now it is with doubt and diffidence that I conclude to send you this communication. My reluctancy has arisen chiefly from a consideration of the claim put forth by leading colored men in the United States, to the effect "that it is unjust to disturb their residence in the land of their birth by a continual call to go to Africa." This claim is, in my opinion, a most just one. Three centuries' residence in a country seems clearly to give any people a right to their nationality therein without disturbance. Our brethren in America have other claims besides this; they have made large contributions to the clearing of their country; they have contributed by sweat and toil to the wealth thereof; and by their prowess and their blood they have participated in the achievement of its liberties. But their master right lies in the fact that they are Christians; and one will have to find some new page and appendage to the Bible, to get the warrant for Christians to repel and expatriate Christians, on account of blood, or race, or color. In fact, it seems to me a most serious thing to wantonly trench upon rights thus solemnly and providentially guaranteed a people, that is, by a constant, ceaseless, fretting iteration of a repelling sentiment.

Of course I do not intend any thing akin to this in my letter. I would not insult the intellect and conscience of any colored man who thinks it his duty to labor for his race on American soil, by telling him that it is his duty to come to Africa. If he is educated up to the ideas of responsibility and obligation, he knows his duty better than I do. And, indeed, generally, it is best to leave individuals to themselves as to the *details* of obligation and responsibility.

"The primal duties shine aloft like stars";—and it is only when men *will* not see them, that we are bound to repeat and re-utter them, until the souls of men are aroused, and they are moved to moral resolution and to noble actions. But as to the *mode, form,* and *manner* of meeting their duties, let the common sense of every man decide it for himself.

My object in writing this letter is not to vex any of our brethren by the iteration of the falsehood that America is not their home, nor by the misty theory "that they will all yet have to come to Liberia." I do not even intend to invite any one to Liberia, glad as I would be to see around me many of the wise and sterling men I know in the United States, who would be real acquisitions to this nation, and as much as I covet their society. I am not putting in a plea for colonization. My object is quite different; in fact it is not a strict compliance with the terms of your letter, for I shall have but little to say about Liberia. But believing that *all* men hold some relation to the land of their fathers, I wish to call the attention of the sons of Africa in America to their "RELATIONS AND DUTY TO THE LAND OF THEIR FATHERS."

And even on such a theme I know I must prepare myself for the rebuff from many—"Why talk to *us* of fatherland? What have *we* to do with Africa? *We* are not Africans; we are Americans. You ask no peculiar interest on the part of Germans, Englishmen, the Scotch, the Irish, the Dutch, in the land of their fathers, why then do you ask it of us?"

Alas for us, as a race! so deeply harmed have we been by oppression that we have lost the force of strong, native principles, and prime natural affections. Because exaggerated contempt has been poured upon us, we too become apt pupils in the school of scorn and contumely. Because repudiation of the black man has been for centuries the wont of civilized nations, black men themselves get shame at their origin and shrink from the terms which indicate it.

Sad as this is, it is not to be wondered at. "Oppression" not only "makes a wise man mad," it robs him also of his self-respect. And this is our loss; but having emerged from slavery, it is our duty to cast off its grave-clothes and resist its deadly influences.

Our ancestors were unfortunate, miserable, and benighted; but nothing more. Their history was a history, not of ignominy and disgrace, but of heathenism and benightedness. And even in that state they exhibited a nobleness of native character, they cherished such virtues, and manifested so much manliness and bravery, that the civilized world is now magnanimous enough to recognize such traits; and its greatest men are free to render their warm eulogies.

When then colored men question the duty of interest in Africa, because they are not Africans, I beg to remind them of the kindred duty of self-respect. And my reply to such queries as I have mentioned above is this: 1. That there is no need of asking the interest of Englishmen, Germans, Dutchmen and others in the land of their fathers, because they have this interest, and are always proud to cherish it. And 2d. I remark that the abject state of Africa is a most real and touching appeal to *any* heart for sympathy and aid. It is an appeal, however, which comes with a double force to every civilized man who has negro blood flowing in his veins.

Africa lies low and is wretched. She is the maimed and crippled arm of humanity. Her great powers are wasted. Dislocation and anguish have reached every joint. Her condition in every point calls for succor—moral, social, domestic, political, commercial, and intellectual. Whence shall flow aid, mercy, advantage to her? Here arises the call of duty and obligation to colored men. Other people may, if they choose, forget the homes of their sires; for almost every European nation is now reaping the fruits of a thousand years' civilization. Every one of them can spare thousands and even millions of their sons to build up civilization in Australia, Canada, New Zealand, South Africa, or Victoria. But Africa is the victim of her heterogeneous idolatries. Africa is wasting away beneath the accretions of civil and moral miseries. Darkness covers the land, and gross darkness the people. Great social evils universally prevail. Confidence and security are destroyed. Licentiousness abounds everywhere. Moloch rules and reigns throughout the whole continent, and by the ordeal of Sassywood, Fetiches, human sacrifices, and devil-worship, is devouring men, women, and little children. They have not the Gospel. They are living without God. The Cross has never met their gaze, and its consolations have never entered their hearts, nor its everlasting truths cheered their deaths.

And all this only epitomizes the miseries of Africa, for it would take a volume to detail and enumerate them. But this is sufficient to convince any son of Africa that the land of our fathers is in great spiritual need, and that those of her sons who haply have ability to aid in her restoration will show mercy to her, and perform an act of filial love and tenderness which is but their "reasonable service."

I have two objects in view in addressing you this letter: *one* relates to the temporal, material interests of adventurous, enterprising colored men; and the *other* pertains to the best and most abiding interests of the million masses of heathen on this continent—I mean their evangelization.

First, I am to speak with reference to the temporal and material interests of adventurous, enterprising and aspiring men in the United States of America. I wish to bring before such persons reasons why they should feel interest in Africa. These reasons are not, I am free to confess, directly and distinctively philanthropic; although I do, indeed, aim at human well-being through their force and influence. But I appeal now more especially to the hopes, desires, ambition, and aspirations of such men. I am referring to that sentiment of self-regard which prompts to noble exertions for support and superiority. I am aiming at that principle of SELF-LOVE which spurs men on to self-advantage and self-aggrandizement—a principle which, in its normal state and in its due degree, to use the words of BUTLER, "is as just and morally good as any affection whatever." In fine, I address myself to all that class of sentiments in the human heart which creates a thirst for wealth, position, honor, and power. I desire the auxiliary aid of this class of persons, and this class of motives, for it is such influences and agencies which are calculated to advance the material growth of Africa. She needs skill, enterprise, energy, *worldly* talent, to raise her; and these applied here to her needs and circumstances, will prove the handmaid of religion, and will serve the great purposes of civilization and enlightenment through all her borders.

There seems to me to be a natural call upon the children of Africa in foreign lands to come and participate in the opening treasures of the land of their fathers. Though these treasures are the manifest gift of God to the negro race, yet that race reaps but the most partial measure of their good and advantage. It has always been thus in the past, and now as the resources of Africa are being more and more developed, the extent of *our* interest therein is becoming more and more diminutive. The slave-trade is interdicted throughout Christendom; the chief powers of earth have put a lien upon the system of slavery; interest and research in Africa have reached a state of intensity; mystery has been banished from some of her most secret quarters; sunlight, after ages of darkness, has burst in upon the charmed regions of her wealth and value; and yet the negro, on his native soil, is but "a hewer of wood and drawer of water"; and the sons of Africa in foreign lands; inane and blinded, suffer the adventurous foreigner, with greed and glut, to jostle them aside, and to seize with skill and effect upon their own rightful inheritance.

For three centuries and upwards, the civilized nations of the earth have been engaged in African commerce. Traffic on the coast of Africa anticipated the discoveries of Columbus. From Africa the purest gold got its characteristic three hundred years ago. From Africa dyes of the greatest value have been carried to the great manufacturing marts of the world. From Africa palm oil is exported by thousands of tons; and now, as the observant eye of commerce is becoming more and more fastened upon this continent, grain, gums, oils of divers kinds, valuable woods, copper and other ore, are being borne from the soil to meet the clamorous demands of distant marts.

The chief item of commerce in this continent has been the "slave-trade." The coast of Africa has been more noted for this than for any thing else. Ever since 1600, the civilized nations of the earth have been transporting in deadly holds, in poisonous and pestilential cabins, in "perfidious barks," millions of our race to foreign lands. This trade is now almost universally regarded as criminal; but in the light of commercial prudence and pecuniary advantage, the slave-trade was as great a piece of folly as it was a crime; for almost beneath their eyes, yea, doubtless, often immediately in their sight, were lying treasures, rivalling far the market value of the flesh and blood they had been so eager to crowd beneath their hatches.

Africa is as rich in resources as India is; not as yet as valuable in products, because she is more unenlightened and has a less skilful population. But so far as it respects mineral and vegetable capacity, there seems to me but little, if any, doubt that Africa more than rivals the most productive lands on the globe. . . .

As with the palm oil, so with maize, sugar-cane, and cotton; civilized men could, with but little difficulty, increase the cultivation of these articles among the natives, and ship them to traders to their own advantage. And this process is the great secret of West African trade: the foreign merchant, by his goods, excites the cupidity of the simple native, who at Fernando Po brings him barwood; at St. Paul, Loanda, beeswax; at Congo, copal and gutta percha; at Accra, maize; at Calabar, black ebony wood; at Bonny and Lagos, palm oil; at Bassa, (Liberia,) camwood; at Lagos, cotton; at Tantamquerry and Gambia, ground nuts and pepper; at Sierra Leone, nearly *all* kinds of African produce; at Elmina, Cape Coast, Accra, and Bassam, gold. By this multiform traffic, yet, be it remembered, in its infancy, and capable of being increased a thousand fold, millions of dollars are being made every year on the coast of Africa.

Now all this flows into the coffers of white men. I mean nothing invidious by this. I state a fact, and am utterly unconscious of any unworthy or ungenerous feeling in stating it. "The earth is the Lord's, and the fulness thereof;" and this "fulness" He has given to MAN, irrespective of race or color. The main condition of the obtainment of it is intelligence, forecast, skill, and enterprise. If the black man—the black man, I mean, civilized and enlightened—has lying before him a golden heritage, and fails to seize upon and to appropriate it, Providence none the less intends it to be seized upon and wills it to be used. And if the white man, with a keen eye, a cunning hand, and a wise practicalness, is enabled to appropriate it with skill and effect, it is his; God gives it to him, and he has a right to seek and to search for a multiplication of it, and when he secures it a right to the use of it, responsible, however, both to God and man for the use of right means to the ends he has before him, and for the moral features of his traffic.

But while conceding that the white man has, in the main, fairly won the present trade of Africa, I cannot but lament our non-participation therein; for the larger advantages of it go to Europe and America, and help to swell the broad stream of their wealth, luxury, and refinement. . . .

And now perhaps you ask—"How shall the children of Africa, sojourning in foreign lands, avail themselves of the treasures of this continent?" I answer briefly, "In the same way white men do." *They* have pointed out the way, let us follow in the same track, and in the use of the like (legitimate) agencies by which trade is facilitated and money is made by them.

Perhaps this is too general, let me therefore attempt something more specific and distinctive.

FIRST, then, I remark that if individuals are unable to enter upon a trading system, they can form associations. If *one* has not sufficient capital, four or six united can make a good beginning. If a few persons cannot make the venture, then a company can be formed. It was in this way the first attempts at trading were made by the Dutch and the English, both in India and Africa. A few men associated themselves together, and sent out their agent or agents, and started a factory. And from such humble beginnings, in the 17th century, has arisen that magnificent Indian Empire, which has helped to swell the vast wealth and the cumbrous capital of England, . . .

Without doubt God designs as great things as these for Africa, and among the means and agencies He will employ, commercial enterprise is most certainly one. To this end, however, high souls and lofty resolves are necessary, as in any other vocation of life. Of course the timid, the overcautious, the fearful—men in whose constitution FAITH is a needed quality, are not fitted for this service. If ever the epoch of negro civilization is brought about in Africa, whatever *external* influences may be brought to bear upon this end, whatever foreign agencies and aids, black men themselves are without doubt to be the chief instruments. But they are to be men of force and energy; men who will not suffer themselves to be outrivalled in enterprise and vigor; men who are prepared for pains, and want, and suffering; men of such invincible courage that the spirit cannot be

tamed by transient failures, incidental misadventure, or even glaring mis-
calculations; men who can exaggerate the feeblest resources into potent
agencies and fruitful capital. Moreover, these men are to have strong moral
proclivities, equal to the deep penetration and the unyielding tenacity of
their minds. No greater curse could be entailed upon Africa than the sudden appearance upon her shores of a mighty host of heartless black bucca-
neers, (for such indeed they would prove themselves,) men sharpened up
by letters and training, filled with feverish greed, with hearts utterly alien
from moral good and human well-being, and only regarding Africa as a
convenient gold-field from which to extract emolument and treasure to
carry off to foreign quarters.

Such men would only reproduce the worst evils of the last three sad centuries of Africa's history; and quickly and inevitably so soil their character
that the *just* imputation would be fastened upon them of that malignant lie
which has recently been spread abroad through Europe and America
against us: that is, of complicity with the slave trade.

It must follow, as a necessity, that the trade and commerce of Africa shall
fall into the hands of black men. At an early day whole fleets of vessels,
manned and officered by black men from the United States and Liberia,
would outrival all the other agencies which are now being used for grasp-
ing West African commerce. Large and important houses would spring
into existence among you all through the States. Wealth would flow into
your coffers, and affluence would soon exhibit itself amid all your associations. The reproach of penury and the consciousness of impotency in all
your relations would rapidly depart, and as a people you would soon be
able to make yourselves a felt element of society in all the relations of life,
on the soil where you were born.

These are some of the *material* influences which would result from this
movement. The moral and philanthropic results would be equally if not
more notable. The kings and tradesmen of Africa, having the *demonstration* of negro capacity before them, would hail the presence of their black
kinsmen from America, and would be stimulated to a generous emulation.
To the farthest interior, leagues and combinations would be formed with
the men of commerce; and thus civilization, enlightenment, and Christianity would be carried to every state, town, and village of interior Africa.
The galling remembrance of the slave-trade on the coast, and of slavery in
America, would quicken the blood and the brain of both parties, and every
wretch of a slave-trader who might visit the coast would have to atone for

his temerity by submitting to the rigid code framed for piracy. And when *this* disturbing and destructive hindrance to African progress was once put down, noble cities, vast agricultural establishments, the seeds of universities, and groundwork of church organizations, would spring up all along the banks, and up the valley of the Niger. . . .

For the carrying out such a plan you have, I repeat myself, you have almost, if not quite, all the needed means and agencies even now at hand. You have, all through the States, men who can at once furnish the capital for the commencement of such a venture. You know I am not wont to exaggerate the wealth of colored men. In such matters I prefer fact to conjecture; for certainly among us on this subject imagination has too often proved "a forward and delusive faculty." Yet I do know of some of our brethren in the States who have become moneyed men, not millionaires, indeed, but men worth their thousands. Some of these men are more prominent individuals than others, and as their names are not unfrequently mentioned in such a connection as this, it may not seem invidious in a like mention on these pages. Some of these persons are acquaintances—a few, old friends of former years, but the most are personally unknown to me. There are Rev. Stephen Smith, William Whipper, Esq., of Philadelphia; Messrs. Knight & Smith, of Chicago, Ill.; Messrs. Cook & Moxly, Buffalo, N. Y.; Youngs & Wilcox, of Cincinnati, &c., &c.

It is possible that in a few instances earnest prejudice against every thing African may cause displeasure at this designation. Any one can see that I have intended nothing discourteous; and it should be remembered that commercial enterprise in Africa has no necessary connection with emigration, or colonization. How great soever the diversities of opinion upon these points, on *this* platform, Douglass and Delany can stand beside the foremost citizens and merchants of Liberia. Hence those men whose feelings are the most averse to any thing like colonization, cannot object to the promotion of trade and the acquisition of wealth. Indeed, I have no doubt that there are thousands who would be glad of a safe investment in any thing wherein there is probability of advantage. Moreover, the fretted mind of our brethren needs distraction from griefs and the causes of griefs. Just now, when darkness shrouds their Southern heavens, what could be more opportune, what more desirable, than such a movement?

In Liberia, we have the noblest opportunities and the greatest advantages. We have a rich and varied soil—inferior, I verily believe, to but few, if any, on the globe. We have some of the proofs and many of the indications of varied and vast mineral wealth of the richest qualities. We have a country finely watered in every section by multitudinous brooks and streams and far-reaching rivers. We have a climate which needs but be educated, and civilized, and tempered by the plastic and curative processes of emigration, clearances, and scientific farming, to be made as fine and as temperate as any land in the tropics can be.

On this soil have been laid the foundations of republican institutions. Our religion is Protestant, with its characteristic tendencies to freedom, progress, and human well-being. We are reaching forward, as far as a young and poor nation can, to a system of common schools. Civilization, that is, in its more simple forms, has displaced ancestral paganism in many sections of the land, has taken permanent foothold in our territory, and already extended its roots among our heathen kin. Our heathen population, moreover, in the immediate neighborhood of our settlements, is but small and sparse; thus saving our civilization from too strong an antagonism, and allowing it room, scope, and opportunity for a hardy growth in its more early days. Active industry is now exhibiting unwonted vigor, and begins to tell upon commerce and the foreign market. . . .

I am not blind to difficulties. I know some of the trials of emigration. I have been called to some of the difficulties, not to say severities, of missionary life. And therefore I shall be free, I trust, from the charge of flippancy. So likewise I am aware of the peculiar obstacles in the way of our brethren in the States. I, too, am an American black man. I, too, have an acquaintance with obstructive idiosyncrasies in them. If you speak of hindrances and difficulties specially theirs, I know all about them.

But I say it deliberately, that the difficulties in the way of our brethren doing a goodly work for Africa, are more subjective than objective. *One of these hindrances is a want of missionary zeal.* This is a marked characteristic of *American* black Christians. I say *American*, for from all I hear, it does not characterize our West Indian brethren; and the infant church of Sierra Leone is already, in sixty years from its birth, a mother of missions. *This* is our radical defect. *Our* religion is not diffusive, but rather introversive. It does not flow out, but rather inward. As a people we like religion—we like religious services. Our people like to go to church, to prayer-meetings, to revivals. But we go to get enjoyment. We like to be made happy by sermons, singing, and pious talk. All this is indeed correct so far as it goes; but it is only *one* side of religion. It shows only that phase of piety which may be termed the *"piety of self-satisfaction."* But if we are true disciples, we should not only seek a comforting piety, but we should also exhibit an effective and expansive one. We should let our godliness exhale like the odor of flowers. We should live for the good of our kind, and strive for the salvation of the world.

Another of these hindrances is what the phrenologists term "*inhabitativeness,*"—the stolid inhabitativeness of our race. As a people, we cling with an almost deadly fixity to locality. I see this on both sides of the Atlantic. Messrs. Douglass and Watkins assail Messrs. Horace Greeley and Gerrit Smith for pointing out this peculiarity of character in our people. But without doubt they tell the truth of us. We are not "given to change." The death of a master, the break-up of a family, may cast a few black men from the farm to the city, but they go no further. We lack speculation. Man has been called a creature,

Looking before and after ———

But not so we. We look where we stand, and but few beyond.

But the enlightened sons of Africa, in distant lands, are called to a far higher work than even this; a work which as much transcends mere civilization as the abiding interests of eternity outvie the transient concerns of time. To wrest a continent from ruin; to bless and animate millions of torpid and benighted souls; to destroy the power of the devil in his strongholds, and to usher therein light, knowledge, blessedness, inspiring hope, holy faith, and abiding glory, is, without doubt, a work which not only commands the powers of the noblest men, but is worthy the presence and the zeal of angels. It is just this work which now claims and calls for the interest and the activity of the sons of Africa. Its plainest statement and its simplest aspect are sufficient, it seems to me, to move these men in every quarter of the world to profound sensibility, to deep resolve, to burning ardor. Such a grand and awful necessity, covering a vast continent, touching the best hopes and the endless destiny of millions of men, ought, I think, to stir the soul of many a self-sacrificing spirit, and quicken it to lofty purposes and noble deeds. And when one considers that never before in human history has such a grand and noble work been laid out in the Divine Providence, before the negro race, and that it rises up before them in its full magnitude now, at the very time when they are best fitted for its needs and requirements, it seems difficult to doubt that many a generous and godly soul will hasten to find its proper place in this great work of God and man, whether it be by the personal and painful endeavors of a laborer in the field of duty, or by the generous benefactions and the cheering incitements which serve to sustain and stimulate distant and tried workers in their toils and trials. "A benefaction of this kind seems to enlarge the very being of a man, extending it to distant places and to future times, inasmuch as unseen countries and after ages may feel the effects of this bounty, while he himself reaps the reward in the blessed society of all those who 'having turned many to righteousness, shine as the stars forever and ever.' "

I am very truly,
Your servant,
ALEX CRUMMELL.

EdwaRd WilMoт BlydEN

Edward Wilmot Blyden was born in St. Thomas, Virgin Islands, in 1832 to free parents who claimed origins in the Ibo people of Africa. The Blydens followed African traditions at home and for two years lived in Venezuela, where young Blyden observed that black people were often exploited. He studied in St. Thomas with the Reverend John Knox, white pastor of the Dutch Reformed Church there, and decided to become a clergyman. In 1850 Blyden was turned down for admission by theological colleges in the United States because he was black, so the idea of emigrating to Liberia appealed to him. He settled in Liberia in 1851, a time when six thousand American blacks made their homes in several communities there.

Blyden believed that Liberia had a special destiny to enhance the prestige of the black race, and to prepare himself for his part he studied theology and teaching. He began to publicly express his pan-African ideas through sermons, public addresses, and writing for Liberian, American, and English publications. He thought the racial integrity of blacks could be achieved only if Europeans kept at a distance; his sense of racial integrity depended on cultural as well as biological and geographical arguments (Berghahn, 50). Thus, his sense of the regeneration of Africa depended on emigration and, as expressed in an excerpt from his influential book *Christianity, Islam and the Negro Race*, published in 1887, a respect for the teaching of Islam in Africa as a way to promote industry and education, which led him to study Arabic.

From 1862 to 1871 Blyden was professor of classics at Liberia College, where one of his colleagues and friends was Alexander Crummell. Between 1850 and 1896, Blyden visited the United States eight times; in 1861 Blyden and Crummell were commissioned by the Liberian government to travel to Britain and America to interest philanthropists in Liberian education and in 1862 to encourage blacks to return to Africa (Logan et al., *Dictionary of American Negro Biography*, 49).

Blyden traveled to Egypt and the Middle East in 1866; in Lebanon he studied Arabic, which he later taught at Liberia College. Blyden's travelogue *From West Africa to Palestine*, published in 1873, is much more of a "traditional" travel narrative than his other works, describing well-known tourist attractions and his observations of the culture. In the excerpt here Blyden expresses the awe he feels in the holy land and his pride in being one of the descendants of Ham, who contributed to ancient Egyptian culture. In one of the pyramids he engraves his name with the word *Liberia* to connect himself to the thousands of other names he saw there. In Jerusalem Blyden compares different cultural and religious practice between Christians, Jews, and Muslims; he also comments on women's veiling in the region and their exclusion from certain forms of prayer.

In Liberia Blyden was often at odds with the mulatto ruling elite, who he believed were bigoted and unpatriotic. In 1871 he narrowly escaped being lynched by his enemies; he fled to Sierra Leone, where he tried to establish a British protectorate to facilitate trade and allow Africans to adapt Western institutions within an African framework (Lynch, 5). Blyden's plans were not fully realized, and he returned to Liberia, where he served as a high school principal, ambassador to Britain, and president of Liberia College. His last official position before his death in 1912 was as director of Muslim education in Sierra Leone.

f r o m
FROM WEST AFRICA TO PALESTINE
(1873)

. . . On the 10th of July, at seven a.m., we anchored in the harbour of Alexandria. I now had before me the renowned land of Egypt. How shall I describe the emotions with which the first sight of this ancient country inspired me? How shall I select and reproduce in an order intelligible to others the thoughts which, in rapid succession, passed through my mind?

I was prepared to find a large harbour, but was greatly surprised at the presence of so large a number of vessels from nearly all parts of the world, and of three or four splendid steam corvettes belonging to the Egyptian government.

I saw in the distance the site of the ancient Pharos, the first great lighthouse constructed in the Mediterranean, and one of the seven wonders of the world. Immediately before me lay the city built by Alexander the Great. What a various history, political, social and religious, has it passed through! When Alexander boasted that he would here build an emporium of commerce that would surpass Tyre, which he had destroyed, and attract the shipping of the world, he little dreamed that the day would come when the most important operations carried on in this city would be by vessels from powerful nations of the west; some of them inhabiting countries then unknown to maritime enterprise. The history of Alexandria since his death has more than realised the dream of the world's conqueror.

About an hour after we anchored a steam-tug came alongside the *Nyanza*, and took off those passengers and their effects who had taken through tickets for India, China, Japan, and Australia. So far as I was concerned the responsibility of the P. & O. Company ceased on the arrival of the steamer at Alexandria. I was therefore obliged to hire a boat to take me ashore. On landing I was very near losing my baggage, amid the wonderful crowd of men and beasts by which I was beset—Negroes, Arabs, Turks, donkeys, camels—in terrifying rivalry for my trunks. I was not disposed to allow anyone to touch my baggage until I could decide upon my destination. At length an Arab, calling himself Hamad, and representing himself as a professed dragoman, came to my assistance, and relieved me of the disagreeable pressure. He assisted me in passing through the Custom House, which was a small affair. I then hired a carriage, and had myself conveyed with my baggage to the United States Consulate-General, where, after exhibiting a letter of introduction from Mr. Adams, the American minister in London, I was most kindly received by Mr. Hale, the Consul-General, a very polite and well-educated gentleman from New England.

Learning from Mr. Hale that the next railway train from Cairo that day would start in about an hour's time, I deposited my baggage in his office, and taking a letter from him to the United States Consul at Cairo, I hastened to the railway station; and, arriving just in time to get a ticket and procure a seat, I was soon whirling up the valley of the Nile at the rate of thirty miles an hour.

I looked at my ticket, and found that it was printed in Arabic characters. I felt a strong desire to retain it as a curiosity, but was obliged to give it up at the end of the journey. . . .

Half an hour after crossing the river, we caught a view of the pyramids in the distance. Here was opened to me a wide field of contemplation, and my imagination was complete "master of the situation." Though we were in an exposed plain, and my companion complained of the intense heat, I did not notice it, so eager was I to gain the pyramids, which seemed further and further to recede the longer we rode towards them. We saw them for three hours before we came up to them.

Just before reaching the pyramids we passed a small village of Arabs, who make their living, for the most part, by assisting travellers to "do" the pyramids. About a dozen of them rushed out as they saw us approaching, with goblets of water, pitchers of coffee, candles, and matches, and engraving knives. The water was very acceptable. I looked at the other articles, and wondered what could be the object of them.

The pyramids stand apparently on a hill of sand, on the borders of the Libyan desert. We had to ascend a considerable elevation—about 130 feet—before getting to the pyramid of Cheops. In the side of this apparent hill of sand, extending from the pyramids of Ghizeh to the smaller pyramids of Abusir and Sakarah, about two miles, are excavated tombs. The pyramids then are at the extremities of an immense city of the dead; they, themselves forming the imperishable tombs of the mighty monarchs who constructed them.

On reaching the base of the great pyramid I tried to find the shady side, but it was impossible to find any shade. On the north side there were several large stones, taken out at the base—leaving huge spaces. Into one of these Ibrahim, myself, and our donkeys entered and shelter ourselves. The Arabs crowded about us, and kept asking question after question, suggesting the pleasure we should enjoy in ascending to the top, and the advantage to be reaped by visiting the interior. But I paid very little attention to them. They addressed me in broken English, French, and Italian. Other thoughts were crowding my mind. I thought of the continuous fatigue I had undergone, without eating anything, sustained only by the object I expected to attain in front, viz., a close inspection of the pyramids. And now that I had gained my point, and sat down to rest under the shadow of a great rock, I could not help feeling that my effort was, after all, but a forcible type of our experience in one-half the pursuits we follow through life. My enchanting dreams and fancies left me completely, as heated, and weary, and hungry, I sat down to rest. How speedily the most cursory experience of the reality often levels to the dust all the mountains built up by the imagination!

Though I cannot say that at the first view of the pyramids they fell below my expectation, still they did not exactly appear what I expected them to be. Their greatness grew upon me as I looked at them. They are something magnificent. (How inadequate that adjective to convey what I mean!)

I had read Longfellow's beautiful description: —

> The mighty pyramids of stone,
> That, wedge-like, cleave the desert airs,
> When nearer seen and better known,
> Are but gigantic flights of stairs.*

But I had supposed that this was merely poetic and ideal, referring to the layer after layer of stone or brick put up "by slow degrees, by more and more," in constructing large edifices: I did not imagine that, in reality, the pyramids were built in steps; but they are really "gigantic flights of stairs"— so that they can be ascended to the very top. Travellers frequently go up. . . .

After gazing in amazement at the outside, I made up my mind, on consultation with Ibrahim as to the safety of the enterprise, to visit the central hall in the interior. Had I known, however, that the performance required so much nerve and physical strength as I found out during the experiment, I should not have ventured. The entrance is first by a very steep and narrow passage, paved with immense stones, which have become dangerously slippery by centuries of use. There are small notches for the toes of those who would achieve the enterprise of entering, distant from each other about four or five feet, showing that they were intended for very tall men who wore no shoes. The modern traveller is obliged to make Hiawathan strides to get the toe of his boot into one of these notches, which are also wearing smooth, so as to make the hold which he gets exceedingly precarious. But for the help of these half-naked, shoeless, and sure-footed Arabs, it would be impossible for Western pilgrims generally to accomplish the feat of visiting the interior. Before entering, the Arabs lighted two candles—an operation which, I confess, somewhat staggered me, as it gave me the idea of sepulchral gloom and ghastliness. I had supposed that the interior of the pyramids was lighted in some way, though I had not stopped to think how. As we had to go down sideways, two attended me, one holding my left hand and the other my right, so that if one slipped the other would be a support. If we had all

*St. Augustine's Ladder.

slipped at once, it is difficult to imagine what would have been the result. The lighted candles were carried in advance. . . .

Here, then, is a very plain dilemma to which we bring our adversaries. Either Negroes existed in those early days or they did not exist. If they did exist, then they must have had a part in the founding of those great empires; if they did not exist, then they are a comparatively youthful race, whose career is yet to be run; and it is unfair to say that they have not achieved anything in the annals of history, especially considering the obstructive influences, already referred to, which have operated upon their country.

But the conjecture is by no means improbable that the particular type or development of this race, spread along the western coast of Africa, in Upper and Lower Guinea, and from which the American continent has been supplied with servile labourers for the last three hundred years is of comparatively recent origin. And this will account for their wonderful tenacity of life, and their rapid increase, like the youthful and elastic Hebrews of old, amid the unparalleled oppressions of their captivity. . . .

The Sphinx, which I gazed at a long while, is a most impressive spectacle. "This colossal and fanciful figure, half human, half animal, the body being that of a lion, was an emblematic representation of the king—the union of intellect and physical power. It was cut out of the solid rock, with the exception of the paws and a portion of the backbone, which are of hewn stone. Its height to the top of the head was sixty-three feet, its length a hundred and forty-three feet, and it measured a hundred and two feet round the forehead. The head-dress is destroyed, and the face is much mutilated, so that the features, which were Egyptian in their character, are scarcely distinguishable. Below its breast and between its paws, which extend fifty feet from the chest, though now covered with sand, are the remains of a small temple and altar, the incense smoke from which ascended to its expanded nostrils."

The veil is worn constantly by all the native females. It takes the place of the western bonnet altogether; in fact, it is more than the bonnet. Like turban or tarbush, which is never off the head of the male, the veil is never away from the head of its mistress. In the house and in the street, at the wash-tub or the ironing-table, in the kitchen, at the well, or in the market, the veil is always present. However ragged and filthy, the veil must be on the head or over the face; and frequently other portions of the body are left altogether exposed in order to cover the face. The Druses and Mussulmans are most particular in requiring that their women shall be closely veiled;

and, through fear of these sects, Jews, Maronites, Greeks, and Protestants keep up the practice. When Protestant females of intelligence are asked why, knowing better, they keep their faces so much concealed, they reply, "Well, we don't care about being closely veiled; but if we don't veil we are liable to be laughed at or insulted by Druses or Mussulmans." In the cities the Mohammedan women are wrapped up from head to foot in white muslin, so as to look very much like sheeted ghosts.

But, after all, there is something graceful in the veil as it is worn by most of the Protestant females. No one who has lived in the East any time would like to see the custom of moderate veiling fall altogether into disuse. How it would shock all the feelings of propriety and reverence, even of the most enthusiastic admirer of western costume, to see a painting of any of the holy women of the Bible in the modern European bonnet and its concomitants! . . .

JERUSALEM

Sept. 9th. — To-day (Sunday) I had the privilege of worshipping in Jerusalem and on Mount Zion in the English cathedral. Rev. Mr. Barclay read the service, and Bishop Gobat preached, from John xvi., 12–14, a truly evangelical, simple, and instructive sermon. Divine service is also celebrated in this church in the Hebrew and German languages. There is no Sabbath in Jerusalem; business is carried on as on other days by Jews and Moslems, who form the great bulk of the population.[1] I saw camels going to and fro with their loads, and every other form of activity engaged in, showing that the people no longer "Remember the Sabbath-day to keep it holy."

September 10th. — Early this morning, in company with the Misses Gobat, who have lived in Jerusalem from childhood, and are full of enthusiastic veneration for its sacred scenes, I went out again through the eastern gate, walked along the Garden of Gethsemane with open Bible in hand, trying to identify localities. We ascended for a little distance the Mount of Olives along what is supposed to have been the usual route of our Saviour to and from Bethany to the city. We then descended into the Valley of Jehoshaphat, and went as far as the Pool of Siloam, of which we tasted the waters. There were a few women washing clothes here. We could gain no admittance into the Garden of Gethsemane. It is surrounded by a stone wall about six feet high, and entered by gates, which are always kept locked in

[1]He means there is no Christian sabbath observed; Jews observe it on Saturday.

the custody of a monk; who was away at the time of our visit. After lingering awhile we entered the city and visited several of the Jewish synagogues. It was now the season of their New Year Festival, and a great many Israelites had come to Jerusalem "for to worship" from various countries. We spent some time at the Spanish and Polish synagogues. Some of the worshippers seemed deeply in earnest; most, however, looked around and stared at us while repeating their prayers. They all had a singular motion of the body, waving to and fro, while reading or chanting, as if in agony. The females, I noticed, were not admitted into the synagogues, but sat in the passages and on the steps, closely veiled. . . .

We reached Bethlehem about three o'clock. The chief place of interest here, is, of course, the Church of the Nativity. This edifice is said to be built over the site where stood the stable in which Christ was born. It is in the shape of a cross, built A.D. 325, by the Empress Helena. Here were pointed out the spot where the babe was lying in the manager when the shepherds made their visit, the place where the wise men offered their gifts, and numerous other localities connected with the Savior's nativity. We spent about an hour in this church; then, paying a short visit to Rev. Mr. Muller, the German missionary at Bethlehem, we left the little town around which cluster so many interesting and sacred associations. . . .

Winding through some narrow, crooked lanes, we reached another most interesting section of the wall of the ancient Temple—the wailing place of the Jews. . . .

After the capture of Jerusalem by Adrian, the Jews were excluded from the city, and it was not till the age of Constantine that they were permitted to approach, so as to behold Jerusalem from the neighbouring hills. At length they were allowed to enter the city once a year, on the day on which it was taken by Titus, in order to wail over the ruins of the Temple; but this privilege they had to purchase of the Roman soldiers.* They are now permitted to approach the precincts of the temple of their fathers, and bathe its hallowed stones with their tears.

No sight in Jerusalem affected me more than that which presented itself in this retired spot, beneath the massive remains of that ancient building. The usual day for wailing is Friday, but, as this was holiday season, they wailed every day, and I had the opportunity of seeing Jews of both sexes, of nearly all ages, from various parts of the earth, lifting up a united cry of lamentation over

*Robinson's Biblical Researches, vol. 1, p. 237.

a desolated and dishonoured sanctuary. The women, for the most part, sat in silence, and the tears rolled down their cheeks. Some of the young girls, as if embarrassed by the presence of spectators, buried their heads in the cavities between the stones and wept. Old men tottered up to the wall, muttering something with trembling lips, and kissed the mighty stones. . . .

Among such a number of conflicting sects the missionary of the Cross finds indeed hard work. Each sect stands off from the other in menacing attitude. In all the cities, and in some whole sections of country, religious feuds and animosities are fearful in their bitterness. Jerusalem is a city of religious controversy, with all "its personal alienations, its exasperating imputations, and its appeals to prejudice and passion." Not unfrequently, at the Church of the Holy Sepulchre, the aid of the Turkish soldiers is invoked to quell the disorders among discordant sects. The Christian world may well pray for the *peace* of the literal Jerusalem.

There is one subject, however, upon which there seems to be remarkable unanimity among the principal sects—Jews, Christians and Moslems—viz., as to the final destiny of Jerusalem; that it is to be the scene of latter-day glories; that the Jews are to be restored to the land of their fathers, and the Messiah is to be enthroned in personal reign in the "City of the Great King." And there seems to be something in the locality which makes one feel that Jerusalem is no ordinary place, whether we regard its past or its future. The most materialistic mind cannot visit the city and leave it without profound emotion. It seems difficult for Christians who have resided any time in the city to escape the impression that God will finally be worshipped on "that mountain," and that all the tribes will flow unto it. . . .

W. E. B. DU BOIS

William Edward Burghardt Du Bois is probably the most well known African-American intellectual. Born on February 23, 1869, in Great Barrington, Massachusetts, Du Bois would live through and participate in most of the major movements for African-American freedom in the twentieth century. After receiving a bachelor of arts degree from Fisk University in 1888, Du Bois went on to become the first African American to receive a doctorate from Harvard University in 1895. Du Bois taught at Wilberforce University and Atlanta University before going on to be one of the organizers of the Niagara Movement and finally joining the National Association for the Advancement of Colored People, where he served as the influential editor of the organization's magazine, *The Crisis*.

Best known for his collection of essays, *The Souls of Black Folk*, Du Bois was a very prolific scholar and essayist, having published several major studies, two autobiographies, as well as works of fiction and a collection of prayers. However, his most influential writings were his monthly columns in *The Crisis*. The selections below are taken from these essays.

Du Bois died in 1963 in Ghana, where he lived as an expatriate during the final years of his extraordinary life.

"LITTLE PORTRAITS OF AFRICA" (1924)
from
THE CRISIS

THE PLACE, THE PEOPLE

Africa is vegetation. It is the riotous, unbridled bursting life of leaf and limb. It is sunshine—pitiless shine of blue rising from morning mists and sinking to hot night shadows. And then the stars — very near are the stars to Africa, near and bright and curiously arrayed. The tree is Africa. The strong, blinding strength of it — the wide deep shade, the burly lavish height of it. Animal life is there wild and abundant — perhaps in the inner jungle I should note it more but here the herb is triumphant, savagely sure — such beautiful shrubbery, such splendor of leaf and gorgeousness of flower I have never seen.

And the people! Last night I went to Kru-town and saw a Christmas masque. There were young women and men of the color of warm ripe horse chestnuts, clothed in white robes and turbaned. They played the Christ story with sincerity, naiveté and verve. Conceive "Silent Night" sung in Kru by this dark white procession with flaming candles; the little black mother of Christ crossing with her baby, in figured blue, with Joseph in Mandingan fez and multi-colored cloak and beside them on her worshipping knees the white wreathed figure of a solemn dark angel. The shepherds watched their flocks by night, the angels sang; and Simeon, raising the baby high in his black arms, sang with my heart in English Kru-wise, *"Lord now lettest thou thy servant depart in peace for mine eyes have seen thy salvation!"*

Liberia is gay in costume — the thrifty Krus who burst into color of a holiday; the proud Veys always well-gowned; the Liberian himself often in white. The children sometimes in their own beautiful skins.

SUNDAY, JANUARY 13, 1924

I have walked three hours in the African bush. In the high bush mighty trees arose draped, with here and there the flash of flower and call of bird. The monkey sentinel cried and his fellows dashed down the great tree avenues. The way was marked — yonder the leopard that called last night under the moon, a bush cow's hoof; a dainty tread of antelope. We leaped the trail of driver ants and poked at the great houses of the white ants. The path rose and wound and fell now soft in green glow, now golden, now shimmery through the water as we balanced on a bare log. There was whine of monkey, scramble of timid unseen life, glide of dark snake. Then came the native farms — coffee, cocoa, plantain, cassava. Nothing is more beautiful than an African village — its harmonious colorings — its cleanliness, its dainty houses with the kitchen palaver place of entertainment, its careful delicate decorations and then the people. I believe that the African form in color and curve is the beautifulest thing on earth; the face is not so lovely—though often comely with perfect teeth and shining eyes,—but the form of the slim limbs, the muscled torso, the deep full breasts!

The bush is silence. Silence of things to be, silence vocal with infinite minor music and flutter and tremble—but silence, deep silence of the great void of Africa.

And the palms; some rose and flared like green fine work; some flared before they rose; some soared and drooped; some were stars and some were sentinels; then came the ferns—the feathery delicate things of grottos and haunts with us, leapt and sang in the sun—they thrust their virgin tracery up and out and almost to trees. Bizarre shapes of grass and shrub and leaf greeted us as though some artist all Divine was playing and laughing and trying every trick of his bewitched pencil above the mighty buildings of the ants.

I am riding on the singing heads of black boys swinging in a hammock. The smooth black bodies swing and sing, the neck set square, the hips sway. O lovely voices and sweet young souls of Africa!

MONROVIA

Monrovia is a city set upon a hill. With coy African modesty her face is half turned from the bold and boisterous ocean and her wide black eyes gaze dreamfully up the Stockton and St. Paul. Her color is white and green and her head of homes rises slowly and widely in spacious shading verandah toward the great headland of Mesurado where the lighthouse screams to wandering ships. Her hair is plaited decently on mighty palm leaves and mangoes; her bare feet, stained with travel, torn with ancient cicatriced wounds drabble in the harbor waters down on Water Street and shun the mud town Plymouth Rock which is Providence Island. Her feet are ugly and old, but oh her hands, her smooth and black and flying hands are beautiful and they linger on roof and porch, in wide-throated grassy street and always they pat and smooth her hair, the green and sluggish palms of her heavy beautiful hair. And there is gold in her hair.

AFRICA

The spell of Africa is upon me. The ancient witchery of her medicine is burning my drowsy, dreamy blood. This is not a country, it is a world—a universe of itself and for itself, a thing Different, Immense, Menacing, Alluring. It is a great black bosom where the Spirit longs to die. It is life so burning, so fire encircled that one bursts with terrible soul inflaming life. One longs to leap against the sun and then calls, like some great hand of fate, the slow, silent crushing power of almighty sleep—of Silence, of immovable Power beyond, within, around. Then comes the calm. The dreamless beat of midday stillness at dusk, at dawn, at noon, always. Things move—black shiny bodies, perfect bodies, bodies of sleek unearthly poise and beauty. Eyes languish, black eyes—slow eyes, lovely and tender eyes in great dark formless faces. Life is slow here. Impetuous Americans quiver in impetuous graves. I saw where the ocean roars to the soul of Henry Highland Garnet. Life slows down and as it slows it deepens; it rises and descends to immense and secret places. Unknown evil appears and unknown good. Africa is the Spiritual Frontier of human kind—oh the wild and beautiful adventures of its taming! But oh! the cost thereof—the endless, endless cost! Then will come a day—an old and ever, ever young day when there will spring in Africa a civilization without coal, without noise, where machinery will sing and never rush and roar, and where men will sleep and think and dance and lie prone before the rising sons, and women will be happy.

The objects of life will be revolutionized. Our duty will not consist in getting up at seven, working furiously for six, ten and twelve hours, eating in sullen ravenousness or extraordinary repletion. No— We shall dream the day away and in cool dawns, in little swift hours, do all our work.

Richard Wright

Richard Wright, one of America's most important and controversial intellectuals, was born in Mississippi on September 4, 1908. After acquiring a degree of literary success unknown to any black writer before him, the author of Native Son, Uncle Tom's Children, and Black Boy left the United States for Paris, where he lived as an expatriate until his death on November 28, 1960. While in Paris Wright became known internationally as a critic of American racism and classicism. By the 1950s Wright began to focus much of his attention on anticolonial struggles in Africa.

In 1954 Wright visited the Gold Coast. Fellow activist and intellectual George Padmore informed Prime Minister Kwame Nkrumah of Wright's desire to visit the Gold Coast, and with a letter of introduction from Nkrumah himself Wright set out on his journey in 1954. That trip resulted in the publication in 1954 of Black Power: A Record of Reactions in a Land of Pathos. The selections here are taken from this powerful and controversial book, which critic Amrit Singh has called "one of the richest texts in the tradition of travel literature" (Singh, Introduction to Black Power, xxi).

from
Black Power: A Record of Reactions in a Land of Pathos (1954)

My money is melting under this tropic sun faster than I am soaking up the reality about me. For two days now I've moped about my hotel room with no visitors or telephone calls. In the newspaper are items telling of monster mass meetings, of vast educational rallies; I'd have liked to have attended those events, but I hear of them only after they have taken place. My frequent visits to the Convention People's Party's headquarters do not elicit any information about what is transpiring, and I cannot escape the feeling that my seeking information has somewhat frightened the African politicians.

I'm of African descent and I'm in the midst of Africans, yet I cannot tell what they are thinking and feeling. And, without the help of either the British or the Africans, I'm completely immobilized. Africa sprawls far inland and my walking jaunts about Accra are no way to see this life. Yet, I cannot just take a train or a bus and go; the more I ask about jungle conditions, the more I'm dismayed. The general state of affairs in the country is not conducive to the safety of wandering tourists. There are but few hotels in Accra, Takoradi, and Kumasi, and their accommodations are of a sort to discourage the heartiest of travelers. Trekking into the interior can only be done with the aid and consent of the government, for, without it, one does not have access to the government resthouses that are stationed at intervals in the jungle. Beyond that, one must depend upon the willingness of the Africans or the British to put one up in their private homes! This does not mean that the British would forbid anyone's going off alone into the jungle to trust his luck, if he was fool enough to want to do it. . . . Neither do I say that this has been expressly arranged; it just works that way.

Each time I entered a store, the Indian or Greek or Syrian merchant wanted an account of my opinions. I suspect that my attitude caused a lot of background talk, for my reactions were open and direct and I could not order them otherwise. When something struck me as being strange, I erupted with questions; when something seemed funny, I laughed; and when I was curious, I dived headlong to uncover the obscurities. . . . Moreover, being obviously of African descent, I looked like the Africans, but I had only to walk upon a scene and my difference at once declared itself without a word being spoken. Over and above these liabilities, I had a background steeped in Communism, yet I was no Communist.

My thought processes were of interest even to the British banker who cashed my travelers' checks.

"Well, sir, what do you think of all this?" he asked me.

"You know, I've only been here a few days," I tried to evade him.

"I mean, don't you think that the people are happy?"

"I've seen so little—"

"Don't you think that we've done a lot for them?"

"I haven't seen very much of life here yet," I stalled.

He knew damn well what I thought, but I was determined not to give him the satisfaction of letting him hear me say it. He leaned forward as he spoke and his tone was low, urgent, confidential:

"You American chaps are three hundred years ahead of these Africans. It'll take a long time for them to catch up with you. I think that they are trying to go too fast, don't *you?* You see, you American chaps are used to living in a white man's country, and these fellows are not."

In his attempt to influence my attitude, he was using the old tried and trusted British technique of divide and rule.

"I don't know about that," I said, smiling at him.

He counted out my pound notes through the barred window.

"Thank you," I said.

"Good morning, sir," he sang out.

"So long," I said.

There was no room for jockeying or making tactical moves in a colony; the European was at close grips with the native who was trapped in the European net of trade and religion. Every casual remark of the dubious stranger had an implied bearing upon policy. Whether you danced or not, whether you were interested in a given scene or not, whether you laughed or not—all of these items were weighed, examined, and filed away in the minds of the upper-class African or British civil servant. A sort of living dossier was kept on you: what you said casually at Mr. So-and-so's luncheon table was discreetly and questioningly served up to you at Mrs. So-and-so's dinner table on the evening of the same day. It was check and double-check.

So far my random observations compel me to the conclusion that colonialism develops the worst qualities of character of both the imperialist and his hapless victim. The European, on duty five hundred miles from the Equator, in the midst of heat and humidity, can never really feel at home and the situation breeds in him a kind of hopeless laziness, a brand of easygoing contempt for human life existing in a guise that is strange and offense to him. Out-numbered, he feels safe only when surrounded by men of his own race and color. Since, for questions of policy, he cannot live with the native, he develops an indifference for the land that grows the food. *His* food is transported over vast distances and at great cost for which the native must pay in the form of taxes. Hence, the European tries without success to convince himself that he is worth all of this bother and care, but he never quite can. His basic concerns are centered upon the wealth of the country, upon doing his job so that no crass criticisms will be heaped upon his head. The social setting produces a chronic suspiciousness about the ultimate meanings of the most ordinary ideas and remarks of the natives, and there is a continuous undertow of concern about the possibility of the native's developing a mood of rebellion, for, at bottom, no matter how jaunty the European pretends to be, he cannot rid himself of the idea that what he and his kind are doing is stealing. . . .

And the native, when he looks at the white man looming powerfully above him, feels contradictory emotions struggling in his heart; he both loves and hates him. He loves him because he sees that the white man is powerful, secure, and, in an absentminded and impersonal sort of way, occasionally generous; and he hates him because he knows that the white man's power is being used to strip him slowly of his wealth, of his dignity, of his traditions, and of his life. Seeing that there is nothing that he can do about it, he loses faith in himself and inwardly quakes when he tries to look into the future in terms of white values that are as yet alien to him. Charmed by that which he fears, pretending to be Christian to merit white approval, and yet, for the sake of his own pride, partaking of the rituals of his own people in secret, he broods, wonders, and finally loses respect for his own modest handicrafts which now seem childish to him in comparison with the mighty and thunderous machinery of the white man.

In the end his own land lies fallow, his skills waste away, and he begins to prefer menial jobs with white families which will enable him to buy tinned food shipped from Europe. He no longer fishes for herring; he buys them in a can; he no longer burns local fats; he depends upon kerosene; he abandons his weaving and buys cloth from Lancashire; he goes to mass and learns to cross himself, and then he goes to the Stool House to propitiate the spirits of his long-departed ancestors.

This afternoon, after taking a nap, I went upon the veranda to escape the humidity of my room. A young African boy was there, wrapped and bundled in his cloth, stretched upon a bench; he glanced at me, then leaped quickly to his feet and hurried off. He turned his head and stared at me as he went around a bend of the veranda. . . . Why had he been so apprehensive? I sat and looked about; the veranda was empty. I had forgotten my cigarettes and went inside my room to fetch them; when I returned the young African was there upon the bench again. Seeing me, he rose at once and walked quickly off. There was no doubt about it; he was afraid. . . . He had thought that I was a European and would be offended at his presence. But what could I say to him? Merely to speak to him might well frighten him even more. . . .

Leslie Alexander Lacy

Leslie Alexander Lacy was born to a prominent black family in Franklin, Louisiana, in 1937. Lacy writes about his very interesting life in his autobiography *The Rise and Fall of the Proper Negro*, published in 1970, from which the selection here is taken. As with many other African-American intellectuals and artists of his generation, Lacy went to Ghana during the Nkrumah years. There he taught and studied political science at the University of Ghana, Legon. The author of six books of nonfiction, Lacy provides the most vibrant picture of Ghana's black American expatriate community we have. On returning to the United States after Kwame Nkrumah was deposed in 1966, Lacy continued to write and teach, primarily in New York and Washington, D.C.

from
The Rise and Fall of the Proper Negro (1970)

BLACK BODIES IN EXILE

Black bodies in Ghana? A Ghanaian friend of mine called us that because he said were weird. "Weird" may not have described us, but we were probably strange to some, disjointed to others. On the whole I think we were a rather fascinating group, joined together in an amorphous community to express from different points of experience and knowledge our dislike and outrage for American racialism. Out of that madness we had come to this West African state, pressed by the words of Countee Cullen—"What is Africa to me?"—hoping to find for an incurable American sickness a drug of identity, a feeling of kinship with Africa and its "strong bronzed men . . . women from whose loins I sprang."

Consciously and unconsciously our presence was not just a second to that motion which had indicted America. More significantly, we were a confirmation, of immense importance, of those black voices—some loud, like Marcus Garvey, some adventurous, like Paul Cuffee, clever, like Martin Robinson Delany, some speaking about the pyramids as our dear Langston did, crying "among the skyscrapers"—which (however romantic, forgotten, or denied) have always, since the first day, damned the New World and cried out for the Old. And in rejecting America, for whatever reason, we had carried forth this glorious history. No, we did not speak Hausa, Twi, Akan, or Ga; our language and values had come from the States, from reservations of America, which had never become *America* because we were of African descent; and that fact—and that alone—established our historical legitimacy. Without arrogance, our presence in the country forged the link between the New World and the Old and made Ghanaian political independence complete. That occurred to me when I saw Du Bois. One of us had made all this possible. Because he had started it. True, there had been slave revolts, other men, other causes, and other forces, past and present, traditional and modern, which produced the complex pattern of independence. But as *Ghana* was the autobiography of Kwame Nkrumah, *African Freedom* was the autobiography of W. E. B. Du Bois. And we were a part of him. Strange, isn't it? I had more history there than I had in America, and by extension, more involvement in the revolution than the average Ghanaian.

It was beautiful—a day-to-day history, a living history. If you entered the country, you probably would see a group of Afros drinking beer at the airport hotel. If you stayed in that hotel or another and watched a television program you liked, you'd have to thank Shirley Du Bois because she was the director. If you wanted a book or speech written or to talk to the editor of the country's leading magazine, the *African Review*, the man to see was Julian Mayfield. Need Julian's magazine in the French edition? See Richard Wright's daughter Julia—absolutely beautiful—but don't touch, because she's got an Algerian husband. Trouble with language? Don't worry, because there's an Afro to teach you at the Institute of Languages. Need an artist? Got three: Tom Feelings, Ted Pontiflet, Herman Bailey. And if you don't like artists, what about a sculptor? Just ask for Ray. Designer? Architect? Max Bond (M.A., Harvard School of Design), Jerry

Bard (M.A., University of Paris). Advisor for a president? Go to Legon and ask for Preston King. Want to have fun, real fun—need a dancer, singer, poetry? See Maya Maka[1] at the Institute of African Studies. Need someone to build what Max designs? See Frank Robertson and the other brothers at All Afro; they deal in heavy industry. Need a good doctor who is developing new techniques in tropical medicine? See Julian's lovely wife, Dr. Ana Livia Corderia. Want a créative children's book? See Jean Bond. Historian? Dr. Lewis. Have bad teeth? See Bobby Lee, and if you don't like him, his pretty wife, Dr. Sarah Lee, is right next door. Business? What kind?—legitimate, illegitimate, honest, underground, some other kind? Well, ask me, and I'll whisper it to you. Need a man of honor and integrity? Got a lot of them, but you can start with Jim Lacy, my namesake. Want a scholar? Well, now, there's Dr. St. Clair Drake, and if he's too radical, see Dr. Martin Kilson. Want some soul? Ask for Jerry Harper. Want a really pretty girl (Southern too) with a lot of talent? Ask for Miss Lucretia Collins. If you want to go back to the States, go see Curtis Morrow; every hurt in our history is in his face. Want to see a happy Afro family? Go to Legon and ask to see the McCleans. Want charm, beauty, and intelligence? See Sylvia Boone; we all love her. Need a French master? See Wendell, he's a good friend of mine and a fine scholar. Want to start a revolution? See Vicky Garvin and Alice Windom. And for the women, how about a lover, a sixty-minute man replete with an authoritarian discussion about the history of China? Go to Tema and ask for Max; he'll fix you up. Need a quick course in journalism? See the director at the Ghana School of Journalism; he is a brother too. Need a photographer who talks a lot? Well, go to Job 600 and get Earl Grant. Want to laugh, have fun, and see black people who have gotten the white man off their backs? Go to the YWCA in Accra any day at noon; you'll find them, sitting at their same table with their Ghanaian friends, having a ball, and you'll probably find me there too.

These people, and many others I have not named, were our tribe in Ghana. Like most tribes, clans, ethnic groups, or whatever, we had leaders and followers, assorted interest-class differentiation and political attitudes. Although each of us had the final say over his individual fate, there tended to be three distinct sectors in the community: the Politicals, the Nonpoliticals, and the Opportunists.

For lack of a better description, the Politicals can be called professional protesters. Many of them had been influenced by the same revolutionary

[1]Maya Angelou.

ideology, and most had had similar activist experiences, in France, America, or England. The Politicals had had, as I did before coming to Ghana, connections—ties or membership involvement—with the white left in the countries they had come form. But they had dissolved or modified these connections for a more pan-Africanist perspective. Most of the men were married to European women, and the black women, except two, were single or divorced and faced the usual problem of chauvinism in a male-dominated society. The majority of the political exiles were near or over thirty, well educated or highly talented in literary and artistic ways. All were religiously loyal to Nkrumah, zealously rationalizing his political moves, and generally, if not always ostensibly, following the ruling party's line.

From the point of view of the government and from the vantage point of their various jobs, this minority in the community had a considerable amount of power. What they said or didn't say carried weight. When the government or party (a procedural distinction, since in substance they were synonymous) wanted an official statement, they were the ones who were consulted. Moreover, since, as a West Indian writer said, "They walked in the corridors of power," they had direct access to the mass media and could be as critical of any political position as they wished—just as long as their stand was not at variance with the prevailing party ideology. Like only a very few others in the country, they had a direct line to the President, as well as intimate associations with some of his key advisors. The President used their skills, including their literary talents, for speech writing; took their advice rather seriously. In every sense, they identified with and were a part of the Ghanaian ruling elite.

Such benefits of power usually carry correlative burdens; and so it was with this Afro elite. They were watchdogs in the community and generally responsible for the activity within it. Negroes believed to be working for the CIA or carrying out subversive activities against the state always sent waves of fear and anxiety through the group. Its position of trust and power was always vulnerable. From inside and outside the party, Nkrumah's enemies were always trying to discredit the Politicals, either to weaken their position as an expatriate force or to embarrass the government. They were also attacked from the inner circle, by Ghanaian and European friends of the president who resented or hated them for their ideology, privileges, or more often than not, simply because they were Afro-Americans. Beyond all this, their power rested upon the overall stability of the CPP. Any day, hour, second, power can shift right or left, depending upon the exigencies of the moment, the strength of the opposition, or unrest in the army. A move to the right would have decreased their power, and a move to the left could have had the reverse effect. Either way, your position would change, and you would inevitably take on more friends or more enemies, probably both.

Being on guard against both external and internal forces coming at your heart produces a strange kind of head. You *must* suspect everyone, since you can never be sure. Everyone, Afro-Americans, even ones you rallied with in Harlem, are potential CIA agents or potential enemies. Every change in government or army and every presidential trip abroad is another headache to consider. In time, therefore, as an exile, you develop what I call a "refugee" mentality. The moves you make appear to reflect political acumen, but in reality they are based on acute anxiety, blind acceptance of an ideology you vaguely comprehend, a confused fusion of the political rhetoric you learned back home (which of course has nothing to do with the present political culture), and equally irrelevant, what you read in the daily newspaper. Naturally, you call all this nonsense "revolutionary," and are so smothered by this cloak that if real agents like the CIA ... if CIA agents came to the country (as I'm sure they did), they could probably move around freely, because nothing in your political training would have prepared you to detect them.

I should say here that this group had a close alliance with the group of South African freedom fighters, which suffered from the same disposition. Small wonder that fascism still rides herd in their country. By default, Julian Mayfield was the unofficial leader of this neurotic contingent. He was very much aware of the psychology of his flock. But little could he do, since he spent most of his hours watching out for the knife against his own neck, trying to convince his immediate supervisor that a monthly magazine should come out each month, and doing his own writing. He worked on the average of fourteen hours a day just to keep ahead.

In the Politicals' behalf—one of their many virtues—they were honest, individuals of integrity, and in spite of their lack of revolutionary sophistication, devoted to their work. They could be trusted and did only what they believed. Also, they believed that Nkrumah was honest and committed and that some of the problems of political change—inevitable in these countries, given the world situation in which independence occurred—would be solved. If more of the Ghanaians had possessed their sense of history and honesty, at the very least there would have been much less corruption.

The Nonpoliticals would have faced the same problems, but fortunately they were not interested in "what was happening." I found that rather amazing, since what was happening would nevertheless affect their lives. Younger, they were the "hippies" of Ghana, and unlike the white hippies in America, had seen the worst in America, the side which had twisted and broken much of their spirit. Psychologically, Africa was good for them. It allowed them moments to think, relax, and feel a sense of development in a changing culture. Unlike the Politicals, with very few exceptions, they lived among the people and learned considerably more about the "real culture" than their radical brothers. Neither were they dogmatic believers. Conditioned by the hard steel of American racism, they were also hard, tough, and cynical; they had patience, a wait-see, or as the Ghanaians say "wait-small," philosophy which gave them a comfortable home among the urban masses. Most were artists and unpublished writers, a few students, and one, maybe two, did nothing. They were for Nkrumah, too, but expressed their support by loving the people they met. They taught the Ghanaian high school youngsters (who always flocked to them because they were "cool") black American music, especially jazz.

Tom Feelings, a talented artist from Brooklyn, led the Nonpoliticals, although neither he nor they wanted, needed, or would have approved had they thought of themselves in that way. But he stood out like a happy little boy, always joyful, always smiling, and drawing the happy children who smiled back. You could see the change in his work. His Brooklyn children looked angry, as our children feel as they grow up. Africa allowed Tom to live his youth all over, and this time he would be black, strong, and free. Tom did not know about their insides, their hurtings, their lack of nourishment—black bodies deformed by malaria, bodies which would not get old. Tom saw what he wanted and needed to see, and that was beautiful, because he created something, made them happy when they saw themselves; and that made him part of their lives.

And Ted Pontiflet, a fine artist too, became the model for many Ghanaian children. When he talked to them about music, I pretended to read, but listened too. The thought of coming to appreciate Charlie Parker, Miles Davis, John Coltrane, and Horace Silver in Africa blew my mind, because I was learning from men, brother men, beautiful men whom I probably would not have met back home. I had come from a mansion; Tom, Ted, Ray, Curtis from tenements, but they were giving and I was taking, because they, collectively and individually, were always closer to what we all were.

Naturally and understandably this group resented the power of the Politicals. Not out of envy, but because the existence of power creates pressures, conformity, obedience, and all our hippies wanted was a new sun, an undiscovered humanity, and as Ray said, "a little time to be me."

The Opportunists were many, always coming, always leaving, always stealing, never feeling—just going along with the tide. When business was right, Nkrumah was right; when business was bad, Nkrumah was bad. Men like these are always around. They are seen in American communities, and they look and smell the same out here.

Leslie Lacy was shaped by the Toms and the Julians. (And once or twice I sold some dollars on the Lebanese black market.) Whatever failings they had, I had. I was of both sectors. Sometimes, through me the community could express a wholeness. Both groups were honest, naïve—each in its own way trying to find itself. When Smith of Southern Rhodesia declared "his country" (isn't that a laugh?) unilaterally independent from Britain, Nkrumah called for the mobilization of a people's army. The Political males stayed up all night convincing me that I should join up with them, even if it meant the loss of citizenship. Finally I felt that it was the logical extension of what I said I believed in, so I—and all the Politicals—signed up. Heading the list were the brothers from the world of music and art, the first volunteers in the country.d The Politicals were surprised. I was not.

Most Ghanaians viewed us, the Afros, as a community, and as far as they were concerned, we were the same breed. The more politically conscious Ghanaians, including some students and intellectuals, were aware of our political differences and levels of involvement and related to us accordingly. But overall, given their own ethnic orientations, they tended to view us as a group, because like any other tribe in the country, we spoke the same language: a language which was critical of America, a language which defended Nkrumah, a tongue which constantly spoke of brotherhood, which never complained about inefficiency or the corruption we knew about. We wanted so much to ask for love that we sometimes lied in order not to hurt someone's feelings; and sometimes we did a little Uncle Tomming (seems strange, doesn't it?) to convince the Ghanaians that, in spite of everything, we were glad to be Home.

And sometimes we didn't want to be around any Ghanaians. Blacks passing through or newly arrived invariably accused us of segregating ourselves from the people. We just said, "Okay, man," or, "Whatever you say, sister," and kept on doing our thing.

Sylvia Ardyn Boone

Sylvia Ardyn Boone, scholar of African and women's art and the first black woman to receive a doctoral degree from the Art History Department at Yale University (1979) as well as the first to be granted tenure (1988) at that university, was born in Mount Vernon, New York, in 1941. Her dissertation "Sowo Art in Sierra Leone: The Mind and Power of Woman on the Plane of the Aesthetic Disciplines" won the Blanshard Prize in History of Art, and she was elected to Phi Beta Kappa.

The author of two important books—*Radiance from the Waters: Ideals of Feminine Beauty in Mende Art,* published in 1986, and *West African Travels: A Guide to Peoples and Places,* published in 1974—Boone expressed an early interest in the African continent. While a student at Brooklyn College, from which she graduated in 1960, Boone traveled to Africa as a participant with Crossroads Africa. Shortly thereafter she studied at the University of Ghana and became one of a large community of African-American expatriates that included W. E. B. Du Bois, Tom Feelings, Julian Mayfield, and Maya Angelou. Boone lived for an extended period of time in countries throughout northern, western, central, and eastern Africa, serving as translator, teacher, researcher, writer, escort-interpreter, guide, and journalist.

Dismayed by the lack of reliable information on Africa for travelers, Boone wrote the travel guide *West African Travels,* which remains one of the best guides of the area. The selections here are taken from the introduction to that volume, which tries to dispel dangerous myths and lies about the continent. Thus, it is one of the rare examples of a travel guide in this volume.

f r o m
WEST AFRICAN TRAVELS (1974)

OMEGA

There is one single key to seeing Africa as it is, not as a reflection of bogus stories you have been told. It is an easy and simple rule, but very hard for Europeans and Americans to follow.

Try to think of every African you meet as a person just like yourself, with the same needs and desires, hopes and dreams. The African, at *his* best, is like *you* at *your* best. When you *both* are striving for the finest of creativity and spirituality, you are alike on a high humanist plane.

Everyone in the world wants great things. Everyone wishes to be beautiful and to live in beautiful surroundings. Everyone wants to build something or to make something grow. Everyone wants to see some idea of his take on material form and life. Everyone loves to feel his intellect stimulated and clicking, whether through a conversation or a poker game. Everyone longs to express his thoughts and feelings and to communicate his conceptions to others. We all yearn for transcendence, for immortal life, to be part of the future.

An African is no different—an obvious fact that must nonetheless be emphasized. Connecting on these wavelengths, being open to these touches, being aware of these aspirations and desires—all these put us in rapport with the Africans we meet.

SPECIAL BENEFITS OF TRAVEL IN AFRICA: AN ATTEMPT TO EXPLAIN

The preacher says it's no secret when you start living a good life. Everyone can see, because you begin to walk better, talk better, look better and act right. The promise is that after your trip to Africa you will be "better."

Travel to Africa has all the benefits of travel to other places, but it also has something *special*. For one friend it is the end of the big-city paranoia that grips us every day. You can walk down the street without terror, get in an elevator without feeling trapped, and there aren't any more of those funny clicks on your phone. The stores don't have convex, reflecting mirrors, and the closed-circuit protection-agency cameras aren't whirring. The bomb isn't going to fall on your head, the world isn't going to end, your life is not in imminent danger—so you can let down your defenses. Because your being is not threatened, you don't have to be tensed for flight or battle.

Your personality is not being shredded by a cascade of words and images on television that corrodes your integrity and self-esteem. No beautiful people, no jet setters, no odious comparisons between yourself and your possessions and the vastly superior minds, bodies and possessions of mannequins and movie stars and public figures constantly splashed on the TV screen. It will occur to you one day on your trip that the voices are not snarling and that the fire-drill bell of alarm and danger isn't ringing, as so often happens in the urban setting. With the pressure cooker off, your better self emerges.

It may be the vividness of colors and shapes. Perhaps it is the endless variety of images, the kaleidoscope of movement and shading. Or the sensation of warmth and leisure, or the feeling of space and ease. Some people say it is the quality of the air—its clarity and cleanliness. Another explains that the primary source of energy is the sun, and in Africa the sun's rays are most direct and most healthful. Whatever it is, it is good for making flowers and people bloom.

VOCABULARY

Most of the words used to refer to Africa and Africans are insulting and pejorative. Common parlance learned from Tarzan movies and television serials is full of words and phrases that demean Africans and hold them in condescension and contempt.

The old vocabulary reveals the values and opinions of the colonialist/imperialist mentality. It says, in effect, Africans are inferior and thus incapable of ruling themselves; it says Africans are children to be managed, brutes to be tamed, wanderers in darkness to be brought to the light. Europeans have the real thing. Africans only the short, underdeveloped version. It is now time to learn a new vocabulary based on modern realities and sensibilities—and facts.

1. *People of African origin are to be called "African," "black" or by nationality.* They are *not* "natives" and they are not "Negroes." The word "native" should never be used. It implies an anonymous person who is inferior and primitive. She is not a "native woman"—rather, she is an African woman; he is not a native of Nigeria, he is a Nigerian.

2. *The word "native" is not used as an adjective either.* You may be tempted to describe something as native—say, his "native" food. Use instead his "local," "traditional" or "customary" food.

3. *"Primitive" and "savage" should be completely eliminated.* No two words are more disparaging and offensive; they should be stricken from your vocabulary. There is no polite substitution for these two words as nouns. As adjectives, for "primitive" one may substitute traditional, rustic, rudimentary, simple, old-fashioned; for "savage," exotic, original, surprising.

4. *The word "tribe" is no longer used;* instead one says "ethnic group" or "people." "Tribe" is another one of those colonial words based on European arrogance and ignorance that fit people into slots and froze them onto little parcels of land. It is ridiculous to refer to ten million Yoruba or five million Akan as a tribe. (Are the eight million Swedes a tribe, or the four million Finns?)

5. *African people are men and women, youths, adolescents, children, boys and girls, as the name fits the age range. No other words are acceptable.* A lovely young African girl is not a maiden . . . how can you tell? Her eighteen-year-old brother is not a young buck or a warrior or a brave; he is, rather, a young man or a youth. If they are both graceful of manner and richly dressed, don't suppose that they are "princess" and "prince." (O, the number of African princes there are!) Their fifty-year-old father is not a "boy," although he does servant's work, and their mother is not a "mammy."

6. *African people wear clothes,* not "costume" or "garb" or "native dress." Learn the names of African clothes, or call them suits, outfits, ensembles or national dress.

7. *Africans speak languages, not "dialects."* They speak in their African languages, or in the "vernacular." At home, as a child, an African learned his mother tongue, not a "native dialect." Aren't there such things as dialects? Yes, and if you are a linguist or an anthropologist discussing classifications of languages, you will be understood by your professional colleagues. But for general purposes such a category applied to African languages is belittling.

8. *African people live in cottages or houses, not in "huts" or "shacks."* Yes, many habitations are small and made of earthen bricks and have thatched roofs. In rural England it would be considered a cottage; call it a cottage when Africans live there too. Houses vary in design and quality, but they are still houses. If you see slums or crumbling buildings, call them that.

9. *Africa is not the "jungle."* Places with thick vegetation are called country, bush or forest. The old jungle image comes from Tarzan movies, with their white man swinging apelike through the trees. The forest belt of Africa is not large compared to the savannah, scrub and desert areas.

10. *African people have medicine,* not "witchcraft" or "juju" administered by witch doctors and medicine men. African folk medicine is a treasure house of knowledge rivaling that of the Chinese; one day it will be appreciated and developed. If AMA scruples prevent you from calling an African medical practitioner a "doctor," refer to him as a "healer" or an "herbalist" or a "traditional doctor." What he practices, then, is traditional healing or herbalism. If he specializes in emotional disorders, he is doing psychic healing.

11. *African people have their own systems of religion and philosophy.* To call their beliefs juju or witchcraft is again disrespectful and mocking. Their religious leaders are priests and priestesses, prophets or holy men, not fetishers. The place of worship is a shrine or temple, not a fetish house, and the objects used in ceremonies are not fetishes or juju.

PEJORATIVE	PREFERRED
1. a) native (noun) Negro	African black man country of origin (Nigerian, Togolese, etc.)
b) native (adjective)	local, customary, traditional
2. a) primitive (noun)	none
b) primitive (adjective)	traditional, rustic, rudimentary, simple, old-fashioned
3. a) savage (noun)	none
b) savage (adjective)	unusual, exotic, surprising, original

PEJORATIVE	PREFERRED
4. tribe	ethnic group, people
5. native, boy, maiden, warrior	man, youth, woman, adolescent
young buck, prince	young man
princess, pickaninny	young woman, child, boy, girl
mammy	none
6. costume, garb, native dress	clothes, outfit, ensemble, national dress
7. dialect	language, tongue, vernacular
8. hut	cottage, house, dwelling
9. jungle	country, bush, forest
10. a) juju, witchcraft (referring to healing practices)	a) folk medicine, herbalism, traditional medicine, psychic healing
b) witch doctor, medicine man (referring to healing practices)	b) doctor, traditional healer, herbalist, psychic healer
11. a) juju, cult, fetish, witchcraft (referring to belief in the Divine)	a) religion, beliefs, customary or traditional religion
b) witch doctor, fetish priest (referring to things spiritual)	b) priest, priestess, prophet
12. a) fetish house (referring to place of worship)	a) shrine, temple
b) fetish, grigri, juju (referring to objects used in worship)	b) talisman, amulet, holy medal, sacred object

4

FRANCE

Since the days of the American Revolution, Americans and African Americans looked to France as a model of freedom, democracy, and equality. During the early nineteenth century the major link between African Americans and France was New Orleans, where many of the French-speaking black elite had studied and pursued careers in France. One example was Victor Sejour, the playwright who was acquainted with Alexandre Dumas (Fabre, 10). Throughout the nineteenth century, abolitionists, artists, and free people of color traveled to that country as a means of experiencing a society that was culturally sophisticated and appeared to be less racist than the United States. Consequently, the possibilities of France entered the African-American mythology well before the Civil War. William Wells Brown and Alexander Crummell visited France, as delegates to the 1849 Peace Congress. The actor Ira Aldridge achieved great fame in France, opening in *Othello* at Versailles in 1866 (Fabre, 18). Frederick Douglass visited France in 1886 and went to see the statue of Alexandre Dumas by Gustave Dore but was angry that the famous writer "had never said one word for his race" (Fabre, 32). In 1879 Amanda Smith (see bio on page 77) stopped in Paris and Italy on her way to preach the gospel in India; she felt that Paris was fashionable and wicked.

Other leaders and artists followed, such as Booker T. Washington, Henry O'Tanner, Edmonia Lewis, Mary Church Terell, W. E. B. Du Bois, and Anna Julia Cooper, who received her doctoral degree from the Sorbonne. However, it wasn't until the end of World War I that less elite African Americans began to travel abroad, pursuing the vision of Paris printed by black American war veterans—of a land of people who loved jazz and who did not frown on interracial liaisons. The most well known and perhaps most successful African American to pursue her dreams in Paris was Josephine Baker. As the black press reported of her success and the high regard the French expressed for her, many others flocked to the city of lights. In fact, Paris might as well have been the second home of the Harlem Renaissance; every major and minor figure of that movement seems to have lived there at some point. Among these are Jessie Fauset, Gwendolyn Bennett, Claude McKay, and Langston Hughes.

Following World War II a newer generation of American blacks flocked to Paris, this time to live as expatriates in explicit protest against American racism. Richard Wright became the dean of black intellectuals and gained an international stage once he moved there. Writers such as Chester Himes, Frank Yerby, and William Gardner Smith followed him. James Baldwin would live in France on and off from 1948 until his death in 1987. For many of these intellectuals the 1950s proved to be a time when Paris lost some of its luster as a site of racial tolerance. For the first time many of the expatriates encountered Africans from France's colonies and were introduced to decolonization struggles in these nations. As independence swept Africa, and when the formerly colonized began to immigrate to the country, mainly in the 1970s and 1980s, France's reputation for racial tolerance lessened among African Americans, especially as sections of the country made frightening turns to the extreme right. Nonetheless, artists such as Barbara Chase Riboud and Dee Dee Bridgewater have still found the country to be far more receptive to their work than the land of their birth.

WilliAm Wells BRown

William Wells Brown was born a slave near Lexington, Kentucky, in 1814, the son of a white father and mulatto mother. Serving under several masters, he was hired out as a tavern keeper's helper, a steward on a Mississippi steamer, a servant, and a printing assistant. He escaped slavery by way of a steamboat in 1834, taking the names Wells Brown from a Quaker benefactor. He worked on Lake Erie steamboats, where he helped other fugitive slaves reach Canada, and later moved to Buffalo, New York, where he organized a black temperance society. Brown met Frederick Douglass at an antislavery meeting and soon became a traveling lecturer on the abolition circuit. His autobiography, *The Narrative of William Wells Brown: A Fugitive Slave*, was published in 1847, two years after Douglass's, and sold ten thousand copies in two years.

In June 1849 Brown was selected by the American Peace Society as a delegate to the International Peace Congress in Paris; Brown's *The American Fugitive in Europe*, published in 1855, describes his experience at the congress, where he met Victor Hugo. With the passing of the Fugitive Slave Law in 1850, Brown found himself stranded in Europe and remained there, earning his living by his pen until his freedom was purchased in 1854.

Brown wrote one of the earliest novels by an African American, *Clotel; or, the President's Daughter*, published in 1853, and his play *The Escape; or, a Leap for Freedom: A Drama in Five Acts* was the first to be published by an African American.

Much of Brown's writing, including his travel sketches from Europe, are meant to counter assertions of the natural inferiority of black people by providing portraits of individuals who overcame obstacles and achieved success, such as his portrait of the versatile trickster figure Joseph Jenkins of London. Both Brown's publications and rhetorical intelligence were used as proof of Negro capability; as a genuine fugitive slave appearing in

England shortly after Harriet Beecher Stowe had made a literary tour, he created quite a stir.

Brown repeatedly illustrates, on the basis of the treatment he receives, what he considers a lack of race-based prejudice in Europe. For example, on the steamer to Edinburgh he wrote, "We found the drawing-saloon almost entirely at our service, and, prejudice against color being unknown, we had no difficulty in obtaining the best accommodation the steamer afforded. This was so unlike the pro-slavery, negro-hating spirit of America ..." He juxtaposes enlightenment ideals abroad with racist attitudes at home but ultimately ends up returning to the land of his birth, where he died in 1884.

from
THE AMERICAN FUGITIVE IN EUROPE: SKETCHES OF PLACES AND PEOPLE ABROAD (1855)

It was a beautiful country through which we passed from Boulogne to Amiens. Straggling cottages which bespeak neatness and comfort abound on every side. The eye wanders over the diversified views with unabated pleasure, and rests in calm repose upon its superlative beauty. Indeed, the eye cannot but be gratified at viewing the entire country from the coast to the metropolis. Sparkling hamlets spring up, as the steam-horse speeds his way, at almost every point, showing the progress of civilization, and the refinement of the nineteenth century.

We arrived at Paris a few minutes past twelve o'clock at night, when, according to our tickets, we should have been there at nine. Elihu Burritt, who had been in Paris some days, and who had the arrangements there pretty much his own way, was at the station waiting the arrival of the train, and we had demonstrated to us the best evidence that he understood his business. In no other place on the whole route had the affairs been so well managed; for we were seated in our respective carriages and our luggage placed on the top, and away we went to our hotels, without the least difficulty or inconvenience. The champion of an "Ocean Penny Postage" received, as he deserved, thanks from the whole company for his admirable management.

The silence of the night was only disturbed by the rolling of the wheels of the omnibus, as we passed through the dimly-lighted streets. Where, a few months before, was to be seen the flash from the cannon and the musket, and the hearing of the cries and groans behind the barricades, was now the stillness of death—nothing save here and there a *gens d'arme* was to be seen going his rounds in silence.

The omnibus set us down at the hotel Bedford, Rue de L'Card, where, although near one o'clock, we found a good supper waiting for us; and, as I was not devoid of an appetite, I did my share towards putting it out of the way.

The next morning I was up at an early hour, and out on the Boulevards to see what might be seen. As I was passing from the hotel to the Place de La Concord, all at once, and as if by some magic power, I found myself in front of the most splendid edifice imaginable, situated at the end of the Rue Nationale. Seeing a number of persons entering the church at that early hour, and recognizing among them my friend the President of the Oberlin (Ohio) Institute, and wishing not to stray too far from my hotel before breakfast, I followed the crowd and entered the building. The church itself consisted of a vast nave, interrupted by four pews on each side, fronted with lofty fluted Corinthian columns standing on pedestals, supporting colossal arches, bearing up cupolas pierced with skylights and adorned with compartments gorgeously gilt; their corners supported with saints and apostles in *alto relievo*. The walls of the church were lined with rich marble. The different paintings and figures gave the interior an imposing appearance. On inquiry, I found that I was in the Church of the Madeleine. It was near this spot that some of the most interesting scenes occurred during the Revolution of 1848, which dethroned Louis Philippe. Behind the Madeleine is a small but well-supplied market: and on an esplanade east of the edifice a flower-market is held on Tuesdays and Fridays.

At eleven o'clock the same day, the Peace Congress met in the Salle St. Cecile, Rue de la St. Lazare. The Parisians have no "Exeter Hall": in fact, there is no private hall in the city of any size, save this, where such a meeting could be held. This hall had been fitted up for the occasion. The room is long, and at one end has a raised platform; and at the opposite end is a gallery, with seats raised one above another. On one side of the hall was a balcony with sofas, which were evidently the "reserved seats."

The hall was filled at an early hour with the delegates, their friends, and a good sprinkling of the French. Occasionally, small groups of gentlemen would make their appearance on the platform, until it soon appeared that there was little room left for others; and yet the officers of the Convention had not come in. The different countries were, many of them, represented here. England, France, Belgium, Germany, Switzerland, Greece, Spain, and the United States, had each their delegates. The assembly began to give signs of impatience, when very soon the train of officials made their appearance amid great applause. Victor Hugo led the way, followed by M. Duguerry, curé of the Madeleine, Elihu Burritt, and a host of others of less note. Victor Hugo took the chair as President of the Congress, supported by vice-presidents from several nations represented. Mr. Richard, the secretary, read a dry report of the names of societies, committees, etc., which was deemed the opening of the Convention.

The president then arose, and delivered one of the most impressive and eloquent appeals in favor of peace that could possibly be imagined. The effect produced upon the minds of all present was such as to make the author of "Notre Dame de Paris" a great favorite with the Congress. An English gentleman near me said to his friend, "I can't understand a word of what he says, but is it not good?" Victor Hugo concluded his speech amid the greatest enthusiasm on the part of the French, which was followed by hurras in the old English style. The Convention was successively addressed by the President of the Brussels Peace Society: President Mahan, of the Oberlin (Ohio) Institute, U.S.; Henry Vincent; and Richard Cobden. The latter was not only the *lion* of the English delegation, but the great man of the Convention. When Mr. Cobden speaks there is no want of hearers. The great power of this gentleman lies in his facts and his earnestness, for he cannot be called an eloquent speaker. Mr. Cobden addressed the Congress first in French, then in English; and, with the single exception of Mr. Ewart, M. P., was the only one of the English delegation that could speak to the French in their own language.

The first day's proceedings were brought to a close at five o'clock, when the numerous audience dispersed—the citizens to their homes, and the delegates to see the sights.

I was not a little amused at an incident that occurred at the close of the first session. On the passage from America, there were in the same steamer with me several Americans, and among these three or four appeared to be much annoyed at the fact that I was a passenger, and enjoying the company of white persons; and, although I was not only insulted, I very often heard the remark, that "That nigger had better be on his master's farm," and "What could the American Peace Society be thinking about, to send a black man as a delegate to Paris?" Well, at the close of the first sitting of the convention, and just as I was leaving Victor Hugo, to whom I had been introduced by an M. P., I observed near me a gentleman with his hat in hand, whom I recognized as one of the passengers who had crossed the Atlantic with me in the *Canada,* and who appeared to be the most horrified at having a negro for a fellow-passenger. This gentleman, as I left M. Hugo, stepped up to me and said, "How do you do, Mr. Brown?" You have the advantage of me," said I. "O, don't you know me? I was a fellow-passenger with you from America; I wish you would give me an introduction to Victor Hugo and Mr. Cobden." I need not inform you that I declined introducing this pro-slavery American to these distinguished men. I only allude to this, to show what a change came over the dreams of my white American brother by crossing the ocean. The man who would not have been seen walking with me in the streets of New York, and who would not have shaken hands with me with a pair of tongs while on the passage from the United States, could come with hat in hand in Paris, and say, "I was your fellow-passenger." From the Salle de St. Cecile, I visited the Column Vendome, from the top of which I obtained a fine view of Paris and its environs. This is the Bunker Hill Monument of Paris. On the top of this pillar is a statue of the Emperor Napoleon, eleven feet high. The monument is built with stone, and the outside covered with a metallic composition, made of cannons, guns, spikes, and other warlike implements taken from the Russians and Austrians by Napoleon. Above twelve hundred cannons were melted down to help to create this monument of folly, to commemorate the success of the French arms in the German campaign. The column is in imitation of the Trajan pillar at Rome, and is twelve feet in diameter at the base. The door at the bottom of the pillar, and where we entered, was decorated above with crowns of oak, surmounted by eagles, each weighing five hundred pounds. The bas-relief of the shaft pursues a spiral direction to the top, and displays, in a chronological order, the principal actions of the French army, from the departure of the troops from Boulogne to the battle of Austerlitz. The figures are near three feet high, and their number said to be two thousand. This sumptuous monument stands on a plinth of polished granite, surmounted by an iron railing; and, from its size and position, has an imposing appearance when seen from any part of the city.

Everything here appears strange and peculiar—the people not less so than their speech. The horses, carriages, furniture, dress and manners, are in keeping with their language. The appearance of the laborers in caps, resembling night-caps, seemed particularly strange to me. The women without bonnets, and their caps turned the right side behind, had nothing of the look of our American women. The prettiest woman I ever saw was without a bonnet, walking on the Boulevards. While in Ireland, and during the few days I was in England, I was struck with the marked difference between the appearance of the women and those of my own country. The American women are too tall, too sallow, and too long-featured, to be called pretty. This is most probably owing to the fact that in America the people come to maturity earlier than in most other countries.

My first night in Paris was spent with interest. No place can present greater street attractions than the Boulevards of Paris. The countless number of cafés, with tables before the doors, and these surrounded by men with long moustaches, with ladies at their sides, whose very smiles give indication of happiness, together with the sound of music from the gardens in the rear, tell the stranger that he is in a different country from his own.

Gwendolyn Bennett

Gwendolyn Bennett was born in Giddings, Texas, in 1902 and spent her youth between Washington, D.C.; Harrisburg, Pennsylvania; and Brooklyn, New York. In the 1920s she began to attend Teacher's College of Columbia University but was discouraged by the racism of that institution. She graduated instead from Pratt Institute and by mid-decade emerged as a talented young artist and poet of the Harlem Renaissance. In 1925 she was granted a travel scholarship by the black sorority Delta Sigma Theta. With the support of the scholarship, Bennett traveled to Paris as an art student. While there she kept a diary, from which the excerpts here are taken. In them we see a vibrant young woman who is initially quite homesick and disoriented, but as she begins to find community with other young people, especially other black Americans, she settles in and becomes much more comfortable. Although infatuated with Paris, like many who precede and follow her, she seeks out a little bit of "Harlem on the Seine." Nowhere is this more evident than in the extraordinary description of a night of champagne, dancing, and flirting at Bricktop's—the famous nightspot owned by African-American expatriate Ada "Bricktop" Smith.

Although Bennett admits to a newfound patriotism toward the United States, she makes a distinction between her longing for home and the feelings she has when she finds herself among white Americans in Paris who by no means seem to fill the void for her.

Her diary is also interesting because it mentions many of the other figures who would become prominent in the Harlem Renaissance. It serves as proof that these individuals had crossed the Atlantic to visit the city of lights, leaving their mark on it and it on them. A consideration of the personal writings, such as this diary, encourages a reevaluation of the geography of the movement that has so come to be associated with Harlem.

After this trip Bennett went on to become a widely respected poet, short-story writer, journalist, and critic. Her art was exhibited and reprinted in journals such as *The Crisis* and *Opportunity*. In the 1930s she taught art to younger artists, such as Jacob Lawrence, and in the 1940s she was accused of being a communist by the House Un-American Activities Committee. She died in 1981.

from
THE DIARIES of GWENdolyN BENNETT
(1925)

Thursday, June 25, 1925

This was my first real day in Paris. Early in the morning, I betook me by taxi to the Latin Quarter. The first place I turned was to the Foyer International des Etudiants. I found out that the Foyer would soon close for vacation and that a room for the summer could not be had before July fifteenth. That was bad enough but they told me further that they did not take art students as residents for the school year. The reason given was because it was their policy to cater to the "more serious minded student." I was to meet Ann Case and her friend at the "Dome" for lunch but they were not there at the time set so I wandered about the Quarter. I found much that amused me, some that interested me, and worlds that made me dreadfully homesick. I went to the Hotel Jeanne d'Arc[1] only to find that Miss Laura Wheeler had moved to Neully. And then back again to the Foyer to see Miss Watson and she not there. Miss Case took me to Madame Mellon's Pension. She couldn't take me in her home until July 3rd. Then with Madame Mellon through the streets until we finally get a room for me at the Hotel Orfila. . . . 18 francs per day including "petite dejueuner." [I had] the proprietor call Aulston Burleigh's number. He came to call on me and I had the shock of my life when they sent him right up to my bed room. He assured me that was quite their way of doing things. I wasn't at all comfortable so we went out. He took me to dinner and then for a long taxi ride all over the city. Paris is a marvelous place . . . words are inadequate to describe it. I was so glad to see Aulston—he was a bit of home. I also went to Le Salon today. Beautiful pictures and stationary.

[1]Later in her diary Bennett notes that this hotel was located on 89 rue Vaneau, "where Jessie Fauset and Laura Wheeler stayed for ever so long."

Saturday June 27

Today one of those queer happenstance occurred which are rather breath-taking. I got up in the morning with the idea that I would look up Anne Cousey, Langotou's friend. I had been to the Foyer and having found nothing of importance there I started down Blvd. St. Michel and had scarcely gone more than thirty yards when I passed a young, nice-looking colored girl. We passed and then we both turned around and she said with infectious impulsiveness, "Are you from America?" And when I answered in the affirmative she said, "You're not by any chance Gwendolyn Bennett." And I answered, "Yes and are you Anne Cousey" . . . and she was. She had come in town but a day to look me up and to attend to a business matter. When I stop to think that we might have missed each other I wonder a bit about these chance meetings.

Tuesday June 30

I went to the Musee des Arts Decoratif today. I walked there from the Quarter and back. The Museum is a marvelous thing. Just think of being able to see Corot's pallet and hat and Delacroix's brush and pipe. I felt fired with a new purpose to do and learn!

There was also an exhibition there of the French painters from the 1800's up until now. I got quite a thrill at seeing so many Manets and Monets in the original.

I was very weary and foot-sore when I stopped on Blvd. St. Michel for tea.

Sunday July 26, 1925

I know that the Fourth of July happened! I say "happened" because that's how I feel about it. To have one's National Holiday roll around when one is in a strange land and can't speak the language is an experience never to be forgotten. A homesickness more poignant and aching than anything I can ever imagine held me in its grip. All day long I did not see or speak to a single one of my compatriots nor did I even hear a word of English spoken. There is this marvelous thing about being here in France. A strange new patriotism has sprung up in me since I've been here in France . . . there are times that I'd give half my remaining years to hear the "Star Spangled Banner" played. And yet even as I feel that way I know that it has nothing to do with the same "home" feeling I have when I see crowds of American white people jostling each other about the American express.

August 2
From the shopping tour we rushed home to dress frantically for the tea-dance to which Louis Jones took the four of us. He took us to a delightful place, in the Bois de Boulagne . . . a very chic place that made me feel that I was a dream-girl in a land of dreams. It must have galled the Americans to death to see us there on a par with them. As Louis and I danced together I heard a group of them saying among themselves, "They dance nicely, don't they? You know they have that native rhythm!" Whoa!

And then to home to drop the girls at their hotel and then Louis and I quickly to a little restaurant in the heart of the Quarter for supper. It was real jolly for us to eat together at this cheap little Pre Fixe pace for 6 francs . . . Louis and I have eaten together at so many chic, expensive places that this was a lovely novelty. . . .

Today we went to Mr. Jenkins' office where Louis played the violin and a Mr. Callilaux accompanied him. It makes my heart swell with pride to know these musicians who are black and yet so wonderful.

Monday August 3
I work hard all morning at the Acadamie de la Grand Chaumiere. The piece was a nude in oil and the first one I had done. Much in the morn-ing's work to discourage me. Art is long!

At night to the Opera again. This time to hear Wagner's "Tolkenguin." The truth of the matter is that I was, really too tired to enjoy anything but the bed tonight. . . . But now and again the sheer beauty of the music that has nothing short of grandeur was able to pierce through even my bodily and mental fatigue. . . . I think though, that the French are perfect asses to have translated it from German into French simply on the strength that they had a war. But then these new world liberalities are lost before the hatred the French bear the Germans. Then too, it is too bad that we Amer-icans will never know a real patriotism.

August 8th, Saturday
I know that Thursday night was a night "out." Mr. Jenkins sponsored the party which was made up of Charlotte, Betty, Tellie, Mercer Cook and wife, Harlod Jackson, Edwin Morgan Mr. Jenkins and myself. First to the Chinese Restaurant in the Rue de L'Ecole de Medicine in the Quarter. We stayed there from 11:30 until 11:45 when Mr. Jenkins joined us. Thence to "LeRoyal" in Montmartre. There much champagne and many cigarettes

and much dancing. I get, in thinking back, a vivid impression of one or two very drunken women and hard, hard faces, and a girl with big baby eyes who affected their over brilliancy and of Tellie just a wee bit tipsy with too much Champaign. For one "charming" moment, Louis rushed up from "Florence's" to dance but one dance. Then at 4:15 A.M. to dear old Brick-top's. The Grand Ave extremely crowded this night with our folks. Lottie Gee there on her first night in town and sings for "Brick" her bit from Shuffle Along—"I'm Just Wild about Harry." Her voice is not what it might have been and she had too much champagne but still there was something very personal and dear about her singing and we colored folks just applauded like mad. "Brick" singing as well as ever her hits—"Insufficient Sweetie" and "I'm in Love Again." Louis came in with all of the clearing quality of a good gust of fresh air and brought with him Albert Smith. He liked to have fallen over when he saw me—1st time in about a month. After the first shock of our unexpected meeting he manages to dance with me and we are both agreeably surprised to find the other such a lovely dancer. Louis dances with me one very lovely dance during the which "Brick" and everybody teases him about how happy he is to have his little brown skin in his arms and he calling me "little lady" and I grinning from ear to ear.

And always the inevitable hot cakes and sausages at "the Duc." Home at 6:30 in the lovely grey morning light.

I shall never quite forget the shock of beauty that I get when the door was opened at "Brick's" and as we stepped out into the early morning streets looking up Rue Pigall there stood Sacred Heart . . . beautiful, pearly Sacre-Coeur as though its silent loveliness were a pointing a white finger at our night's debauchery. I wished then that so worthy an emotion as I felt might have been caught forever in a poem but somehow the muse refuses to work these days.

JESSIE REDMON FAUSET

Jessie Redmon Fauset, novelist, poet, essayist, and editor, was one of the most influential contributors to the Harlem Renaissance. Born in Camden County, New Jersey in 1882, and raised and educated in Philadelphia, Fauset went on to receive a bachelors degree from Cornell University and a masters degree in French from the University of Pennsylvania. At Cornell she was elected into Phi Beta Kappa. Although primarily known for her four novels, Fauset is also recognized as a powerful literary editor of *The Crisis*, which helped to launch the careers of Langston Hughes, Zora Neale Hurston, Claude McKay, Jean Toomer, Countee Cullen, and other younger writers of the period.

Only recently, through the work of black feminist literary critics, have Fauset's extraordinary nonfiction writings come to the attention of a broader public. Widely traveled, Fauset devoted a great deal of her nonfiction to her trips to places throughout Europe and North Africa. These essays, which appeared in *The Crisis*, are among the very best of Fauset's work. The selection here is a portrait of Paris on the occasion of her return to a city with which she first fell in love as a young student. Here she reveals a Paris quite different from the romantic, center of Western culture that captivated her own earlier trips. Consequently, we see Fauset at her best—when she is describing the ordinary, the mundane, with her characteristic elegant eloquence.

"YARROW REVISITED" (1925)
from
THE CRISIS

This is not the Paris of my student days nor even the Paris of the second Pan-African Congress held three months ago. I seem to glimpse in the memories of those visits an enchanted city of gay streets, blue skies, of romantically historic monuments, a playground, a court of justice of the world. Everyone was possessed of a fine courtesy; attendants were kind and generous, though even then a little too conscious, for an American, of the possibility of tips; there was a delicious sense of *laisser-aller.*

Perhaps the difference lies in the season. I have never been here before so late in the year. One speaks of France and its golden weather as though that condition were perpetual. It is only October but the skies are drab, the days are grey and every twenty-four hours rain falls, steady, penetrating, soaking. The boulevards are still full, even crowded, but with Frenchmen now, not tourists; one meets with as much courtesy here, no more, no less, than anywhere else. In brief, life in Paris is life the civilized world over. But there is one exception.

I am glad to have had those golden memories of former visits. Yet I am glad to be here now in this workaday season. "Life as she is—" that is what I want to know even if it is different to the verge of disappointment from preconceived notions. Truth is best. Yet dreams are fine stuff too. In the last of those three poems of Wordsworth on Yarrow—Yarrow Unvisited, Visited, Revisited, there are, I remember, these words:

> The visions of the past
> Sustain the heart in feeling
> Life as she is—

It is precisely because of those visions that I am eager to know life. French life "as she is."

Just as the weather is by no means always golden and gay, so French living is not always a thing of joy and laughter.

I am not living in the vicinity of the gay, wide boulevards. I lived there three years ago. Nor am I in the "Quartier Latin," the famous student quarter; I spent some months there when I was a student. From both of these former environments my faulty impressions. No this time I am installed high up in a small quiet hotel on a rather narrow but busy side street though still near the "quarter." It is far, far from the *Boulevard des Italiens.* But it is right in the heart of a teeming business and residential section.

I love comfort, I love ease. I do not consider laziness a crime. I hate to move. Yet so determined am I to see "Life as she is" that with as much joy as reluctance have I mapped out this plan:

Two weeks in a cheap pension (Already over, thank God!)
A month in this small, comfortable hotel. (There is a fireplace
   in my room.)
A month in a "good" French family.
A month in a first-class pension.
After that such travel as my remaining means and time
   may permit.

The pension held, as I suspect all cheap boarding houses do, the elements of unspeakable dreariness. It was a large house built inevitably of stone, set romantically, I thought at first, far, far back in a courtyard to which one gained access by one of those thick, slowly moving doors set flush in a stone arch-way. It is this type of architecture, the lack of our projecting steps, the flatness of doors and windows which give me at any rate the effect in certain quarters of Paris of living in a fortified city. Within the house was a broad winding stair-case built beautifully in an open well so that one might stand on the ground floor and glimpse the roof ceiling. It was the only beautiful thing in that house. Within two days I found it was not so "romantic" to lie in a courtyard for the sun practically never penetrated the house. Oh that dampness! I, fresh from America with its steam heat and its auxiliary appliances of gas and oil, gas logs and accessible fireplaces, could understand Esau's quittance of his birthright for a mess of pottage. I'd have handed over the birthrights of all my friends and relations for an ordinary gas heater with fixtures.

Incidentally I do not "get" the French attitude toward this matter of heating. Of course for a few extra daily cents I was able to get thawed out in the pension. They made a fire in my room of "*charbons*"—a sort of charcoal nugget of a beautiful oval shape. But they made it with surprise. "No one has a fire yet, Mademoiselle." The hotels advertise *chauffage centrale* (central heating) but of my dozen acquaintances who live in hotels only one bears testimony to the turning on of that heat. And that, she declares, produces an effect more by auto-suggestion than by actual warmth. A clever American who has lived in Paris for several years tells me that hotel-keepers say: "Oh yes we have central heating but of course the heat is not turned on yet because the winter hasn't really come." This sort of thing keeps up till the middle of January when the refrain changes to "Well it isn't worth while turning it on now for it will soon be spring!" I think there is something to this story for when I came to this hotel my first inquiries were with regard to heat. The manager said "naturally the heat is not turned on yet." The garçon, Albert, expressed some surprise at my desire for a fire in my room and explained as he made it that the heat would be turned on tomorrow. A week later, the maid, in response to a searching inquiry, declared that the heat would be turned on soon. "Tomorrow?" I asked with an interest purely academic for my woodfire was merely blazing. "Oh, no not tomorrow," she rejoined aghast at the thought of setting so close a date, "but certainly within a few days."

In the pension a line from a melancholy hymn of my Presbyterian childhood comes back to me: "Change and decay in all around I see." The diningroom was negligible with a sort of shabby comfort. But the salon spoke of the decayed grandeur of other days. It was white and gold; a soiled white and cracked and faded gold. There were many tapestried chairs reduced to a monotone of dinginess and innumerable knick-knacks and bibelots such as I have not seen since in that same childhood I visited the homes of various great-aunts. And about the boarders there was this same air of dessication. An old, old lady, a widow I judged from her deep black and her son of perhaps 55; another old lady, once the matron I should say of some frightfully corrective institution, erect and with a terrible, raucous voice; four or five depressed young men, bookkeepers, clerks, hopelessly nondescript. The food was nondescript too.

Life in the pension is not French life only: it is life everywhere in similar environment. Only I had not thought of finding it in France.

Rue de Sevres which leads from the Boulevard Montparnasse, where my friends live, to my street is an impressively busy place. There are all sorts of businesses here jumbled close side by side, delicatessens, bakeries, milliners' establishments, hardware stores, jewelers, photographers, a cutlery. Out of the apparent confusion rises gradually some appreciation of the unexpectedly hard common sense of the French which says: "One has to have all these things in order to live; why not have them all close at hand?"

One would never have to walk a mile for a camel here either a literal or a figurative one. If French people elected to use camels they would be found, I am quite sure, along Rue de Sevres tethered a bit too near perhaps to the exposed cheeses and the cuts of meat. It is this decidedly logical hard matter-of-factness which is, I am beginning to think, the Frenchiest quality about the French. One sees it cropping out in all sorts of ways. This is the sort of thing which is at once back of the spectacle of the irreproachably dressed househalfler emerging from the bakery with a large half load of bread tucked unwrapped under his arm and that other different spectacle of the exposure of the human form upon the French stage to a degree totally unparalleled by any theater in America. "Life," says the Frenchman without cynicism, "is bread and is also shining flesh. Why bother to wrap up the one or to disguise the other?"

Such busy people! Gone in this section of the city at least is that illusion of Paris the play-ground of the world. I have never seen people work so hard in my life nor with such seriousness. It is true that they lose the time from twelve or twelve-thirty until two every day. Small shops close; the manicurist with a glance at her clock cannot do your hands now for see "it will take forty-five minutes at least. It is half-past eleven now and I close at twelve. Some other time perhaps mademoiselle?" But the remaining hours! Suzanne, the maid at the pension, eyes my trunk dubiously. "I am not sure that I can carry it up, Mademoiselle. I may have to call the concierge!" Albert in the hotel carries terrible trunks, loads and loads of heavy, heavy linen huge baskets of wood all day, all day he trudges up and down, apparently never thinking of using the elevator. His aspect is not the least bit servile yet I do not remember seeing any one so consciously a servant. Or perhaps his heavy air is due to a dull inner wonderment. Was it for this I crouched day and night in the trenches? I have heard Dr. DuBois speak many times of that something in colored Americans which simply will not let them work too long or too hard. That has been God's greatest gift.

Yet there is something about Paris. In the beginning I said that life in Paris is the same as life in the civilized world over but that there was one exception. In Paris I find myself more American than I ever feel in America. I am more conscious of national characteristics than I have ever been in New York. When I say: "We do that differently in America," I do not mean that *we* do that differently in Harlem, or on "You" Street in Washington, or on Christian Street in Philadelphia. I mean that Americans white and black do not act that way. And I recall now as I write that practically all the public buildings here bear on them the legend: "Liberté, Egalité, Fraternité" I was busy at lunchtime today and so missed my dejeuner. *I shall go out presently and have tea and I shall have it at the first tea room which takes my fancy.* This is also something to be considered in reviewing French "life as she is."

HAZEL SCOTT

Hazel Scott was heralded as a piano prodigy when she made her debut at age three in 1923. The gifted child would go on to become widely known for her talent, glamour, and activism. Born in 1920 in Port of Spain, Trinidad, she moved with her family to the United States at age four. At age eight she won a scholarship to the Juilliard School of Music but did not attend the school until she was sixteen. Throughout her career Scott appeared on Broadway, in Hollywood movies, and in nightclubs throughout the United States. She is perhaps best known for popularizing classical music by playing boogie-woogie versions of well-known pieces.

In 1945 Scott married Adam Clayton Powell, a U.S. congressman from Harlem, with whom she had a son. Quite political in her own right, Scott was harassed by the House Un-American Activities Committee. Because she was accused of being a communist sympathizer, her television show, the first to be hosted by a black woman, was canceled in 1950. Following a divorce from Powell in 1956, Scott moved to Paris, where she lived until 1967. the selection here is taken from the article "What Paris Means to Me," which Scott published in *Negro Digest* in 1961. It gives us a portrait of a Paris ripe with the political activity of a younger generation of African students as well as another view of the black artist in Paris. Here we read of Scott's encounter with one of her mentees, Billie Holiday, at the end of her career, in a city that seems to have lost some of its enthusiasm for the black American entertainer.

Scott died in 1981.

"WHAT PARIS MEANS TO ME" (1961)
f r o m
NEGRO DIGEST

Three years in Paris rehabilitated me.

I went there originally for three weeks to rest and play an engagement. Before I left America, unknown to anyone, Adam and I had a little talk. I was not too happy with the work situation here and I was not happy personally. Adam said, "If you are not happy here why don't you stay over there a while and work."

The three weeks stretched out to three years. They were filled, for the most part, gay, fun-filled, work-filled years. After a year, Skipper, my son, joined me. We took a large apartment in Paris, which we still have, and occasionally, we went down to Cannes to live with friends on the Riviera.

During this period I entertained at clubs all over the continent and in North Africa and the Near East. My three years out of America were three years of much needed rest, not from work, but from racial tension; and by that I do not mean that I never run into racism. That would not be true. But whenever I encountered racism in any form, it was so rare that it was an exception rather than the rule and it stuck out as an incident. I'm not going to say that France is paradise, but I will say this: You can live anywhere if you've got the money to live. You can go anywhere if you've got the money to go and whomever you marry or date is your business. . . .

A friend told me upon Billie Holiday's return to the United States, she called me the Queen of the Mau Maus. She meant this as a compliment. She said it because of the affection and esteem the African students in Paris hold for me. . . .

My Paris is not the city of champagne and caviar. My Paris is a pot full of red beans and rice and an apartment full of old friends and glasses tinkling and the rich, happy sound of people laughing from the heart. My Paris is the warmth of the big Thanksgiving dinners I had every year for my old and dear friends. My Paris is the enchantment of wandering through an old museum, hand in hand with an old friend from Hollywood, lost in the wonder of Rodin. My Paris is the magic of looking up the Champs Elysées from the Place del la Concorde and being warmed by the merry madness of the lights. My Paris is like the very first time you realize you are in love, like the very first time you are kissed.

Paris is all this and more, but it is also pain. While I was there, some of my dearest friends died and some were murdered. I lost Lester Young and Billie Holiday. And I went to the very door of death myself after a serious operation.

Lester, who is (not was) such a beautiful individual, came to see me every day during my recuperation and we listened for hours on end to Frank Sinatra's album, Only the Lonely. It pains me to remember he went from my apartment to an airplane which took him to America and death.

Paris is Billie Holiday, too. I remember her one night, toward the end, singing a bitter blues, trying to say everything, trying to explain everything within the confines of twelve bars. She had been robbed, again, and she was blue. Sitting there in the Mars Club in Paris, listening to this woman who represents (not represented) so many years of my life, sitting there remembering how she used to protect me and curse me and run me home when I was 15 and working on 52nd Street in New York, I was overcome by all the tragedy, all the greatness and all the beauty of her life.

I had my own problems too. Anna Lucasata had just collapsed and I was sort of in-between and wandering. While wondering where I was going and what I was doing, I began to cry. Billie stopped, gripped my arm and dragged me to a back room and slammed the door. "The next time you begin to feel like this," she said, "just remember that you've got Skipper and Lady only has a little Chihuahua and Lady's making it. And another thing: Never let them see you cry." Isn't that a wonderful, fantastic thing to say? "Never let them see you cry."

I learned a lot in Paris about people and about myself. One does not look into the face of death, as I have, and come away worrying about pettiness and cattiness and gossip and conforming. It seems that every time I am near death, someone or something is asking me over and over, How stupid can you get? This last time, when I spent a month in bed, I got the message. I am not likely to forget it. Love is important. Love. Some people go to their graves without ever learning that simple lesson.

COUNTEE CULLEN

Countee Cullen was born in March 1903 and later became one of the most prolific and celebrated writers of the Harlem Renaissance. Although he is known primarily for his poetry, Cullen translated classical works and published a novel, children's fiction, plays, and essays. Furthermore, he was the editor of the important anthology *Caroling Dusk*, published in 1927.

The selection here originally appeared in *The Crisis* in June 1929. In it he addresses the stereotype of the "rude" French by countering their daily "courtesies" with the absence of such civilities in the United States. Although he never explicitly compares the French response to blacks to that of the United States, it is clearly implied here.

"COUNTEE CULLEN ON FRENCH COURTESY"
from
THE CRISIS

Paris, March 1, 1929

One may reasonably be expected after a six months' sojourn in a strange land to arrive at some definite opinion of the people. All the labels and tags should by this time be sifted and assorted. I recall that it has taken singularly less time for many visitors to America to arrive at the most definite and erroneous conclusions about us, and that many white excursionists on a rapid and casual visit to Negro quarters have satisfactorily, to their thinking, pigeonholed the entire race, with astonishing celerity, if with dubious acuteness. After all, the tendency to generalize is so inately human that it should be pardoned. Moreover, the truth of any matter is an elusive and many colored thing. Therefore, it is with little faith in my own observations that after my half year's stay among them, walking their streets, talking to them when I could do so without seeming offensively inquisitive, that I find myself thinking of the French as a people of consummate politeness, of a most enlightened tolerance, and of a sad impecunity.

The manners of the French are amazing, and must occasion foreigners, especially the younger element of Americans and the suddenly and vulgarly well-to-do, many moments of acute embarrassment. For it has never seemed to me that politeness has played a large part in American living. It is true that Southerners, both black and white, lay strenuous and oft repeated claims to an exclusive lien on hospitality. But that is another matter. A politeness of the French variety cannot conceivably exist in a section of the country where one group despises the other and merely grudgingly tolerates its continued existence. The American pace in general is too swift to allow the display of social solicitudes that one thinks of in connection with politeness *à la française*. It is a brand that cannot thrive on hurry. There, probably, is the reason it has reached so genteel a growth among the French. Though Negroes are mythically accredited with the world's most comprehensive understanding of the importance of leisure, I doubt that even we can even slightly approach the Gallic appreciation of that blissful state. It seems that, for the French, tomorrow is a far more important time than either yesterday or today; for tomorrow may be done all that he put off doing yesterday, all that he will probably delay doing today. He is very like the schoolboy dallying with the lessons that he knows must eventually be learned, but only at the last moment.

"Sir" and "Madam" and "Ma'am" have long since disappeared from current American speech, unless there be parts of the country where they are held over as interesting relics of antebellum days. Nowadays one answers questions crisply with a short curt, hurried, "yes" or "no"; trappings are obsolete; it is not even required that children be hampered with them in their relations with their parents or with their teachers. Perhaps such expressions would have a false ring in a democratic country. I recall an incident that occurred not so long ago in New York when, in a mood of singular amiability and humility, I answered "yes, ma'am" to a question put to me by a lady. It was so much wasted abasement, for the lady informed me that in these enlightened times no one said "ma'am" any more, nor "sir."

Now that I think of it, a possible explanation occurs to me. At the time, the lady, though far on the shady side of life, was still a maiden, technically speaking. Since then she has managed to edge into the marital state, and may have changed her mind about those obsolete expressions. After all, "Madam," in her case, was truly inappropriate, and may have smacked of a smirking levity on my part. But in France, it is the mark of the stranger, of the crude man from across the waters, not to employ these ancient impedimenta of politeness. An excellent thesis, I am sure, one that would warm the hearts of the sovereign board of any of our American universities would be: "How Many Times Per Day Are 'Monsieur,' 'Madame,' and 'Mademoiselle' Used in French Conversation and What is the General Effect of Such Extravagance on the Morale of American Visitors?"

What purchaser in an American store has not at some time in his experience had that guiltiest of feeling induced in him by the surliness of a storekeeper suddenly called from his newspaper, his lunch, or a choice bit of gossip, that he, the buyer, was actually being favored far and away above his natural deserts in being allowed to make a purchase at that particular moment? But whatever your purchase in a French store, be it a bit of bread that you must carry through the streets with no more hygienic covering than your naked hand, a bottle of wine, or an automobile, your visit to the Frenchman's shop has all the earmarks of a social call. On entering, you are at once most solicitously bid good day; if it is your second visit to that particular store, your health is a subject of vital importance to the proprietor; and because your wife has not accompanied you this morning (having been with you yesterday) he is breathless in his anxiety lest any fatality may have occurred to her during the night. And when you depart with your badly tied package of little things falling every way but right, your total expenditure having amounted to about twenty-four cents in American currency, it is the sheerest ill breeding for you not only not to wish the proprietor a good day, but to hope that you will see him again.

To one accustomed to the manners of passengers riding the Interborough Rapid Transit Lines, the politeness encountered on the Paris subway, or Metropolitan, seems incredible. One does not kick, scratch, shunt, jostle, or tickle the person in front of him out of his path as he nears the station where he desires to exit. But gently, suavely, softly, he begins in time to ask those in front of him if it is their intention to descend at the next station. If such is not the case, they squeeze aside into themselves and allow him to pass, until by a gradual process of elimination, the polite passenger finds himself at the door when the train glides into the station. Of course, this form of social consideration could not as easily be employed in the subways of New York, as the natural temperament of the people would be against it.

In some quarters I have heard French politeness explained away as having a commercial basis. I doubt seriously that this is so, that any commercial consideration could so change and modify an entire people. It seems to me something innate, a natural inherent streak, something fine and delicate, left over perhaps, as a French lady told me, from the days when France had kings and a court through whose vices shown the virtue of impeccable manners. The lady, who is an arch royalist even now, decries what seem to me the most magnificent manner I have ever encountered. To her these are nothing, compared with the manners of those days that are gone forever (for even she has no hopes for the return of a royalist regime). Not having smelled the flower in its dewy days, I can only say that if it be a bit wilted now, it still exhales a rare and charming savor.

JAMES BALDWIN

Playwright, novelist, essayist, and civil rights activist James Baldwin was one of the most prolific and well known writers of his time. Born in 1924, Baldwin was recognized as a major literary talent even before the publication in 1953 of his first novel, *Go Tell It on the Mountain*. Throughout his adult life, he lived between the United States and Europe, especially France, although he lived in Switzerland and Turkey as well. Nonetheless, he returned frequently to the United States to teach, to write, and most important to participate in the movements for black rights, especially in the 1960s. His powerful essays are among the most important of that decade.

Baldwin first visited Paris at the age of twenty-four, and some of his most eloquent essays were written about his experiences as an expatriate. Of Paris he wrote, "In Paris, I began to see the sky for what seemed to be the first time. It was borne in on me—and it did not make me feel melancholy—that sky had been there before I was born and would be there when I was dead. And it was up to me, therefore, to make of my brief opportunity the most that could be made."

The selection here analyzes the complex meeting of American blacks with American whites and francophone Africans on the streets of Paris.

James Baldwin died at his home in St. Paul de Vence in the South of France on November 30, 1987.

"ENCOUNTER ON THE SEINE:
BLACK MEETS BROWN" (1955)
from
NOTES OF A NATIVE SON

In Paris nowadays it is rather more difficult for an American Negro to become a really successful entertainer than it is rumored to have been some thirty years ago. For one thing, champagne has ceased to be drunk out of slippers, and the frivolously colored thousand-franc note is neither as elastic nor as freely spent as it was in the 1920's. The musicians and singers who are here now must work very hard indeed to acquire the polish and style which will land them in the big time. Bearing witness to this eternally tantalizing possibility, performers whose eminence is unchallenged, like Duke Ellington or Louis Armstrong, occasionally pass through. Some of their ambitious followers are in or near the big time already; others are gaining reputations which have yet to be tested in the States. Gordon Heath, who will be remembered for his performances as the embattled soldier in Broadway's *Deep Are the Roots* some seasons back, sings ballads nightly in his own night club on the Rue L'Abbaye; and everyone who comes to Paris these days sooner or later discovers Chez Inez, a night club in the Latin Quarter run by a singer named Inez Cavanaugh, which specializes in fried chicken and jazz. It is at Chez Inez that many an unknown first performs in public, going on thereafter, if not always to greater triumphs, at least to other night clubs, and possibly landing a contract to tour the Riviera during the spring and summer.

In general, only the Negro entertainers are able to maintain a useful and unquestioning comradeship with other Negroes. Their nonperforming, colored countrymen are, nearly to a man, incomparably more isolated, and it must be conceded that this isolation is deliberate. It is estimated that there are five hundred American Negroes living in this city, the vast majority of them veterans studying on the G.I. Bill. They are studying everything from the Sorbonne's standard *Cours de Civilisation Française* to abnormal psychology, brain surgery, music, fine arts, and literature. Their isolation from each other is not difficult to understand if one bears in mind the axiom, unquestioned by American landlords, that Negroes are happy only when they are kept together. Those driven to break this pattern by leaving the U.S. ghettos not merely have effected a social and physical leave-taking but also have been precipitated into cruel psychological warfare. It is altogether inevitable that past humiliations should become associated not only with one's traditional oppressors but also with one's traditional kinfolk.

Thus the sight of a face from home is not invariably a source of joy, but can also quite easily become a source of embarrassment or rage. The American Negro in Paris is forced at last to exercise an undemocratic discrimination rarely practiced by Americans, that of judging his people, duck by duck, and distinguishing them one from another. Through this deliberate isolation, through lack of numbers, and above all through his own overwhelming need to be, as it were, forgotten, the American Negro in Paris is very nearly the invisible man.

The wariness with which he regards his colored kin is a natural extension of the wariness with which he regards all of his countrymen. At the beginning, certainly, he cherishes rather exaggerated hopes of the French. His white countrymen, by and large, fail to justify his fears, partly because the social climate does not encourage an outward display of racial bigotry, partly out of their awareness of being ambassadors, and finally, I should think, because they are themselves relieved at being no longer forced to think in terms of color. There remains, nevertheless, in the encounter of white Americans and Negro Americans the high potential of an awkward or an ugly situation.

The white American regards his darker brother through the distorting screen created by a lifetime of conditioning. He is accustomed to regard him either as a needy and deserving martyr or as the soul of rhythm, but he is more than a little intimidated to find this stranger so many miles from home. At first he tends instinctively, whatever his intelligence may belatedly clamor, to take it as a reflection on his personal honor and good-will; and at the same time, with that winning generosity, at once good-natured and uneasy, which characterizes Americans, he would like to establish communication, and sympathy, with his compatriot. "And how do *you* feel about it?" he would like to ask, "it" being anything—the Russians, Betty Grable, the Place de la Concorde. The trouble here is that any "it," so tentatively offered, may suddenly become loaded and vibrant with tension, creating in the air between the two thus met an intolerable atmosphere of danger.

The Negro, on the other hand, via the same conditioning which constricts the outward gesture of the whites, has learned to anticipate: as the mouth opens he divines what the tongue will utter. He has had time, too, long before he came to Paris, to reflect on the absolute and personally expensive futility of taking any one of his countrymen to task for his status in America, or of hoping to convey to them any of his experience. The American Negro and white do not, therefore, discuss the past, except in considerably guarded snatches. Both are quite willing, and indeed quite wise, to remark instead the considerably overrated impressiveness of the Eiffel Tower.

The Eiffel Tower has naturally long since ceased to divert the French, who consider that all Negroes arrive from America, trumpet-laden and twinkle-toed, bearing scars so unutterably painful that all of the glories of the French Republic may not suffice to heal them. This indignant generosity poses problems of its own, which, language and custom being what they are, are not so easily averted.

The European tends to avoid the really monumental confusion which might result from an attempt to apprehend the relationship of the forty-eight states to one another, clinging instead to such information as is afforded by radio, press, and film, to anecdotes considered to be illustrative of American life, and to the myth that we have ourselves perpetuated. The result, in conversation, is rather like seeing one's back yard reproduced with extreme fidelity, but in such a perspective that it becomes a place which one has never seen or visited, which never has existed, and which never can exist. The Negro is forced to say "Yes" to many a difficult question, and yet to deny the conclusion to which his answers seem to point. His past, he now realizes, has not been simply a series of ropes and bonfires and humiliations, but something vastly more complex, which, as he thinks painfully, "It was much worse than that," was also, he irrationally feels, something much better. As it is useless to excoriate his countrymen, it is galling now to be pitied as a victim, to accept this ready sympathy which is limited only by its failure to accept him as an American. He finds himself involved, in another language, in the same old battle: the battle for his own identity. To accept the reality of his being an American becomes a matter involving his integrity and his greatest hopes, for only by accepting this reality can he hope to make articulate to himself or to others the uniqueness of his experience, and to set free the spirit so long anonymous and caged.

The ambivalence of his status is thrown into relief by his encounters with the Negro students from France's colonies who live in Paris. The

French African comes from a region and a way of life which—at least from the American point of view—is exceedingly primitive, and where exploitation takes more naked forms. In Paris, the African Negro's status, conspicuous and subtly inconvenient, is that of a colonial; and he leads here the intangibly precarious life of someone abruptly and recently uprooted. His bitterness is unlike that of his American kinsman in that it is not so treacherously likely to be turned against himself. He has, not so very many miles away, a homeland to which his relationship, no less than his responsibility, is overwhelmingly clear: His country must be given—or it must seize—its freedom. This bitter ambition is shared by his fellow colonials, with whom he has a common language, and whom he has no wish whatever to avoid; without whose sustenance, indeed, he would be almost altogether lost in Paris. They live in groups together, in the same neighborhoods, in student hotels and under conditions which cannot fail to impress the American as almost unendurable.

Yet what the American is seeing is not simply the poverty of the student but the enormous gap between the European and American standards of living. *All* of the students in the Latin Quarter live in ageless, sinister-looking hotels; they are all forced continually to choose between cigarettes and cheese at lunch.

It is true that the poverty and anger which the American Negro sees must be related to Europe and not to America. Yet, as he wishes for a moment that he were home again, where at least the terrain is familiar, there begins to race within him, like the despised beat of the tom-tom, echoes of a past which he has not yet been able to utilize, intimations of a responsibility which he has not yet been able to face. He begins to conjecture how much he has gained and lost during his long sojourn in the American republic. The African before him has endured privation, injustice, medieval cruelty; but the African has not yet endured the utter alienation of himself from his people and his past. His mother did not sing "Sometimes I Feel Like a Motherless Child," and he has not, all his life long, ached for acceptance in a culture which pronounced straight hair and white skin the only acceptable beauty.

They face each other, the Negro and the African, over a gulf of three hundred years—an alienation too vast to be conquered in an evening's good-will, too heavy and too double-edged ever to be trapped in speech. This alienation causes the Negro to recognize that he is a hybrid. Not a physical hybrid merely: in every aspect of his living he betrays the memory of the auction block and the impact of the happy ending. In white Americans he finds reflected — repeated, as it were, in a higher key — his tensions, his terrors, his tenderness. Dimly and for the first time, there begins to fall into perspective the nature of the roles they have played in the lives and history of each other. Now he is bone of their bone, flesh of their flesh; they have loved and hated and obsessed and feared each other and his blood is in their soil. Therefore he cannot deny them, nor can they ever be divorced.

The American Negro cannot explain to the African what surely seems in himself to be a want of manliness, of racial pride, a maudlin ability to forgive. It is difficult to make clear that he is not seeking to forfeit his birthright as a black man, but that, on the contrary, it is precisely this birthright which he is struggling to recognize and make articulate. Perhaps it now occurs to him that in his need to establish himself in relation to his past he is most American, that this depthless alienation from oneself and one's people is, in sum, the American experience.

Yet one day he will face his home again; nor can he realistically expect to find overwhelming changes. In America, it is true, the appearance is perpetually changing, each generation greeting with short-lived exultation yet more dazzling additions to our renowned façade. But the ghetto, anxiety, bitterness, and guilt continue to breed their indescribable complex of tensions. What time will bring Americans is at last their own identity. It is on this dangerous voyage and in the same boat that the American Negro will make peace with himself and with the voiceless many thousands gone before him.

5

RUSSIA

*F*or generations of African Americans, the esteem with which the Russian people held their national poet, the mixed-race Pushkin, has created an image of Russia as a nation free of racial prejudice. The widespread reception and appreciation of classically trained black performers—such as the Shakespearean actor Ira Aldridge, the opera singer Roland Hayes, and the multitalented Paul Robeson—only added to the African-American romance with the country. In the nineteenth century, as Russia moved from a peasant class to a revolution that avowed to eliminate class, it seems that African-American travelers to Russia cannot ignore the class conflict or its connection to race. Finally, for many left-leaning twentieth-century black intellectuals—the official stance of the International Communist Party on race relations in the United States—their support of black organizing efforts and of high-profile cases, such as that of the Scottsboro boys, served as evidence of the possibilities of Soviet-style communism.

The excerpts chosen for this section reveal the changing nature of African-American images of Russia. Nancy Prince paints a portrait of the elegance and pageantry of the Russian court in the early nineteenth century. For Prince, Russia is a place where she is a member of the court, an independent businesswoman, and an employer of servants and apprentices. Yet Prince describes with detail her version of the Decembrist Rebellion in St. Petersburg in 1825 with its violent aftermath. Her position within the court may account for her admiration for the tsar and empress. She makes only brief mention of the serfs, and she observes and compares their situation with slaves in the United States.

The three African-American men of the twentieth century included here are concerned primarily with the intellectuals and the workers. Traveling to the young Soviet Union shortly after the Revolution of 1917, all three see in Soviet society a model for dealing with the class and racial politics of the United States. Claude McKay and Langston Hughes make constant comparisons between the Soviet Union and the United States. All three hold wide romantic views of the Russian Revolution, the Russian state, and the Russian people. In 1929 McKay addressed the Fourth Congress of the Third Communist international about race relations in the Communist International States. Harry Haywood first went to Russia as a student and eventually became a high-ranking official in the Communist Party of the United States. Although Hughes never joined the party, he clearly admired its politics. Ever the wanderer, Hughes left Moscow and traveled throughout the central Asian Soviet republics, where he met and made connections with many ethnic minorities, some of whom were brown-skinned people with whom Hughes identified.

Activist and poet Audre Lorde traveled outside Moscow as well, but her trip took place in the 1970s after the exposure of Stalin's atrocities and during the Cold War. Lorde was also a leftist, but unlike McKay, Hughes and Haywood—or perhaps because of them and their eventual disillusion with the Communist Party—the realities of Soviet Life prohibited her from entirely romanticizing it. She applauds the standards and availability of health care and education but questions the treatment of Jews and the silences around the plight of African Americans.

Andrea Lee, the youngest writer here, is a child of the Cold War who traveled to Russia during the last decade of that era. She can celebrate the efficiency of the public transportation system but likens the "propagandized" versions of history and the state-sponsored news radio to an Orwellian nightmare.

NANCY PRINCE

Nancy Prince traveled to Russia in 1824, when she married Nero Prince, an African-American man from Massachusetts who had worked as a cook and was bound to St. Petersburg to serve in the tsar's guard. Prince's affiliation with the court offered opportunities that had not been available in New England; she ran a clothing-making business and employed a servant, a journeywoman, and apprentices to sell her garments to the empress. More than in any other section of her narrative, when describing Russia Prince turns to observation in the tradition of Western travel writing. She also admires Empress Alexandra, who provides an example of a white woman of privilege and power, duty, and warmth—characteristics that Prince clearly admires. The empress takes an interest in Prince not only by supporting her business but also by having her children's matron encourage Prince to distribute Bibles to the poor. Prince observes that the peasants in Russia are slaves and are treated poorly, but in comparison with American slavery they are not separated from their families or sold; mobility is limited in each case, but the serfs can at least develop a community identity with others of their class. As she writes in *A Narrative of the Life and Travels of Mrs. Nancy Prince*, Prince left Russia for health reasons in 1833 after residing there for nine years; Mr. Prince, who was to have returned afterward, died abroad. Before writing her narrative, Prince gave a talk in the Boston area about her Russian experiences.

f r o m

A NARRATIVE OF THE LIFE AND TRAVELS
OF MRS. NANCY PRINCE (1853)

May, 1825. I spent some time visiting the different towns in the vicinity of St. Petersburg. In the fall of the same year, the Emperor retired to a warmer climate for the health of the Empress Elizabeth. January, 1826, the corpse of Alexander was brought in state, and was met three miles from the city by the nobles of the court; and they formed a procession, and the body was brought in state into the building where the imperial family were deposited. March, of the same year, the corpse of Elizabeth was brought in the same manner. Constantine was then king of Poland, he was next heir to the throne, and was, unanimously voted by the people, but refused and resigned the crown in favor of his brother Nicholas. The day appointed the people were ordered to assemble as usual, at the ringing of the bells; they rejected Nicholas; a sign was given by the leaders that was well understood, and the people great and small rushed to the square and cried with one voice for Constantine. The emperor with his prime minister, and city governor, rode into the midst of them, entreating them to retire, without avail; they were obliged to order the cannons fired upon the mob; it was not known when they discharged them that the emperor and his ministers were in the crowd. He was wonderfully preserved, while both his friends and their horses were killed. There was a general seizing of all classes, who were taken into custody. The scene cannot be described; the bodies of the killed and mangled were cast into the river, and the snow and ice were stained with the blood of human victims; as they were obliged to drive the cannon to and fro in the midst of the crowd, the bones of those wounded, who might have been cured, were crushed. The cannon are very large, drawn by eight horses, trained for the purpose. The scene was awful; all business was stopped. This deep plot originated in 1814, in Germany, with the Russian nobility and German, under the pretense of a Free Mason's Lodge. When they returned home they increased their numbers and presented their chart to the emperor for permission, which was granted. In the year 1822, the emperor being suspicious that all was not right, took their chart from them. They carried it on in small parties, rapidly increasing, believing they would soon be able to destroy all the imperial branches, and have a republican government. Had not this taken place, undoubtedly they would at last have succeeded. So deep was the foundation of this plot laid, both males and females were engaged in it. The prisonhouses were filled, and thirty of the leading men were put in solitary confinement, and twenty-six of the number died, four were burned. A stage was erected and faggots were placed underneath, each prisoner was secured by iron chains, presenting a most appalling sight to an eye-witness. A priest was in attendance to cheer their last dying moments, then fire was set to the faggots, and those brave men were consumed. Others received the knout, and even the princesses and ladies of rank were imprisoned and flogged in their own habitations. Those that survived their punishment were banished to Siberia. The mode of banishment is very imposing and very heart-rending, severing them from all dear relatives and friends, for they are never permitted to take their children. When they arrive at the gate of the city, their first sight is a guard of soldiers, then wagons with provisions, then the noblemen in their banished apparel guarded, then each side, conveyances for the females, then ladies in order, guarded by soldiers.

Preparations were now being made for the coronation of the new Emperor and Empress. This took place September, 1826, in Moscow, 555 miles south-east from St. Petersburg. All persons engaged in the court were sent beforehand, in order to prepare for the coming event. After his majesty's laws were read, as usual on such occasions, those who wished to remain in his service did so, and those who did not were discharged. . . .

The present Emperor and Empress are courteous and affable. The Empress would often send for the ladies of the court at 8 oclock in the evening to sup with her: when they arrive at the court they form a procession and she takes the lead. On entering the hall, the band strikes up; there are two long tables on each side, and in the midst circular tables for the Imperial family. The tables are spread apparently with every variety of eatables and desserts, but everything is artificial, presenting a novel appearance. When the company are seated, the Emperor and Empress walk around the tables and shake hands with each individual, as they pass. The prisoners of war who are nobles, are seated by themselves with their faces veiled. There is a tender or waiter to each person, with two plates, one with soup and the other with something else. After a variety of courses, in one hour they are dismissed by the band. They then retire to another part of the palace to attend a ball or theatrical amusements. At the Empress' command they are dismissed. She carries power and dignity in her countenance, and is well adapted to her station. And after her late amusements at night, she would be out at an early hour in the morning, visiting the abodes of the distressed, dressed in as common apparel as any one here, either walking, or riding in a common sleigh. At her return she would call for her children, to take them in her arms and talk to them. "She riseth while it is yet night and giveth meat to her household and a portion to her maidens, she stretcheth out her hands to the poor, yea, she reacheth out her hands to the needy; she is not afraid of the snow, for all her household are clothed in scarlet." Then she would go to the cabinet of his Majesty; there she would write and advise with him.

The Russian ladies follow the fashions of the French and English. Their religion is after the Greek Church. There are no seats in their churches; they stand, bow, and kneel, during the service. The principal church is on the Main street. There are the statues of the great commanders that have conquered in battle. They are clad in brass, with flags in their hands, and all their ancient implements of war are deposited there. The altar is surrounded by statues of the Virgin Mary and the twelve apostles. When Russia is at war, and her armies are about to engage in battle, it is here that the Emperor and his family and court, come to pray for victory over the enemy. The day they engaged in battle against the Poles, the Empress Dowager took her death; she was embalmed and laid in state six weeks in the hall of the winter palace. I went a number of times to see her, and the people pay her homage, and kiss the hands of that lump of clay. All religion is tolerated, but the native Russians are subject to the Greek Church. There are a number of institutions in St. Petersburg where children of all classes have the privilege of instruction. The sailors' and soldiers' boys enter the corps at the age of seven, and are educated for that purpose. The girls remain in the barracks with their parents, or go to some institution where they are instructed in all the branches of female education. There are other establishments, where the higher classes send their children. . . .

The city houses are built of stone and brick, and twice the thickness of American houses. They are heated by Peaches, of similar construction to our furnaces; the outside of which is faced with China tiles, presenting a very beautiful appearance. The village houses are built of logs corked with oakum, where the peasants reside. This class of people till the land, most of them are slaves and are very degraded. The rich own the poor, but they are not suffered to separate families or sell them off the soil. All are subject to the Emperor, and no nobleman can leave without his permission. The mode of travelling is principally by stages which are built something like our omnibusses, with settees upon the top railed and guarded by soldiers, for the purpose of protecting the travellers from the attacks of wild beasts. The common language is a mixture of Sclavonian and Polish. The nobility make use of the modern Greek, French and English. I learned the languages in six months, so as to be able to attend to my business, and also made some proficiency in the French. My time was taken up in domestic affairs; I took two children to board, the third week after commencing housekeeping, and increased their numbers. The baby linen making and childrens' garments were in great demand. I started a business in these articles and took a journeywoman and apprentices.

ClaudE McKAy

Claude McKay was born in Jamaica in 1889. In the early twentieth century he migrated to the United States, where he gained a reputation as a talented young black writer. Originally invited to Russia by John Reed in 1920, McKay did not visit the Soviet Union until 1921. While there he attended the Fourth Congress of the Third Communist International in Moscow and met and talked with Leon Trotsky and other officials of the Communist Party. The excerpts here originally appeared in *The Crisis* and are taken from the early days of that trip. By the time of his return to the United States in 1934, McKay had become disillusioned with the Communist Party. He died in 1949.

"SoviET RussiA aNd tHE NEqRo" (1923) *f r o m* THE Crisis

Though Western Europe can be reported as being quite ignorant and apathetic of the Negro in world affairs, there is one great nation with an arm in Europe that is thinking intelligently on the Negro as it does about all international problems. When the Russian workers overturned their infamous government in 1917, one of the first acts of the new Premier, Lenin, was a proclamation greeting all the oppressed peoples throughout the world, exhorting them to organize and unite against the common international oppressor—Private Capitalism. Later on in Moscow, Lenin himself grappled with the question of the American Negroes and spoke on the subject before the Second Congress of the Third International. He consulted with John Reed, the American journalist, and dwelt on the urgent necessity of propaganda and organizational work among the Negroes of the South. The subject was not allowed to drop. When Sen Katayama of Japan, the veteran revolutionist, went from the United States to Russia in 1921 he placed the American Negro problem first upon his full agenda. And ever since he has been working unceasingly and unselfishly to promote the cause of the exploited American Negro among the Soviet councils of Russia.

With the mammoth country securely under their control, and despite the great energy and thought that are being poured into the revival of the national industry, the vanguard of the Russian workers and the national minorities, now set free from imperial oppression, are thinking seriously about the fate of the oppressed classes, the suppressed national and racial minorities in the rest of Europe, Asia, Africa and America. They feel themselves kin in spirit to these people. They want to help make them free. And not the least of the oppressed that fill the thoughts of the new Russia are the Negroes of America and Africa. If we look back two decades to recall how the Czarist persecution of the Russian Jews agitated Democratic America, we will get some idea of the mind of Liberated Russia towards the Negroes of America. The Russian people are reading the terrible history of their own recent past in the tragic position of the American Negro to-day. Indeed, the Southern States can well serve the purpose of showing what has happened in Russia. For if the exploited poor whites of the South could ever transform themselves into making common cause with the persecuted and plundered Negroes, overcome the oppressive oligarchy—the political crackers and robber landlords—and deprive it of all political privileges, the situation would be very similar to that of Soviet Russia to-day.

In Moscow I met an old Jewish revolutionist who had done time in Siberia, now young again and filled with the spirit of the triumphant Revolution. We talked about American affairs and touched naturally on the subject of the Negro. I told him of the difficulties of the problem, that the best of the liberal white elements were also working for a better status for the Negro, and he remarked: "When the democratic bourgeoisie of the United States were execrating Czardom for the Jewish pogroms they were meting out to your people a treatment more savage and barbarous than the Jews ever experienced in the old Russia. America," he said religiously, "had to make some sort of expiatory gesture for her sins. There is no surfeited bourgeoisie here in Russia to make a hobby of ugly social problems, but the

Russian workers, who have won through the ordeal of persecution and revolution, extend the hand of international brotherhood to all the suppressed Negro millions of America."

I met with this spirit of sympathetic appreciation and response prevailing in all circles in Moscow and Petrograd. I never guessed what was awaiting me in Russia. I had left America in September of 1922 determined to get there, to see into the new revolutionary life of the people and report on it. I was not a little dismayed when, congenitally averse to notoriety as I am, I found that on stepping upon Russian soil I forthwith became a notorious character. And strangely enough there was nothing unpleasant about my being swept into the surge of revolutionary Russia. For better or for worse every person in Russia is vitally affected by the revolution. No one but a soulless body can live there without being stirred to the depths by it.

I reached Russia in November—the month of the Fourth Congress of the Communist International and the Fifth Anniversary of the Russian Revolution. The whole revolutionary nation was mobilized to honor the occasion, Petrograd was magnificent in red flags and streamers. Red flags fluttered against the snow from all the great granite buildings. Railroad trains, street cars, factories, stores, hotels, schools—all wore decorations. It was a festive month of celebration in which I, as a member of the Negro race, was a very active participant. I was received as though the people had been comprised of, and were prepared for, my coming. When Max Eastman and I tried to bore our way through the dense crowds, that jammed the Tverskaya Street in Moscow on the 7th of November, I was caught, tossed up into the air, and passed along by dozens of stalwart youths.

"How warmly excited they get over a strange face!" said Eastman. A young Russian Communist remarked: "But where is the difference? Some of the Indians are as dark as you." To which another replied: "The lines of the face are different, the Indians have been with us long. The people instinctively see the difference." And so always the conversation revolved around me until my face flamed. The Moscow press printed long articles about the Negroes in America, a poet was inspired to rhyme about the Africans looking to Soviet Russia and soon I was in demand everywhere— at the lectures of poets and journalists, the meetings of soldiers and factory workers. Slowly I began losing self-consciousness with the realization that I was welcomed thus as a symbol, as a member of the great American Negro group—kin to the unhappy black slaves of European Imperialism in

Africa—that the workers of Soviet Russia, rejoicing in their freedom, were greeting through me.

Russia, in broad terms, is a country where all the races of Europe and of Asia meet and mix. The fact is that under the repressive power of the Czarist bureaucracy the different races preserved a degree of kindly tolerance towards each other. The fierce racial hatreds that flame in the Balkans never existed in Russia. Where in the South no Negro might approach a *"cracker"* as a man for friendly offices, a Jewish pilgrim in old Russia could find rest and sustenance in the home of an orthodox peasant. It is a problem to define the Russian type by features. The Hindu, the Mongolian, the Persian, the Arab, the West European—all these types may be traced woven into the distinctive polyglot population of Moscow. And so, to the Russian, I was merely another type, but stranger, with which they were not yet familiar. They were curious with me, all and sundry, young and old, in a friendly, refreshing manner. Their curiosity had none of the intolerable impertinence and often downright affront that any very dark colored man, be he Negro, Indian or Arab, would experience in Germany and England.

In 1920, while I was trying to get out a volume of my poems in London, I had a visit with Bernard Shaw who remarked that it must be tragic for a sensitive Negro to be an artist. Shaw was right. Some of the English reviews of my book touched the very bottom of journalistic muck. The English reviewer outdid his American cousin (except the South, of course, which could not surprise any white person much less a black) in sprinkling criticism with racial prejudice. The sedate, copperhead "Spectator" as much as said: no "cultured" white man could read a Negro's poetry without prejudice, that instinctively he must search for that "something" that must make him antagonistic to it. But fortunately Mr. McKay did not offend our susceptibilities! The English people from the lowest to the highest, cannot think of a black man as being anything but an entertainer, boxer, a Baptist preacher or a menial. The Germans are just a little worse. Any healthy looking black coon of an adventurous streak can have a wonderful time palming himself off as another Siki or a buck dancer. When an American writer introduced me as a poet to a very cultured German, a lover of all the arts, he could not believe it, and I don't think he does yet. An American student tells his middle class landlady that he is having a black friend to lunch: "But are you sure that he is not a cannibal?" she asks without a flicker of a humorous smile!

But in Petrograd and Moscow, I could not detect a trace of this ignorant snobbishness among the educated classes, and the attitude of the common workers, the soldiers and sailors was still more remarkable. It was so beautifully naive; for them I was only a black member of the world of humanity. It may be urged that the fine feelings of the Russians towards a Negro was the effect of Bolshevist pressure and propaganda. The fact is that I spent most of my leisure time in non-partisan and anti-bolshevist circles. In Moscow I found the Luxe Hotel where I put up extremely depressing, the dining room was anathema to me and I grew tired to death of meeting the proletarian ambassadors from foreign lands, some of whom bore themselves as if they were the holy messengers of Jesus, Prince of Heaven, instead of working class representatives. And so I spent many of my free evenings at the Domino Café, a notorious den of the dilettante poets and writers. There came the young anarchists and menshevists and all the young aspiring fry to read and discuss their poetry and prose. Sometimes a group of the older men came too. One evening I noticed Pilnyak the novelist, Okonoff the critic, Feodor the translator of Poe, an editor, a theatre manager and their young disciples, beer-drinking through a very interesting literary discussion. There was always music, good folk-singing and bad fiddling, the place was more like a second rate cabaret than a poets' club, but nevertheless much to be enjoyed, with amiable chats and light banter through which the evening wore pleasantly away. This was the meeting place of the frivolous set with whom I eased my mind after writing all day.

The evenings of the proletarian poets held in the Arbot were much more serious affairs. The leadership was communist, the audience working class and attentive like diligent, elementary school children. To these meetings also came some of the keener intellects from the Domino Café. One of these young women told me that she wanted to keep in touch with all the phases of the new culture. In Petrograd the meetings of the intelligentzia seemed more formal and inclusive. There were such notable men there as Chukovsky the critic, Eugene Zamiatan the celebrated novelist and Maishack the poet and translator of Kipling. The artist and theatre world were also represented. There was no communist spirit in evidence at these intelligentzia gatherings. Frankly there was an undercurrent of hostility to the bolshevists. But I was invited to speak and read my poems whenever I appeared at any of them and treated with every courtesy and consideration as a writer. Among those sophisticated and cultured Russians, many of them speaking from two to four languages, there was no overdoing of the correct thing, no vulgar wonderment and bounderish superiority over a Negro's being a poet. I was a poet, that was all, and their keen questions showed that they were much more interested in the technique of my poetry, my views on and my position regarding the modern literary movements than in the difference of my color. Although I will not presume that there was no attraction at all in that little difference!

On my last visit to Petrograd I stayed in the Palace of the Grand Duke Vladimir Alexander, the brother of Czar Nicholas the Second. His old, kindly steward who looked after my comfort wanders round like a ghost through the great rooms. The house is now the headquarters of the Petrograd intellectuals. A fine painting of the Duke stands curtained in the dining room. I was told that he was liberal minded, a patron of the arts, and much liked by the Russian intelligentzia. The atmosphere of the house was theoretically non-political, but I quickly scented a strong hostility to bolshevist authority. But even here I had only pleasant encounters and illuminating conversations with the inmates and visitors, who freely expressed their views against the Soviet Government, although they knew me to be very sympathetic to it.

During the first days of my visit I felt that the great demonstration of friendliness was somehow expressive of the enthusiastic spirit of the glad anniversary days, that after the month was ended I could calmly settle down to finish the book about the American Negro that the State Publishing Department of Moscow had commissioned me to write, and in the meantime quietly go about making interesting contacts. But my days in russia were a progression of affectionate enthusiasm of the people towards me. Among the factory workers, the red-starred and chevroned soldiers and sailors, the proletarian students and children, I could not get off as lightly as I did with the intelligentzia. At every meeting I was received with boisterous acclaim, mobbed with friendly demonstration. The women workers of the great bank in Moscow insisted on hearing about the working conditions of the colored women of America and after a brief outline I was asked the most exacting questions concerning the positions that were most available to colored women, their wages and general relationship with the white women workers. The details I could not give; but when I got through, the Russian women passed a resolution sending greetings to the colored women workers of America, exhorting them to organize their forces and send a woman representative to Russia. I received a similar message from the Propaganda Department of the Petrograd Soviet which is managed by

Nicoleva, a very energetic woman. There I was shown the new status of the Russian women gained through the revolution of 1917. Capable women can fit themselves for any position; equal pay with men for equal work; full pay during the period of pregnancy and no work for the mother two months before and two months after the confinement. Getting a divorce is comparatively easy and not influenced by money power, detective chicanery and wire pulling. A special department looks into the problems of joint personal property and the guardianship and support of the children. There is no penalty for legal abortion and no legal stigma of illegitimacy attaching to children born out of wedlock.

There were no problems of the submerged lower classes and the suppressed national minorities of the old Russia that could not bear comparison with the grievous position of the millions of Negroes in the United States to-day. Just as Negroes are barred from the American Navy and the higher ranks of the Army, so were the Jews and the sons of the peasantry and proletariat discriminated against in the Russian Empire. It is needless repetition of the obvious to say that Soviet Russia does not tolerate such discriminations, for the actual government of the country is now in the hands of the combined national minorities, the peasantry and the proletariat. By the permission of Leon Trotsky, Commissar-in-chief of the military and naval forces of Soviet Russia, I visited the highest military schools in the Kremlin and environs of Moscow. And there I saw the new material, the sons of the working people in training as cadets by the old officers of the upper classes. For two weeks I was a guest of the Red navy in Petrograd with the same eager proletarian youth of new Russia, who conducted me through the intricate machinery of submarines, took me over aeroplanes captured from the British during the counter-revolutionary war around Petrograd and showed me the making of a warship ready for action. And even of greater interest was the life of the men and the officers, the simplified discipline that was strictly enforced, the food that was served for each and all alike, the extra political educational classes and the extreme tactfulness and elasticity of the political commissars, all communists, who act as advisers and arbitrators between the men and students and the officers. Twice or thrice I was given some of the *kasha* which is sometimes served with the meals. In Moscow I grew to like this food very much, but it was always difficult to get. I had always imagined that it was quite unwholesome and unpalatable and eaten by the Russian peasant only on account of extreme poverty. But on the contrary I found it very rare and sustaining when cooked right with a bit of meat and served with butter—a grain food very much like the common but very delicious West Indian rice-and-peas.

The red cadets are seen in the best light at their gymnasium exercises and at the political assemblies when discipline is set aside. Especially at the latter where a visitor feels that he is in the midst of the early revolutionary days, so hortatory are the speeches, so intense the enthusiasm of the men. At all these meetings I had to speak and the students asked me general questions about the Negro in the American Army and Navy, and when I gave them the common information known to all American Negroes, students, officers and commissars were unanimous in wishing that a group of young American Negroes would take up training to become officers in the Army and Navy of Soviet Russia.

The proletarian students of Moscow were eager to learn of the life and work of Negro students. They sent messages of encouragement and good will to the Negro students of America and, with a fine gesture of fellowship, elected the Negro delegate of the American Communist party and myself to honorary membership in the Moscow Soviet. . . .

Russia is prepared and waiting to receive couriers and heralds of good will and interracial understanding from the Negro race. Her demonstration of friendliness and equality for Negroes may not conduce to promote healthy relations between Soviet Russia and democratic America, the anthropologists of 100 per cent pure white Americanism may soon invoke Science to prove that the Russians are not at all God's white people. I even caught a little of American anti-Negro propaganda in Russia. A friend of mine, a member of the Moscow intelligentzia repeated to me the remarks of the lady correspondent of a Danish newspaper: that I should not be taken as a representative Negro for she had lived in America and found all Negroes lazy, bad and vicious, a terror to white women. In Petrograd I got a like story from Chukovsky, the critic, who was on intimate terms with a high worker of the American Relief Administration and his southern wife. Chukovsky is himself an intellectual "westerner," the term applied to those Russians who put Western-European civilization before Russian culture and believe that Russia's salvation lies in becoming completely western-ized. He had spent an impressionable part of his youth in London and adores all things English, and during the world war was very pro-English. For the American democracy, also, he expresses unfeigned admiration. He has more Anglo-American books than Russian in his fine library and considers the literary section of the New York *Times* a journal of a very high standard. He is really a maniac of Anglo-Saxon American culture. Chukovsky was quite incredulous when I gave him the facts of the Negro's status in American civilization.

"The Americans are a people of such great energy and ability," he said, "how could they act so petty towards a racial minority?" And then he related an experience of his in London that bore a strong smell of *cracker* breath. However, I record it here in the belief that it is authentic for Chukovsky is a man of integrity: About the beginning of the century, he was sent to England as correspondent of a newspaper in Odessa, but in London he was more given to poetic dreaming and studying English literature in the British Museum and rarely sent any news home. So he lost his job and had to find cheap, furnished rooms. A few weeks later, after he had taken up his residence in new quarters, a black guest arrived, an American gentleman of the cloth. The preacher procured a room on the top floor and used the dining and sitting room with the other guests, among whom was a white American family. The latter protested the presence of the Negro in the house and especially in the guest room. The landlady was in a dilemma, she could not lose her American boarders and the clergyman's money was not to be despised. At last she compromised by getting the white Americans to agree to the Negro's staying without being allowed the privilege of the guest room, and Chukovsky was asked to tell the Negro the truth. Chukovsky strode upstairs to give the unpleasant facts to the preacher and to offer a little consolation, but the black man was not unduly offended:

"The white guests have the right to object to me," he explained, anticipating Garvey, "they belong to a superior race."

"But," said Chukovsky, "I do not object to you, I don't feel any difference; we don't understand color prejudice in Russia."

"Well," philosophized the preacher, "you are very kind, but taking the scriptures as authority, I don't consider the Russians to be white people."

LANGSTON HUGHES

Poet, playwright, novelist, autobiographer, and essayist Langston Hughes is one of the most well known and beloved African-American writers. Born in 1902 in Joplin, Missouri, Hughes began his worldly wanderings as a young man. Throughout his life he wrote about his travel adventures from places such as France, the west coast of Africa, and Central America. Hughes served as a correspondent for black newspapers during the Spanish Civil War and traveled extensively throughout the Soviet Union and Asia. The excerpts here are taken from his trip to the Soviet Union in 1933. Having first gone with a group of young African Americans who were supposed to make a film, Hughes remained in the Soviet Union after the film project fell through. During that time he traveled throughout the vast nation, discovering and writing about the diversity of the Soviet people. Hughes met Soviet writers (including Maxim Gorky), attended conferences, and visited trade union sessions, factories, and schools. Hughes also helped translate the work of Russian poets. This dispatch appeared in *The Crisis*.

"GOING SOUTH IN RUSSIA" (1934)
f r o m
THE CRISIS

To an American Negro living in the northern part of the United States the word *South* has an unpleasant sound, an overtone of horror and of fear. For it is in the South that our ancestors were slaves for three hundred years, bought and sold like cattle. It is in the South today that we suffer the worst forms of racial persecution and economic exploitation — segregation, peonage, and lynching. It is in the Southern states that the color line is hard and fast, Jim Crow rules, and I am treated like a dog. Yet it is in the South that two-thirds of my people live: a great Black Belt stretching from Virginia to Texas, across the cotton plantations to Georgia and Alabama and Mississippi, down into the orange groves of Florida and the sugar cane lands of Louisiana. It is in the South that black hands create the wealth that supports the great cities—Atlanta, Memphis, New Orleans, where the rich whites live in fine houses on magnolia-shaded streets and the Negroes live in slums restricted by law. It is in the South that what the Americans call the "race problem" rears its ugly head the highest and, like a snake with its eyes on a bird, holds the whole land in its power. It is in the South that hate and terror walk the streets and roads by day, sometimes quiet, sometimes violent, and sleep in the beds with the citizens at night.

Two springs ago I came almost directly out of this American South to the Soviet Union. You can imagine the contrast. No need for me to write about it. And after a summer in Moscow, I found myself packing up to go South again—but, this time, South under the red flag. I was starting out from Moscow, capital of the new world, bound for Central Asia to discover how the yellow and brown peoples live and work there. I wanted to compare their existence with that of the colored and oppressed peoples I had known under capitalism in Cuba, Haiti, Mexico, and my own United States. I wanted to study the life of these dark people in the Soviet Union, and write a book about them for the dark races of the capitalist world.

On the train I had a lot of time to think. I thought how in the thirty years of my life I had seldom gotten on a train in America without being conscious of my color. In the South, there are Jim Crow cars and Negroes must ride separate from the whites, usually in a filthy antiquated coach next to the engine, getting all the smoke and bumps and dirt. In the South, we cannot buy sleeping car tickets. Such comforts are only for white folks. And in the North where segregated travel is not the law, colored people have, nevertheless, many difficulties. In auto buses they must take the seats in the rear, over the wheels. On the boats they must occupy the worst cabins. The ticket agents always say that all other accommodations are sold. On trains, if one sits down by a white person, the white person will sometimes get up, flinging back an insult at the Negro who has dared to take a seat beside him. Thus it is that in America, if you are yellow, brown, or black, you can never travel anywhere without being reminded of your color, and oft-times suffering great inconveniences.

I sat in the comfortable sleeping car on my first day out of Moscow and remembered many things about trips I had taken in America. I remembered how, once as a youngster going alone to see my father who was working in Mexico, I went into the dining car of the train to eat. I sat down at a table with a white man. The man looked at me and said, "You're a nigger, ain't you?" and left the table. It was beneath his dignity to eat with a Negro child. At St. Louis I went onto the station platform to buy a glass of milk. The clerk behind the counter said, "We don't serve niggers," and refused to sell me anything. As I grew older I learned to expect this often when traveling. So when I went South to lecture on my poetry at Negro universities, I carried my own food because I knew I could not go into the dining cars. Once from Washington to New Orleans, I lived all the way in the train on cold food. I remembered this miserable trip as I sat eating a hot dinner on the diner of the Moscow-Tashkent express.

Traveling South from New York, at Washington, the capital of our country, the official Jim Crow begins. There the conductor comes through the train and, if you are a Negro, touches you on the shoulder and says, "The last coach forward is the car for colored people." Then you must move your baggage and yourself up near the engine, because when the train crosses the Potomac River into Virginia, and the dome of the Capitol disappears, it is illegal any longer for white people and colored people to ride together. (Or to eat together, or sleep together, or in some places even to work together.) Now I am riding South from Moscow and am not Jim-Crowed, and none of the darker people on the train with me are Jim-Crowed, so I make a happy mental note in the back of my mind to write home to the Negro papers: "There is no Jim Crow on the trains of the Soviet Union."

In the car ahead of mine there is a man almost as brown as I am. A young man dressed quite ordinarily in a pair of tan trousers and a nondescript grey coat. Some Asiatic factory worker who has been to Moscow on a vacation, I think. We talk a little. He asks me what I do for a living, and I ask him what he does. I am a writer. He is the mayor of Bokhara, the Chairman of the City Soviet! I make a note in the back of my mind: "In the Soviet Union dark men are also the mayors of cities," for here is a man who is the head of a very famous city, old Bokhara, romantic Bokhara known in stories and legends the world over.

In the course of our conversation, I learned that there were many cities in Central Asia where dark men and women are in control of the government. And I thought about Mississippi where more than half of the population is Negro, but one never hears of a colored person in the government.

In fact, in that state Negroes cannot even vote. And you will never meet them riding in the sleeping car.

Here, there were twelve of us going South from Moscow, for I was traveling with a Negro group from Mezhrabpom Film on a tour of the Soviet Union.

Kurbanov, for that was the name of the young Uzbek from the Bokhara Soviet, came often to talk to us. He was a mine of information about the liberation of Central Asia and the vast changes that have come about there after the Revolution. Truly a land of Before and After. Before the Revolution, emirs and khans, mullahs and beys. After the Revolution, the workers in power. Before, one-half of one per cent of the people illiterate. Now, fifty per cent read and write. Before, education solely for the rich, mostly in religious schools; and no schools in the villages. Now, free schools everywhere. Before, the land was robbed of its raw materials for the factories of the Russian capitalists. Now, there are big plants, electric stations, and textile mills in Asia. Before, no theatres, no movies, no modern culture. Now, national art encouraged and developed everywhere. Before, Kurbanov said, the natives were treated like dogs. Now, that is finished, and Russian and native, Jew and gentile, white and brown, live and work together. Before, no intermarriages of white and brown, now there are many. Before, Kurbanov himself was a herd-boy in the mountains. Now, he is the Chairman of a city soviet, the mayor of a large and ancient city. Truly, Soviet Asia is a land of Before and After, and the Revolution is creating a new life that is changing the history of the East.

We gathered these things not only from our Uzbek comrade, but from many other passengers we met on the long train during the five days and nights southeast to Central Asia. There was a woman librarian from Leningrad, who had been home on a vacation going back to the work of which she spoke with pride—the growth of the library at Tashkent, the large number of books in the native languages with the new Latin alphabet that were now being published, and the corresponding growth of native readers. There was a young Red Army man who told us of the camaraderie and understanding growing up between lads of widely different environmental backgrounds in the Red Army School at Tashkent. There was a Russian merchant privileged to help in the building of new industries in an ancient and once backward, but now awakening Asia. And there were two young Komsomol poets going from Moscow to work on publications for the encouragement of national literature in the young writers of Soviet Asia.

One night, we held a meeting with the members of the train crew not then on duty. Our Negro group and the workers of the express exchanged information and ideas. They told us about their work and their part in the building of socialism. We told them about the conditions of Negro labor in America, about the crisis abroad, about Al Capone and the Chicago bandits, and the bootleggers and bankers of Broadway. We found that they knew, as their comments and questions indicated, a great deal more about America than the average American knows about the Soviet Union. And we learned that their working conditions are superior to those of American railway workers—particularly in regard to the train porters. Here, in each coach, there is a compartment with berths where the crew might rest. The Negro porters on American trains have no such conveniences. Here, on the sleeping cars, there are two attendants. In the U.S.A. a single man takes care of a car, working throughout a long trip, and perhaps managing to catch a little sleep on the bench in the men's toilet. Our porters depend on tips for a living, their wages being extremely low. These things we told the crew of the Moscow-Tashkent express and they, in turn, sent back through us their greetings to the Negro railway workers of America.

So, with our many new and interesting comrades of the train, the days on the road passed quickly. First, the rich farm lands slid by outside our windows; stations where peasant women from the kolkhozes sold chickens and cheese and eggs; then the Volga at sunset, famous old river of song and story; a day or so later, Orenburg where Asia begins and camels are in the streets; then the vast reaches of the Kirghiz steppes and the bright tip of the Aral Sea like silver in the sun.

On the day when we passed through the Kazakstan desert, the Fortieth Anniversary of Gorky's literary life was being celebrated throughout the Union. The Komsomol poets and the crew of our train organized a meeting, too. At a little station where the train stopped in the late afternoon, we all went on to the platform and short speeches were made in honor of Gorky and his tremendous work. (Even in the heart of the desert, this writer whose words throb with the lives of the common people, was not forgotten.) Nomad Kazaks, the men in great coats of skins, the women in white headdresses, gathered around, mingling with the passengers. One of the young poets spoke; then a representative of the train crew; and someone from the station. My speech in English was translated into Russian, and again into the Kazak tongue. Then the meeting closed. We sent a telegram to Comrade Gorky from the passengers of the train, and another from our Negro group. And as the whistle blew, we climbed back into our coaches, and the engine steamed on through the desert pulling the long train deeper into Asia. It was sunset, and there was a great vastness of sky over sand before the first stars came.

Late the following afternoon, we saw a fertile oasis of water and greenery, cotton growing and trees in fruit, then crowds of yellow faces and bright robes at the now frequent stations. At evening we came to the big city of Tashkent, the great center of the Soviet East. There we were met by a workers' delegation including brown Asiatics, fair-skinned Russians, and an American Negro engineer, Bernard Powers, from Howard University, now helping to build roads across Asia.

Audre Lorde

Poet, essayist, activist, and autobiographer Audre Lorde was born in New York City in 1934. Traveling frequently as part of political delegations, Lorde wrote of these experiences as a means of making connections between progressive political struggles around the world.

The selection here is taken from travel journals published in *Sister Outsider*, based on a two-week trip to Russia in 1976 as an American observer to the African-Asian Writers Conference. It was sponsored by the Union of Soviet Writers. Like Hughes, Lorde also traveled through the southern part of the country. Although her observations about the country and the people are less romantic than the previous selections, she notes that their distance toward her is simply part of the national character and not racism. However, the Russian intellectuals she meets are condescending and patronizing toward their invited guest. Lorde also notes the Soviet silence around homosexuality and Russian Jews. Finally, she questions the sincerity of Soviet support for the social and political struggles of African Americans.

"Notes from a Trip to Russia"
from
Sister Outsider:
Essays and Speeches (1984)

The flight to Moscow was nine hours long, and from my observations on the plane, Russians are generally as unfriendly to each other as Americans are and just about as unhelpful.

There was a marvelously craggy-faced old blue-eyed woman in her seventies wearing a babushka, with a huge coat roll. On the plane everyone had one kind of huge coat roll or another except me. When I stepped out into the Moscow weather I realized why. But this woman was sitting in the seat right in front of me. She was traveling alone and was too short to wield her roll easily. She tried once, and she tried twice, and finally I got up and helped her. The plane was packed: I'd never seen a plane quite so crowded before. The old woman turned around and looked at me. It was obvious she did not speak English because I had muttered something to her with no reply. There was in her eyes a look of absolutely no rancor. I thought with a quick shock how a certain tension in glances between American Black and white people is taken for granted. There was no thank you either, but there was a certain kind of simple human response to who I was. And then as she turned to sit back down, under her very dowdy cardigan I saw on her undersweater at least three military-type medals complete with chevrons. Hero of the Republic medals, I learned later. Earned for hard work.

This is something that I noticed all over: the very old people in Russia have a stamp upon them that I hope I can learn and never lose, a matter-of-fact resilience and sense of their place upon the earth that is very sturdy and reassuring. . . .

My tourist guide's name was Helen, a very pleasant and attractive large-boned young woman in her thirties. She was born in the East, near Japan, and her father, who'd been a military man, was dead. She lived with her mother now, and she said that she and her mother had to learn to do a lot of things for themselves since there are so few men around these days and service is so hard to get by. . . .

We would pass from time to time incredibly beautiful, old, uncared for Russian-Orthodox-style houses, with gorgeous painted wooden colors and outlined ornate windows. Some of them were almost falling down. But there was a large ornate richness about the landscape and architecture on the outskirts of Moscow, even in its grey winter, that seemed to tell me immediately that I was not at home. . . .

Before dinner I took a short walk. It was already growing dark, but down the street from the hotel was the Stadium stop on the Metro, which is a subway. I walked down there and into the Metro station and I stood in front of the escalators for awhile just watching the faces of the people coming and going. It felt like instant 14th Street of my childhood, before Blacks and Latins colored New York, except everyone was much more orderly and the whole place seemed much less crowded. The thing that was really strangest of all for the ten minutes that I stood there was that there were no Black people. And the token collector and the station manager were women. The station was very large and very beautiful and very clean—shockingly, strikingly, enjoyably clean. The whole station looked like a theater lobby—bright brass and mosaics and shining chandeliers. Even when they were rushing, and in Moscow there's always a kind of rush, people lack the desperation of New York. One thing that characterized all of these people was a pleasantness in their faces, a willingness to smile, at least at me, a stranger. It was a strange contrast to the grimness of the weather. . . .

I was interviewed by Oleg this evening, one of the officials of the Union of Soviet Writers, the people who had invited me to Russia and who were footing the bill. In my interview with him I learned the hotel that we're staying in was originally a youth hostel and Oleg apologized because it was not as "civilized," so he said, as other Moscow hotels. I came across this term civilized before, and I wondered whether it was a term used around Americans or whether it meant up to American standards. Increasingly I get a feeling that American standards are sort of an unspoken norm, and that whether one resists them, or whether one adopts them, they are there to be reckoned with. This is rather disappointing. But coming back to the hotel, I notice that the fixtures here are a little shabby, but they do work, and the studio beds are a bit adolescent in size, but they are comfortable. For a youth hostel it's better than I would ever hope for. Of course, I can't help but wonder why the African-Asian Conference people should be housed in a youth hostel, particularly an "uncivilized" one, but I don't imagine that I'll ever get an answer to that. All hotel rooms cost the same in the Soviet Union. . . .

Oleg does not speak English, or does not converse in English. Like many other people I was to meet during my stay in Russia, he understands English although he does not let on. Oleg said through Helen that he wants me to know it was very important for us to meet other writers and that the point of the Conference was for us to get together. I thanked him for the twenty-five rubles I had been given as soon as I arrived here in Moscow, which I have been told was a gift from the Union of Soviet Writers for pocket money. I spoke of the oppressed people all over the world, meeting to touch and to share, I spoke of South Africa and their struggle. Oleg said something very curious. "Yes, South Africa is really very bad. It is like a sore upon the body that will not heal." This sounded to me both removed and proprietary. Unclear. Willy, my south African poet friend, lives in Tanzania now and he may be here, which I am very excited about. . . .

We traveled south to Uzbekistan for the Conference, a five hour journey that became seven because of delays. . . .

As we descended the plane in Tashkent, it was deliciously hot and smelled like Accra, Ghana. At least it seemed to me that it did, from the short ride from the airport to the hotel. The road to the city had lots of wood and white marble all around broad avenues, and bright street lights. . . . We arrived tired and hot, to a welcome that would make your heart grow still, then sing. Can you imagine 250 of us, weary, cramped, hungry, disoriented, overtalked, underfed? It is after dark. We step out of the plane and there before us are over a hundred people and TV cameras, and lights and two to three hundred little children dressed in costumes with bunches of flowers that they thrust upon each of us as we walked down the ramp from the plane. "Surprise!" Well, you know, it was a surprise. Pure and simple and I was pretty damn well surprised. I was surprised at the gesture, hokey or not, at the mass participation in it. Most of all, I was surprised at my response to it; I felt genuinely welcomed.

So off to the hotel we went and I had the distinct feeling here, for the first time in Russia, that I was meeting warm-blooded people; in the sense of contact unavoided, desires and emotions possible, the sense that there is something hauntingly, personally familiar—not in the way the town looks because it looked like nothing I'd ever seen before, night and the minarets—but the tempo of life felt hotter, quicker than in Moscow; and in place of Moscow's determined pleasantness, the people displayed a kind of warmth that was very engaging. They are an Asian people in Tashkent, Usbeki. They look like the descendants of Ghengis Khan, some of whom I'm sure they are. They are Asian and they are Russian. They think and speak and consider themselves Russian, for all intents and purposes so far as I can see, and I really wonder how they manage that. On the other hand, the longer I stayed the more I realized some of the personal tensions between North Russian and Uzbek are national and some racial.

There are only four sisters in this whole conference. In the plane coming to Tashkent, I sat with the three other African women and we exchanged chitchat for 5½ hours about our respective children, about our ex-old men, all very, very heterocetera. . . .

Tashkent is divided into two parts. There's the old part that survived the huge earthquake of 1966, and there's the newer part which is on the outskirts of old Tashkent. It's very new and very modern, rebuilt in a very short time. . . . The old part, which is really the center of Tashkent, looks very, very much like a town in Ghana or Dahomey, say Kumasi or Cotonou. In the daylight it looks so much like some parts of West Africa that I could scarcely believe it. . . . If Moscow is New York, Tashkent is Accra. It is African in so many ways—the stalls, the mix of the old and the new, the corrugated tin roofs on top of adobe houses. The corn smell in the plaza, although the plazas were more modern than in West Africa. Even some flowers and trees, Calla lilies. But the red laterite smell of the earth was different.

The people here in Tashkent, which is close to the Iranian border, are very diverse, and I am impressed by their apparent unity, but the ways in which the Russian and the Asian people seem to be able to function in a multinational atmosphere that requires of them that they get along, whether or not they are each other's favorite people. And it's not that there are no individuals who are nationalists, or racists, but that the taking of a state position against nationalism, against racism is what makes it possible for a society like this to function. And of course the next step in that process must be the personal element. I don't see anyone attempting or even suggesting this phase, however, and that is troublesome, for without this step socialism remains at the mercy of an incomplete vision, imposed from the outside. We have internal desires but outside controls. But at least there is a climate here that seems to encourage those questions. I asked Helen about the Jews, and she was rather evasive. I think, saying only that there were Jews in government. The basic position seems to be one of a presumption of equality, even though there is sometimes a large gap between the expectation and the reality. . . .

When Fikre, an Ethiopian student at Patrice Lumumba University and I went shopping in the market [a] Moslem woman . . . came up to me in the marketplace, and she brought her little boy up to me asking Fikre if I had a little boy also. She said that she had never seen a Black woman before, that she had seen Black men, but she had never seen a Black woman, and that she so much liked the way I looked that she just wanted to bring her little boy and find out if I had a little boy too. Then we blessed each other and spoke good words and then she passed on. . . .

We went later that afternoon to another meeting of solidarity for the oppressed people of Somewhere. The only thing that I was quite sure of was that it was not for the oppressed Black people of America, which point, of course, I had questioned a number of days before and was still awaiting a reply. So we stood in the hot sun at the porcelain factory and it baked my brains and I thought about a lot of things. The peoples of the Soviet Union, in many respects, impress me as people who can not yet afford to be honest. When they can be they will either blossom into a marvel or sink into decay. What gets me about the United States is that it pretends to be honest and therefore has so little room to move towards hope. I think that in America there are certain kinds of problems and in Russia there are certain kinds of problems, but basically, when you find people who start from a position where human beings are at the core, as opposed to a position where profit is at the core, the solutions can be very different. I wonder how similar human beings are at the core here, either, although there is more lip service done to that idea than in the U.S. . . .

The last few days after we returned to Moscow I got to meet one woman I had noticed all through the Conference. She was an Eskimo woman. Her name was Toni and she's Chukwo. They are from the part of Russia closest to Alaska, the part that wasn't sold by the Russians, across the Bering Straits. Toni did not speak English and I didn't speak Russian, but I felt as if we were making love that night through our interpreters. I still don't know if she knew what was going on or not, but I suspect that she did.

I had been extremely moved by her presentation earlier in the day. We sat down to dinner, about ten of us, and Toni starting speaking to me through our interpreters. She said that she had been searching for my eyes in the crowd all through her speech because she felt as if she were talking to my heart. And that when she sang the little songs that she did, she sang it for a beginning that she hoped for all of our people. And this lady cast, let me tell you, a very powerful spell. There are only fourteen thousand Chukwo people left. In her speech at one point she said, "It is a very sad thing when a whole people ceases to exist." And then she sang a little song which she said her people sing whenever something new happens. Her dark round eyes and seal-heavy hair flashed and swung in time to her music. It sent a chill down my spine at the time, because although there are 21 million Black Americans, I feel like we're an endangered species too, and how sad for our cultures to die. I felt as if we alone, of all the people at the Conference, shared that knowledge and that threat, Toni and I. At dinner Toni kept telling me how beautiful I was, and how it was not only my beauty that she would carry with her always but my words, and that we should share our joys as well as our sorrows, and someday our children would be able to speak freely with each other. She made a toast after toast to women and to their strength. All of this was through our interpreters. I was trying to decide what to make of this when Toni got up, moved over, and sat down beside me. She touched my knee and kissed me, and so we sat all through dinner. We held hands and we kissed, but any time we spoke to each other, it was done through our interpreters, blond Russian girls who smirked as they translated our words, I suppose Toni and I connected somewhere in the middle of the Aleutians.

She kissed my picture on my book before she got up, thanked us for dinner, and went off with the male Latvian delegate from Riga.

HARRY HAYWOOD

Communist activist and theorist Harry Haywood was born in South Omaha, Nebraska, in 1898. After serving in France during World War I, Haywood was recruited into the African Blood Brotherhood (a secret Black Nationalist organization) and the Young Workers League. Both organizations were affiliated with the Communist Party of the United States (CPUSA). Throughout his life Haywood sought to reconcile Marxism-Lenism with black nationalism. In 1926 he traveled to the Soviet Union as a student. He remained there until 1930, during which time he theorized and advocated the National Revolutionary Movement for Self-Determination and an autonomous republic for black people in the Black Belt. By 1930 this became the official position of the party. In 1931 he was chosen to head the Communist Party's Negro Department. From this post he organized the Scottsboro campaign. Haywood was appointed to the politburo of the CPUSA. In 1937 he fought in the Lincoln Brigade of the Spanish Civil War and then joined the Merchant Marines during World War II to organize the Communist National Maritime Union. After the party dropped its advocacy of an autonomous black republic in 1944, Haywood became more involved in black nationalist efforts, especially in Chicago, where he influenced a younger generation of black activists, most notably Amiri Baraka and Kwame Toure. He died there in 1985. The selection here describes his days as a student in Moscow.

f r o m
Black Bolshevik (1978)

Needless to say, Blacks attracted the curiosity of the Muscovites. Children followed us in the streets. If we paused to greet a friend, we found ourselves instantly surrounded by curious crowds—unabashedly staring at us. Once, while strolling down Tverskaya, Otto and I stopped to greet a white American friend and immediately found ourselves surrounded by curious Russians. It was a friendly curiosity which we took in stride. A young Russian woman stepped forward and began to upbraid and lecture the crowd.

"Why are you staring at these people? They're human beings the same as us. Do you want them to think that we're savages? Eta ne kulturnya! (That is uncultured!)" The last was an epithet and in those days a high insult.

"Eta ne po-Sovietski! (It's not the Soviet way!)" she scolded them.

At that point, someone in the crowd calmly responded: "Well, citizens, it's a free country, isn't it?"

We were not offended, but amused. We understood all this for what it was.

There was one occasion when Otto, Farmer, Bankole and I were walking down Tverskaya. Bankole, of course, stood out—attracting more attention than the rest of us with his English cut Savil-Row suit, monocle and cane—a black edition of a British aristocrat. We found ourselves being followed by a group of Russian children, who shouted: "Jass Band . . . Jass Band!"

Otto, Farmer and I were amused at the incident and took it in stride. Bankole, however, shaking with rage at the implication jerked around to confront them. His monocle fell off as he shouted: "Net Jass Band! Net Jass Band!" As he spoke, he hit his cane on the ground for emphasis.

Evidently, to these kids, a jazz band was not just a group of musicians, but a race or tribe of people to which we must belong. They obviously thought we were with Leland and Drayton, the musicians I had met in Berlin. They had been a big hit with the Muscovites. We pulled Bankole away, "C'mon man, cut it out. They don't mean anything."

In the Soviet Union, remnants of national and racial prejudices from the old society were attacked by education and law. It was a crime to give or receive direct or indirect privileges, or to exercise discrimination because of race or nationality. Any manifestation of racial or national superiority was punishable by law and was regarded as a serious political offense, a social crime.

During my entire stay in the Soviet Union, I encountered only one incident of racial hostility. It was on a Moscow streetcar. Several of us Black students had boarded the car on our way to spend an evening with our friend MacCloud. It was after rush hour and the car was only about half filled with Russian passengers. As usual, we were the objects of friendly curiosity. At one stop, a drunken Russian staggered aboard. Seeing us, he muttered (but loud enough for the whole car to hear) something about "Black devils in our country."

A group of outraged Russian passengers thereupon seized him and ordered the motorman to stop the car. It was a citizen's arrest, the first I had ever witnessed. "How dare you, you scum, insult people who are the guests of our country!?"

What then occurred was an impromptu, on-the-spot meeting, where they debated what to do with the man. I was to see many of this kind of "meeting" during my stay in Russia.

It was decided to take the culprit to the police station which, the conductor informed them, was a few blocks ahead. Upon arrival there, they hustled the drunk out of the car and insisted that we Blacks, as the injured parties, come along to make the charges.

At first we demurred, saying that the man was obviously drunk and not responsible for his remarks. "No, citizens," said a young man (who had done most of the talking), "drunk or not, we don't allow this sort of thing in our country. You must come with us to the militia (police) station and prefer charges against this man."

The car stopped in front of the station. The poor drunk was hustled off and all the passengers came along. The defendant had sobered up somewhat by this time and began apologizing before we had even entered the building. We got to the commandant of the station.

The drunk swore that he didn't mean what he'd said, "I was drunk and angry about something else. I swear to you citizens that I have no race prejudice against those Black gospoda (gentle men)."

We actually felt sorry for the poor fellow and we accepted his apology. We didn't want to press the matter. "No" said the commandant, "we'll keep him overnight. Perhaps this will be a lesson to him." . . .

AndREA LEE

Andrea Lee was born in Philadelphia in 1953 and graduated from Harvard/Radcliffe Colleges in the early 1970s. The excerpt here is taken from her first book, *Russian Journals*, published in 1981. The book traces Lee's travels through Russia from 1978 to 1979 with her husband, a graduate student in Russian history. The book received a National Book Award nomination. Lee is also the author of the novel *Sarah Phillips*, published in 1984.

f r o m
RUSSIAN JOURNALS (1981)

The tower in which we will live for most of the next ten months is one of the landmarks of Moscow, an absurd thirty-two-story wedding cake of gray and red granite, set above the city in the Lenin Hills. This titanic building, the main dormitory of Moscow State University, is a monument of the pompous and energetic style of architecture nicknamed "Stalin Gothic." Seen from a distance, it suggests a Disney version of a ziggurat; its central spire, like the Kremlin towers, holds a blinking red star. Inside, as in a medieval fortress, there is everything necessary to sustain life in case of siege: bakeries, dairy store, a fruit and vegetable store, a pharmacy, a post office, magazine kiosks, a watch-repair stand—all this in addition to classrooms, and student rooms, and cafeterias. On the outside, it bristles with a daft excess of decoration that is a strange twentieth-century mixture of Babylonian, Corinthian, and Slavic: there are outsized bronze flags and statues, fadence curlicues, wrought-iron sconces—even a vast reflecting pool decorated with metal water lilies the size of small cabbages. As I climb the endless stairs and negotiate the labyrinth of mustysmelling hallways, I feel dwarfed and apprehensive, a human being lost in a palace scaled for giants.

I came to this odd new home with my husband on a summer evening two days ago, when exhaustion from long-distance travel gave every new sight the mysterious simplicity and resonance of a dream. I had my first glimpse of the Soviet Union as we broke through a cloud barrier near Sheremetyevo Airport, and found ourselves flying low over a forest of birch and evergreen, dotted with countless small ponds. There was an almost magical lushness and secrecy about this flattish northern landscape that I found powerfully attractive; suddenly I remembered that my earliest visions of Russia were of an infinite forest, dark as any forest that stretches through a child's imagination, and peopled by swan maidens, hunter princes, fabulous bears, and witches who lived in huts set on chicken legs. Tied to Russia by no claims of blood or tradition, I still felt, while very young, an obscure attraction to this country that I knew only from its violent, highly colored folklore; its music, through which ran a similar vein of extravagance; and the dark political comments of adults. It seemed to me to be a mysterious counterweight to the known world of America—a country, like the land at the back of the north wind, in which life ran backward and the fantastic was commonplace.

Our disembarkment and passage through customs at Sheremetyevo were standard chaos, involving a long, dazed wait in a crowded room traversed from time to time by hot breezes smelling sweetly of cut grass. Only one memory remains with me from those hours: the sight of a Pioneer excursion group of twenty small girls who seemed, by their Asiatic faces and straight black hair, to be Siberian. They all wore the blue shorts, white shirts, and red neckerchiefs that I had seen in pictures, as well as ornately curled hair bows that gave them a queer geisha look, and as I studied them with the dreamy precision of fatigue, all twenty stared back at me with an avid, unadorned curiosity. Standing beyond the customs barrier was a young man who introduced himself in English as Grigorii, a journalism student sent to meet us by the university's office of foreign affairs. Grigorii was a dark-haired young man in his twenties, with very small eyes behind enormous round glasses and a pinched, rather gnomish body in a large, baggy suit; the impression he gave was that he had melted down slightly inside his clothing. He led us outside to a black Volga, a Soviet car that looks like a cross between a Rambler and a Plymouth. A shortlegged driver, wearing a checked cap pulled down very far over his ears, stowed our bags, and soon we were speeding down a road with the vaguely horrifying sense of freedom one feels only when going through absolutely strange territory in a strange car. It was dark by now, and the smell of fields and forest rushed in through the windows. Grigorii had discovered that we both spoke Russian, and had grown garrulous. "So you are a student of Russian history?" he was saying to Tom. "I myself am extremely interested in American history—especially in your Civil War. Two years ago I even wrote a paper on the Great Barbecue."

"The what?" asked Tom.

"The Great Barbecue—the turning point of the Reconstruction period. Don't tell me you haven't heard of it!" (Grigorii pronounced the word "barbecue" with the gleeful relish of a Frenchman saying "Marlboro.")

"I haven't," said Tom, and as the car slid through the darkness Grigorii illuminated for us this lost part of American history, mentioning feudal remnants, the industrial bourgeoisie, and the struggle of the working class. Listening to his small, dry, pedantic voice mention names and places I'd never heard of, I wondered what Marxist looking-glass we'd stepped through. Where on earth were we? Was he talking about the same America we had just left?

When the monstrous silhouette of the university tower appeared on the skyline, Grigorii paused to point it out proudly. "Impressive, isn't it?" he said. "It's the most luxurious dormitory in the Soviet Union—every year hundreds of tourists come to visit it. It's a city block in circumference; some other time I will give you the figures on its height and number of windows. I'm sorry that we won't be passing the reflecting pool tonight, but there is a very handsome giant barometer that I will show you. I feel very lucky to live there. We'll be neighbors, so to speak!"

"Hurrah!" I whispered to Tom, and he dug his elbow into my ribs. Then we sat silently as the black tower grew larger against the sky.

Our arrival meant passing through a gatehouse, climbing a great many stairs, crossing a chilly marble hall, and threading through a maze of corridors on a path that led at last to a long ride in an elevator, and some kind of fuss with an old woman over a key. Although it was only about nine o'clock in the evening, a charmed stillness seemed to reign in the dormitory; we saw very few students. Instead, there seemed to be inordinate numbers of *babushki*—old women—in semi-official posts, knitting and nodding in dark corners like watchful beldames out of a Grimms tale. The *babushka* of the keys, a tiny creature with a fierce squint under a cowled white shawl, watched us struggle with the door to our room and then turned to whisper portentously to a still smaller companion, *"Ischo Amerikantsy"* (More Americans).

When Grigorii left us, we flicked a switch, and in the sudden bright light, faced our living quarters for a year. They were what Russians call a *blok*—a minute suite consisting of two rooms about six feet by ten feet each, a tiny entryway, and a pair of cubicles containing, between them, a toilet, a shower and washstand, and several large, indolent cockroaches. The two main rooms were painted the dispiriting beige and green of institutional rooms around the world, and furnished, rather nicely, with varnished chairs, tables, bookcases, and two single beds. (I've since discovered that our rooms represent great luxury, since Russian students in the same building often live four and six to such quarters.) Each room held a radio that tuned in to only one station—Radio Moscow—and at this particular moment, news was being broadcast by a woman with an excited, throaty voice. "Today," she said, "the Party Government delegation of the Democratic Republic of Vietnam, led by Comrades Le Duan and Pham Van Dong visited the Kirovsky factory in Leningrad. . . . In front of the monument to V. I. Lenin in Factory Square, there took place a meeting of Soviet-Vietnamese friendship. . . . The Leningraders arrived at the meeting with flowers, red flags, and signs in honor of the unbreakable friendship. . . . The people gathering together greeted the emissaries of the heroic Vietnamese people with warm applause . . ." The news went off, and on came a medley of Komsomol songs delivered stalwartly by what sounded like an entire nation of ruddy-cheeked young patriots. "You can't turn this thing off," said Tom, fiddling with the radio knob. Indeed, like one of Orwell's telescreens, our official radios could be turned down to inaudible, but never turned off. I began to giggle hysterically, and to calm myself, walked over to the window, from which I could see, illuminated by a spotlight on one of the pediments of the building, a gigantic bronze flag.

A bit later, in one of the fits of witless energy that sometimes replace exhaustion, we decided to take the metro into Red Square. Everyone describes the Moscow subway system, so I won't, except to say that it is as clean and efficient as they write, and that it is awesome, for an American, to see the veins of a city lined with marble, gilt, and mosaic instead of filth and graffiti. It was in the subway that night that I first endured the unblinking stare of the Russian populace, a stare already described to me by Tom and by friends who had been in the Soviet Union before. "You will never not be stared at," they told me, advising me to stare back coolly and steadily, especially at the shoes of my tormentors, since the average Soviet shoe is an embarrassment of cracked imitation leather. When we got on at the University metro stop, the scant group of passengers included two minute, humpbacked *babushki*; a pretty fresh-faced girl of eighteen or nineteen, who opened her mouth to yawn and revealed two aluminum teeth; a fat young mother in a minidress and platform shoes, who held a baby tightly swaddled in a ribbon-bound blanket; a group of stylish young men dressed in greasy American jeans and vinyl snap-front jackets. They all looked us up and down with undisguised fascination and whispered comments to their neighbors. Although we were dressed in what we thought was a neutral, inconspicuous fashion, the clothes we had on—cotton pants and shirts—now seemed infinitely newer, crisper, better cut than anything anyone else had on; my sandals, also, seemed to fascinate everyone. So we sat, practically riddled with stares, in the dim light of the rocking subway car, breathing an atmosphere heavy with odors of sharp tobacco, sausage, and perspiring human flesh. Tom drew a deep, happy breath. "It still smells like Russia," he said.

PART III

6

TRUTH SEEKERS:
STATESMEN, SCHOLARS,
AND JOURNALISTS
(FROM 1930 TO THE
CIVIL RIGHTS ERA)

African-American statesmen, scholars, and journalists as diverse as Frederick Douglass, Ida B. Wells-Barnett, and James Weldon Johnson have traveled as representatives or well-known critics of the U.S. government. In this section we include travelers who served in official capacities as diplomats, scholars, journalists, and students of race and class relations in foreign lands and in less official capacities as observers who gain new insight into the land of their birth. Whether they are serving in an official government capacity, as delegates to professional or artistic conferences, or as students or scholars, these twentieth-century voyagers traveled to a world that was very different from that of their predecessors. They left an America in the throes of an emerging civil rights movement and, as is the case with Martin Luther King in India, were heralded as heroes of that movement. Carl Rowan casts a more critical eye on India than does King and in so doing is less likely to suggest that the United States might learn something from this nation.

These selections also demonstrate that in some cases travelers find what they are looking for. This is most evident with Booker T. Washington, who assures readers that blacks in America have it far better than does the European working class. Sue Bailey Thurman's investigations of Mexico lead her to suggest that African Americans strongly consider the land south of the border as a possible tourist site and alternative home. For Angela Davis, as late as the 1960s blacks in America still have it pretty bad; Davis became further radicalized in Europe, and the possibility of change brought on by revolutionary political action in the United States called her back home.

Booker T. Washington

During his lifetime, Booker T. Washington would emerge as one of the most important, complex, and controversial figures in American history. Born a slave in 1856, Washington is best known as the founder of Tuskegee Institute in Alabama. He was also a major political figure in the late nineteenth and early twentieth centuries. In addition to heading Tuskegee Institute, Washington also founded the National Negro Business League and was an early proponent of political accommodation and economic advancement as an ideology of self-help for African Americans.

The selection here is taken from *The Man Farthest Down* (1912), Washington's observations during his travels in Europe. It is believed that the text was actually written by sociologist Robert Park, who worked closely with Washington early in his career. Throughout much of the book Washington compares the conditions of African Americans with those of the emerging white European working class and finds American blacks to be faring better than their European counterparts. Surely this would have appealed to many of the white industrialists from whom he sought support.

"Naples and the Land of the Emigrant" (1912)
from
The Man Farthest Down

I had crossed Europe from north to south before I got my first glimpse of an emigrant bound for America. On the way from Vienna to Naples I stopped at midnight at Rome, and in the interval between trains I spent an hour in wandering about in the soft southern air—such air as I had not found anywhere since I left my home in Alabama.

In returning to the station my curiosity was aroused, as I was passing in the shadow of the building, by what seemed to me a large vacant room near the main entrance to the station. As I attempted to enter this room I stumbled over the figure of a man lying on the stone floor. Looking farther, I saw something like forty or fifty persons, men as well as women, lying on the floor, their faces turned toward the wall, asleep.

The room itself was apparently bare and empty of all furniture. There was neither a bench nor a table, so far as I could see, in any part of the room. It seems that, without any expectation of doing so, I had wandered into the room reserved for emigrants, and came accidentally upon one of the sights I most wanted to see in Italy—namely, a party of emigrants bound for America.

As near as I could learn, these people were, for the most part, peasants, who had come in from the surrounding country, carrying what little property they possessed on their backs or tied up in little bundles in their arms, and were awaiting the arrival of the train that was to take them to the port from which they could take ship for America.

I confess it struck me as rather pathetic that, in this splendid new and modern railway station, in which the foreign traveller and the native Italian of the upper classes were provided with every convenience and luxury, so little thought had been given to the comfort of these humble travellers, who represent the people in Italy who pay proportionately most of the taxes, and who, by their patient industry and thrift, have contributed more than any other class to such progress as Italy has made in recent years.

Later on I had an opportunity to pass through the country from which perhaps the majority of these emigrants had come. I travelled through a long stretch of country where one sees only now and then a lonesome shepherd or a wretched hut with one low room and a cowstall. I also visited some of the little villages which one sees clinging to the barren hilltops, to escape the poisonous mists of the plains below. There I saw the peasants in their homes and learned something of the way in which the lowly people in the rural districts have been neglected and oppressed. After that I was able to understand that it was no special hardship that these emigrants suffered at Rome. Perhaps many of them had never before slept in a place so clean and sanitary as the room the railway provided them.

Early the next morning, as my train was approaching Naples, my attention was attracted by the large number of women I saw at work in the fields. It was not merely the number of women but the heavy wrought-iron hoes, of a crude and primitive manufacture, with which these women worked that aroused my interest. These hoes were much like the heavy tools I had seen the slaves use on the plantations before the Civil War. With these heavy instruments some of the women seemed to be hacking the soil, apparently preparing it for cultivation; others were merely leaning wearily upon their tools, as if they were over-tired with the exertion. This seemed quite possible to me, because the Italian women are slighter and not as robust as the women I had seen at work in the fields in Austria.

I inquired why it was that I saw so many women in the fields in this part of the country, for I had understood that Italian women, as a rule, did not go so frequently into field work as the women do in Austria and Hungary. I learned that it was because so many of the men who formerly did this work had emigrated to America. As a matter of fact, three fourths of the emigration from Italy to America comes from Sicily and the other southern provinces. There are villages in lower Italy which have been practically deserted. There are others in which no one but women and old men are left behind, and the whole population is more than half supported by the earnings of Italian labourers in America. There are cities within twenty miles of Naples which have lost within ten years two thirds of their inhabitants. In fact, there is one little village not far from the city of which it is said that the entire male population is in America.

Ten days later, coming north from Sicily, I passed through the farming country south of Naples, from which large numbers of emigrants go every year to the United States. It is a sad and desolate region. Earthquakes, malaria, antiquated method of farming, and the general neglect of the agricultural population have all contributed to the miseries of the people. The land itself—at least such portion of it as I saw—looks old, wornout, and decrepit; and the general air of desolation is emphasized when, as happened in my case, one comes suddenly, in the midst of the desolate landscape, upon some magnificent and lonely ruin representing the ancient civilization that flourished here two thousand years ago.

Statistics which have been recently collected, after an elaborate investigation by the Italian Government, show that, in a general way, the extent of emigration from southern Italy is in direct ratio to the neglect of the agricultural classes. Where the wages are smallest and the conditions hardest, there emigration has reached the highest mark. In other words, it is precisely from those parts of Italy where there are the greatest poverty, crime, and ignorance that the largest number of emigrants from Italy go out to America, and, I might add, the smallest number return. Of the 511,935 emigrants who come to North and South America from Italy in 1906, 380,615 came from Sicily and the southern provinces.

One of the most interesting experiences I had while in Europe was in observing the number of different classes and races there are in Europe who look down upon, and take a hopeless view of, certain of their neighbours because they regard them as inferior. For example, one of the first things I learned in Italy was that the people in northern Italy look down upon the people of southern Italy as an inferior race. I heard and read many times while I was in Italy stories and anecdotes illustrating the childishness, the superstition, and the ignorance of the peasant people and the lower classes generally in southern Italy. In fact, nothing that I have known or heard about the superstition of the Negro people in America compares with what I heard about the superstition of the Italian peasants. What surprised me more was to learn that statistics gathered by the Italian Government indicate that in southern Italy, contrary to the experience of every other country, the agricultural labourers are physically inferior to every other class of the population. The people in the rural districts are shorter of stature and in a poorer condition generally than they are in the cities.

For all these reasons I was the more anxious to learn for myself what these people were like. I wanted to find out precisely in what this inferiority of the southern Italian consisted, because I knew that these people were very largely descended from the ancient Greeks, who, by reputation at least, were the most gifted people the world has ever known.

The city of Naples offers some advantages for studying the southern population, since it is the port at which the stream of emigration from the small towns and farming districts of the interior reaches the sea. The exportation of labourers to America is one of the chief businesses of that city. It was at Naples, then, that I gained my earliest first-hand acquaintance with the Italians of the south.

I think the thing that impressed me most about Naples was the contrast between the splendour of its natural surroundings, the elegance and solidity of its buildings, and the dirt, disorder, and squalor in which the masses of the people live. It was early morning when I arrived in the city for the first time. The sun, which was just rising over the black mass of Vesuvius, flooded the whole city and the surrounding country with the most enchanting light. In this soft light the gray and white masses of the city buildings, piled against the projecting hillside to the right and stretching away along the curving shores to the left, made a picture which I shall never forget.

Some of this sunshine seemed to have got into the veins of the people, too, for I never saw anywhere so much sparkle and colour, so much life and movement, as I did among the people who throng the narrow streets of Naples. I never heard before so many curious human noises or saw such vivid and expressive gestures. On the other hand, I never saw anywhere before so many beggars, so many barefooted men, so many people waiting at the station and around the streets to pick up a casual job. It seemed to me that there were at least six porters to every passenger who got off the train, and these porters were evidently well organized, for I had the experience of seeing myself and my effects calmly parcelled out among half a dozen of them, every one of whom demanded, of course, a separate fee for his services.

My experience in Europe leads me to conclude that the number of casual labourers, hucksters, vagabonds, and hunters of odd jobs one meets in a city is a pretty good index of the condition of the masses of the people. By this measure I think that I should have been able to say at the outset that there was in Naples a larger class living in the dirt, degradation, and ignorance at the bottom of society than in any other city I visited in Europe. I make this statement even though cities like Catania and Palermo, in Sicily, which are surrounded by an agricultural population just as wretched, are little, if any, better than Naples in this respect.

Very few persons who go to Naples merely as sightseers ever get acquainted, I suspect, with the actual conditions of the people. Most travellers who see Naples are carried away by the glamour of the sunshine, the colour, and the vivacity of the Italian temperament. For that reason they do not see the hard struggle for existence which goes on in the narrow streets of the city, or, if they do, they look upon the shifts and devices to which this light-hearted people are driven in order to live as merely part of the picturesqueness of the southern life and people.

I have been more than once through the slums and poorer quarters of the coloured people of New Orleans, Atlanta, Philadelphia, and New York, and my personal observation convinces me that the coloured population of these cities is in every way many per cent. better off than the corresponding classes in Naples and the other Italian cities I have named. As far as the actual hardships they have to endure or the opportunities open to them, the condition of the Negroes in these cities does not compare, in my opinion, with that of the masses of the Italians in these southern Italian cities.

There is this difference also: the majority of the Negroes in the large cities of the South and North in the United States are from the country. They have been accustomed to range and wander in a country where life was loose and simple, and existence hardly a problem. They have not been accustomed to either the comforts or the hardships of complex city life. In the case of the Italians, life in the crowded, narrow streets, and the unsanitary intimacy and confusion in which men, goats, and cattle here mingle, have become the fixed habit of centuries.

It is not an unusual thing, for instance, to find a cow or a mule living in close proximity, if not in the same room, with the rest of the family, and, in spite of the skill and artistic taste which show themselves everywhere in the construction and decoration of the buildings, the dirt and disorder in which the people live in these buildings are beyond description. Frequently, in passing through the streets of these southern cities, one meets a herd of goats wandering placidly along over the stone pavements, nibbling here and there in the gutters or holding up in front of a house to be milked.

Even where the city government has made the effort to widen and improve the streets, let in air and sunlight, and maintain sanitary conditions, the masses of the people have not yet learned to make use of these conveniences. I recall, in passing along one of these streets, in the centre of the city, which had been recently laid out with broad stone sidewalks and built up with handsome three and four story stone buildings, seeing a man and a cow standing on the sidewalk at the corner of the street. It seemed to me that the natural thing would have been to let the cow stand in the street and not obstruct the sidewalk. But these people evidently look upon the cow as having the same rights as other members of the population. While the man who owned the cow was engaged in milking, a group of women from the neighbouring tenements stood about with their pitchers and gossiped, awaiting their turn at the cow.

This method of distributing milk—namely, by driving the animal to the front door and milking while you wait—has some advantages. It makes it unnecessary to sterilize the milk, and adulteration becomes impracticable. The disadvantage is that, in order to make this method of milk delivery possible, the cow and the goat must become city dwellers and live in the same narrow streets with the rest of the population. Whatever may be true of the goat, however, I am sure that the cow is not naturally adapted to city life, and where, as is true in many instances, whole families are forced to crowd into one or two rooms, the cow-stall is likely to be still more crowded.

Under these conditions I am sure that the average cow is going to be neither healthy nor happy.

For my purposes it is convenient to divide the life of Naples into three classes. There is the life of the main avenues or boulevards, where one sees all that is charming in Neapolitan life. The buildings are handsome, streets are filled with carriages, sidewalks are crowded with handsomely dressed people. Occasionally one sees a barefooted beggar asleep on the marble steps of some public building. Sometimes one sees, as I did, a woman toiling up the long street side by side with a donkey pulling a cart. There are a good many beggars, but even they are cheerful, and they hold out their hands to you with a roguish twinkle in their eyes that somehow charms the pennies out of your pocket.

Then there is the life of the narrower streets, which stretch out in an intricate network all over the older part of the city. Many of these streets contain the homes as well as the workshops of the artisan class. Others are filled with the petty traffic of hucksters and small tradesmen. In one street you may find a long row of pushcarts, with fish and vegetables, or strings of cheap meat dangling from cords, surrounded by a crowd, chaffering and gesticulating—Neapolitan bargain-hunters. In another street you will find, intermingled with the little shops, skilled artisans with their benches pushed half into the street, at work at their various tasks. Here you will see a wood-carver at his open doorway, busily engaged in carving out an elegant bit of furniture, while in the back of the shop his wife is likely to be engaged in getting the midday meal. A little farther along you may meet a goldsmith, a worker in iron or in copper. One is making a piece of jewellery, the other is mending a kettle. In these streets one sees, in fact, all the old handicrafts carried on in much the same manner and apparently with the same skill that they were carried on three hundred years ago.

Finally, there are the narrower, darker, dirtier streets which are not picturesque and into which no ordinary traveller ventures. This seldom-visited region was, however, the one in which I was particularly interested, for I had come to Naples to see the people and to see the worst.

In the neighbourhood of the hotel where I stayed there was a narrow, winding street which led by a stone staircase from the main thoroughfare up the projecting hillside to one of those dark and obscure alleyways for which Naples, in spite of the improvements which have been made in recent years, is still noted. Near the foot of the stairs there was a bakery, and not far away was the office of the State Lottery. The little street to which I refer is chiefly inhabited by fishermen and casual labourers, who belong to the poorest class of the city. They are the patrons also of the lottery and the bakery, for there is no part of Naples that is so poor that it does not support the luxury of a lottery; and, I might add, there are few places of business that are carried on in a filthier manner than these bakeries of the poorer classes.

I was passing this place late in the afternoon, when I was surprised to see a huckster—I think he was a fish vender—draw up his wagon at the foot of this stone staircase and begin unhitching his mule. I looked on with some curiosity, because I could not, for the life of me, make out where he was going to put that animal after he had unhitched him. Presently the mule, having been freed from the wagon, turned of his own motion and began clambering up the staircase. I was so interested that I followed.

A little way up the hill the staircase turned into a dark and dirty alleyway, which, however, was crowded with people. Most of them were sitting in their doorways or in the street; some were knitting, some were cooking over little charcoal braziers which were placed out in the street. One family had the table spread in the middle of the road and had just sat down very contentedly to their evening meal. The street was strewn with old bottles, dirty papers, and all manner of trash; at the same time it was filled with sprawling babies and with chickens, not to mention goats and other household appurtenances. The mule, however, was evidently familiar with the situation, and made his way along the street, without creating any surprise or disturbance, to his own home.

I visited several other streets during my stay in Naples which were, if possible, in a worse condition than the one I have described. In a city where every one lives in the streets more hand half the time, and where all the intimate business of life is carried on with a frankness and candour of which we in America have no conception, there is little difficulty in seeing how people live. I noted, for example, instances in which the whole family, to the number of six or seven, lived in a single room, on a dirt floor, without a single window. More than that, this one room, which was in the basement of a large tenement house, was not as large as the average one-room Negro cabin in the South. In one of these one-room homes I visited there was a blacksmith shop in one part of the room, while the family ate and slept in the other part. The room was so small that I took the trouble to measure it, and founded it 8 × 13 feet in size.

Many of these homes of the poorer classes are nothing better than dark and damp cellars. More than once I found in these dark holes sick children and invalid men and women living in a room in which no ray of light entered except through the open door. Sometimes there would be a little candle burning in front of a crucifix beside the bed of the invalid, but this flickering taper, lighting up some pale, wan face, only emphasized the dreary surroundings. It was a constant source of surprise to me that under such conditions these people could be so cheerful, friendly, and apparently contented.

I made some inquiry as to what sort of amusements they had. I found that one of the principal forms of amusement of this class of people is gambling. What seems stranger still, this vice is in Italy a Government monopoly. The state, through its control of the lottery, adds to the other revenue which it extracts from the people not less than five million dollars a year, and this sum comes, for the most part, from the very poorest part of the population.

There are, it seems, something like 1,700 or 1,800 offices scattered through the several large cities of Italy where the people may buy lottery tickets. It seemed to me that the majority of these offices must be in Naples, for in going about the city I saw them almost everywhere, particularly in the poorer quarters.

These lottery offices were so interesting that I determined to visit one myself and learn how the game was played. It seems that there is a drawing every Saturday. Any one may bet, whatever amount he chooses, that a number somewhere between one and ninety will turn up in the drawing. Five numbers are drawn. If you win, the lottery pays ten to one. You may also bet that any two of the five numbers drawn will turn up in succession. In that case, the bank pays the winner something like fifty to one. You may also bet that three out of five will turn up, and in case you win the bank pays 250 times the amount you bet. Of course the odds are very much against the player, and it is estimated that the state gets about 50 per cent. of all the money that is paid in. The art of the game consists, according to popular superstition, in picking a lucky number. In order to pick a lucky number, however, one must go to a fortune-teller and have one's dreams interpreted, or one must pick a number according to some striking event, for it is supposed that every event of any importance suggests some lucky number. Of course this makes the game more interesting and complicated, but it is, after all, a very expensive form of amusement for poor people.

From all that I can learn, public sentiment in Italy is rapidly being aroused to the evils which cling to the present system of dealing with the agricultural labourer and the poorer classes. But Italy has not done well by her lower classes in the past. She has oppressed them with heavy taxes; has maintained a land system that has worn out the soil at the same time that it has impoverished the labourer; has left the agricultural labourers in ignorance; has failed to protect them from the rapacity of the large landowners; and has finally driven them to seek their fortunes in a foreign land.

In return, these emigrants have repaid their native country by vastly increasing her foreign commerce, by pouring back into Italy the earnings they have made abroad, by themselves returning with new ideas and new ambitions and entering into the work of building up the country.

These returned emigrants have brought back to the mother country improved farming machinery, new methods of labour, and new capital. Italian emigrants abroad not only contribute to their mother country a sum estimated at between five and six million dollars annually, but Italian emigration has awakened Italy to the value of her labouring classes, and in doing this has laid the foundation for the prosperity of the whole country. In fact, Italy is another illustration that the condition of the man at the bottom affects the life of every class above him. It is to the class lowest down that Italy largely owes what prosperity she has as yet attained.

Angela Davis

Angela Davis was born into a middle-class black family in Birmingham, Alabama, in January 1944. Growing up in the segregated South helped shape the young Davis's political consciousness. She would go on to become one of America's most controversial figures. As a teenager Davis left Birmingham for New York to attend the Elizabeth Irwin High School, a private all-girls institution where she was first introduced to Marxism. This early radicalism led her to Brandeis University in Waltham, Massachusetts, where she studied with Herbert Marcuse. On graduation from Brandeis in 1965, Davis went to Frankfurt, Germany, to study philosophy with the noted Frankfurt School theorist Theodor Adorno. As such, she followed in the footsteps of W. E. B. Du Bois and Mary Church Terrell, both of whom had spent student years in Germany.

In 1969, California Governor Ronald Reagan fired Davis from her job as a professor of philosophy at UCLA because of her membership in the American Communist Party. By 1970 Davis's name was at the top of the FBI's Ten Most Wanted List for having been accused of providing the young Jonathan Jackson with the arms he used to take a judge and jurors hostage from the Marin County Courthouse in 1970.

The excerpt here describes her experience in Germany and closes with her desire to return to the United States to join the black freedom struggle.

f r o m
Angela Davis: An Autobiography
(1974)

... When I boarded the boat sailing for Germany, Watts was burning. I felt again the tension of the Janus head—leaving the country at that time was hard for me. But in a little more than a week, I was on the other side of the ocean.

My stipend consisted of the boat fare and a hundred dollars a month— for rent, food, tram fare to and from the university, books, and whatever else I needed. As I searched the city for a room, the agencies kept telling me, "*Es tut uns leid, aber wir haben keine Zimmer für Ausländer.*" "Sorry but we don't have rooms for foreigners," their attitude clearly implying, "Our rooms are only for good Aryans."

In historical time, twenty years is not very long—half the people I saw on the streets, and practically all the adults, had gone through the experience of Hitler. And in West Germany, unlike the German Democratic Republic, there had been no determined campaign to attack the fascist and racist attitudes which had become so deeply imbedded.

Eventually, after days of reading the fine print of the *Frankfurter Allgemeiner*, I found a little room near the zoo, on the top floor of a postwar apartment building—like the *chambre de bonne* I had lived in in Paris. The family to whose apartment the room was attached seemed to be exceptional, as far as the masses of West Germans were concerned. They were curious and concerned about the condition of Black people in the United States and they never failed to draw the appropriate parallels between the Nazi oppression of the Jews in their country and the repression of my people in the United States. They repeatedly invited me to their apartment for dinner and discussions. In the beginning when my German was not very polished, these discussions helped me orient myself to the language.

During the first few weeks, I didn't understand a word of what Adorno was saying. Not only were the concepts difficult to grasp, but he spoke his own special aphoristic variety of German. It was a consolation to discover that most German students attending his lectures for the first time were having almost as much trouble understanding Adorno as I.

I saw old friends from previous trips to Europe, and entered into new friendships as well. It was a great relief to find that not too far from me lived a young Black man from Indiana who had been stationed in Frankfurt as a GI and had decided to stay on to pursue his studies in literature at the university. We were good friends throughout my stay in Germany. I was friendly with a group of Haitian students, a Black South African and two couples who, like myself, had come from the United States to study with Adorno.

I was paying eighty marks a month for my room—practically a quarter of the hundred dollars I had to live on. Almost inevitably, when the end of the month approached, I was eating nothing but *Quark* (something between yogurt and cottage cheese), and writing my parents for a few dollars to tide me over until the next check came in. I was very relieved to find a room on Adalbertstrasse, near the university, which cost only a few marks a month. It was in a massive old building of crumbling red brick, an abandoned factory which the owner rented out I imagine in order to avoid paying a watchman.

The three floors of one side were occupied by a sculptor who fashioned huge abstract metal forms which he kept in the courtyard. The side I moved into had been taken over by a group of students, all as poor as I. The entire place cost us seventy-five marks (less than twenty dollars) a month, and it could comfortably accommodate up to five people in the little nooks that had served as offices when the factory was in operation.

It was a dilapidated old abandoned building with dirty cement floors, no showers—not even hot water—and no central heating, only potbellied coal stoves. But paying only about five dollars a month for rent and a few more dollars for coal during the winter months, I could afford to eat a little better—even buying meat a couple of days a week—and was able to buy more books and a new blouse once in a while. As throughout Europe, cultural events could always be attended by students at a great discount, so for about fifty cents, I could see a movie or go to the theater, the opera, the ballet or a museum.

During the spring of my first year there, all the students who had received scholarships from the exchange program were given a trip to Berlin from whatever section of Germany they happened to be living in. Anxious to see Socialist Germany, I spent most of the time in Berlin, the capital of the German Democratic Republic. Each day, I walked across at Checkpoint Charlie—the border point for people with passports from capitalist countries.

Crowds of white tourists from the United States would be standing in line, probably waiting to cross the border in order to tell people they had seen the other side of the "wall"—so they could say, in Kennedy's war-filled words, *"Ich bin ein Berliner,"* that is, I am ready to fight communism. The tourists were always complaining about the wait. But I never had any trouble—each time I went across, I would receive the signal to go on only a few moments after I had shown my passport. This was their way of showing their solidarity with Black people.

Claudia and Margaret Burnham's stepbrother Bob had recently come through Frankfurt, stayed a while at the "factory" and then gone on to study at the Brecht Theater in Berlin. Through him, I was introduced to several people in the GDR who showed me around the city. Living in Bob's apartment building was a group of Cubans—the national director of the ballet and several of his assistants. I was amazed at their youth—the director was in his early twenties and the rest around the same age. They talked about their efforts to more fully integrate the African element of Cuban culture into their classical dances and described the way in which they were developing the old Yoruba dances which, before the revolution, had been restricted to the remote areas of the country where Black people still retained African customs.

Esther and James Jackson, old friends of my parents from Birmingham, were in Berlin at the time. Jim, the International Affairs Director of the Communist Party, U.S.A., was representing the party at the May Day celebration. I spent an evening with them. We talked about the old days when Jim had been underground, and how puzzled I had been as a child, seeing those sinister white men following us all over New York looking for him; Jim was one of the lucky ones whom the FBI never succeeded in tracking down. We discussed the socialist transformation of the GDR and its active campaign against the remnants of fascism in the mentality of the people. The next day I watched the parade, participated in the May Day Festivities and then went on back through Checkpoint Charlie to catch my plane for Frankfurt.

When the West German police said they were going to detain me at the airport, I was certain they were going to accuse me of being too friendly with the people in the GDR—and, of course, they would have been correct. But, according to them, the reason they wouldn't let me board the plane had to do with my failure to check out with the Frankfurt police when I had moved, some months before, out of the room near the zoo, and had not registered with the police station near the factory. I could never get used to the incredible bureaucracy in which one must become embroiled merely as a prerequisite for living an ordinary life. Everyone, citizen or foreigner, not registered at the nearest police station—and there was no lack of them—was technically liable to arrest, including those visiting with friends for only a few days. Although I had registered when I moved into the first place (the process is called *Anmeldung*—announcing one's arrival), it had not crossed my mind to tell them I was leaving (called *Ausmeldung*) and to go through the *Anmeldung* at the Adalbertstrasse police station. The West Berlin police were serious: they were talking about deporting me. It took several hours before I could persuade them that my failure to register had been an innocent omission. After it was all over and they had left the threat of deportation hanging over me unless I cleared myself the next day with the Frankfurt police, I was still positive that the harassment was a little retaliatory action for my trip to the GDR.

Frankfurt was a very intensive learning experience. Stimulating lectures and seminars conducted by Theodore Adorno, Jürgen Habermass, Professor Haag, Alfred Schmidt, Oscar Negt. Tackling formidable works, such as all three of Kant's Critiques and the works of Hegel and Marx as well (in one seminar, we spent an entire semester analyzing about twenty pages of Hegel's *Logic*).

Most of the students living in the factory studied either philosophy or sociology. Many were members of S.D.S.—Sozialistischer Deutscher Studentenbund, the German Socialist Student League. And they were very seriously striving to arrive at some form of practical resistance capable of ultimately overturning the enemy system. Aside from the concern with the social contradictions inside their own country, they consistently tried to force an internationist awareness among their members. I participated in rallies and demonstrations directed against U.S. aggression in Vietnam. Those of us who were not citizens had to be especially careful because an arrest would mean a sure deportation. One demonstration, which took place outside the U.S. Embassy, was particularly dangerous. Chanting "U.S. *raus*, U.S. *raus*, U.S. *raus aus Vietnam!*" and "Ho, Ho, Ho Chi Minh!" the crowds of demonstrators were attacked almost immediately by mounted police. One young woman was trampled under the hooves of the horses. Since it had been decided beforehand that we would resist this expected attack, the agreed upon hit-and-run, disruptive tactics were put into operation. The idea was to move along the main street leading to the center of the city, disrupting the functioning of the tramway. As the crowds of demonstrators marched down the main street on the sidewalks on both sides of the street, some would periodically separate from the group and sit down on the tramway tracks. Watching the approach of the police, they waited until the very last moment to run into the refuge of the crowd. Not all of us made it. When it was my turn to do the sitting and running, I had to make sure I was fast enough to reach the safety of the crowd, not wanting to have a case foisted upon me by the West German courts. After several hours of sitting and running, and a sizeable number of arrests, we made it to the Hauptwache, the center of the city, and listened to an arousing speech by Rudi Dutsche, the Chairman of S.D.S., who was later shot in the head by a would-be assassin who said he was inspired by the assassination of Martin Luther King.

Toward the end of my second year, a mass student demonstration, organized by S.D.S. in Berlin protesting the visit by the Shah of Iran, was attacked by the Shah's security, aided by the West Berlin police, with such terrible force that it ended in the death of a student — Ben Ohnesorge, who was attending his first political protest. The response throughout West Germany was swift and intense. In Frankfurt, there were mass gatherings, demonstrations and teach-ins.

I was most impressed by the consciousness of the student movement when I heard about the Berlin campaign led by S.D.S. against the movie *Africa Adio*, directed by two Roman playboy-types, dealing with the ousting of the colonialists from Africa. Not only was this movie thoroughly racist in that it depicted the African Liberation Fighters as aggressors against the pure, educated, civilized whites, but the directors went so far as to stage actual killings in order to do on-the-spot documentary coverage of Africa. S.D.S. members in Berlin tore up a theater which refused to boycott the film.

Students and workers were being drawn en masse into the area of political protest in Germany. At the same time, great upheavals were taking place in the States.

My decision to study in Frankfurt had been made in 1964, against the backdrop of relative political tranquillity. But by the time I left in the summer of 1965, thousands of sisters and brothers were screaming in the streets of Los Angeles that they had observed the rules of the game long enough, too long.

Watts was exploding; furiously burning. And out of the ashes of Watts, Phoenix-like, a new Black militancy was being born.

While I was hidden away in West Germany the Black Liberation Movement was undergoing decisive metamorphoses. The slogan "Black Power" sprang out of a march in Mississippi. Organizations were being transfigured—The Student Non-Violent Coordinating Committee, a leading civil rights organization, was becoming the foremost advocate of "Black Power." The Congress on Racial Equality was undergoing similar transformations. In Newark, a national Black Power Conference had been organized. In political groups, labor unions, churches and other organizations, Black caucuses were being formed to defend the special interests of Black people. Everywhere there were upheavals.

While I was reading philosophy in Frankfurt, and participating in the rearguard of S.D.S., there were young Black men in Oakland, California, who had decided that they had to wield arms in order to protect the residents of Oakland's Black community from the indiscriminate policy brutality ravaging the area. Huey Newton, Bobby Seale, li'l Bobby Hutton—those were some of the names that reached me. One day in Frankfurt I read about their entrance into the California Legislature in Sacramento with their weapons in order to safeguard their right (a right given to all whites) to carry them as instruments of self-defense. The name of this organization was the Black Panther Party for Self-Defense.

The more the struggles at home accelerated, the more frustrated I felt at being forced to experience it all vicariously. I was advancing my studies, deepening my understanding of philosophy, but I felt more and more isolated. I was so far away from the terrain of the fight that I could not even analyze the episodes of the struggle. I did not even have the knowledge or understanding to judge which currents of the movement were progressive and genuine and which were not. It was a difficult balance I was trying to maintain, and it was increasingly hard to feel a part of the collective coming to consciousness of my people.

I am certain that what I was feeling was a variation and reflection of the same feelings that were overwhelming larger and larger numbers of Black people abroad. Many others of us must have felt pained, when reading about some new crisis in the struggle at home, to be hearing about it secondhand.

I had thought mine was the perfect dilemma: the struggle at home versus the need to remain in Frankfurt until the completion of my doctorate, for I was certain that Frankfurt was far more conducive to philosophical studies than any other place. But each day it was becoming clearer to me that my ability to accomplish anything was directly dependent on my ability to contribute something concrete to the struggle.

Adorno had readily agreed to direct my work on a doctoral dissertation. But now I felt it would be impossible for me to stay in Germany any longer. Two years was enough. I arranged for an appointment with Adorno at the Institute and explained to him that I had to go home. In my correspondence with Marcuse, he had already agreed to work with me at the University of California in San Diego, where he had accepted a position after having been practically pushed out of Brandeis for political reasons. I wanted to continue my academic work, but I knew I could not do it unless I was politically involved. The struggle was a life-nerve; our only hope for survival. I made up my mind. The journey was on.

Arthur A. Schomburg

Bibliophile, curator, and writer Arthur Alfonso Schomburg was born in San Juan, Puerto Rico, on January 24, 1874. While a young man in Puerto Rico, he began to collect photographs and books about the presence of blacks in Puerto Rico. After coming to New York in 1891, Schomburg worked as a teacher of Spanish and also served as secretary of the Las Dos Antillas Cuban Revolutionary Party in New York—a party devoted to freeing Cuba and Puerto Rico from Spain. Schomburg traveled throughout the world in search of books and other documents of significance to the history of blacks throughout the world. Schomburg died in 1938. The Schomburg Center for Research in Black Culture, located in Harlem, was founded on his collection and until this day is the most important archive of black history and culture.

"My Trip to Cuba in Quest of Negro Books" (1933)
from
Opportunity

Diego Colon, the son of the famous navigator known to us as Columbus, was governor of Hispaniola when he appointed Captain Diego Velasquez in 1511 to embark forthwith an expedition to colonize the island of Juana, now known as Cuba. With him on the same mission was Father Bartolome de Las Casas, Hernan Cortez and some three hundred men. These intrepid men landed not far from Santiago de Cuba, where during the year 1521 the first slaves were introduced. However, Africans were introduced with the first expedition. These were those who knew the Spanish language and had been born and reared in the province of Andalucia, especially from the cities of Sevilla and Cadiz where to this day the street known as "Cuesta de Negros" still survives.

Cuba is endeared to the memory of Estevanico the guide that will be remembered as the real discoverer of the Seven Cities of Cibola, in what is now known as Arizona. Estevanico was born in Amazor, North Africa, lived in Spain and thence was taken to Cuba where we find him on the Florida expedition that met disaster with only four saved. His next enterprise was with Marcos de Niza the missionary friar, whose exploits have been lucidly explained by Captain Jaramilo. Herman Cortez the conqueror of the Aztecs had quite a number of Negroes in his military expedition. One of the curious incidents of this memorable conquest is the fact that Juan Garirdo, a Negro was the first who planted and harvested wheat in America and Juan Cortez another Negro, a comic actor or clown had come to Mexico from Cuba, making them unique characters in that early epoch.

The first entry of slaves in Cuba can be shown by documents in the Archives of the Indies; subsequent reports on African slaves covers a vast period of exceedingly interesting data of their enormous service rendered to the development of the Americas during discovery and colonization.

Doctor Juan Jerez Villarreal, the historian member of the Club Atenas, is happy in reflective eloquence, when in the president's beautiful office he speaks of Manuel Velasquez, colored, a graduate from the University of Alcala de Henares, Spain, founded by Cardenal Ximenes who held adverse views to Las Casas on the question of slavery. Velasquez was a personal friend of Charles V, to whom he frequently wrote from Santiago de Cuba protesting against the treatment to which the natives had to submit. He is attributed with having opened the first school in the island. Other schools were opened by Lorenzo Mendez and Mariano Moya, lieutenants in the battalion of colored men of Habana. There was also a friar, a mulatto named Tellez, who taught Latin in the convent of the Dominican order. The first Negro librarian was born at Bayamo in 1758. He was Manuel Socorro Rodriguez and held the office at Santa Fe de Bogota, in Central America. The earliest Negro women doing something unusual in the field of semi-professional activity are Teodora and Micaela Gines, bandolin players in the orchestra that rendered music in the churches of Santiago de Cuba during the year 1580.

The representative colored men of Habana have come together in a very laudable undertaking, the establishment of a club called Atenas. The

Cuban government has given paternal solicitude to this establishment. A survey of the membership roll shows many men in governmental affairs. Among these is found the Honorable Juan Gualberto Gomez, the grand old man of Cuba, member of the Spanish Abolition Society now in his eighty-third year, actively engaged in writing his memoirs. Not so long ago President Machado placed on his breast the most cherished, the highest decoration—Carlos Manuel de Cespedes—the Republic can bestow on her sons. The services rendered by this patriot are beyond words for me to give my meed of praise. Under the notorious Spanish regime he was twice banished to imprisonment in those infamous African penal institutions for his rebellious activities in behalf of his country.

The Club Atenas publishes an official bulletin, a very interesting magazine beautifully illustrated, printed on the finest glazed paper, to which most of its bronzed writers have contributed their share of artistic and creative labors. But foremost there is Juan Gualberto Gomez who pleaded his own cause with forensic and judicious mind. "From early youth and within my sphere of action, circumstances have placed me here where I was born. I have been active for the independence of Cuba, my father-land, liberty and the progress of the Cuban Negro." If you were to entertain any doubts of the heights attained by colored men in the sister republic and their heritage, let us again listen to the great commoner. "We are no longer pariahs, we are not proscribed to a national life, we share public life in all its degrees and spheres. We have entered by casting our votes just like the whites but as Negroes mixed in the same urn. We have passed through the beautiful gates of opposition to win judicial positions and to share honors in the legislative chambers of the nation and in the executive council. We have entered by popular election in the provincial councils and in the municipal chambers. We have taken active part in all battles, municipal, provincial and national of our country. That alone represents to my understanding, an appreciable advance, for it shows our effective influence more or less in the government of our people. Today the schools of the republic are wide open to all its citizens regardless of color; the halls of our national university are graduating colored students in all branches of human knowledge. All this has been accomplished in less than a quarter of a century." Don Juan Gualberto Gomez was writing as early as 1871 when in Madrid he joined hands with those enlightened minds that gave Puerto Rico its full measure of freedom from the tentacles of the slave monster in 1873. He served as president of the united societies of colored people of Cuba when they presented Rafael Maria de Labra with an art object by the notable Picault, symbolizing the genius of Liberty, the gift of the colored people to their benefactor. President Thorndike of the Atenas Club graciously took me to see Gomez, my friend of nearly forty years. I could not but think how time has crystalized the service given by him to his country and how the love of his fellow men had enshrined him while yet in our midst.

Among the great number of poems which Cuba has produced from the times of Juana Pastor in 1815 and Placido with his "Plegaria" to the "Songoro Cosongo" of Nicolas Guillen, a contemporary, there is a plethora of works, varied, indifferent, fair and some of beauty and charm. Francisco Manzano, the slave, gave us his Autobiography and Zafira, a drama in verse. Madden, an Irishman who served Great Britain in Cuba as representative to curb the evil effects of the slave trade, speaking of Manzano, said, "Who can read the Autobiography of this poet without feeling horror and the greatest bitterness against society."

Were we to argue that this was a dramatic incident, the sound of our voice would stop right here, but beside this sable bard we have Antonio Medina Cespedes, whose poetical works received merited literary considerations from his critics. He was a self-educated school master in Habana, his home was the *pabulum* where colored children received alphabetical instruction. His poetical works are well esteemed to this day for their classical style and excellent dramatic construction. In 1849 he published Ladoiska, a drama in five acts in verse. Later Guajiro Generoso, the dramatic comedy, Rogerio the Bandit, and Jacobo Girondi all in measured strains. Medina is revered as the father of primary education in Habana.

We believe Placido is better known to the world than any other Cuban poet. He was shot to death for alleged participation in an insurrection that was concocted in the brains of the Spanish authorities out of fear. We cannot read his poems without a tender feeling for his untimely death. Who can withhold lamentation for the unfortunate end of Placido, Echemendia, Manzano, all men of genius who suffered in the ignominious crucible of slavery, solely because they possessed rare gifts.

Senor Domingo Figarola-Caneda, president of the literary academy, is the person who has sought to remove the thorns from this poet's brow. After careful and exhaustive investigation he has lifted Placido from the depths of infamy and crowned him with martyrdom. The singer of Xiconteca, the genius from a maternity home is now kindly remembered the blot on his memory having been forever removed.

The club Atenas carries an open account of $1,800 in order to erect a suitable monument to the memory of this great singer in the Yumuri Valley in plain view of the hallowed sod where he fell pierced by leaden bullets. Not until such a memorial is erected, can the minds of the colored people rest in peace, now that Doctor Caneda has removed the veil of shame from his memory.

While consulting a person well versed on the present trend of Cuban literature, I was asked if I were conversant with the two writers whose creative contributions to the domain of letters, just now are on every critic's tongue. No? "Then you should know them." While in Habana it was my good fortune to meet Senor Carlos M. Trelles whose bibliography of the colored writers is so necessary for a view of the subject and Doctor Coronado of the National Library who showed me rare tomes by these colored poets. Senor Lizaso was also kind enough to give an opinion of the contemporary colored poets of the island. Thus armed I sallied forth like Don Quixote on my pilgrimage.

Regino Boti was born in the eastern section of Cuba, educated at Barcelona, Spain and the University of Habana in law. Some of his best works are "Arabescos Mentales," "El Mar y la Montana Hipsipilas with some literary notations on Ruben Dario. Senor Lizaso in his critical anthology "La Moderna Poesia" writes eloquently of Boti who gives us notable literary and critical observations of the great figures of Hispano-American literature.

In 1892 Ghirardo Jimenez saw the light of day in Santiago de Cuba where he attended college. He received his medical degree from the University of Habana. His poetical works are many. "La Selva Interior" shows him as a modern poet who describes the ordinary with marked originality.

Regino Pedroso, a native Habanese, young, witty, brilliant, many of whose verses are based on fable themes, also writes from keen and minute observation of human nature. In "The Road to Bagdad" we have a set of sonnets written with the seductive charm of the East. It has all the suavity, delicacy and sonorous sweetness for which he has been acclaimed by his countrymen.

Since the publication of Lizaso's anthology at Madrid 1926, there has appeared another bard whose work has attracted the attention of every Cuban critic.

A young man of excellent personality winning ways, every inch "to the manner born," a person of culture and refinement, is Nicolas Guillen whom I met at the Club Atenas, the author of the "Songoro Cosongo" that recently moved the Cuban literati to hail him as one of her ablest sons. In this small book, a new form, new ideas, a novel change, has come to the old established school.

Guillen's work, "Songoro Cosongo," was printed in three hundred numbered copies which were presented to his admirers and friends. Neither love nor money could buy a copy but faithful Pastor Argudin gave his copy to the Schomburg Collection. The book has been reviewed in every Spanish speaking country and is regarded as one of the most unusual literary achievements in the last two decades, Spain's great philosopher Manuel Unamuno has sung its praises extravagantly.

For quaint beauty, charm of expression, harmony of theme, musical austerity, I know of no poet that can surpass this young bard, when he recreates the customs, traditions and chants of his people. Nearly every oem in the Songoro Cosongo has been set to music by native composers.

But it is not only in the field of letters that we find the artistic gifts of Cuba's colored people. There is Pastor Algudin, a great artist who has won laurels at home as well as abroad. In Spain his canvasses are in famous galleries. The murals that adorned the Cuban building at the Seville's exposition were Algudin's handiwork. The painter took me to see the Capitolio, a replica of our House of Congress, only more lavish, looking like an Aladdin's palace set down for some beautiful hour's pleasure in the center of a lovely park, even to the thirty carat diamond imbedded on the floor directly under the dome. Here we looked on three canvasses by Algudin hanging on the walls, a tribute to his brush, mind and heart.

Gustavo E. Urrutia contributes a page called "Ideales de una Raza" in the great daily paper "El Diario de la Marina." He is a well known writer, architect, publicist, critic. His plans for the memorial to Columbus at Santo Domingo were so bold and impressive that the Journal of Cuban Architecture printed them in full. But Urrutia beside these attributes is a great personality, keen in invective and a defender of racial traditions to the very marrow. He sees great beauty in the early customs of the Africans who were brought to Cuba and since then have contributed their melody and songs to the cultural development of the Cuban nation from the days of Velasquez. To Urrutia we owe the critical knowledge of Nanigocult and the discovery of Guillen's poetry.

How much has been left unsaid. There is Ramon Ramos, the sculptor whose bronze monument to the mother of the Maceo's adorn one of the

city parks. Domingo Argudin Lombrillo sculptor and art critic, Lino D'ou
Ayllon, historian; Emilio Rivero Merlin, painter; Jose Manuel Jimenez,
professor of music in the Conservatory of Berlin. To American Negroes
interested in the cultural development of their race, a trip to Cuba would
be an inspiration and a revelation that might astound them.

KATHERINE DUNHAM

Born in Chicago in 1909, Katherine Dunham is a world renown dancer, choreographer, anthropologist, and writer. After studying modern dance and ballet, Dunham founded the Chicago Negro School of Ballet in the early 1930s. While in Chicago she also enrolled at the University of Chicago, where she studied with Melville Herskovtz. Her doctoral thesis, "Dances of Haiti," was published in Spanish, French, and English. In 1937 she received a Guggenheim to support her work in Haiti, Jamaica, Martinique, and Trinidad. In Haiti, she was initiated into Vaudun in 1935 and has maintained a spiritual connection with that nation until the present. This selection comes from *Island Possessed* (1969), Dunham's memoir of that trip.

Dunham's scholarship informed her choreography and led to the opening of the Katherine Dunham School of Arts and Research in New York in 1943. Here, Dunham trained many generations of dancers, including Eartha Kitt and Arthur Mitchell (founder of the Dance Theater of Harlem).

from
Island Possessed (1969)

It was with letters from Melville Herskovits, head of the Department of Anthropology at Northwestern University, that I invaded the Caribbean — Haiti, Jamaica, Martinique, Trinidad, passing lightly over the other islands, then Haiti again for the final stand for the real study.

When I arrived in Haiti, not long after the exodus of the Marines, there were still baptized drums hidden in hollow tree trunks and behind waterfalls. President Stenio Vincent paid deference to "folklore" for the sake of the growing interests of tourists in the island, but an air of secrecy clothed all the serious ceremonies and it was not the policy of the first government after the Occupation to sponsor young women visitors in investigations that might verify to the world outside what has been a crucial problem to Haitian statesmen since the independence: the irreconcilable breach between the thin upper crust of the Haitian elite—who would have liked to be rulers of the land, participating in the revolution only to get rid of the French and the bubbling, churning ferment of the black peasants, who rally were by numbers and by historical content and character and humanness, I was to find, the true Haitian people. . . .

Of my kind I was a first—a lone young woman easy to place in the clean-cut American dichotomy of color, harder to place in the complexity of Caribbean color classifications; a mulatto when occasion called for, an in-between, or "griffon" actually, I suppose; most of the time an unplaceable, which I prefer to think of as "noir"—not exactly the color black, but the quality of belonging with or being at ease with black people when in the hills or the plains or anywhere and scrambling through daily life along with them. . . .

Of my first day in Port-au-Prince I have two memories. One is the pink sugar-cake cathedral that never ceases to draw attention whether the voyager arrives by sea or air. It is set as a sort of pale coral vaginal opening leading into the mountains, to Canapé Vert and Pétionville and La Boule and God knows where else I may not have seen. Scattered around this Delphic beauty without rhyme or reason except to torment tourists—the slums of Port-au-Prince extended at that time from Pont Beudette to Carrefours— that is, what might be called the suburban area from the left of the bay in the center of which the cathedral nestles to the extreme right which follows the other protective arm of the bay, in the direction of Source Leclerc, which I was to know later. There is a magnificent royal palm grove just on the ocean, the truly painful beauty of which sheltered ordure, yaws (skin syphilis) infested parents and babies, stray cats too clever to be caught, skinned, and eaten, pigs holding bones together with skin. . . . The slums extended past "cribs" run by my now dear friend Madame Nadier, past the swimming pool and tennis courts of caste and color-restricted Club Thorland, past the mud huts of Carrefours, then well south on to the uncharted roads to the next city of any size, Leongane. They were slums unequaled in parts of the world which I have known since then, and they are hard to rival in Lima, Peru, of not so long ago, the favelas of Brazil, massed sampan river housing in Hong Kong, or the clusters of tin and paper huts bordering a bridge on the road to Rufisque, just outside Dakar in Senegal, West Africa. . . .

In those days the first social regulation in Haiti was to stay closely knit to your own color or degree of black-white blood-mixture grouping—which was actually a caste, being exclusive, endogamous, inherent, nontransferable, immutable. The immutable part I found to have an escape clause, expressed in an old Haitian proverb: "Mulatre pauvre—neg'; neg' riche—mulatre!" or, a poor mulatto becomes a black, a rich black a mulatto. Of course, this was true only on the surface. In a last analysis the Rouziers, [two Haitian sisters Dunham has met] though obliged to resort to innkeeping to save the family silverware and preserve the antimascassars, would never really be "black" in Haiti; and daughters of families I have known, who were educated in books, and rich, I have seen sit out dance after dance at fancy dress balls because they were just too dark of skin color to make the social grade and fell behind the mulatto standard in features and hair texture. In the eighteenth-century, Moreau de Saint-Mery, the most descriptive and perhaps unbiased of the historians and chroniclers of Saint-Domingue, notes the forty gradations of mixtures recognized at the time of his writing between black and white, with sometimes Arawak or Carib Indian blood thrown in. Haiti of today recognizes the following: mulatto, marabou, griffon, black.

When the exact degree of blood mixture had been forgotten or could not be determined, as in my case, or in the cases of Haitians expatriated and married abroad for generations, materialities of money and manners entered in, along with those intangibles that make up a large part of all such judgments, even those considered scientific and rational.

It seemed best to give the Rouzier sisters and the few pensioners of the Hotel Excelsior time to sort out my position in this complex caste system in order not to run the risk of upsetting them, as I had the immigrations officer who came to meet our homey little Royal Netherlands Lines boat, as it dropped anchor in the bay of Port-au-Prince that June morning in 1936.

Ralph J. Bunche

Ralph J. Bunche, born in 1904, was a scholar, diplomat, and international civil servant. After finishing first in his class from Jefferson High School in Los Angeles, Bunche went on to graduate summa cum laude from UCLA in 1927 and to receive a doctoral degree in political science from Harvard University, making him the first African American to receive a doctorate in that discipline. After helping to found the political science department at Howard University, Bunche went on to head the Division of Dependent Affairs in the Office of Special Political Affairs for the U.S. State Department. Bunche ended his career with the United Nations, where he became the "architect" of the U.N. Peacekeeping Operation. Although involved in international affairs throughout the remainder of this career, Bunche remained active in the African-American quest for civil rights in the land of his birth.

The selection here is taken from *An African American in South Africa,* a collection of journal entries documenting his stay in South Africa from 1936 to 1937 edited by Robert R. Edgar, who adapted the bracketed material in the text. Because these notes were written without an audience in mind, according to Edgar, Bunche's comments are "unguarded" and "candid" (4).

f r o m
"An African American in South Africa" (1937)

September 29 Cape Town
Room steward woke me up at 5:50 a.m. Dressed, finished packing, and went on deck to see Cape Town nestling beautifully at the foot of Table Mountain. A striking picture. Got through immigration officer okay after a wait of half an hour and a payment of a £ 5 deposit for "good behavior." I'm allowed to stay until December 31st. Then went back on deck and saw Abe Desmore on the dock with two white men whom I later met as Snitcher and Swanstein. Couldn't get the customs declaration straight on deck, so I got my bags together and went down to meet Desmore et al. Turned customs business over to a [Thomas] Cook's agent and finally got through without paying any duty (though customs officer tried to soak me £ 2.10 for my bedding, etc.) by arranging for Cook's to store the tropical equipment for me and to hold it until I am ready to leave South Africa. Cook's representative said I can have the stuff whenever I want it.

Went out to Snitcher's beach cottage for a ham and egg breakfast. It was then only 8:30. Then Swanstein drove me by Cook's and I got plenty of mail, including a fat letter from Ruth and one each from Joan and Jane. Then out to Mrs. Gool's . . . where I am staying. Fine new stucco bungalow and very modern. Her 15 year old daughter is beautiful. They are Malays. Mrs. Gool is attractive, left-wing and talks a mile a·minute. Reminds me of Katherine Beard House up high right near the mountain.

Went down to Cook's and Post Office to mail letters in p.m. Strolled about a bit and watched [a] negro and his woman sing, clown and dance on his hands at the Parade. Drunken white men loafing and enjoying show. One snapped a picture with his hand over the lens.

I have a nice large room and all of my things were put away when I came back this p.m. Dr. Schapera called—will see him at 10 a.m. tomorrow. I met Snitcher's brother and Sam Kahn. Negroes so mixed up here the place looks like Harlem.

September 30

Up too late and had to take cab to university [of Cape Town] for my appointment with Schapera.

University lying at foot of majestic mountain rising in background. Looking away from Jameson Hall, I see a great range of mountains in the near distance, blue-hazed, some snow-capped still.

Schapera is small, trim, reserved and cold-eyed, but he was quite friendly. I had a long talk with him. He had received a letter from the High Commissioner extending me the privilege of visiting Basutoland. He advised me to do so. He introduced me to his seminar students, and I remained for it. It consisted of his reading from one of the chapters in a new book he's writing and asking for criticisms. He told me there are about fifty colored students at the university. Told me I might be able to visit him at his hotel but would not be allowed to eat with him there.

No Jim Crow on buses, but colored and natives* can only ride 2nd and 3rd [class] on trains—even on the train to Mowbray for the University.

Went to the University by train to Mowbray. Rode 1st class on train—no segregation. Saw colored and blacks mostly in 3rd class coaches (wooden seats), but a good sprinkling of colored in 2nd class. [I was] only colored in my coach in 1st on return.

Lavoratories marked "For European Gentlemen" in Cape Town ry. [railway] station. No such designation in station at Mowbray.

Heard a fattish, bald, dark-brown Negro soap-boxing at the Parade. He apparently represents the African National Congress. Inveighing vs. the "pick-me-up" raids[†] on the location and the government's brewing of Kaffir beer.[‡]

---

*"Native" refers to an African. At the time of Bunche's visit, "native" had generally been discarded by Africans who resented its paternalistic overtones. Bunche also used the word "colored"; I have kept Bunche's spelling throughout the text. In the American context, "colored" referred to anyone of Negro descent. In the South African context, it was spelled "colored" and generally meant anyone of mixed descent. However, the term is loosely defined and, in South Africa law, can mean anyone who is regarded as neither African nor European.

[†]Pick-me-ups or pickup vans are police vans. Eslanda Robeson described the pick-me-up as a cross between a dog-catcher's wagon and a police patrol wagon. Africans call it simply "pickup." If they cannot show a pass or permit to be out on the streets, they are seized, loaded into these vans, and taken to jail (*African Journey* [1945], 72).

[‡]Kaffir beer is any home-brewed beer made from malted grains, usually sorghum.

Used American Negro as example constantly. Said they have brains and wealth and don't stand for foolishness. Says American Negro says Africa belongs to Africans, and are ready to come back home, but are Africans ready to receive them? Advocates joining the U.N.I.A. and spoke highly of Garvey.*

Says brown men (colored) are afraid of guns and "run 25 miles an hour" whenever they see one. But says guns only make the native "wild" and the more he sees the wilder he gets. Says Indians are chasing the white man out of India and African must regain his own country too. Says if white man "doesn't play the game" he will be chased out. Says Japanese are chasing white[s] out of China, especially Russians, and apparently that this is a good thing.

Said American Negroes can strike, but South African natives can't and warned that being dressed up didn't make a person a human being. American Negro demanded to be treated as human beings and are equal of any people in world. Praised Joe Louis[†] as a great man—a black man and world champion. No white man in all of Africa can challenge him.

Attacked Smuts.[‡] Said natives must join organizations and use their power. Crowd snickered as he began, but he soon had many nodding their heads in approbation. He spoke vigorously and often cursed. A few white[s] stood by listening; others walked boldly back and forth between him and the crowd. He had a girl selling copies of the Bantu Word. Police not far away, but they didn't molest him.

A short distance away another native was speaking to a crowd in Bantu. Called Dutchmen "dumb." Pointed to a picture of Negroes marching in Courier and said: "See here how 10,000 American black men march to show the world that they are equal to any people on earth." Said black men in Africa asleep.

Denounced poor whites in South Africa—said they would take all black men's jobs. Attacked the rich. Said rich are sitting on their riches, on the gold and diamonds that rightfully belong to the natives, and that time had come for poor men to demand their share. Said white men had robbed natives of their own gold and diamonds in their own country. But said native is changing. He is oppressed by white man's laws—liquor laws, poll-

*Marcus Garvey.
[†]The American boxer.
[‡]Jan Smuts, South African prime minister (1939–48).

taxes, pass laws, etc., and white man must change them and give him good laws or native is ready to die. Being starved to death anyway.

Said native is shoved off on location because white man doesn't want him hear him, and then white man invades the black man's location with "pick-me-up." Natives say white man must stay away from his place.

Attacked religion. Says bishops give natives only religion. Natives shouldn't fall for it—God doesn't help lazy men—helps only those who think and act for themselves. Says "a blinking bishop" prayed (in [news] papers last night) for the war in China to end and this drew a big laugh.

One native speaking to another in "fancy" English. One sporting a new watch.

"Ken you tell me the time, I do not suppose?"

"Ah yes, eet is quarter to the clock."

"Oh god-damn, let again!" . . .

October 9

Signs in court house: "Male witnesses colored"; "Female witnesses colored"; "Male-European"; "Female-European." The rooms are at opposite ends of corridor. In Civil Court D, Snitcher arguing civil damage suit for a colored plaintiff who was abused, and allegedly unlawfully arrested and prosecuted by a guard on a suburban train. Harry demanding £ 250 damages. Harry's arguments very potent. The magistrate is quiet, dignified and honest enough looking. The magistrate takes his own notes on the case, noting citations carefully. Harry avoids the color issue.

Harry described the plaintiff as a "respectable, dignified colored man, who wouldn't use the abusive language defendants charge him with."

Snitcher demanded that opposing attorney (a government attorney defending a government worker) cease referring to his adult colored plaintiff (a middle-aged dignified man with a flowing moustache) as a "boy."

Colored fellow behind me says colored [and] natives are treated terribly on the trains and that most of guards are recruited from the country. Says this is first case of its kind and [it] will have a good influence.

Harry said bilingualism is general in courts, tho not universal. Said there are no laws requiring Jim Crow in Cape Town, but that public discriminations have never been tested in courts here. Thinks common law capable of interpretation to the effect that, e.g., a proprietor of a bioscope, holding a license from the state, could be compelled to admit the general public without discrimination. [His] only fear is that a favorable decision and attendant publicity would lead to a positive segregation law. But this would probably be counterbalanced by educational value of such a fight to non-European community. At least it would clarify and define the existing anomalous situation, which is much like D.C. in re absence of laws. Tacit agreement between groups re separate groups.

Used a lavatory boldly marked "For Europeans Only" in Snitcher's building. . . .

October 16
Effendi, the Turkish reporter for the Standard, claims Turkey is the only country in the world entirely free of race prejudice. He says English are responsible for the introduction of race prejudice here, as black and white (Dutch) were getting on very well before the English came. . . .

October 17
Saw a native group of about 25 in baptism ceremonies in sea at Woodstock beach. Church of Christ group. Cold, raw, windy day. Singing hymns (strange) and Bible printed in Xhosa. Weird harmony. Only three women; one with a baby on her back. One English speaking native in the group—a little cringing, bearded fellow, dressed like a dandy, told me they are from Langa and have about one hundred members in their flock. Pastor was a tall, brownskinned, serious-eyed, bearded native. In short testimonial sermons after the baptisms (in English), one native, while quoting the scripture like Ford quotes the party line, stated that the scriptures and religion made no provision for the color-bar. . . .

October 18
There was virtual Jim Crow at the Dutch Church meeting, for the colored all occupied entire rows and the whites similarly. There was no race mixture on any particular row, though the rows were mixed—sort of alternating. There was a tall, tense looking [man] in frock coat, who seemed to be a sort of door-keeper, page boy, messenger. No fraternization between black and white delegates.

Saw "Sister Nannie," the mountainous, black sister who got the King's medal recently (Dr. Gow also received one several years ago) for her work in running a hostel for "unfortunate girls"—i.e., a place where they can drop their fatherless babes. She's connected with the Dutch Reformed Church, and was all dressed up in a nurse's uniform, serving tea to the delegates.

Reagon a pompous, conceited ass in an Emmett Scott sort of way. Thinks himself a great leader and financier. Talks of the people as though they are children or subjects who would flounder and perish without his astute hands.

He makes all sorts of extravagant claims for the A.P.O. Says it is the only South African non-European organization that has ever done anything. Poppy cock! He didn't even mention the I.C.U. or the African [National] Congress.

He runs a couple of "semifraternal" business enterprises—building associations, industrial insurance and the A.P.O. burial association, out of all of which he undoubtedly gets his ample cut. He's a smooth and fluent talker.

October 22

These American consuls and legation secretaries are pretty lousey when they are confronted with an American Negro. Went down largely on Gow's advice to see the American Consul-General today—a Mr. Denby—just to ask a single question about my permit—and largely on Reverend Gow's advice. He was a fairly young, blue-eyed guy who said he hails from D. C. and has been here ten months. He was just as taciturn, curt and unsympathetic as the guy at the Legation in London was. The only place they treated me decently was in Paris. . . .

Colored medical students can't go beyond the third year at the University of C.T. because they can't get clinical work there, so they must complete their work abroad. They aren't allowed to work on colored patients even for these are needed by the white students!

Very little colored business, but Indians have a number of shops, though small, up Hanover Street. Some colored printers, some small builders etc. But there is no real bourgeoisie. The teachers tend to affect the psychology of the bourgeois class, but have no economic foundation for it. . . .

November 6 Basutoland

Visited Ladybrand, a little town in the Orange Free State, nestling in a valley. Here, as in most Afrikander rural towns, the Dutch Reformed Church is the central feature and towers above all else in the town as one approaches it. . . .

[They say] in old days the chiefs court was given more discretion in deciding cases. But today the chiefs are arbitrary. Many abuses by chiefs deciding cases today.

The chief keeps the fines and abuses his power. In the old days the chief heard cases themselves. But today most of the chiefs let their "chairman" of court hear the cases. Existing chiefs are corrupt and "multiply like locusts" due to polygamy. (Bull says one of Richards' forthcoming proclamations is to limit the no. of chiefs.)

In the old days only the sons of chiefs first wife were recognized as his heirs. But now the chiefs have often insisted that the sons of other chiefs divide their domains amongst all these sons.

In the old days there was mutual love between the chief and his people. This is changed today—because the chiefs are out for self and gain.

The situation is changed today because of the British government. Before the British, people could desert the bad chiefs (the Basuto rarely killed them). This is impossible today. The chiefs have indirectly gotten privilege and security under indirect rule.

The alternatives of the Basuto today are to either stay under bad chiefs or go into the union—"out of frying pan into the fire." They admit that the masses of people still cling to the chiefs—but the signs are that they are slowly breaking away from the chiefs. They will still plough for the chiefs, even tho they don't like it.

Chief Setsomi in the Leribe District was thrashed by his people for maladministration and had to be hospitalized. They cited another instance of a native subject firing (tho missing) a gun point-blank at a chief because the chief had expropriated his horses.

Another common abuse by chiefs is in unjust reallocation of lands. "The chiefs take advantage of commoners."

They admit the fund. [fundamental] conflict between the educated African and the chief, tho they say that the chiefs are under the misapprehension that the educated natives hate them.

The masses of natives still regard the hereditary chief as having a special status and would prefer a bad hereditary chief to an efficient, educated commoner (educ. [educated] chief might be too efficient).

A system of elected chiefs wouldn't work now people are not too advanced.

There is a power of appeal from the decisions of chiefs; but there are not many appeals tho some are upheld. Those who appeal from decisions of chief are left in his bad graces.

[The chiefs] find native masses bitterly opposed to incorporation, due to rough experiences in working for Boers and at hands of union police. [The Basotho] fear pass system also. Many Basutos in jail in the union merely for being without passes. They are also opposed to union taxes—e.g., dog, bicycle, beer taxes. All of the chiefs are against incorporation and the masses of natives follow their chiefs.

Many Europeans—traders and officials—in Basutoland also opposed to incorpor. [incorporation].

Basutos prefer to go to mines rather than to farms in union. But many young men who go to mines come back—broken in health with mine diseases—yet the young men are eager to go. Many younger men who go to mines desert their families at home and never return.

Without incorpor., how will Basutoland support its population?

Prospecting for minerals not allowed in Basutoland—the chiefs are opposed to it. "They won't hear of mining here." Afraid of losing their land to whites. For same reason, the chiefs are opposed to the introduction of railroads in Basutoland.

There is much cattle raiding still in Basutoland. Armed raiders (local) steal livestock and sell them in the union [of South Africa].

The chiefs are much more wealthy than the rest of the people. The educated native does accumulate more wealth than the others.

Complaint that "a matric" (one who has passed the matriculation exam.) returning from Fort Hare and entering the Civil Service in Basutoland gets only £3 per month. A native policeman without any education gets as much.

There are 4 govt. intermediate schools and they pay from £3 to £10 per mo.

They were all impressed by what I told them of the color unity among Amer. Negroes. . . .

November 7

The native women (and some men) buy a lot of hair pomade and use it. But they haven't acquired the straightening iron yet.

A question is continually in my mind: How can this handful of whites keep these millions of blacks down?

The blacks can't be but so dumb—they show too much adeptness at handling the white man's contraptions—bicycles, cars, carpentry, forges, football cricket, languages, etc.

November 8

Left Maseru at 8 [A.M.]. "Alexander," the much mouthed Sesuto, driving, Ma and Pa Bull in back seat.

All along the road the natives were industriously ploughing the fields. They appear to be a real peasant people—farmers and herders, though the men are scarce and one sees mainly women and children in the fields. The men are at the mines. They use oxen before the plough and sometimes as many as full span.*

Umbrellas seem very popular with the native women. I saw many of them along the route—walking down road with babies on back, strolling across fields and even on horse back—with umbrellas unfurled.

We saw scores of neat, unobtrusive villages on hills and mountain. Many are a ruddy-brown color—built with red clay. Many use the local sand stone for part of their huts. The huts blend into the background thatched tops. Some square and some round. Mrs. Bull says that the square huts are thot [thought] to be "more advanced" than the round [ones].

We attend a court in Masupha's village in Leribe. The court is held every day but Sunday. The court is presided over by the chairman of the court and not Chief Masupha, who has gone into town and taken some members of the court with him.

The court is held outside with members of the court seated on chairs underneath trees. Moshesh established custom of holding courts under a Monkhoane tree,[†] and most village courts continue it. Spectators perched in a circle about the court on rocks. The members of the court are nominees of the chief—headmen and elders. They serve at pleasure of the chief.

The first case we observed is over a cow. The plaintiff is a ragged old man who claimed that a cow he has bought has been sold by the husband of the defendant, a old widow, and that a substitute cow was being pawned off on him.

The widow sat under a Mexican aloe (cactus) plant, her grown daughter squatting beside her. She claimed that she knew nothing about the change. The litigants and the court yelled back and forth at each other with questions and answers.

The cow, it develops, had been sold by the son to another party. Due apologies were made to the plaintiff at the time and he was offered the return of the £2 he had paid for the animal—but this plaintiff refused because he maintained that the cow belonged to him in the first place.

The old lady defendant got very "hot" and proceeded to bawl out the court, telling the chief questioner on the court to "shut up," and claiming

---

*Depending on the weight of a plough and the strength of the oxen, a full span can vary from two to eight oxen.

†The monkhoane, or parsley, tree (*Heteromorpha arborescens*) has a special association with moshoeshoe's birthplace, Menkhoaneng, "the place of monkhoane trees."

that the plaintiff had misrepresented the facts and that the court's questions favored the plaintiff.

The case was complicated by the fact that the cow had had 4 calves—during period of dispute, and is sure involves ownership.

The court finished its questioning and reserved it decision until after it had held later deliberation on the case.

Another case was called. 2nd case: defendant had married and had to pay "bohali" (lobola). He paid 13 of the 16 cattle demanded for his wife, and chief ordered him to [pay] the other 3. A chief's messenger was sent out to collect the other 3 cattle.

Messenger set out to collect them and he demanded a fee of 2/6. But defendant didn't have it at the moment, and then messenger seized 1/2 [a] bag of peas.

Defendant says he now has the 2/6 and wishes his peas back. Messenger hasn't shown up yet and so case was postponed for the time being.

3rd case: land dispute between 2 headmen. The defendant was a tall young fellow and a headman, who talks very rapidly and eloquently. He refuses to give a statement to the court because he alleges that the plaintiff has introduced some extraneous issues into the case that he is unprepared to discuss.

The plaintiff is a fat man with khaki suit. He claims that case is not heard by plaintiffs chief because that is plaintiff's father and therefore the defendant demanded a change in venue to this court.

The defendant claims that plaintiff took 2 fields because the plaintiff claimed they belonged to a man who had moved away from the defendant's village and plaintiff claimed the fields because he is higher in rank (as son of a chief) than defendant.

Court orders defendant to go and write down all his objections.

Had a short conference with the District Officer, Mr. Cannon. He discussed the difficulties with the "educated" natives, who are "too far advanced" for their people, and who criticize the chiefs. He dismissed them by saying "if they don't like it here, they can go elsewhere."

Cannon told us that the head chief in the district is Masupha Molapo, who is "acting" for his brother, Motsoene Molapo, "who has been virtually deposed" because he has outbursts of temper. Cannon says all chiefs must be deposed through the paramount chief, on the recommendation of the administration, however, Cannon complained that old Motsoene doesn't accept the situation too well and keeps sticking his nose into district affairs. . . .

November 8

Ficksburg-Bloemfontein. Drunken, talkative Basuto chief in my compartment. Got in while I was out. Was insistent that he had right to stay though he had only a 2nd class ticket. Ticket examiner put him out with a sharp command. He came by later and apologized. I then invited him [in] and he told me he is a cousin of Chief Masupha, whose village I had just left. Says he got his education at Fort Hare. I told him I am American Negro and he waxed effervescent about how American Negroes like [have pride in] their color and understand and sympathize with the African. Said Sesutos are a great people, but they need education and great leaders. Said Richards, the Resident Commissioner of Basuto[land], is a fine man and shows love for black man externally, but deep in his heart, he is like all white men. Wants to break the African. Says Basutos are excellent politicians.

He told me I ought to see the Council of Chiefs at Maseru next week—then I would hear some fine speeches.

I was put into a smelly compartment at Ficksburg, even though it was a double compartment all to myself.

Ludicrousness of putting me in a jim crow compartment (the jim crow on these South African trains are the coaches marked reserved). The bedding boys always occupy one compartment in them; the native 3rd class coaches are usually on either side, even if it is 1st class, and having a white water in a blue monkey suit to serve me my meals here, and to bow to me and inquire "will that be all, Sir?" and "Is that satisfactory, Sir?"

I'm a curiosity because I travel first class—even the chief travels only second. The ticket examiner very pleasantly inquires what I'm travelling for, and the waiter, seeing all the equipment in my photo apparatus bay while [I am] down changing film in my Rollieflex, asked me if I'm "selling them."

I told ticket examiner in answer to his inquiry that I was doing research in cultural anthropology for the S.S.R.C.* He just gave me a queer look and walked out.

I'm transcribing these notes on the train—over a bumpy roadbed and in relative comfort at that—thanks to Mr. Bull, who told me that writing in a train is relatively easy, if one puts a pillow in one's lap.

*The Social Science Research Council, Bunche's funding organization.

MARTIN LUTHER KING, JR.

Martin Luther King, Jr., was born in 1929. Before the age of forty he would become one of America's most internationally known and respected leaders. After leading the Montgomery bus boycott, which successfully challenged segregation on public accommodations throughout the South, King visited India. Because King's political strategies and philosophies had been greatly influenced by Mahatma Gandhi, this trip was quite significant for him. The selection here is taken from an article about that trip that first appeared in *Ebony* magazine in 1959. The article and its place of publication are very important. Because *Ebony* was the publication most read by African Americans, it served as a forum for shaping and informing black households throughout the nation. Here King does not address this audience about the struggles with which they are most familiar; rather, he makes connections between their own struggles and those of a people thousands of miles away. Also, the article is significant in that it demonstrates King's growing class consciousness and his emergence as a statesmen of international prominence who comments not only on domestic issues but on foreign ones as well. Within less than a decade, King would fall prey to an assassin's bullet at the age of thirty-nine.

"MY TRIP TO THE LAND OF GANDHI" (1959)
from
Ebony

For a long time I had wanted to take a trip to India. Even as a child the entire Orient held a strange fascination for me—the elephants, the tigers, the temples, the snake charmers and all the other storybook characters.

While the Montgomery boycott was going on, India's Gandhi was the guiding light of our technique of nonviolent social change. We spoke of him often. So as soon as our victory over bus segregation was won, some of my friends said: "Why don't you go to India and see for yourself what the Mahatma, whom you so admire, has wrought."

In 1956 when Pandit Jawaharlal Nehru, India's prime minister, made a short visit to the United States, he was gracious enough to say that he wished that he and I had met and had his diplomatic representatives make inquiries as to the possibility of my visiting his country some time soon. Our former American ambassador to India, Chester Bowles, wrote me along the same lines.

But every time that I was about to make the trip, something would interfere. At one time it was my visit by prior commitment to Ghana. At another time my publishers were pressing me to finish writing *Stride Toward Freedom*. Then along came Mrs. Izola Ware Curry. When she struck me with that Japanese letter opener on that Saturday afternoon in September as I sat autographing books in a Harlem store, she not only knocked out the travel plans that I had but almost everything else as well.

After I recovered from this near-fatal encounter and was finally released by my doctors, it occurred to me that it might be better to get in the trip to India before plunging too deeply once again into the sea of the southern segregation struggle.

I preferred not to take this long trip alone and asked my wife and my friend, Lawrence Reddick, to accompany me. Coretta was particularly interested in the women of India and Dr. Reddick in the history and government of that great country. He had written my biography, *Crusader Without Violence*, and said that my true test would come when the people who knew Gandhi looked me over and passed judgment upon me and the Montgomery movement. The three of us made up a sort of three-headed team with six eyes and six ears for looking and listening.

The Christopher Reynolds Foundation made a grant through the American Friends Service Committee to cover most of the expenses of the trip and the Southern Christian Leadership Conference and the Montgomery Improvement Association added their support. The Gandhi Memorial Trust of India extended an official invitation, through diplomatic channels, for our visit.

And so on February 3, 1959, just before midnight, we left New York by plane. En route we stopped in Paris with Richard Wright, an old friend of

Reddick's, who brought us up to date on European attitudes on the Negro question and gave us a taste of the best French cooking.

We missed our plane connection in Switzerland because of fog, arriving in India after a roundabout route, two days late. But from the time we came down out of the clouds at Bombay on February 10, until March 10, when we waved goodbye at the New Delhi airport, we had one of the most concentrated and eye-opening experiences of our lives. There is so much to tell that I can only touch upon a few of the high points.

At the outset, let me say that we had a grand reception in India. The people showered upon us the most generous hospitality imaginable. We were graciously received by the prime minister, the president and the vice-president of the nation; members of Parliament, governors and chief ministers of various Indian states; writers, professors, social reformers and at least one saint. Since our pictures were in the newspapers very often it was not unusual for us to be recognized by crowds in public places and on public conveyances. Occasionally I would take a morning walk in the large cities, and out of the most unexpected places someone would emerge and ask: "Are you Martin Luther King?"

Virtually every door was open to us. We had hundreds of invitations that the limited time did not allow us to accept. We were looked upon as brothers with the color of our skins as something of an asset. But the strongest bond of fraternity was the common cause of minority and colonial peoples in America, Africa and Asia struggling to throw off racialism and imperialism.

We had the opportunity to share our views with thousands of Indian people through endless conversations and numerous discussion sessions. I spoke before university groups and public meetings all over India. Because of the keen interest that the Indian people have in the race problem these meetings were usually packed. Occasionally interpreters were used, but on the whole I spoke to audiences that understood English.

The Indian people love to listen to the Negro spirituals. Therefore, Coretta ended up singing as much as I lectured. We discovered that autograph seekers are not confined to America. After appearances in public meetings and while visiting villages we were often besieged for autographs. Even while riding planes, more than once pilots came into the cabin from the cockpit requesting our signatures.

We got a good press throughout our stay. Thanks to the Indian papers, the Montgomery bus boycott was already well known in that country. Indian publications perhaps gave a better continuity of our 381-day bus strike than did most of our papers in the United States. Occasionally I meet some American fellow citizen who even now asks me how the bus boycott is going, apparently never having read that our great day of bus integration, December 21, 1956, closed that chapter of our history.

We held press conferences in all of the larger cities Delhi, Calcutta, Madras and Bombay—and talked with newspapermen almost everywhere we went. They asked sharp questions and at times appeared to be hostile but that was just their way of bringing out the story that they were after. As reporters, they were scrupulously fair with us and in their editorials showed an amazing grasp of what was going on in America and other parts of the world.

The trip had a great impact upon me personally. It was wonderful to be in Gandhi's land, to talk with his son, his grandsons, his cousins and other relatives; to share the reminiscences of his close comrades, to visit his ashrama, to see the countless memorials for him and finally to lay a wreath on his entombed ashes at Rajghat. I left India more convinced than ever before that nonviolent resistance is the most potent weapon available to oppressed people in their struggle for freedom. It was a marvelous thing to see the amazing results of a nonviolent campaign. The aftermath of hatred and bitterness that usually follows a violent campaign was found nowhere in India. Today a mutual friendship based on complete equality exists between the Indian and British people within the commonwealth. The way of acquiescence leads to moral and spiritual suicide. The way of violence leads to bitterness in the survivors and brutality in the destroyers. But, the way of nonviolence leads to redemption and the creation of the beloved community.

The spirit of Gandhi is very much alive in India today. Some of his disciples have misgivings about this when they remember the drama of the fight for national independence and when they look around and find nobody today who comes near the stature of the Mahatma. But any objective observer must report that Gandhi is not only the greatest figure in India's history but that his influence is felt in almost every aspect of life and public policy today.

India can never forget Gandhi. For example, the Gandhi Memorial Trust (also known as the Gandhi Smarak Nidhi) collected some $130 million soon after the death of "the father of the nation." This was perhaps the largest, spontaneous, mass monetary contribution to the memory of a single individual in the history of the world. This fund, along with support from the Government and other institutions, is resulting in the spread and development of Gandhian philosophy, the implementing of his constructive program, the erection of libraries and the publication of works by and about the life and times of Gandhi. Posterity could not escape him even if it tried. By all standards of measurement, he is one of the half-dozen greatest men in world history.

I was delighted that the Gandhians accepted us with open arms. They praised our experiment with the nonviolent resistance technique at Montgomery. They seem to look upon it as an outstanding example of the possibilities of its use in Western civilization. To them as to me it also suggests that nonviolent resistance *when planned and positive in action* can work effectively even under totalitarian regimes.

We argued this point at some length with the groups of African students who are today studying in India. They felt that nonviolent resistance could only work in a situation where the resisters had a potential ally in the conscience of the opponent. We soon discovered that they, like many others, tended to confuse passive resistance with nonresistance. This is completely wrong. True nonviolent resistance is not unrealistic submission to evil power. It is rather a courageous confrontation of evil by the power of love, in the faith that it is better to be the recipient of violence than the inflictor of it, since the latter only multiplies the existence of violence and bitterness in the universe, while the former may develop a sense of shame in the opponent, and thereby bring about a transformation and change of heart.

Nonviolent resistance does call for love, but it is not a sentimental love. It is a very stern love that would organize itself into collective action to right a wrong by taking on itself suffering. While I understand the reasons why oppressed people often turn to violence in their struggle for freedom, it is my firm belief that the crusade for independence and human dignity that is now reaching a climax in Africa will have a more positive effect on the world, if it is waged along the lines that were first demonstrated in that continent by Gandhi himself.

India is a vast country with vast problems. We flew over the long stretches, from north to south, east to west; took trains for shorter jumps and used automobiles and jeeps to get us into the less accessible places.

India is about a third the size of the United States but has almost three times as many people. Everywhere we went we saw crowded humanity — on the roads, in the city streets and squares, even in the villages.

Most of the people are poor and poorly dressed. The average income per person is less than seventy dollars per year. Nevertheless, their turbans for their heads, loose-flowing, wrap-around *dbotis* that they wear instead of trousers and the flowing saris that the women wear instead of dresses are colorful and picturesque. Many Indians wear part native and part Western dress.

We think that we in the United States have a big housing problem, but in the city of Bombay, for example, over a half-million people sleep out of doors every night. These are most unattached, unemployed or partially employed males. They carry their bedding with them like foot soldiers and unroll it each night in any unoccupied space they can find—on the sidewalk, in a railroad station or at the entrance of a shop that is closed for the evening.

The food shortage is so widespread that it is estimated that less than thirty percent of the people get what we would call three square meals a day. During our great depression of the 1930s, we spoke of "a third of a nation" being "ill-housed, ill clad and ill fed." For India today, simply change one-third to two-thirds in that statement and that would make it about right.

As great as is unemployment, under-employment is even greater. Seventy percent of the Indian people are classified as agricultural workers and most of these do less than two hundred days of farm labor per year because of the seasonal fluctuations and other uncertainties of mother nature. Jobless men roam the city streets.

Great ills flow from the poverty of India but strangely there is relatively little crime. Here is another concrete manifestation of the wonderful spiritual quality of the Indian people. They are poor, jammed together and half starved but they do not take it out on each other. They are a kindly people. They do not abuse each other—verbally or physically—as readily as we do. We saw but one fist fight in India during our stay.

In contrast to the poverty-stricken, there are Indians who are rich, have luxurious homes, landed estates, fine clothes and show evidence of overeating. The bourgeoisie—white, black or brown—behaves about the same the world over.

And then there is, even here, the problem of segregation. We call it race in America; they call it caste in India. In both places it means that some are considered inferior, treated as though they deserve less.

We were surprised and delighted to see that India has made greater progress in the fight against caste "untouchability" than we have made here in our own country against race segregation. Both nations have federal laws against discrimination (acknowledging, of course, that the decision of our Supreme

Court is the law of our land). But after this has been said, we must recognize that there are great differences between what India has done and what we have done on a problem that is very similar. The leaders of India have placed their moral power behind their law. From the Prime Minister down to the village councilmen, everybody declares publicly that untouchability is wrong. But in the United States some of our highest officials decline to render a moral judgment on segregation and some from the South publicly boast of their determination to maintain segregation. This would be unthinkable in India.

Moreover, Gandhi not only spoke against the caste system but he acted against it. He took "untouchables" by the hand and led them into the temples from which they had been excluded. To equal that, President Eisenhower would take a Negro child by the hand and lead her into Central High School in Little Rock.

Gandhi also renamed the untouchables, calling them "Harijans" which means "children of God."

The government has thrown its full weight behind the program of giving the Harijans an equal chance in society—especially when it comes to job opportunities, education, and housing.

India's leaders, in and out of government, are conscious of their country's other great problems and are heroically grappling with them. The country seems to be divided. Some say that India should become Westernized and modernized as quickly as possible so that she might raise her standards of living. Foreign capital and foreign industry should be invited in, for in this lies the salvation of the almost desperate situation.

On the other hand, there are others—perhaps the majority—who say that Westernization will bring with it the evils of materialism, cut-throat competition and rugged individualism; that India will lose her soul if she takes to chasing Yankee dollars; and that the big machine will only raise the living standards of the comparative few workers who get jobs but that the greater number of people will be displaced and will thus be worse off than they are now.

Prime Minister Nehru, who is at once an intellectual and a man charged with the practical responsibility of heading the government, seems to steer a middle course between these extreme attitudes. In our talk with him he indicated that he felt that some industrialization was absolutely necessary; that there were some things that only big or heavy industry could do for the country but that if the state keeps a watchful eye on the developments, most of the pitfalls may be avoided.

At the same time, Mr. Nehru gives support to the movement that would encourage and expand the handicraft arts such as spinning and weaving in home and village and thus leave as much economic self-help and an autonomy as possible to the local community.

There is a great movement in India that is almost unknown in America. At its center is the campaign for land reform known as Bhoodan. It would solve India's great economic and social change by consent, not by force. The Bhoodanists are led by the saints Vinoba Bhave and Jayaprakash Narayan, a highly sensitive intellectual, who was trained in American colleges. Their ideal is self-sufficiency. Their program envisions:

1. *Persuading* large landowners to give up some of their holding to landless peasants.
2. *Persuading* small landowners to give up their individual ownership for common cooperative ownership by the villages;
3. *Encouraging* farmers and villagers to spin and weave the cloth for their own clothes during their spare time from their agricultural pursuits.

Since these measures would answer the questions of employment, food and clothing, the village could then, through cooperative action, make just about everything that it would need or get it through bartering and exchange from other villages. Accordingly, each village would be virtually self-sufficient and would thus free itself from the domination of the urban centers that are today like evil lodestones drawing the people away from the rural areas, concentrating them in city slums and debauching them with urban vices. At least this is the argument of the Bhoodanists and other Gandhians.

Such ideas sound strange and archaic to Western ears. However, the Indians have already achieved greater results than we Americans would ever expect. For example, millions of acres of land have been given up by rich landlords and additional millions of acres have been given up to cooperative management by small farmers. On the other hand, the Bhoodanists shrink from giving their movement the organization and drive that we in America would venture to guess that it must have in order to keep pace with the magnitude of the problems that everybody is trying to solve.

Even the government's five-year plans fall short in that they do not appear to be of sufficient scope to embrace their objectives. Thus, the three five-year plans were designed to provide twenty-five million new jobs over a fifteen-year period but the birth rate of India is six million per year. This means that in fifteen years there will be nine million more people (less those who have died or retired) looking for the fifteen million news jobs. In other words, if the planning were one hundred percent successful, it could not keep pace with the growth of problems it is trying to solve.

As for what should be done, we surely do not have the answer. But we do feel certain that India needs help. She must have outside capital and technical know-how. It is in the interest of the United States and the West to help supply these needs and *not attach strings to the gifts.*

Whatever we do should be done in a spirit of international brotherhood, not national selfishness. It should be done not merely because it is diplomatically expedient, but because it is morally correct. At the same time, it will rebound to the credit of the West if India is able to maintain her democracy while solving her problems.

It would be a boon to democracy if one of the great nations of the world, with almost four hundred million people, proves that it is possible to provide a good living for everyone without surrendering to a dictatorship of either the "right" or "left." Today India is a tremendous force for peace and nonviolence, at home and abroad. It is a land where the idealist and the intellectual are yet respected. We should want to help India preserve her soul and thus help to save her own.

CARL T. ROWAN

Journalist and government official Carl T. Rowan was born in 1925 in Ravenscroft, Tennessee, where he attended Tennessee State University. After being drafted into the military, Rowan went on to attend Oberlin College. He graduated from Oberlin in 1947 and received his master's degree in journalism in 1948 from the University of Minnesota. By 1950 he was one of the first African-American reporters at a major daily newspaper, the *Minneapolis Tribune*.

President John F. Kennedy appointed Rowan deputy assistant secretary of state, and in 1963 President Lyndon Johnson appointed him to head the U.S. Information Agency.

Rowan is the author of several books; the excerpt here is taken from *The Pitiful and the Proud*, published in 1956. This selection chronicles his travels throughout India as a black man.

"A COLORED BROTHER LOST"
f r o m
THE PITIFUL AND THE PROUD (1956)

Our quarrel with racism is that it substitutes the accident of skin color for judgment of men as men. Counter-racism would have us do the same: to lump white men by their supposed racial grouping and govern our acts and reactions accordingly. It is our task to rise above this noxious nonsense.

— CARLOS ROMULO,
at the Bandung Conference

The Indian Airlines DC3 shook and wrenched violently as we flew through angry gray clouds filled with rain waters that soon would pour down on already-ravaged Assam. A fat, bearded man, an odd sight with his long hair and the dangling, glittering jewelry hanging from the lobes of his ears, groaned each time the plane hit an air pocket and shook his insides. He was a pathetic sight as he opened his mouth to vomit, only to find that nothing but air now was left in his massive belly.

I gripped the arms of my seat, trying to forget both the discomfort and the hazard of monsoon-flying by gazing out between clouds at the marvelous blue peaks which glistened in the rays of sunlight that fought their way through the roaring rumble of clouds and mists.

Finally we were descending for a landing at Gauhati. Now I could understand what an Indian writer meant when he described the hills as the ornaments of Assam "as are the stars in a peacock's feather." The hills would tower with beauty, some wearing ugly clouds the way a gorgeous woman might use a so-so hat to emphasize her own beauty. Others merged with the blue of distant skies, forging splendid vistas for all who gazed from the supine plains below.

This was Assam, the land of majestic green woodlands, of the stealthy tiger, the sly leopard and the slithering serpent. Here was that land of malaria and mountains and primitive spiritual doctrines about which my West had heard so much. Other than that, Assam was known to many only as a land of earthquakes and floods. I had heard of Cherrapunji, which claimed the reputation as the wettest spot in the world, lying green and helpless under some 300 inches of rain a year. Even now, I knew, the monsoon once again had battered the hills and plains, pushing torrential streams into the great Brahmaputra River, spreading it over its banks into the fertile plains and across fallow lands, destroying human habitation and animal life. Whole villages were being swept away, much in the manner in which thousands died in the tidal waves that occasionally swept across the Japanese islands.

Assam also was known to outsiders as the site of two of history's great earthquakes. In 1897 the valleys and the hills had rumbled and coughed up disaster, leaving at least 1,540 persons dead. In August, 1950, the earth heaved and shook itself into gruesome contortions as the hills disintegrated and the landscape turned topsy-turvy under a destructive force equal to that of a million atomic bombs. After this, one of the worst earthquakes in Indian history, the Assamese counted up almost 2,000 dead.

Few Americans, other than missionaries and a few tourists lucky enough to learn about the lovely cool hill stations called Shillong and Darjeeling, had ever set foot in Assam. In fact, Assam is little known to the rest of India because it is remote from the center of Indian life. Assam is the easternmost wing of a subcontinent criss-crossed by hills and valleys inhabited by peoples of different races and ethnological loyalties. So in India, Assam to many is a land of witchcraft and magic, of animism and wild tribes, locked in by the bordering states of Tibet and Bhutan to the north, the Himalayan mountain ranges to the northeast, Burma and Manipur to the east and southeast, East Pakistan to the west and southwest. The state is connected to the rest of India only by a narrow strip of land between Bhutan and Nepal.

After our plane landed, I stood for almost an hour under a vast tin-roofed structure that appeared to be a cross between a hangar and a Quonset hut. Finally all the baggage was loaded aboard an ancient old bus. I started to board the bus when the driver opened the rear door and I was almost knocked off my feet in a mad scramble for seats. The driver caught my arm and said, "You sit up front." I stood stunned for a moment until he pointed to a small area of the bus near the driver which had been partitioned off. I took a seat and later found that I was riding first-class, a privilege foreigners get automatically. The bus delivered us to the Indian Airlines office from which I took a rickshaw to Circuit House, a state-government-run residence usually reserved for guests of state. Somehow, I had wangled a room there.

I found Gauhati little different from the rest of India as far as the eye could judge living conditions or the educational standards of the people. Most of all, I learned within twelve hours after arrival that the mind of India was about the same all over. My first evening there, I lectured at B. Barooah College, part of Gauhati University. I talked for half an hour about the press; students questioned me for an hour and a half about international politics and race relations in America. Their questions were sharp and incisive, going to the heart of the strengths and weaknesses of America. Still, I was impressed by the fact that rarely did a questioner begin by saying, "Is it a fact . . . ?" Most of them began, "Now, isn't it a fact . . . ?" I was startled at one point when a young man asked, "Now, isn't it true that at the train station in Tucson, Arizona, there are signs on toilets and water fountains saying: 'For White Gentlemen,' and 'For Colored Men'?" I smiled as I observed that the young man read his questions from a piece of paper which he held behind the heads of the students in front of him, as had been the practice of a number of questioners. . . .

I had been in India a month, and hardly for a single day had I been able to forget that I was a Negro. "Inherently, you are one of us," an Indian would say. "Now, you tell us the real story about the treatment of your race in America," others would say. I strove desperately to be honest in pointing out the areas in which racial injustice exists, but at the same time to give Indians a realistic picture of the significant changes taking place in American race relations. Yet college students and principals insisted on introducing me as a heroic character who had dashed to India just a step ahead of Simon Legree's whip. At the Imperial Bank at New Delhi an official was reluctant to cash a bank draft because he did not believe I was an American.

"Were you born in America?" he asked as he looked unbelievingly at my passport.

"I was born there. My parents were born there. As far back as I've cared to look, all my ancestors were born there," I said.

"Are many of you dark-skinned Americans allowed to go about with this kind of money?" he asked, referring to my draft for 6,500 rupees (about $1,350).

This kind of incident was rare, but questions never ceased about whether Negroes can own property or vote, whether they are lynched with regularity, permitted to marry white people or allowed to live outside all-Negro neighborhoods. But it was August 3 when I finally saw the fullest implications of race among the 365,000,000 people of India.

Nitish Chakravarty, Gauhati correspondent for the *Hindustan Standard*, turned out to be an excellent host, although I had been warned in Calcutta to treat him with suspicion. Several Indian newspapermen there had misgivings about his political affiliations. Chakravarty seemed to me to be no more than an extremely idealistic young man who was genuinely happy to have the opportunity to arrange speeches for an American Negro. On many occasions, as we talked, he expressed to me a feeling of closeness which I made no effort to destroy.

Yet I was not prepared for the display of racial feeling that broke forth when I went before a group of Gauhati newspapermen to talk about the role of the press in social change. I had been lecturing only a few minutes when S. C. Kakati, assistant editor of the *Assam Tribune*, the only English language daily in that state, muttered to me, "We want to get some special questions."

I was shocked at what I considered an unbelievable display of rudeness. I paused and said to the newspapermen, "Apparently I'm wasting my time by lecturing about newspapers and social change. This gentleman indicates he simply wants answers to a few questions. Your chairman asked me to speak for half an hour. If you prefer to ask questions, however, I shall stop my speech here and let you ask them."

The group showed a spontaneous eagerness to get to the question period. I had been warned beforehand that in the group were three admitted Communists and an unknown number of sympathizers. The atmosphere got quite warm. Then a thick-lipped, dark-skinned newsman named P. E. Shanker, who worked for Press Trust of India, India's equivalent of Associated Press, said to me, "Mr. Rowan, I must say that I'm a little disappointed with some of your answers."

"Well, I'm sure you understand, sir, that I answer to suit only my conscience and not necessarily your expectations," I said.

"Well, I came only because I thought you would say things differently," he replied. "I came because I saw your picture in the *Assam Tribune*. I looked at it and I looked at my dark hand and I said, 'Here comes one of us.' I thought I'd come out to hear an American Negro journalist. When one of your white officials came up, many of us would not come out. Some who did refused to shake hands with him. We trust you, and we speak to you frankly, because there is a common bond of color. We hate the white man because he is the cause of all the trouble in Asia today. We respect you, but we hate white America."

I looked around to see nods of agreement.

"What unkindness has America done to you and your country that would lead you to hate her?" I asked.

"Military aid to Pakistan," he cried bitterly. "That is why we now distrust her. We think she is a warmonger. We think she wants to dominate Asia to make it her market."

"I think that is sheer nonsense," I said. "Let's not get involved in a lot of moralistic remarks and charges with no facts behind them. Tell me, where in America's history do you find evidence that she ever dominated any people for economic or ulterior reasons?"

"You see," Shanker replied, "we have been oppressed by the white man for so long. And you have been ruled by the white man. That is why I say we can feel close to you and trust you. But we dare not trust the white man."

Once again heads shook in agreement.

"Now we are going to tell you some things we would not tell a white American," Shanker continued. "We resent your country dropping those atomic bombs on the colored people of Japan. We resent your atomic tests in the Pacific. I say that if there is a dispute between a Western nation and an Asian nation, we automatically side with the Asian nation unless the evidence to the contrary is overwhelming."

In silence the newspapermen stared at me—their "dark-skinned brother."

"Mr. Shanker, as much as any newspaperman likes the flattering notion that he is being told something other newspapermen are not told," I said, "I simply cannot buy all this 'bond of color' nonsense. You see, if I accept your theory that we colored people are all alike in a good way, is it not logical for someone else to accept the bigot's theory that we are all alike in a bad way?

"Having experienced the pains of racism, even as you say, I still cannot accept your theory for a moment. I think it ridiculous to argue that you can trust all colored men, but no white men.

"But I am going to play along with you on this 'common bond of color' business and see how far I can stretch it. I am about to say some things I could not say if it were not as one 'colored brother' to another. First, I think you are a phony, hammering into the minds of your colleagues a theory you cannot believe yourself. Not long ago you expressed fear and hatred of Pakistan's Moslems—men of color. A few minutes ago you were damning my country because of its dealing with Chiang Kai-shek, Syngman Rhee and Bao Dai—all men of color—men whom you obviously do not trust."

"Why do you defend those white devils?" broke in Kakati. "Why do you go around saying there has been progress. We all know that there never has been a Negro president of the United States."

"What does that prove? If I said no man with pink shorts ever has been president, does it mean that nobody with pink shorts has any liberties?" I asked.

"Furthermore," cut in another Indian, "we think American whites are warmongers. We dislike that because we are not a warlike people."

"Hold it," I shouted. "I've heard that too many times, and I've kept silent out of fear of offending your countrymen. But I'm about to test those bonds of color again. Will you tell this colored brother what you unwarlike fellows were doing during the riots at partition? Was that just a game of cops and robbers in which thousands died? Those Indian divisions at Kashmir—are they there just to fall over and plead non-violence if Pakistanis move into Kashmir? Even the minor violence in connection with foreign pockets was an expression of your unwarlike nature, is that it?"

He dodged my question, shouting, "The Portuguese and French imperialists have no right to possessions in India. They must go."

"Fine, suppose we agree that they must go," I said. "What I say to you is that you adopt this unwarlike pose, but you use violence when you think it is morally justified; yet, you label as warmongers another people who only stand ready to use force in a situation where they think the moral necessity is just as obvious and impelling."

"If you claim to be unwarlike, why are you making hydrogen bombs?" Shanker demanded. "Is it not warmongering and emotionalism?"

"We are experimenting with hydrogen bombs for the same reason India is building an army: we feel the day may come when we are forced to use those bombs, although we hope not. We build bombs because we know a potential enemy builds bombs—although you seem to imply that this bomb-building is a one-way street. You must know that last December [1953] my country offered to stop building bombs and to use the money saved to help undeveloped ares of the world if the Russians would stop. The Russians haven't agreed. You cry that we are hysterical because we act in the face of the threat of communism. Is it hysteria when you talk about a threat of Pakistan in Kashmir?"

"That is different, very different," answered Shanker. "We know the Moslems. We know their history. We know they will attack."

"Isn't it rather odd that you can dig back through history to convince yourself that the Moslems are a real menace but that you cannot see recent history—what happened to six hundred million people, some of them as close by as your neighboring Tibet—and conclude that communism is a real menace?" I asked.

"You disappoint me greatly," said Shanker. "I fear the insidious capitalist influence has robbed us of a colored brother."

"Now you see," I said, "you just can't trust some of us colored people."

The newsmen began to file out, some stopping to shake hands with me, a few even expressing approval of the things I had said. Others muttered to themselves. I looked at my watch and saw that the argument had lasted three and a half hours. I left the meeting room and walked back to my room in Circuit House where I sat, a "colored brother lost," thinking about the frightening implications of what I had regarded as an effort to impose thought control by color solidarity. A few minutes later I heard several voices near the compound and I looked out to see the newspapermen returning with a distinguished-looking, gray-haired gentleman. I stepped to the door just as Shanker yelled to me, "We're coming after you again."

Shanker introduced the new gentleman as Debeswar Sarma, a member of Parliament from Jorhat, in North Assam, and former Speaker of the Assam Assembly. This time Sarma did all the talking, going over the same old racial ground over which Shanker and his colleagues had gone, although Sarma was much more subtle. He would preface most of his allegations with regard to the United States with, "I stand to be corrected, but . . . we think your country recognizes Russia but not China because the Chinese are Asians . . . we think the press is preparing your people for war. . . ." After each allegation, I felt compelled to say, "Now since you stand to be corrected, pause and let us see if I can do a bit of correcting. . . .

This meeting lasted an hour and a half, and when it was over I was filled with a frightening realization that here was an inverse racialism which was as much a threat to peace and to man's dignity, to his intellectual being, as was the kind of racism under which I had suffered. I knew then that there existed a great need to make it obvious to Indians that people of different races and backgrounds can build a solidarity of mutual interests and goals and a mutual regard for liberty, and not be self-doomed to recurrent conflict by such a superficial thing as color. I recalled that the public relations man for one state government had said to me, "Your visit is important to us not so much for what you are saying as for who is saying it. It means so much for our people to see that a colored man supports his government in a predominantly white country. With all our language difficulties, we need so much to convince the people of India that a unified democracy can be molded out of a polyglot community."

Those were kind words, and deep inside my mind I accepted them as truth. I found that I had said to the newsmen the only thing that could be said by an individualist who believed deeply that color is too insignificant a thing to govern either men's rights or their actions. But the emotional part of me was disturbed; there was frustration, and I wondered what Shanker might have said about his colored brother lost had he been aware that just three days earlier I had received the following letter from my wife:

Dearest Carl,
. . . We are now home safely after the long drive from Buffalo. I drove all the way and made unexpectedly good time, arriving at Ludington, Mich., several hours before the ferry on which we had reservations was to leave. The earlier ferry was full, so we had to spend the night there.

We went to one motel, which advertised a vacancy, but the woman looked at me and the boys and said, "We don't take colored here." She appeared half drunk, so I didn't bother with her. We went down the road and got motel space without trouble. . . .

7

VISITORS, TOURISTS, AND "OTHERS"

The travelers in this section are mostly writers, but some are educators and activists; that may account for their self-consciousness as they confront the meaning of identity and displacement in the "contact zones" of foreign travel. Gwendolyn Brooks and June Jordan, two of America's most relevant poets, write of their longing to connect with the Africans and Bahamians they observe during their journeys but also note the sense of privilege and otherness they feel in relation to local blacks. As African Americans they are also tourists with a great deal of freedom and mobility. Colleen McElroy, on the back of a motorcycle in the Australian outback, wants to be a "daughter come home" to the aborigines she meets but finally cannot. Travel allows Jordan to analyze not only race but also the connections and differences that cut across class, gender, and ethnicity; she draws on her experiences as a professor and of the politics of tourism to imagine the perspective of her black maid Olive and the poor women in the market with whom she haggles. "We are not particularly women any more; we are parties to a transaction designed to set us against each other."

For these travelers the landscapes that unfold before them evoke memories of home and childhood—comparisons and sensory perceptions abound, suggesting the liminality of travel as a state of being in-between. Doubleness and paradoxes are commonplace.

Florence Ladd and Vincent Carter create portraits in their travelogues—Ladd of Carrie Sembene, an African-American woman living in Africa, and Carter of Bern, Switzerland. Unlike many of the authors in this collection, Carter displaces reference to himself as he writes of city and country lifestyles, describing the conformity and anxieties he senses in the Swiss psyche.

These travelers remind us of the richness of the genre and the hybridity that enables them to fashion accounts that meet the specific goals of their journey. In any case we get a stronger sense of the person through her representation of encounters with otherness and the longing for transformation that seems to be an integral part of every voyage.

Gwendolyn Brooks

Throughout her extraordinary career, Gwendolyn Brooks has published numerous volumes of poetry, a novel, children's literature, and an autobiography. In 1950 she became the first African American to receive the Pulitzer Prize. Born in Topeka, Kansas, in 1917, Brooks was raised in Chicago, where her talent was recognized and nurtured by her family and community. In the 1960s Brooks's work became much more self-consciously political, clearly bearing the influence of a younger generation of black writers of the Black Arts Movement.

The selection here is taken from Brooks's autobiography, *Report from Part One*. Although her work had begun to display affinities for black nationalism, here she describes a trip to Kenya and to Tanzania, where she is recognized not as an African but as an American.

"African Fragment" (1972)
f r o m
Report from Part One

Nairobi, Kenya.

Many many whites, sun-browned, wealthy, flying to the land of the black man.

When the whites on the plane speak of Africa they speak with an affected heartiness, with a glass possessiveness, with nervous bluster.

The first blacks I see in Africa enter the white man's big bird, quickly bob and dip about, cleaning out the trash.

Nairobi. I gulp down the Nairobi midnight air. I stride erectly from the plane to the airport. I tell myself, "I don't care what *any*body says; this is BLACKland—and I am *black*."

In my room, a wastebasket covered with "leopard" cloth. A "Renoir" on a wall. (White women. Pensive white women, plumply sitting.) There is a fat elephant on my key.

Saturday night—the boom-booming of the "Kenya Resident Band," playing nothing in particular, but that very loudly. Loud, red, precipitate music. Howls, off somewhere, loud laughs. . . .

On Sunday morning people, little troops of them, are out. I see them from my window. There is a bunch-dress woman, baby on back, walking beside her husband—who holds a two-inch daughterlet by the tiny hand. I leave the Panafric Hotel, strike out into the sunshine. It is cool enough to wear a jacket. I have put on my blue jacket, tying the belt behind me. Once all the pavement decline of the hotel, I begin to scream inside myself. I notify myself "The earth of *Africa* is under my feet!" Above me, white clouds! Blue, blue sky!

A little boy behind his father on a bicycle at first smiles in response to my own hot just-out-of-the-U.S. smile, then changes his mind and sticks a white tongue out at me, clutching his father all the while.

Black people are everywhere, in bright-colored robes, long gowns tied at the waist, kerchiefs, western trousers and shirts and jackets, western short skirts and separates. I look about at my brothers and sisters, and I am aware of both a warm joy and in inexpressible, irrepressible sadness. For these people, who resemble my "relatives" on Chicago's Forty Seventh and King Drive, or on Thirty Sixth and Calumet, or in the depths of the West Side, are neatly separate from me. In the New Land, my languages were taken away, the accents and nuances of my languages were taken away. I know nothing of Swahili nor of any other African language. Therefore, the chattering blacks around me might just as well be twittering birds. I say "Good morning!" "Hello!" "Hi!" (For as yet I do not even know their "Jambo!") Sometimes they smile, nod and mutter something, sometimes they look blankly at me and say nothing. Sometimes they carefully look away from me.

I think to myself "How long it has taken me to secure for myself the accents, nuances, subtleties of the *English* language!" "I do not have," I say to myself, "another fifty-four years to learn the languages that are rightfully mine!"

The men keep their hair short. (I see an exact copy of balladeer Terry Callier.) Many of the "better off" black men wear black suits. The black cloth looks dull—almost rusty. It is to be observed that the people, in general, admire what is European. But the women's hair and headdress try to rebel—try *not* to "abandon the hut." I see the naturals—naturally—but no "big" naturals. I see tall twists of colored cloth on the lifted heads of the women.

Sgt. Ellis Avenue . . . I see sudden bright recognitions, long warm steady handshakes. I walk and walk and walk. I take pictures with my daughter's little camera. This arouses, variously, curiosity, anger, suspicion, superior impatience. I can tell that some of the people are wondering why I am taking *their* pictures: after all, *I* am the oddity.

Bravely, I enter a downtown grocery store. I do not know enough about the money; I dream embarrassment. I buy cans of orange juice, and wafers and sardines. I buy "*Puf!*" And I manage very well. I offer the Indian saleswoman a large note, and she gives me change, without ever discovering how little I know about "her" money.

Africa. A writer is tempted not to worry about "writing it up"; is tempted just to "let" it beautifully be!

"Mother Africa."

The people here carry on their lives with—it seems—scarcely a thought of their stolen brothers and sisters over the way there, *far* over the way. They have their home problems. I think if all of us up and packed and CAME, some very careful explaining would have to be done. Some mighty sure lessons would have to come through. Otherwise their widening eyes and ears might EXPLODE.

Many Africans, stopping everything at midday, lie down in the nearest grassy place. Oblivious to opinion; faces down or faces up. In bright or dusty clothes.

The cars are after you. They rape as they wish, they rip around corners, aiming their passion here and there. They eye, and *aim.*

There is quietness around me. The voices may rise in rich laughter, but they are chiefly subdued. The young women's voices are appealingly soft, often lightly musical.

I do not see the "pimp" walk affected by many young black men "back home." Here, the walk of a young man is usually full of fresh air and gentle bounce! Or it may be a sort of loose lope.

Gatheru: ". . . Africans—after *all*, it IS *their* country. . . ." When you really *feel* that, Africans of the straight blood, when all the millions of you really *feel* that, along with the knowing your woes will be done.

A little collection of fast walkers turns down a road. I turn, too: I follow them. They enter a comely church, All Saints Cathedral. I think, "How happy my mother would be to know that, on my first Sunday in Africa, I am going to church." In the church, the congregation is black, but there is mixed black and white sitting on the platform, and the somber choir is mixed black and white. For the somber black-robed black at the podium there is one fervent minute of emotional release: "As Tubman said," *he* says with rising stridency, "oh mastuh—don't send yo' *son!*—come yo' SE'F!"

A small man at a newspaper "stand" a few steps away from the church points to a pile of newspapers and asks *at* me "*New York Times?*" It is, I feel, an insult! What, in Africa, on my first day in Africa, do I want with the *New York Times?*

In an Indian bookshop. "You look like a Tourist," says the Indian bookshopkeeper to an Indian shopper in dark glasses and a tall wide floppy black hat. "Oooh *oooh*," she squeals. "I certainly don't *feel* like one!"
Aren't they both tourists? Yes, they are tourists in this land that belongs to *blacks*.

The Third World concept seems to me, at this time, too large for blacks to tackle. There is now-*urgent* business. I want blacks—*right now*—to forge a black synthesis, a black union: so tight that each black may be relied on to protect, enjoy, listen to, and warmly curry his fellows. That, at this time, is business enough.

Back at the hotel. It is an expensive hotel, a "tourist" hotel, and the life in it is certainly not representative of African life in Africa. My friend Era Bell Thompson, international editor of *Ebony Magazine*, has given me the telephone number of Margaret Kenyatta, mayor of Nairobi and daughter of Jomo Kenyatta, and it is my intention to ask her about families, African families ("may I stay with one of them?") and about students, African students ("may one of them show me every aspect of Nairobi, pleasant and unpleasant?"). It is her home number that I have and she is quickly reached. She is surprised to hear from me. (A letter of introduction that Era Bell has sent her is not to reach her until I am back in Chicago.) But she replies to my questions with an invitation to visit her at the City Council next morning. . . .

I wash, change, and descend to the dining room. I am served a good meal by non-committal waiters. *Hurry hurry hurry.* Yield us your plate, so we can be rid of your presence, and can give "your" place at table to another. The handsome dining room is crowded. I ask a waiter about the availability of coffee ice cream. He looks frightened, and begins a six-minute conference with another waiter, who immediately looks as harried. . . .

"SONNY!" imperiously calls the "superior white" man to the black man. SONNY! Come. Do my bidding, *slave.* . . .

Upstairs. My room is on the fourth floor. Out comes my fat elephant key. I enter cautiously, looking up, down, and all around. Ravenous, zig-zagging insects, huge and strange, are what I am looking for, what I fear, anticipate. And in *spite* of the fact that I've lined all the window louvre openings with tissue, there is a disturbance in the globe! But I'm weapon-ready at least. I seize my "Puf!", handy right there at the door. Armed with this canned courage, I stand upon a teetery chair, leer, and—*Puf!—Puf!—Puf!*

I have slain my first, and only, African beast.

It is dark here at fifteen minutes after seven. Most of my week here is going to be cloudy, and it will rain on two of my days.

When I go to bed—looking for flying spiders, jumping roaches and sprinting mosquitoes in every direction (in "all" of Africa, I never saw these!)—I am cold. Cold in Africa! In my ignorance of my mother-home, this seems odd.

Only on this second night of my Nairobi visit do insistent pictures of my "old" life nudge me. I am surprised by sharply illustrated memories of dandelions in my parents' Champlain Avenue back yard, so cherished in my childhood; sandpails; graduations; Chicago bus-boardings; Papa, who wanted no soup on the last day of his life, no fruit juice, but "a lamb chop:"

(we wouldn't give it to him—how cruel, thoughtless, or unimaginative); playmates loved and hated; Reverend Lightfoot at my wedding. But quickly these pictures pack themselves away. And again it is *Africa* that is real.

The City Council Building is a large and wide white beauty.

I have been brought to it from the Panafric Hotel by a handsome chauffeur in a handsome and long black limousine. On my arrival two stalwarts, one on each side, have escorted me up the fine white stairs and up, up into Miss Kenyatta's outer office, where a pretty and efficient young woman with pleasant unsmilingness has coffee brought in to me, coffee with cream and brown sugar, by a young man in tan jacket who *does* smile.

When Miss Kenyatta comes in from who knows what great duty, she take me into her private office. She has more coffee brought in to me. Anxiously she watches me as I drink it. "Is that all right?" During our exchange she says this again and again. The translation is: I hope this which I am doing pleases and aids you.

She is strong. Her beautiful face and the attractive ampleness of her figure say Strength, Security, Means-To-Effect,-Begin,-And-Bring-To-An-End.

I look around me. A heater, named "Valor"; red with still flame. On the wall to my left, a picture of Miss K., in her ceremonial robes of royal red and black. On the wall across from her picture is a large likeness of her father, the just Jomo, whose strength seems powerfully to start into the room, perhaps to say, "Now, *look*, Daughter"; or, perhaps, "COUNTRY-MEN!" I see open boxes of shining insignia—medals, decorations, possibly. These sit, quietly proud, under *her* picture.

What do we talk of? Of Era Bell Thompson, of her concern for Era Bell's weariness. ("She works too hard.") Of Era Bell's various writings. Of the possibility that I might want more coffee. Of the University of Nairobi, which I want to see and to which she telephones. Fredrick Waweru will talk to me at half past two, and, if possible, secure for me a young man or woman who will introduce me to Nairobi family life. We talk of poetry. Yes, she likes some poetry. She likes p'Bitek. "Do you mean the man who wrote 'The Song of Lawino?' Okot p'Bitek?" "Yes." I tell her of my excited admiration of this poet. She smiles, controlled empathy in her smile.

She takes me through a door in her office to a long room filled with gaily-covered couches and chairs (I remember green patterns, and white), where she has me sign her guest book. Then I am returned to the outer office, where she and her secretary speak to each other chiefly of the inadequacy of the telephones that morning—using the softly, affectionately confiding voices that I find so many Africans reserve for friendly conversation among themselves.

Margaret Kenyatta's chauffeur is instructed to take me to the University of Nairobi. Mr. Waweru, I am to find, is the assistant registrar. I tour the beautiful university . . . sit for a while in a large empty room in the Education Building—"Ed. 120"—which is furnished with many chairs cushioned in deep-bright blue. I go out, stride across the grounds, smiling here and there. It seems that *all* of the girls have soft feminine voices! I leave the school grounds and very carefully cross a car-crazy street. I find a nice little shop, and go in to buy gifts for friends. I had been told by Nora, who had attended the university for six weeks the summer before, to trade with care and wit; so whenever the nice young man quotes a price, I look surprised, skeptical, delicately alarmed. He understands the game, of course, and plays with a quiet geniality. He lowers all prices, but not greatly.

Loaded with loot, I return to the university, and find Mr. Waweru.

To my requests to meet families, to be introduced to families, to be taken into homes, Miss Kenyatta's last word had been that "these things" must be arranged—I should have written long ago, and "something" might have been arranged, I am told by Fredrick Waweru: "Your time is so short, and you gave no advance notice; the best time for these social meetings is on the weekend. Take my wife and me, for example. We would have been pleased . . . But my wife works as a nurse, and I'm busy here all week . . . My mother and father live far away . . . When are you leaving?"

"Saturday."

"The weekend!" he exclaims in relief. "You see?"

I see.

So. Miss K. knows no student to recommend to my company, and Mr. W., *if he hears of one*, will let me know.

"We don't want you disappearing," says Fredrick Waweru. "You don't want just anyone for a guide, because we wouldn't want you to just sort of disappear."

"Good gosh, no!" and I shudder, remembering that I have just read in a newspaper there of the disappearance of two white Americans. When I exclaim and shudder, Mr. W. really opens up, and laughs with warm friendship before the image of it all: me disappearing, you see—utterly, utterly disappearing, with no trace ever and whatsoever. . . .

He is generous. He informs me of the curriculum, of the different schools in the combine and of their offerings. He says that at the next graduation there will be at least ten doctors coming from their school of medicine. "The next year this will be doubled; and soon. . . ." He talks of the school of journalism. He says, too, in answer to my eager question, that poet p'Bitek is still a member of the university staff, but is, at the time, some thirty miles away. He makes a telephone call. The conversation, with whomever, is carried on in quick, cheery "African"—Swahili? Yoruba? I certainly and sorrowfully do not know.

"Are you coming back to Nairobi from Dar es Salaam? No; from Dar es Salaam I shall go to Cairo, and from Cairo to London, and from London to Chicago. "P'Bitek will definitely be here at the university on the twenty-eighth and twenty-ninth, so, if you can rearrange your travel plans, he could see you here."

In any event, I leave copies of Broadside Press books and Third World Press books for Okot p'Bitek and for Mr. Waweru himself, autographing those that are my own. (I had left copies of my books with Miss Kenyatta, who looked pleased to have them.)

I request a cab. Mr. Waweru summons a servitor, who on arrival is told to take me downstairs, and to get a cab for me. I shake hands with Mr. W., and look into his eyes for the last time. It has been interesting, observing those eyes; one is impressed by the level silence of the eyes. You *have* to think of the eyes of lions, looking with calm neither warm nor cool at the intruder, who may or may not be welcome. During our time together— about forty minutes—his messages have been well lined up, and he has spoken at a steady rate, fluent, but *not* super-fast as he tells me he fears.

Downstairs the cab is a long time coming. I stand in one of the arched doorways, watching the people. A small spinning girl, about four, with almost no hair, is engaged and petted by many passers-through. She throws back her head at each notice, and gazes coquettishly at her admirer. She gives words to each. African words. "She, too, speaks an African language," I muse despondently. "I, at *fifty*-four, do not."

I see worried-looking white professors, with lines across perspiring brows. I see big-naturaled, Edwardian-jacketed, tight-trousered, "pimp" walking American "dudes." Here again are the strong but modest young African girls who, when they speak at all, speak with that shy musical soft-ness I am beginning to revere. And I am fascinated by the African male stu-dents, short, tall, graceful or agreeably wobbly, who when they recognize each other greet each other with a warm affection so beautiful I wish urgently that I might be a part of it.

Profound handshakes, handshakes of earnest fellowship delightfully spice this campus.

"It's coming," says a young man, leaning out of the wee office which holds telephones, a table, and two attendants. So I thank him, and go out to the road to find "it."

I do not want to see Miss Kenyatta again, distinctive though she is. I do not, on this little trip, want a thoroughly official flavoring of my impressions. I want my impressions to be spontaneous. At another time I could enjoy, if allowed, a richer acquaintance with this firm mayor of Nairobi—would enjoy talking honestly and piercingly (if that is possible: perhaps it is not) of matters that really scrape up out of the heart, rather than of coffee, poet preferences and mutual acquaintance.

Coffee *does* seem, however, a serious matter here! For a cloud had come over the face of Miss Kenyatta's cautiously friendly secretary when I first declined coffee *or* tea, so I quickly changed my mind and accepted the steaming coffee served with a pitcher of cream, a bowl of brown sugar crystals. Served in a green and white cup, on a green and white chipped saucer. And as for poesy—well, when I told Miss Kenyatta that I keep buying copies of *The Song of Lawino* to give away, she looked at me, for the first time, as though I *might* be a decent and interesting human being, instead of just another nosy, needling 'nited States-er, cluttering up her country and her time. "Call me tomorrow," she had said warmly when we parted, "and let me know how you make out at the University of Nairobi. I am not a scholar, and I do not know much about these matters. But call me. Is that all right?"

I call the next afternoon. A man answers. He knows no English, and will not bring any one else to the telephone. But I want only to assure her that I have "made out" just fine, just fine. And I do not call again.

In all the places I visit, in all the Nairobi streets I roam, I encounter only one dashiki-wearer. A man of about thirty, hymn-singing in the All Saints Cathedral.

Monroe Sharp left Chicago four years ago, and is making Tanzania his home. "Our African relatives here," he informs me, "have got *some* doubts about us. 'Well, Afro-AMERICANS,' they like mutter, *'you're* not going to come over here and take over *our own* country!' For," goes on Monroe, "they know that the Afro-Ams have, in general, more education and skills than have they—that they can't compete therein—and, before they know it, a takeover by their little long-lost brothers and sisters COULD occur. 'We're not about to let that happen,' vow those Africans aware of a threat-potential."

Other Sharp warnings. Don't come over, Afro-Americans, expecting everything to move as it does in the United States. Americans are, above all, pragmatic. If things don't *move*, they're geared to *find out why* there's no motion. They automatically *do* something about the failure or faltering. But in Tanzania, it might take a couple of months to secure a needed part from, say, England. And there are other reasons why gallopings cannot be effected. Some are rooted deep in ancient awes, fears, and prejudices. Eggs, perhaps, cannot be eaten by the women of one area because there is a fear that fertility will be hindered. And—one witch doctor is being hunted in regard to sixty "murders" of children: in this case, perhaps, sixty boys have been lined up and *whacked*; circumcisions!—all done by an old, a traditional knife—poisonous, of *course*.

Come, says Monroe. But come willing to ask questions and to receive answers and to endure hardships.

THE AFRICANS! They insist on calling themselves Africans and their little traveling brothers and sisters "Afro-Americans" no matter *how* much we want them to recognize our kinship.

Says Monroe of "the Africans:" "They can appreciate a nice angry spirit. But they ain't goin' to stand for you comin' over here and blowin' up the Hotel Kilimanjaro because *Nixon's* stayin' there."

SUE BAILEY THURMAN

Educator, reformer, lecturer, author, musician, and religious worker Sue Bailey Thurman is perhaps best known as the wife of the influential theologian Dr. Howard Thurman. However, this multitalented woman was a leader in her own right. A club woman throughout her life, Thurman was the founder and editor of the NCNW's journal, the editor of the YWCA's journal, and the founder of the Howard University Faculty Wives Association. In addition, she collected and assembled "Dolls for Democracy," an exhibit of faces of African-American women fashioned by sculptor Meta Vaux Warrick Fuller. Widely read and broadly traveled, Thurman contributed articles and essays about her travels to the leading African-American and Quaker journals of her day. The selection here is taken from an article that first appeared in *The Crisis* and documents her travels to Mexico. In this piece she urges African Americans to pursue travels in this "colored country" in addition to or perhaps instead of Europe. For Thurman, as for black travelers before and after her, Mexico provided a much better racial climate for African Americans.

"HOW FAR FROM HERE TO MEXICO?" (1930)
from
THE CRISIS

The inspiration of the title calls back to those sultry summers of long ago when the children of my childhood gathering at nightfall ended the day with the favorite game:

"How far from here to Mexico?

"Threescore miles and ten."

"Can I get there by candlelight?"

"Yes, if the old gray witch doesn't catch you on the way!"

Tonight in a quiet street in Mexico City I am again measuring the distance that lies between the United States and Mexico, but this time it is in terms of that which separates the American Negro from the land and inhabitants of our neighbor of the South. I have not often made my steps this way. Negroes are little known and seldom encountered here for only the very rare occasion brings Negroes from America to this place. Two young women came with the Hubert Herring Seminar, auspices of the Committee on Cultural Relations with Latin America, in 1931. In the same year a writer and an educator, newlywed, chose a honeymoon to Mexico via Vera Cruz. Our poet, Langston Hughes has made visits here to see his father who came long ago and elected to stay. More recently grooms accompanied the American entourage which came in for the International Polo Matches. And there was a jazz orchestra, one of the latest visitors, whose scheduled engagement met with ill-fortuned results. Now comes *La Imitacion de la Vida* which has been showing in Mexico City for several weeks and is dated for sometime ahead in the outlying districts of the city. I saw it again in Mexico just to make a study of the Mexican reactions. Much of it could not be transplanted to this Latin soil and be understood. But it was surprising how much of it could be and with what clear insight the audience took in the various nuances of its purport and meaning. There were expressions of "Mucho!" in praise of the acting of Louise Beavers. But from all indications the film held no "surprise element" for the Mexican theatregoers. It was as they expected it to be, if indeed it would be any kind of imitation at all! Its theme was concerned with the life and work of a devoted Negro servant, in which part we have appeared most often in real life among them.

NEGROES UNKNOWN

They have seen us in the role of grooms, jazz orchestras or menial laborers employed at the whim of some American family or business firm resident in Mexico. They have seen the segregation of the Negro begin at Laredo, Tex., and extend north to Popular Bluff, Mo. They have gazed from drawing rooms bearing them onward to Washington or to city consulates, out upon the narrow streetways and dingy hovels of the segregated sections of our American cities. They have learned of us from the American white man in their midst, usually a southerner, who faithfully reflects in his own life the attitude of the United States itself toward its racial minority groups. Mexicans, themselves, know nothing about our artists or craftsmen, our educators, business or professional men, newspaper editors, if they suspect us of having newspapers, or students in contemporary life in America. Lacking such a vast range of intelligence it is small wonder that one's application for passport ("permit" it really is), should be held so long before being accorded the simple courtesy and deference due under the tourists-laws governing all Americans other than Negroes. They cannot believe that we are actually citizens of the United States, and where the idea is accepted it is taken to be a matter of little moment, rendered invalid by its limiting provisos.

It is pleasant, indeed, that Louise Beavers can act and that as an actress she has been recognized by audiences in Mexico. But I am more concerned with the fate in Mexico of Louise Beavers the person, and I admit being genuinely distressed that the case has been such that had she applied for admission here, on any provocation of her own, purely as an American woman, she might have chosen another place to visit during the interminable period in which she would have waited for the permission to be granted without payment of bond.

It is more regrettable when one remembers that loveliness is here to sell at a rate of exchange in love of pure beauty! Natural beauty—a glimpse of proud Popacatepetl drowsing above the tropical valleys; henna, blue and olive landscapes, a gay backdrop for Santa Anita. Spiritual beauty—Chapultopec Park and the national band concerts; Mexican songs with guitar accompaniment strumming far into the night; lively feet dancing the *Jarabe*; slow-moving feet offering gardenias; swift, gliding feet, scarce touching the pavement; off to the new future of Mexico!

BETTER THAN EUROPE

It should not be too difficult to persuade some of us to leave off the trek to Europe for a while, long enough to explore the mysteries of the other Americas. Or must we wait for the very young Negroes, world-seekers of tomorrow, who will wander far and wide forcing their destiny into far-away places; there to be found at home in the language and culture, and at home in having come to the end of their quest for the "other soul." Happily, some with only a few years of age have begun already with books of travel, and international periodicals cleverly written to allure their childish wanderlust. Others whose privilege is too occasional to be considered a commonplace, receive the impetus through vicarious experiences in the foreign language classroom. These know the incommunicable fascination of being initiated into the language through the medium of one in whom the culture of the language has found a voice. Here—in the example of the excellent Professor Spratlin who directed my first studies in Spanish—the induction into Hispanic culture is made through contact with one who offers in his personal culture a unique scroll of the civilization.

This is looking forward to that future when one will no longer settle down to the toil of making new culture paths in American living, until he has first heard the teacups rattling in many different languages, and made himself a part of all the comparative life vouchsafed for him through travel.

Herein is a new path to self-discovery and to the state of invulnerableness in which one is sure of what he knows. Its security has been recently summarized in the bold and vigorous utterance of a young Mexican of today: "It is something to have found *my* relationship to the social and political evolution of the three Americas. Circumstances may not overcome this wisdom, for, I have within myself the germ of all reform!"

Mrs. Thurman was directed by the chief of the immigration department in Mexico City, (in Spanish)—Dirrecion General de Poblacion, Antonio Hidalgo, to advise all Negro tourists interested in a trip to Mexico to apply at the nearest consulate where permits should be granted at once without any difficulty. If there is difficulty,—communicate the trouble to the Mexican Ambassador in Washington, Castillo Najera, and send a copy of the correspondence to Antonio Hidalgo, Chief of Immigration. Orders have been issued to Washington that no difficulties were to be placed in the way of Negro tourists entering the country and that they were to enjoy the same facilities as anyone else.

VINCENT CARTER

Little is known about Vincent Carter, the author of *The Bern Book: A Record of a Voyage of the Mind*, published in 1970. Carter was born in Kansas City, Missouri, in 1924. After working for the Union Pacific Railroad, he entered Lincoln University, just outside Philadelphia, and then went to Wayne State. Following his education, he traveled to Paris and then to the capital of Switzerland, Bern, where he settled as an expatriate. While there, Carter wrote novels and autobiographical, philosophical meditations on his experiences and observations as a black man living in Bern. The book is complex, difficult, and exciting. It clearly belongs to a tradition of black experimental writing, which has received far too little attention from literary critics and historians.

"The City"
f r o m
The Bern Book: A Record of the Voyage of the Mind (1970)

... The old section of the city of Bern presented to my consciousness a feeling of patient, fearful watchfulness. It was so gray and heavy and low and close together, like a crowd of old men huddled around a secret. Upon viewing the town from a high place, the grayness and the heaviness seemed to spiral into varying shades from the center of town toward its periphery. The age of the town, it seemed, should have been determinable from the concentric rings, which traced its movement in time and space from one level to another, as it ascended the gentle grade, rising from the banks of the emerald river, Aare.

The little knot in the center I imagined to have been the original seed—
planted by the powerful Duke of Zähringer—from which Bern grew, and
the successive rings to have indicated the movement of the farmers from
the surrounding villages to various convenient places, where they gathered
in order to trade with their city neighbors and where the need for tradesmen and shops soon after arose, which place synthesized and grew in population and importance until it became the capital of the nation, and the
capital of the nation became the host to the community of nations known
as Europe, housing the embassies and legations not only of Europe, but of
every major power in the world.

Although Bern is surrounded by green fields and orchards (drive fifteen
minutes in any direction from the center of the city and you are in the
country) it is a city which is principally inhabited by the *Beamter*, or civil
servant, who comes from every canton in the nation and is a part of the
diplomatic complements of visiting nations.

The land and the houses were (and are now) the property of the wealthy
burgher who rose to power as the city, and consequently the federation,
grew. However, Zürich became the center of the nation's economic interests, while Bern's major role became ultimately political.

The capital of Switzerland and the diplomatic center for world media-
tion, in order to meet the needs of the ever-growing bureaucracy, had to
have houses and shops and produce, in order to sustain its role in the western community of nations. As a result, the city has developed in a peculiar
way, for because of its peculiar position in relation to its neighbors
(Switzerland does not have enough natural resources to exist independently) it must depend upon quiet, peaceful, profitable relations with its
neighbors, all of whom are more powerful that it is.

Bern, therefore, has the air of a brightly polished shop with a full stock of
goods on display with which to satisfy her own needs and attract the fearsome
but necessary strangers. Its thick gray stones house the stores, which are supplied by the peasant farmers and by trade procurement, and thick bars on the
bank windows protect the currencies of the entire world, and the banks are
in turn backed by an economic-political policy of careful conservatism,
which is inspired by the awesome view of the mountains on clear *Föhn* days.

Contrary to the city citizen's life, the peasant's life is relatively secure.
He has the house (with many improvements, of course) which his grandfather had. He rises at dawn, just like farmers everywhere, and goes to bed
with the chickens. Because he works very hard his hands are gnarled like

the trees in his thickets and his face is rough and leathery from relentless windlashings. Though his eyes are bleary, he wears no glasses.

He has a stout wife and sturdy children. They are over there, tossing hay in the field. He has cows. They are tinkling on the hillside above. He can read, write and figure, and there is a man in town on market days, in front of the Metropole cinema, to explain the new machines. He has several. There is a thick silver watch with a heavy chain in his trousers pocket, but he seldom looks at it because he is used to reading the time by gazing beneath a down-cupped palm at the sun. His daughter, however, has a shiny new gold wristwatch. The boys can take care of themselves; the oldest, if he will only settle down, will have the farm, but it is the girl who worries him. He dresses her up in fine city clothes and buys her a big new American car, in which to ride to town on market days. A good dowry will get her a respectable city man, a doctor maybe.

In the city the land is all taken. The young man or woman who wishes to make his way in life is perforce confronted with the problem of finding a "place," a little piece of earth, upon which to plant his feet solidly and be.

The secure man has a job with a living salary, graded advancement and retirement at the age of sixty-five. He lives at the end of a parallel avenue with a wife who bears his children and keeps his apartment in order. The children go to elementary and commercial school, in order to become tradesmen, businessmen (the story of Horatio Alger is very well known in Switzerland) or they go to the gymnasium and to the university, in order to become doctors of medicine, national economics or engineers.

To make his way in life easier the buildings and streets, as well as the patina on all imposing statues, are thoroughly scrubbed and polished, and the street signs are freshly painted. Every turn to the right and to the left, every curve and curving tendency is clearly indicated. He can make no mistake, whether on foot or on wheels. Nor can he err in matters of form. All of the standards by which he lives are prescribed so clearly that there can be no room for doubt. The heel of every respectable citizen's shoe is level, nor does the rust thereon embarrass the foot of his knitted sock, though, in spite of the vigilant needle and thread, a hole frequently appears in her hose. But by and large, all the wild threads are dutifully snipped away and the mere outward signs of poverty are hard put to improvise.

Unlike his grandfather in the country, the city citizen is apt to be a little soft and round from a lack of regular exercise and from overeating. His hands feel boneless when you shake them. Upon the fourth finger of his left hand he wears a ring made of a precious metal, offset by a precious stone. Upon his left wrist he wears a Swiss wristwatch, which protrudes proudly from an immaculately starched cuff. The watch he checks daily at six, twelve and six o'clock when he listens to the news. He often wears glasses and he has a slightly ailing heart, a troublesome liver and the nerves of his arms and legs are often inflamed.

The city differs from the country only in degree, which degree, however, imposes a greater variety of ethical situations upon the inhabitants of the city than are imposed upon the inhabitants of the country. This means that the simple, clear, almost instinctive conservatism, which constrains the thoughts and actions of the country folk (who are protected from foreign influences by the mere fact of their isolation and their work) manifest itself in the city in ways which are as various as its function.

In the city the emphasis is upon form. To belong to the society means to conform to its norms. And there is no escape because, though the city is larger and more complex than the country, it is very small as compared to the capital cities of the world. Relatively speaking, the society of the city, like that of the country, is very intimate. One lives a public life simply because one cannot avoid being observed by one's neighbors. One result is that any radical or nonconformist element in the city, like the well-nurtured "wild life" surrounding the countryside, is hard put to improvise.

Therefore, one walks wearily down the straight, narrow avenue, looking neither to the left nor to the right (in the daytime) because the ubiquitous eyes of the dangerous strangers from the powerful nations beyond the mountains are upon you, because of the imposing stares of the strangers from the next canton, because of the accusing eyes of the lovers who occupy the parallel beds who gave birth to strange children, now dead, except for the memory of projected first names and finally because of the empty stares in the eyes of the strangers who face each other over coffee in brightly illuminated kitchens at half-past seven in the morning.

Nervous tensions carve deep intricate patterns into the secret places of the city citizen's consciousness and dilate the pupils of his eyes with subversive desperation—as he registers surprise at the crowded intersection when the stoplight flashes Go! Centuries of accumulated anxiety augments fears, in order to silence which, he eats, drinks, insulates his body with stout pairs of long woolen underwear and covets his wife and his secretary not merely in order to satisfy his appetite, but in order to store up provisions, as it were, in the event of an eminently novel catastrophe.

JUNE JORDAN

June Jordan was born in Harlem in 1936. She has established a reputation as a poet, essayist, and activist. She has also written children's books, a biography, a novel, several plays and poetry collections. The selection here, taken from Jordan's collection *Essays Moving Towards Home: Political Essays*, which explores the tension between the black traveler from the United States in a black island nation and as such reveals the complexities of class and nationality that idealistic notions of blackness often mask.

"REPORT FROM THE BAHAMAS" (1989)
f r o m
MOVING TOWARDS HOME:
· POLITICAL ESSAYS

I am staying in a hotel that calls itself The Sheraton British Colonial. One of the photographs advertising the place displays a middle-aged Black man in a waiter's tuxedo, smiling. What intrigues me most about the picture is just this: while the Black man bears a tray full of "colorful" drinks above his left shoulder, both of his feet, shoes and trouserlegs, up to ten inches above his ankles, stand in the also "colorful" Caribbean salt water. He is so delighted to serve you he will wade into the water to bring you Banana Daiquiris while you float! More precisely, he will wade into the water, fully clothed, oblivious to the ruin of his shoes, his trousers, his health, and he will do it with a smile.

I am in the Bahamas. On the phone in my room, a spinning complement of plastic pages offers handy index clues such as CAR RENTAL and CASINOS. A message from the Ministry of Tourism appears among these

travellers tips. Opening with a paragraph of "WELCOME," the message
then proceeds to "A PAGE OF HISTORY," which reads as follows:

> New World History begins on the same day that modern Bahamian his-
> tory begins—October 12, 1492. That's when Columbus stepped
> ashore—British influence came first with the Eleutherian Adventures of
> 1647—After the Revolutions, American Loyalists fled from the newly
> independent states and settled in the Bahamas. Confederate blockade-
> runners used the island as a haven during the War between the States,
> and after the War, a number of Southerners moved to the Bahamas . . .

There it is again. Something proclaims itself a legitimate history and all it
does is track white Mr. Columbus to the British Eleutherians through the
Confederate Southerners as they barge into New World surf, land on New
World turf, and nobody saying one word about the Bahamian people, the
Black peoples, to whom the only thing new in their island world was this
weird succession of crude intruders and its colonial consequences.

This is my consciousness of race as I unpack my bathing suit in the
Sheraton British Colonial. Neither this hotel nor the British nor the long
ago Italians nor the white Delta airline pilots belong here, of course. And
every time I look at the photograph of that fool standing in the water with
his shoes on I'm about to have a West Indian fit, even though I know he's
no fool; he's a middle-aged Black man who needs a job and this is his job—
pretending himself a servile ancillary to the pleasures of the rich. (Compared to his options in life, I am a rich woman. Compared to most of the
Black Americans arriving for this Easter weekend on a three nights four
days' deal of bargain rates, the middle-aged waiter is a poor Black man.)

We will jostle along with the other (white) visitors and join them in the
tee shirt shops or, laughing together, learn ruthless rules of negotiation as
we, Black Americans as well as white, argue down the price of handwoven
goods at the nearby straw market while the merchants, frequently toothless
Black women seated on the concrete in their only presentable dress, humble themselves to our careless games:

"Yes? You like it? Eight dollar."

"Five."

"I give it to you. Seven."

And so it continues, this weird succession of crude intruders that, now,
includes me and my brothers and my sisters from the North.

This is my consciousness of class as I try to decide how much money I can spend on Bahamian gifts for my family back in Brooklyn. No matter that these other Black women incessantly weave words and flowers into the straw hats and bags piled beside them on the burning dusty street. No matter that these other Black women must work their sense of beauty into these things that we will take away as cheaply as we dare, or they will do without food.

We are not white, after all. The budget is limited. And we are harmlessly killing time between the poolside rum punch and "The Native Show on the Patio" that will play tonight outside the hotel restaurant.

This is my consciousness of race and class and gender identity as I notice the fixed relations between these other Black women and myself. They sell and I buy or I don't. They risk not eating. I risk going broke on my first vacation afternoon.

We are not particularly women anymore; we are parties to a transaction designed to set us against each other.

"Olive" is the name of the Black woman who cleans my hotel room. On my way to the beach I am wondering what "Olive" would say if I told her why I chose The Sheraton British Colonial; if I told her I wanted to swim. I wanted to sleep. I did not want to be harassed by the middle-aged waiter, or his nephew. I did not want to be raped by anybody (white or Black) at all and I calculated that my safety as a Black woman alone would best be assured by a multinational hotel corporation. In my experience, the big guys take customer complaints more seriously than the little ones. I would suppose that's one reason why they're big; they don't like to lose money anymore than I like to be bothered when I'm trying to read a goddamned book underneath a palm tree I paid $264 to get next to. A Black woman seeking refuge in a multinational corporation may seem like a contradiction to some, but there you are. In this case it's a coincidence of entirely different self-interests: Sheraton/cash=June Jordan's short run safety.

Anyway, I'm pretty sure "Olive" would look at me as though I came from someplace as far away as Brooklyn. Then she'd probably allow herself one indignant query before righteously removing her vacuum cleaner from my room: "and why in the first place you come down you without your husband?"

I cannot imagine how I would begin to answer her.

My "rights" and my "freedom" and my "desire" and a slew of other New World values; what would they sound like to this Black woman described on the card atop my hotel bureau as "Olive the Maid"? "Olive" is older than I am and I may smoke a cigarette while she changes the sheets on my bed. Whose rights? Whose freedom? Whose desire?

And why should she give a shit about mine unless I do something, for real, about hers?

It happens that the book that I finished reading under a palm tree earlier today was the novel *The Bread Givers*, by Anzia Yezierska. Definitely autobiographical, Yezierska lays out the difficulties of being both female and "a person" inside a traditional Jewish family at the start of the twentieth century. That any Jewish woman became anything more than the abused servant of her father or her husband is really an improbable piece of news. Yet Yezierska managed such an unlikely outcome for her own life. In *The Bread Givers*, the heroine also manages an important, although partial, escape from traditional Jewish female destiny. And in the unpardonable, despotic father, the Talmudic scholar of that Jewish family, did I not see my own and hate him twice, again? When the heroine, the young Jewish child, wanders the streets with a filthy pail she borrows to sell herring in order to raise the ghetto rent and when she cries, "Nothing was before me but the hunger in our house, and no bread for the next meal if I didn't sell the herring. No longer like a fire engine, but like a household of hungry mouths my heart cried, 'herring—herring! Two cents apiece!' who would doubt the ease, the sisterhood of conversation possible between that white girl and the Black women selling straw bags on the streets of paradise because they do not want to die? And is it not obvious that the wife of that Talmudic scholar and "Olive," who cleans my room here at the hotel, have more in common than I can claim with either one of them?

This is my consciousness of race and class and gender identity as I collect wet towels, sunglasses, wristwatch, and head towards a shower.

I am thinking about the boy who loaned this novel to me. He's white and he's Jewish and he's pursuing an independent study project with me, at the State University where I teach whether or not I feel like it, where I teach without stint because, like the waiter, I am no fool. It's my job and either I work or I do without everything you need money to buy. The boy loaned me the novel because he thought I'd be interested to know how a Jewish-American writer used English so that the syntax, and therefore the cultural habits of mind expressed by the Yiddish language, could survive translation. He did this because he wanted to create another connection between us on the basis of language, between his knowledge/his love of Yiddish and my knowledge/my love of Black English.

He had been right about the forceful survival of the Yiddish. And I had become excited by this further evidence of the written voice of spoken language protected from the monodrone of "standard" English, and so we had grown closer on this account. But then our talk shifted to student affairs more generally, and I had learned that this student does not care one way or another about currently jeopardized Federal Student Loan programs because, as he explained it to me, they do not affect him. He does not need financial help outside his family. My own son, however, is Black. And I am the only family help available to him and that means, if Reagan succeeds in eliminating Federal programs to aid minority students, he will have to forget about furthering his studies, or he or I or both of us will have to hit the numbers pretty big. For these reasons of difference, the student and I had moved away from each other, even while we continued to talk.

My consciousness turned to race, again, and class.

Sitting in the same chair as the boy, several weeks ago, a graduate student came to discuss her grade. I praised the excellence of her final paper; indeed it had seemed to me an extraordinary pulling together of recent left brain/right brain research with the themes of transcendental poetry.

She told me that, for her part, she'd completed her reading of my political essays. "You are so lucky!" she exclaimed.

"What do you mean by that?"

"You have a cause. You have a purpose to your life."

I looked carefully at this white woman; what was she really saying to me?

"What do you mean?" I repeated.

"Poverty. Police violence. Discrimination in general."

(Jesus Christ, I thought: Is that her idea of lucky?)

"And how about you?" I asked.

"Me?"

"Yeah, you. Don't you have a cause?"

"Me? I'm just a middle-aged woman: a housewife and a mother. I'm a nobody."

For a while, I made no response.

First of all, speaking of race and class and gender in one breath, what she said meant that those lucky preoccupations of mine, from police violence to nuclear wipe-out, were not shared. They were mine and not hers. But here she sat, friendly as an old stuffed animal, beaming good will or more "luck" in my direction.

In the second place, what this white woman said to me meant that she did not believe she was "a person" precisely because she had fulfilled the traditional female functions revered by the father of that Jewish immigrant, Anzia Yezierska. And the woman in front of me was not a Jew. That was not the connection. The link was strictly female. Nevertheless, how should that woman and I, another female, connect, beyond this bizarre exchange?

If she believed me lucky to have regular hurdles of discrimination then why shouldn't I insist that she's lucky to be a middle class white Wasp female who lives in such well-sanctioned normative comfort that she even has the luxury to deny the power of the privileges that paralyze her life?

If she deserts me and "my cause" where we differ, if, for example, she abandons me to "my" problems of race, then why should I support her in "her" problems of housewifely oblivion?

Recollection of this peculiar moment brings me to the shower in the bathroom cleaned by "Olive." She reminds me of the usual Women's Studies curriculum because it has nothing to do with her or her job: you won't find "Olive" listed anywhere on the reading list. You will likewise seldom hear of Anzia Yezierska. But yes, you will find, from Florence Nightingale to Adrienne Rich, a white procession of independently well-to-do women writers. (Gertrude Stein/Virginia Woolf/Hilda Doolittle are standard names among the "essential" women writers.)

In other words, most of the women of the world—Black and First World and white who work because we must—most of the women of the world persist far from the heart of the usual Women's Studies syllabus.

Similarly, the typical Black History course will slide by the majority experience it pretends to represent. For example, Mary McLeod Bethune will scarcely receive as much attention as Nat Turner, even though Black women who bravely and efficiently provided for the education of Black people hugely outnumber those few Black men who led successful or doomed rebellions against slavery. In fact, Mary McLeod Bethune may not receive even honorable mention because Black History too often apes those ridiculous white history courses which produce such dangerous gibberish as The Sheraton British Colonial "history" of the Bahamas. Both Black and white history courses exclude from their central consideration those people who neither killed nor conquered anyone as the means to new identity, those people who took care of every one of the people who wanted to become "a person," those people who still take care of the life at issue: the ones who wash and who feed and who teach and who diligently decorate straw hats and bags with all of their historically unrequired gentle love: the women.

> Oh the old rugged cross
> on a hill far away
> Well I cherish the old rugged cross.

It's Good Friday in the Bahamas. Seventy-eight degrees in the shade. Except for Sheraton territory, everything's closed.

It so happens that for truly secular reasons I've been fasting for three days. My hunger now has reached nearly violent proportions. In the hotel sandwich shop, the Black woman handling the counter complains about the tourists; why isn't the shop closed and why don't the tourists stop eating for once in their lives. I'm famished and I order chicken salad and cottage cheese and lettuce and tomato and a hard boiled egg and a hot cross bun and apple juice.

She eyes me with disgust.

To be sure, the timing of my stomach offends her serious religious practices. Neither one of us apologizes to the other. She seasons the chicken salad to the peppery max while I listen to the loud radio gospel she plays to console herself. It's a country Black version of "The Old Rugged Cross."

As I heave much chicken into my mouth tears start. It's not the pepper. I am, after all, a West Indian daughter. It's the Good Friday music that dominates the humid atmosphere.

> Well I cherish the old rugged cross

And I am back, faster than a 747, in Brooklyn, in the home of my parents where we are wondering, as we do every year, if the sky will darken until Christ has been buried in the tomb. The sky should darken if God is in His heavens. And then, around 3 p.m., at the conclusion of our mournful church service at the neighborhood St. Phillips, and even while we dumbly stare at the black cloth covering the gold altar and the slender unlit candles, the sun should return through the high gothic windows and vindicate our waiting faith that the Lord will rise again, on Easter.

How I used to bow my head at the very name of Jesus: ecstatic to abase myself in deference to His majesty.

My mouth is full of salad. I can't seem to eat quickly enough. I can't think how I should lessen the offense of my appetite. The other Black woman on the premises, the one who disapprovingly prepared this very tasty break from my fast, makes no remark. She is no fool. This is a job she needs. I suppose she notices that at least I included a hot cross bun among my edibles. That's something in my favor. I decide that's enough.

I am suddenly eager to walk off the food. Up a fairly steep hill I walk without hurrying. Through the pastel desolation of the little town, the road brings me to a confectionary pink and white plantation house. At the gates, an unnecessarily large statue of Christopher Columbus faces me down, or tries to. His hand is fisted to one hip. I look back at him, laugh without deference, and turn left.

It's time to pack it up. Catch my plane. I scan the hotel room for things not to forget. There's that white report card on the bureau.

"Dear Guests:" it says, under the name "Olive." "I am your maid for the day. Please rate me: Excellent. Good. Average. Poor. Thank you."

I tuck this memento from the Sheraton British Colonial into my notebook. How would "Olive" rate *me*? What would it mean for us to seem "good" to each other? What would that rating require?

But I am hastening to leave. Neither turtle soup nor kidney pie nor any conch shell delight shall delay my departure. I have rested, here, in the Bahamas, and I'm ready to return to my usual job, my usual work. But the skin on my body has changed and so has my mind. On the Delta flight home I realize I am burning up, indeed.

So far as I can see, the usual race and class concepts of connection, or gender assumptions of unity, do not apply very well. I doubt that they ever did. Otherwise why would Black folks forever bemoan our lack of solidarity when the deal turns real. And if unity on the basis of sexual oppression is something natural, then why do we women, the majority people on the planet, still have a problem?

The plane's ready for takeoff. I fasten my seatbelt and let the tumult inside my head run free. Yes: race and class and gender remain as real as the weather. But what they must mean about the contact between two individuals is less obvious and, like the weather, not predictable.

And when these factors of race and class and gender absolutely collapse is whenever you try to use them as automatic concepts of connection. They may serve well as indicators of commonly felt conflict, but as elements of connection they seem about as reliable as precipitation probability for the day after the night before the day.

It occurs to me that much organizational grief could be avoided if people understood that partnership in misery does not necessarily provide for partnership for change: *When we get the monsters off our backs all of us may want to run in very different directions.*

And not only that: even though both "Olive" and "I" live inside a conflict neither one of us created, and even though both of us therefore hurt inside that conflict, I may be one of the monsters she needs to eliminate from her universe and, in a sense, she may be one of the monsters in mine.

I am reaching for the words to describe the difference between a common identity that has been imposed and the individual identity any one of us will choose, once she gains that chance.

That difference is the one that keeps us stupid in the face of new, specific information about somebody else with whom we are supposed to have a connection because a third party, hostile to both of us, has worked it so that the two of us, like it or not, share a common enemy. *What happens beyond the idea of that enemy and beyond the consequences of that enemy?*

I am saying that the ultimate connection cannot be the enemy. The ultimate connection must be the need that we find between us. It is not only who you are, in other words, but what we can do for each other that will determine the connection.

I am flying back to my job. I have been teaching contemporary women's poetry this semester. One quandary I have set myself to explore with my students is the one of taking responsibility without power. We had been wrestling ideas to the floor for several sessions when a young Black woman, a South African, asked me for help, after class.

Sokutu told me she was "in a trance" and that she'd been unable to eat for two weeks.

"What's going on?" I asked her, even as my eyes startled at her trembling and emaciated appearance.

"My husband. He drinks all the time. He beats me up. I go to the hospital. I can't eat. I don't know what/anything."

In my office, she described her situation. I did not dare to let her sense my fear and horror. She was dragging about, hour by hour, in dread. Her husband, a young Black South African, was drinking himself into more and more deadly violence against her.

Sokutu told me how she could keep nothing down. She weighed 90 lbs at the outside, as she spoke to me. She'd already been hospitalized as a result of her husband's battering rage.

I knew both of them because I had organized a campus group to aid the liberation struggles of Southern Africa.

Nausea rose in my throat. What about this presumable connection: this husband and this wife fled from that homeland of hatred against them, and now what? He was destroying himself. If not stopped, he would certainly murder his wife.

She needed a doctor, right away. It was a medical emergency. She needed protection. It was a security crisis. She needed refuge for battered wives and personal therapy and legal counsel. She needed a friend.

I got on the phone and called every number in the campus directory that I could imagine might prove helpful. Nothing worked. There were no institutional resources designed to meet her enormous, multifaceted, and ordinary woman's need.

I called various students. I asked the Chairperson of the English Department for advice. I asked everyone for help.

Finally, another one of my students, Cathy, a young Irish woman active in campus IRA activities, responded. She asked for further details. I gave them to her.

"Her husband," Cathy told me, "is an alcoholic. You have to understand about alcoholics. It's not the same as anything else. And it's a disease you can't treat any old way."

I listened, fearfully. Did this mean there was nothing we could do?

"That's not what I'm saying," she said. "But you have to keep the alcoholic part of the thing central in everybody's mind, otherwise her husband will kill her. Or he'll kill himself."

She spoke calmly, I felt there was nothing to do but to assume she knew what she was talking about.

"Will you come with me?" I asked her, after a silence. "Will you come with me and help us figure out what to do next?"

Cathy said she would but that she felt shy: Sokutu comes from South Africa. What would she think about Cathy?

"I don't know," I said. "But let's go."

We left to find a dormitory room for the young battered wife.

It was late, now, and dark outside.

On Cathy's VW that I followed behind with my own car, was the sticker that reads BOBBY SANDS FREE AT LAST. My eyes blurred as I read and reread the words. This was another connection: Bobby Sands and Martin Luther King Jr. and who would believe it? I would not have believed it; I

grew up terrorized by Irish kids who introduced me to the word "nigga."
And here I was following an Irish woman to the room of a Black South
African. We were going to that room to try to save a life together.

When we reached the little room, we found ourselves awkward and
large. Sokutu attempted to treat us with utmost courtesy, as though we were
honored guests. She seem surprised by Cathy, but mostly Sokutu was
flushed with relief and joy because we were there, with her.

I did not know how we should ever terminate her heartfelt courtesies
and address, directly, the reason for our visit: her starvation and her
extreme physical danger.

Finally, Cathy sat on the floor and reached out her hands to Sokutu.

"I'm here," she said quietly, "Because June has told me what has happened to you. And I know what it is. Your husband is an alcoholic. He has
a disease. I know what it is. My father was an alcoholic. He killed himself.
He almost killed my mother. I want to be your friend."

"Oh," was the only small sound that escaped from Sokutu's mouth. And
then she embraced the other student. And then everything changed and I
watched all of this happen so I know that this happened: this connection.

And after we called the police and exchanged phone numbers and plans
were made for the night and for the next morning, the young South African
woman walked down the dormitory hallway, saying goodbye and saying
thank you to us.

I walked behind them, the young Irish woman and the young South
African, and I saw them walking as sisters walk, hugging each other, and
whispering and sure of each other and I felt how it was not who they were
but what they both know and what they were both preparing to do about
what they know that was going to make them both free at last.

And I look out the windows of the plane and I see clouds that will not
kill me and I know that someday soon other clouds may erupt to kill us all.

And I tell the stewardess No thanks to the cocktails she offers me. But I
look about the cabin at the hundred strangers drinking as they fly and I
think even here and even now I must make the connection real between
me and these strangers everywhere before those other clouds unify this
ragged bunch of us, too late.

FloreNce CawtHorNe Ladd

Florence Cawthorne Ladd was born in 1932 in Washington, D.C., where she attended prestigious Dunbar High School before going to Howard University. Following her graduation from Howard, she went on to receive a doctoral degree in psychology from the University of Rochester. Throughout her career Ladd worked as a researcher and professor. She also served as dean of students of Wellesley College, executive director of Oxfam, and director of the Bunting Institute of Radcliffe College. In 1996 Ladd published her first novel, *Sarah's Psalm*, the story of a beautiful, brilliant African-American graduate student who travels to Senegal to research her dissertation on a famous African novelist and filmmaker. While there she falls in love with the subject of her dissertation, thereby beginning an extraordinary life filled with travel, art, and politics. The selection here is taken from Ladd's travel journey and describes her meeting with the woman who inspired the title character of her novel.

"EXCERPTS FROM A DAKAR DIARY" (1983)
f r o m
SAGE

5 July 1982

Wil Petty called for Michael and me at 7 p.m. to take us to the residence of the U.S. Ambassador who hosted the official U.S. Independence Day reception for the diplomatic community. The garden of the residence was the setting for the party. Tables decorated with red, white and blue bunting were laden with hors d'oeuvres and American whiskey, gin, bourbon and Coca-Cola. I asked for white wine and was directed to the "table for the French where there are wines and champagne."

The Ambassador and Wil greeted guests, men uniformly dressed in business suits, and women in an array of styles—African women in colorful and traditional gowns, the other women in cocktail dresses or evening gowns. (My long Mexican cotton was appropriately formal and exotic.)

Mich seemed quite at ease in the company of ambassadors. Amazing 12-year-old grace! Smiling and nodding he moved among them, at first sipping a Coke and later champagne.

I was one in the circle of guests that had surrounded John Franklin to hear his views on African-Vatican relations when his eloquent monologue ceased. His eyes had shifted beyond us to the entrance. Aware of the silence he had created in the circle, he said, "One of my favorite people has arrived." He excused himself and strode through the throng to embrace her.

Carrie Sembene had arrived. Everyone seemed to take notice. She was alone. She was wearing a long peach crepe gown with one shoulder strap and a peach feathered headband around her forehead—lovely with her cocoa coloring. She was radiant, royal and more beautiful than I had remembered.

Carrie remembered! She remembered our first meeting two years ago. She inquired about Drimmer who had introduced us. I told her that I had hoped to see her, to discuss a "piece" I was writing. She suggested dinner at their home on Wednesday evening. She met Mich. Their son, Mousa, is Mich's age. Mich is eager to meet him.

7 July 1982

Late afternoon. We went to the Cultural Affairs Office to visit Wil and wait for Carrie who soon arrived. She drove us to Yoff where their house is dramatically perched on a rocky bluff above the Bay. Michael and Mousa met but could not exchange words. A brief greeting from Ousmane who was engaged in a long telephone conversation. Carrie, the boys, and I went outside. The surf crashed rhythmically against the boulders. There was—and perhaps always is—a high wind. Carrie and I placed two chairs in a sheltered corner of the patio and watched Michael, Mousa and Mousa's chickens. Rocks, sea, sand and red clay surround their domestic sanctuary.

We began with laments (Carrie with an expatriate's passion and concern) about the Reagan administration, the conservative surge in U.S. politics, and the effects on international currencies. They had been to the Cannes Festival. Sembene was one of thirteen film directors honored. Carrie recommended "Yol" and "Missing." We moved from films to books. Their neighbor and friend, Fatou Sow, is completing a manuscript on Senegalese women.

It was time to mention the "piece." I told Carrie that I had started a short story about her and that I wanted to interview her for I knew too little about her life to complete it. Carrie was surprised, amused, and, to my surprise, flattered.

But she would not be interviewed. She would not tell me any more than I already knew. "The fantasy is richer than the reality," she insisted. "Write it. It is your story." She pointed out that the issues of everyday life would confuse the story. (To appreciate the portrait of a life, one should view it from a distance—like pointillism; stand at a distance from the canvas to see the artist's work, intentions.)

Ousmane joined us. He spoke of the Cannes Festival and his recent film work in Senegal Orientale. Carrie, from time to time, injected an opinion, reinforced or took issue with a remark. I listened to Ousmane but looked at Carrie. Forceful, she offers opinions without sounding opinionated, gives advice with the clarity, confidence and assurance of a much older woman. If she has any insecurities and uncertainties, they are not apparent. Insightfully and intelligently, she gets to the heart of the matter. She supports and promotes Ousmane, but maintains her own identity and presents a well-defined self.

Dinner was *chez* Fatou and Pathe. We strolled along sand-covered, ill-defined streets for a distance of approximately four blocks. We passed four or five houses, generous, recently built, handsome architecturally. Pathe greeted us. Fatou and their three children appeared. Fast movement, agitated grace, wiry bodies, alert eyes. Pathe's intensity was immediately evident. Bearded, with penetrating eyes that peered through glasses, he was the intellectual match for Fatou's sharp mind—indeed, for us all.

Pathe rushed into an account of an evening of readings and spirited discussion at his bookstore. He told Carrie that she should write again. I suggested that Carrie write an autobiography and mentioned that I had started a short story about her. Carrie protested, claiming the details of her life would not claim anyone's attention.

"Carrie," according to Sembene, "in American literature is a witch." He said it as if to acknowledge that he has been bewitched. He reminded us and himself that he has relied on her magic. Carrie is a good witch.

What I know of Carrie's life is a contemporary fairy tale: from a black middle class Chicago family; began a doctoral program (Comparative Lit?) at the University of Indiana where she was drawn to the novels and films of Sembene. She traveled to Senegal to meet the subject of her dissertation. They met, married, and have a splendid son. It is an academic fairy tale. Not yet 40, Carrie enjoys an intellectually rich, stimulating international lifestyle. Her generous spirit invites and inspires a vast intercontinental network of admirers and friends. Mention that you have been to Dakar and immediately you are asked, "Did you meet Carrie Semebene?" She is a magical, contemporary fairy queen.

To bring the subject to a close, Carrie said emphatically, with finality, "It is your story. Go back to America and write it."

Who is Carrie? What is she to me? She is my younger, keener, more daring self. She symbolizes the evolving universal kinship among women, living out the relationship between African and Afro-American women. She represents the nobility, distinction, energy, ambition and openness that I find in the friends I call sisters. They, too, are Carrie.

It is not my story. Nor solely your story, Carried. It is our story. We must tell our story.

Toni Cade Bambara

Toni Cade Bambara was born in 1939 in New York, where she grew up in a politically and culturally vibrant Harlem community. A distinguished writer, activist, and documentary filmmaker, Bambara was one of the exciting new voices to emerge among a bevy of black women writers during the Black Power Movement. Bambara published two edited volumes, *The Black Woman* (1970) and *Tales and Stories for Black Folks* (1971); two collections of short stories, *Gorilla, My Love* (1972) and *The Sea Birds Are Still Alive* (1977); and one novel, *The Salt Eaters* (1980), before her death in December 1995. In addition to her writing, Bambara taught at City College of New York, Rutgers University, Duke University, Spelman College, and numerous other traditional and nontraditional teaching settings.

Although Bambara spent most of her life in New York, Atlanta, and Philadelphia, she also traveled extensively, and her travel greatly influenced her writing. Following a trip to Cuba in 1973 and to Vietnam in 1975, Bambara became convinced that "writing is a legitimate way, an important way, to participate in the empowerment of the community that names me" (Evans, 42). Toni Cade Bambara's travels and her consciousness of liberation struggles worldwide allowed her to identify and articulate important commonalities and connections between those engaged in struggle and to turn her creative attention to settings other than the urban settings of her early fiction. Her short story "The Sea Birds Are Still Alive" is a product of these efforts. This selection is from an interview with Bambara and fellow filmmaker Louis Massiah.

"How She Came By Her Name" (1996)
from
Deep Sightings and Rescue Missions: Fiction, Essays, and Conversations

You have traveled extensively around the world. You have been to Cuba, Sweden, Vietnam, Laos, India, Nigeria, Jamaica, Barbados. You have often traveled as a delegate. What is that experience like, and why is that important to you?

When you are a member of a delegation, you have responsibility before you go, while you are there, and when you come back. Before you go, you want to contact your constituency and find out what they want to know about that country. Also, what kind of solidarity they wish to express with the people of that country, and what sort of materials they would like to send. For example, when we went to Cuba, we took diaphragms, blood plasma, and penicillin. When folks went to Guinea-Bissau, building materials. To Brazil, mops, because none of the maids have mops. In the spring of 1975 I was part of a delegation called the North American Academic Marxist-Leninist Anti-Imperialist Feminist Women. It used to take us ten minutes to introduce ourselves. We were invited by the Women's Union of North Vietnam to come as a delegation and to do what delegates do, like raising critical questions such as: What was the infant mortality rate before the Revolution? What is now? What was the rate of literacy before the Revolution? What is it now? Who were the people on the bottom strata, and what position do they hold now? What are their prospects for the next ten years? I was always interested in the personal stories and would ask, "Who were you then and who are you now?" We were invited in the spring to go to Vietnam, but they had the victory in the spring, which was unexpected, so the Women's Union needed to go around and visit the socialist camp and thank people for their solidarity during the struggle. So we were put on hold. Many of us had already quit our jobs, sublet our apartments, turned off our phones etc. I sat down and wrote, and that became *The Sea Birds*

Are Still Alive. Most of those stories had not been published; been hanging around the house, and they were completed during that spring and sum-mer.

In Vietnam we were also interested in bringing back things for our constituency; we would have to give a debriefing and a report of some kind and had to shape it in some palatable way. Children gave us cards to give to the children here expressing solidarity. When I got back, one of the tasks I had was to deliver this information to my constituency. I decided to do it the way I knew how to do. I wrote a short story in seven sections. I would read a section then, then we would have music, somebody would get up and read the greeting cards that the children had made. Then I would read another section based on stories I had been told, then someone would show some slides and posters, then I would read another section. It went on like that. That story line became the title story in *The Sea Birds Are Still Alive*.

NTOZAKE SHANGE

Poet, playwright, and novelist Ntozake Shange was born in Trenton, New Jersey, in 1948. The daughter of a physician and an educator, Shange spent much of her youth in St. Louis, where she was exposed to the arts and where she met W. E. B. Du Bois and other African-American luminaries who visited her family's home. In 1976 Shange's brilliant, controversial play *For Colored Girls Who Have Considered Suicide When the Rainbow Is Enuf* established her as a major literary talent. Shange's poems, plays, novels, and essays all exhibit a cosmopolitan sense of self as a black woman of the African diaspora.

The selection here describes Shange's trip to Nicaragua during the rule of the Sandinistas—poet revolutionaries—with whom Shange identifies.

"All It Took Was a Road/Surprises of Urban Renewal" (1998)
from
If I Can Cook / You Know God Can

From the very start, black music authorized a private autonomous, free, and even rebellious rhythm on the part of the listener or dancer, instead of subjecting him or her to a dominant, foreseeable, or prewritten pattern.

— CARLOS FUENTES,
The Buried Mirror

Between Managua and Bluefields there are many, many mountains. Until the short-lived victory of the Sandinistas in 1981, there was no road. So

Nicaragua was a fairly schizophrenic little country with the black people on one side of the mountain and the mestizos and blancos on the other, while Amerindians made a way for themselves in the jungles as best they could. It was very important that there be no connection between the East and West Coast populations. That way myths and distance could weaken any resistance to the reign of the dictator Somoza, if the threat of being "disappeared" was insufficient. When the freeways came through our communities, the African-American ones, my home was disappeared along with thousands of others. We were left with no business districts, no access to each other; what was one neighborhood was now ten, who lived next door was now a threatening six or eight highway lanes away, if there at all. Particularly hurt were the restaurants and theaters where a community shares food and celebrates itself. This we already know is a deathblow to our culture, extroverted, raucous, and spontaneous.

Anyway, I was in Nicaragua traveling to the house in which Nicaragua's revered poet Rubén Dario was born and raised before his sojourn to Europe. Here, a black North American coming from Managua going vaguely in the direction of the Atlantic coast, where people like me lived, would eventually see me, too. I was anxious, divining this reunion of another lost portion of the Diaspora. This anxiety didn't last long, however, for no sooner had I begun to be acutely aware of my "racial" difference from everyone around me (poets though they were, like me, in a nation of poets), than someone's radio blasted Willie Colón and Celia Cruz singing "Usted Abuso." The bus rang out with every imaginable accented Spanish singing, all swaying to my *salsero preferido* (favorite salsa singer). The South Bronx had survived and pulled a trick on the Major Deegan. The blockade against Cuba lacked a sense of rhythm. But it didn't stop there. Next came Stevie Wonder and Michael Jackson rockin' our little bus through a war-torn, earthquake-ravaged land. The tales of our people's incompetency and addition to failure must be very bad jokes indeed.

Even more important was running into Nicaraguan poet Carlos Johnson. He reminded me of a painter friend of mine from Nashville, except for the West Indian tinge to his English. At the front porch of his house, Rubén Dario met us with a poem. Then came many poems from me, that to this very day stem from that moment of underestimating who and what I come from.

"My Song for Hector Lavoe"

Mira / tu puedes ir conmigo /
hasta managua and/the earthquake was no more a surprise /
than you / con su voz / que viene de los dioses / and the
swivel of hips de su flaca / as you dance or / when she
sucks the hearts / out of the eggs of / tortugas / anglos die to
see float about / while all the time we dance around
them / split up / change
partners and fall madly in love . . . porque
nosotros somos an army of marathon dancers / lovers / seekers
and / we have never met an enemy we can't outlive.

It turned out that Carlos used the racismo of the ruling class to his own advantage by wandering "aimlessly" around Managua as if he were an itinerant musician, like all black people, saxophone case in hand. Only this poet's musical instrument was an AK-47, which was used strategically to undermine the Somoza regime and lead to what we nostalgically now call La Victoria. I heard this story and others like it once we'd made it back to Managua, full of deep, sweet black rum, black music, and relentless appetites.

In what we could call a tropical ice house, a dance hall under a thatched roof, open to the night air and the call of romance, we dance to something called Nicason, a *mezcla* (mixture) of reggae, beguine, and cumbé with a ranchero overlay. You see, road or no road, we connect to the culture of the people we live with, whether they like us or not, or even if they've never seen one of us: they know James Brown. In the sweat and swivel of dancing, being hungry for more of life, and each other, we ate *huevos de tortugas*, everybody. . . .

That night in Managua we were able to cover the scars of war with poetry, music, and abandon ourselves to the impulses of our bodies in the night heat and each other's arms. The volcano where Somoza dropped the bodies of anyone for any reason was covered with mist and clouds. I only thought once about the house I grew up in that had disappeared and been resurrected as a police station. The thought broke my heart, but the fact of all of us let me hold my head high.

Colleen McElroy

Born in St. Louis, Missouri, in 1935, Colleen McElroy is a prolific essayist and poet. After receiving her doctoral degree in ethonolinguistics from the University of Washington, McElroy went on to become a professor of English at her alma mater. In 1983 she became the first black woman promoted to full professor at that institution. In 1985 her collection of poems, *Queen of the Ebony Isles*, received the American Book Award. McElroy's writings are inspired and influenced by her travels, which have included excursions to Europe, South America, Japan, Majorca, Africa, and Asia.

In 1997 McElroy published a volume of her own travel writings, *A Long Way from St. Louie*, from which the excerpt here is taken.

"No Stops Until Darwin" (1997)
from
A Long Way from St. Louie

In 1994 I took a motorcycle trip across the Australian desert. Fifty-eight years old and on the back of a Harley, a handsome Australian driver guiding me through Aboriginal Land. It was great. At least I thought it was. Something to talk about with the folks back home.

My son said: Are you crazy? You could've been killed out there. I reminded him of the accident I'd had less than ten city blocks from my house. The sweet sports car I'd owned for eighteen years, folded around me like a handkerchief.

My lover said: You never get up at 4:30 in the morning for me. I said: You're not a big red rock in the middle of the Australian desert.

My daughter said: *Mo*-ther! the word stressed with reminders of my responsibilities to her. I said: Hey, you're going to Russia for two years! "That's different," she said. I didn't bother to tell her that the difference was a matter of who was traveling.

And I didn't bother to say anything to my own mother. They've become bookends in my life—my daughter, the Missionary, and my impatient mother—they alternate between scolding me and making sure I've packed everything I'll need.

"You need to stay home," my mother said. "I don't know what you're looking for out there." "Me neither," I said. "But I'll tell you when I find it."

And each time, I have told her what I found. This time, how long it took to get my body stirring at four o'clock in the morning, even with the anticipation of watching the sunrise paint Ayers Rock from earth brown to fuschia. Four A.M., and I crawled out of bed to watch the sun do what it does so well every day without me. "This had better be good," I told the driver. "I only get up this early for babies and airplanes, and thank goodness I no longer have to get out of bed for a baby." My driver, David, looked as if he'd heard it all before. I blinked sleep from my eyes and tried to concentrate on the thermos of sweetened tea I'd brought with me. But even the sugar refused to take hold. It was winter in Australia and cold in the desert at that time of morning. Everyone in our caravan was stomping around, trying to bring enough blood to their hands and feet so they could set up camera equipment. I was huddled on the back of the Harley with my trusty point-and-shoot set for automatic consecutive photos. "You call that little thing a camera?" David asked in his delectable Australian accent. At four in the morning, I was having trouble thinking of his accent as delectable, so I answered snidely, "I don't care what name you give it as long as it comes when I call it," and went back to my tea. After that, everyone left me alone to mutter to myself.

Even in a group, I can manage to travel alone. In fact, as a black woman, that's easy to do. Most often I'm the lone black female on the trip—sometimes making folks rethink the notion that black women never travel except to Africa and the Caribbean, sometimes an uncomfortable reminder of America's racial history—but always I am aware that my vision of the world will differ from that of my usual travel companions. Not that I need to travel to be reminded that I see the world differently. Sometimes that realization takes no more than discussing a movie. For example, I say I cannot understand how a contemporary film director can make a movie on the streets of downtown New York without having any black people in the scene. "What happened to the black folks?" I say. "Did they send them all to Reikers? All the cleaning ladies and bankers, the bus drivers and shop clerks, the messengers and cabbies? All the black women shopping Bloomingdale's and Sak's?" But my friends, those who haven't lived in big cities or have never found themselves excluded on the basis of color, give me puzzled looks. They haven't noticed that black people were missing from scenes that were supposed to reflect the general American public. Often I'm given a lecture on the filmmaker's right to be selective about who is included in a film depicting reality. "Selective?" I repeat. "Sounds like some kind of warped Darwinist theory of evolution," I tell them, "but fortunately, life isn't like that. Like my grandma said: Black people are everywhere."

Everywhere I went, in big cities like Sydney, Melbourne, and Brisbane there were references to Aboriginal culture. But if I hadn't really been looking for them, I could have left the country believing that there were very few Aborigines living in Australia. I don't mean in the Outback. On any given day, I could find a dozen tour guides competing for the chance to take me to Aboriginal Land. But in the cities, Aboriginals were only symbols. Their country had been turned into a world of white faces where they'd become, like Ralph Ellison's Invisible Man, conspicuous by their absence. Yet, every public park was infested with blonds playing the didgeridu, and every shopping mall had an art center of tourist souvenirs— wood carvings and cloth emblazoned with dreamtime images, ethnicity for sale, "genuine made in the Bush," white shopkeepers told me. "Aborigines don't like the city," I was told. But I took a second look. Under the cloak of urbanization, they worked in banks, hospitals, law offices, and schools. Some owned homes in the suburbs. Some were mixed bloods but of Aboriginal descent nonetheless. Book stores stocked special sections with their stories: *Portraits of our Elders, Inside Black Australia, Aboriginal Folktales.* Traditional stories and emerging writers. "Last aisle, third shelf from the bottom," I was told. Just like home, I thought. What was it that Darwin had theorized: The struggle for survival between individuals is based on continuous variations.

We were on the highway heading toward King's Canyon beyond Ayers Rock and the Olgas Mountains when I saw it—a sign that read: No Stops Until Darwin.

"How far to Darwin?" I asked. "Several thousand kilometers," David said.

I grunted. That's a helluva lot bigger than Texas, I thought. "How long would it take to get there?"

"Well, you've got to get off the Gunbarrel Highway and back onto the Lasseter, then take the main road. Ten days, a week, if you're lucky."

"So there's nothing between here and Darwin?" "Depends on how you look at it," he laughed. When I didn't laugh too, he added, "Rest easy, luv. It's just a little Outback humor."

I never found out whether he meant his laughter or the sign, because just then he swerved to avoid a frilled lizard sunning itself in the red dust. of the road. It raised its head, ignoring us as it paid homage to the sun, the frill flared about its neck like a monarch's ruff. "I hear tell, they used to eat those things back in the Bush," David said. Then we roared off, the Harley spewing dust, King's Canyon in front of us, the lizard on the road behind us looking down its nose at the passing world.

Ayers Rock: Uluru, sacred place for the Anangu, the Aboriginal people. Even from a distance, it is clear that Uluru is no ordinary mesa. It rises in majestic splendor out of the dust of the desert, a landscape of brick red sand and spinifex scrub brush, the horizon occasionally broken by a lone tree — and, of course, by Uluru, the rock itself, thrust abruptly some 1,200 feet above the desert like a giant rust-colored beast come to slumber under an endless sky. No one fails to find it magnificent, its sheer size and steepness massed on the plate of the desert. I think of it as rising up like a mountain, but the Anangu believe it fell from the heavens. They regard the rock as a sacred place, each crevasse, cave, and indentation blessed with spiritual powers. They take a dim view of tourists who climb it, but that doesn't stop the tourists. Throughout the day, they crawl, mostly on all fours, up the perpendicular sides to the top of the rock. From a distance, they look like a line of ants crawling up a giant sugar cube. In fact, that's what the Aborigines call them: minga, the Anangu word for ants — all those white folks, the Germans and French, the Americans and Italians, the Aussies and Kiwis, crawling up the side of the sacred rock. "Have you climbed Ayers Rock?" I was asked later. I answered, "No, but I didn't climb Notre Dame, either." What's one sacred place, more or less? I thought. My answer was met with a puzzled look. "How could you pas up such an opportunity?"

Uluru became my whole reason for visiting Australia. I wanted to partake of the Uluru Experience, as it is called, and so, motorcycle parked, I hiked around Ayers Rock, an outsider's walkabout approved of by the Aborigines. In predawn light, the rock was muddy brown and looked anything but spiritual, probably because I was out of bed at an ungodly hour and the only spiritual experience I was really interested in was sleep. But I trudged ahead, moving quickly in the cold windy air of early morning. The cold surprised me, since I still insisted on holding to the illusion that the word *desert* meant heat. But an icy wind whistled against the sides of the Uluru. As dawn approached, the ranger, a young woman from Melbourne who led the hike around the rock, took us to a sheltered recess. We ate breakfast as the sun rose against the eastern face of Uluru, colors spreading in layers on Uluru's surface: from the deep brown of night to gray brown to mauve, pink, orange, and finally to bright red as the sun engulfed the sky. It was definitely worth getting up at the crack of dawn, and my point-and-shoot camera was as trustworthy as a Labrador retriever. Uluru seemed to beckon photographers, its slopes and valleys sensual as a woman's body. A shift in angles, and the light and shadows offered new surprises. Turn one corner, and suddenly I was staring at a waterfall that came out of nowhere but tumbled down the rock as if it followed stair steps. Turn another corner, and the surface was sandy dry, lizards and insects the only signs of life. I could see cave openings high up on the sheer face of the rock, no visible footpaths leading to them. "That's a ritual cave," the ranger told us. "Only Aborigines can enter." It's no wonder, I thought, looking at the steep climb.

We had been standing near a cave opening at the base of the rock, watching the sunlight spread in our direction. As light erased the shroud of darkness, the cave walls came alive with paintings. Here a warrior. There a woman and child. There a kangaroo, a snake, a ribbon of sunlight, the desert dreaming itself. I remembered the rock paintings I'd seen on cave walls in Spain, where stories also were told in figures that symbolized the real world and the world of the spirits. At Uluru, the ranger elaborated upon legends of the ancient ones, pulling the tales from the drawings, the spirit of the desert, the verbal art of Ayers Rock which was detailed as surely as the Gutenberg tradition might detail a story in alphabet and script. The sun grew stronger and warmed us. For a while, we were silent, then, as the ranger ended a story of Aboriginal dreamtime, a young man from Scotland gestured toward the symbols and figures on the walls. "So," he said, "it is no' a real story, eh? They jus' pull all this from the imagination?"

On the desert, I began to believe nothing was real. At any given moment, I was convinced that even the desert itself lived in a dream of the mythical past. By midday, the heat had forced us into shirt-sleeves and I couldn't remember the chilly air of early morning. By midday, the desert was cloaked in shades of russet and ochre, clumps of pink paper flowers and yellow rattle pods blooming near billabongs that still bore traces of the great sea that once covered Australia. In places, saltwater shield shrimp lay dormant in the dry beds of rock pools where spinifex grass was clumped like Texas sagebrush. The ranger picked up several shrimp. They rested in her hand like badges, their backs flattened into the shield shape that cushions them against accidents. "They wait for the rains," she said, "then they come to life. In the span of one rainy season, some will live and die. Mate, lay eggs, then fall into a half-life when the dry season comes." In her hand, the shrimp were stony as fossils. I asked if they were sleeping. "Not sleep as we know it," she said. "Just waiting. But they scurry like beetles when the rains come." When she tossed them back into the spinifex, they sounded like sand falling to the ground.

A thorny devil darted out of the clump of spinifex and disappeared almost before we caught a glimpse of it. For some strange reason, it was a lizard I'd liked the moment I'd seen one, maybe because it was so homely, like an old scab with doleful eyes or a cactus stalk on legs. "That one's a pet," the ranger said. "Well, as much of a pet as you can expect a lizard to be." "What do you feed it?" I asked. She laughed. "You don't really feed a thorny devil. You just let it have its run. Keep it out of traffic. I saved that one from a tumble with a tour bus. Sometimes they take off in the wrong direction." I remembered the ochre-colored lizards I'd seen on my way to the shower building that morning. Half-hidden in the shadows on the edge of the walkway, they were barely discernable in the light from the cabin door, but something had made me stop. They were waiting as if to let me know that the path had been theirs for centuries and I was nothing more than a newcomer. They gave me a look that said: What's your problem? So I stood there until they decided to let me walk past, making their point with a slight flick of the head before they slipped out of the halo of light and vanished back into the deeper shadows, their passing no more than a faint trail left in the sand.

In a village on the desert west of Yulara, I stand under the shadow of a paperbark shelter and watch an Aboriginal woman decorate bowls with ancient designs: lizards, birds, turtles, and snakes, their trails painted in geometric patterns. Several unfinished bark tapestries are resting against a corner post in back of the hutch. In the next lean-to, a man carves snake and bird tracks into spear heads. I've been standing there for nearly ten minutes before the woman speaks. "You a daughter come home?" she asks. She never looks up. In fact, she hasn't looked up since I arrived. Her voice, in a gravelly overlay of Australian English and her own language, startles me. For a second, I'm not sure I understand her. I cup my hand behind my ear. This time, her question is more distinct. "You from Oz?" she asks. "Oz?" I repeat before I remember that Oz is a shortened way of saying Australia. "No," I say. Several other women enter the lean-to. They inspect me. Will I pass for a daughter come home? I wonder. But my nose is not flat enough, my hair not straight enough, my brow not strong enough.

"You don't look Aboriginal, but you'll get around alright," Sloan Baybury told me. He had become my unofficial guide in Brisbane. We'd spent the afternoon in the museum at the Queensland Cultural Center. Sloan knew one of the curators, and after we left the convention hall, he managed to get me an introduction. He said he was impressed with my speech on oral traditions. He was an archeologist, and I was flattered when he called me an international researcher, but as I walked through the museum, international became a matter of opinion. Every room reminded me of how little I knew of the connection between Aboriginal and Pacific cultures. We went from rooms full of shields and spears to rooms filled with pottery and paperbark patterns. One room held an enormous freestanding exhibition of beautifully decorated didgeridus suspended from the ceiling like slender acrobats—so many that for a moment, I could imagine myself lost inside the music of the instrument. In the ethnography of myths and totems, the museum exhibits spelled out a small portion of the history of Aboriginal cultures. I tried my best to hold up my end of the discussion, asking what I hoped were intelligent questions about differences between the art of Australia's Northern Territory and that of the Southern Territory, and how much cultural exchange there was between the Aborigines and the people white Australians called Kanakas, who had been captured in the Pacific and brought to Australia as slaves. "How do you make the distinction," I asked, "between those who were enslaved and the disenfranchised?" The curator looked slightly embarrassed, most likely because Kanaka, like Negro, was a colonialist term. But Sloan grinned, pleased that I had not accepted the standard spiel. "You know more than the average bloke who comes here to give a talk on folk culture," Sloan said. I told him I had my reasons, but he brushed his hand against my cheek and said, "That's pretty obvious. But it takes more than color to make a match, luv."

A woman is painting a serving bowl with birds and mythical bunyip.
Another woman sits beside her and continues weaving a basket she's
brought to the lean-to. Two others stand nearby, watching me. "You a
daughter come home?" she asks. "You come from around W.A.?" Her name
is Caralee, or something that sounds close to that. My ear has retreated into
the sounds of my childhood and refuses to distinguish any words that do not
hold a Missouri accent. My hearing is dulled; sounds are snarled. I catch a
word here, a word there. I say, "No, not W.A." Caralee goes on with her
work without looking up. "Eh, from the Queen," one woman says. I think
they mean Queensland. They all grin at me. "No, the U.S.," I say. "America." They give me a look that is both sad and disappointed. Home doesn't
stretch that far, they seem to say. "She needs some tucker," Caralee says.
This brings a round of giggles, but they gesture to a seat, a log stump
smoothed across the top. I have been accepted, up to a point, but more than
I had expected to be. The women stir the cooking fire.

I begin to talk about the wooden serving bowl Caralee is painting. It is
remarkably beautiful, close to one of the designs I'd seen in the museum
in Brisbane: a pattern of concentric circles in pale ochre denoting the
movement of birds, and surrounding those, ghostlike bunyip in bright
blue—arms, legs, and tails all akimbo under the red ochre limbs of trees
folded around the edge of the bowl. The women pull something that looks
like a split log closer to the fire. With flat sticks, they begin to rake the bark
pulp. I'm thinking about blue bunyip and trees with limbs like arms, so I
don't notice that there's something moving under the edge of the flat sticks.
Then I see it: a worm, pale and plump on the end of a stick, then plop—
into the fire. "Tucker," they say. "Eat." Another hits the fire. Then another.
Witchetty grubs, a delicacy, I remember. It takes all my nerve to keep from
leaping away, my stomach in my mouth.

I tell myself: Chill out, McElroy. But witchetty grubs are crawly things,
and I hate bugs. I remember an awful encounter with bugs in Kansas City
before I moved to the Pacific Northwest. I'd been standing by the garbage
cans, dreaming of an ocean that seemed light-years away from that prairie
town, and because I'd been daydreaming, I was still holding the lid to the
can, not paying attention its resident predators. The cockroaches in Kansas
have wings, and they move like guerrilla warriors, fast and heading for
cover. One flew in my ear. My neighbor, watching me from her kitchen
window, swore I invented a dance that had not been seen on this planet
before that day. All I know is that for days after, I flushed my ear with warm

water, but still I heard the flutter of wings against the drum. As far as I'm concerned, a worm is nothing more than a bug without wings, and witchetty grubs qualify. I watch the grubs nose blindly from the heart of the wood. I shudder. There's a slight crackle of flames. They could be clams, I tell myself. Or escargot. Or those chocolate covered ants sold in Africa. But I've seen the grubs move, and I've long since come to the conclusion that I'm a carnivore with a delicate stomach. "Eat what you shoot," my father told me. I was ten years old, but had managed to bag one poor chicken hawk that boiled for days and was still tough. That was my last hunting trip. I even walk away from a crab boil. If it's already cooked, I'll eat it. Just don't ask me to watch it die. The women scoop the grubs from the fire and giggle. I rub my stomach and cough. "Not today," I say, praying they'll believe I'm hopelessly ill. We bargain for a shallow serving dish instead. I'm no longer thought of as a daughter, just outsider. I take the best offer on a dish painted with the images of witchetty grubs. I leave behind the birds and blue bunyip nesting in the limbs of mythical trees. I tell myself that I've made the best of what was probably a touchy situation.

I talk to myself quite a bit when I'm traveling. It eases the tension and helps me check my expectations. Sometimes it keeps me from being pulled into the madness of someone else's conversation. On a bus between Cairns and Moseman Gorge, Rosie, an Aussie tourist from Perth, described fourteen ways of making meat pies, in detail. There seemed to be no connection with the tour and Rosie's need to let us know her finesse with meat pastry combinations, unless you count the bus driver's penchant for telling dirty jokes in dialect. On that trip, I learned more words in Australian slang for a woman's private anatomy than I ever knew existed. In the end, I had a choice: Rosie or the driver. My only relief was when we left the bus to take a close-up look at a scenic view. But as soon as we took our seats again, Rosie was there to fill in the gaps between the bus driver's bad jokes and announcements of other sights to see. Only those in the back of the bus missed Rosie's endless meat pie advisories. I, unfortunately, had garnered a seat in the front, near Rosie. She had a face not unlike the giant wrasse, a fish I'd seen a couple of days earlier while diving in the Great Barrier Reef. The wrasse appeared in a school of smaller fish and seemed to take charge, examining every diver with an expression full of corporate meanness, as if it were there to determine your next promotion. As my Aunt Claudia would say—and she was the meanest of all my mother's sisters—they looked like they wouldn't lend a crippled man a crutch. I was holding my breath, a lifeline of oxygen stuck in my mouth, my legs steadily cycling for balance. The wrasse didn't back off. Neither did Rosie.

We were sitting under the dome of a double-decker, Queensland rolling by in waves of farms, small towns, mountain streams, and incredibly lush green forests. After a week of red sands and spinifex, this gave me a chance to recover my memory of landscapes that looked like Seattle. Early on, Rosie explained that she was from Perth, "Freemantle, really. We've got all the modern conveniences, eh?" She nodded to her husband, but he'd fallen into some kind of trance, his eyes glazed over. Early on, it was obvious that Rosie was less interested in what she might see on her fortnight away from Perth than in what she could say—or rather, for some inexplicable reason, how she could describe meat pies. So I became my own tour guide. While Rosie lectured on red pies versus brown pies, I made mental note of the several species of evergreens growing side by side with tropical vines. While she allowed that spinach pies were best with four eggs, not two, I examined the mist hanging over the gorge like a bridal veil. Who could possibly want so many variations on meat pies? I thought as I counted the number of brush fires clearing the land so that one more suburb could be built. Only those whose mental illness drives them to describe their obsessions in public, I told myself. Of all the tour buses in all the world, she had to pick mine, I sighed. At the end of the day, as the bus wheezed onto the highway back to Cairn's, Rosie's parting shot was full of onions and carrots and how lean the meat should be. "Never buy from a Koori," she said. "They're cannibals. Eat anything, they will." I closed my eyes just as we passed a field smoldering under a farmer's brush fire. I was back cooking witchetty grubs, except they all looked like Rosie. My serving dish was almost full, but nobody would touch the stuff.

"We couldn't have survived without the aborigines," Eric says. I'm on another tour, this one into the Daintree Rain Forest. I've traded in Rosie for a smaller group: the guide, Eric, a German family with two teenagers, a lesbian couple from Sweden, and me. It's a manageable size. The adults keep to themselves, except to fend off teenage angst. The boy, fifteen, wants to personally dismantle the Daintree; the girl, seventeen, is repulsed by it all. Has she read the German version of the *Barbie Doll Book of Teenage Etiquette*? Eric leads us quickly along a well-marked trail into dense underbrush. He tells us he's from Perth. I gulp. How could Hermes, god of travelers, cast bad karma my way twice on the same trip? I hope you're not Rosie's neighbor, I think, imagining endless days of meat pies.

Eric explains Australia's origins. "Forty million years ago . . ." he begins. My brain turns off. I haven't yet come to terms with the fact that the paint I saw on Egyptian tombs was done some four thousand years ago, but a million! Eric shows us red gum trees and hoop vines, three different varieties of wattle with spiky orange-and-yellow buds that look like cactus berries, tea trees with sap that heals insect bites, and blunt leaf plants good for cuts and scrapes. "I've seen those before," I say. "In Malaysia." "Right," Eric says. "Same botanical family. Just a variation." The fifteen year old snarls at me; the seventeen year old yawns. Eric digs around the base of a tree. "The first settlers ate these," he said. Not witchetty grubs again, I think. But it's a seed, brown and shiny as a walnut, and it doesn't move. "The Aborigines showed them how. Kept them from starving to death," Eric says. The fifteen year old is game for something new. He pops one in his mouth and spits it out almost in the same breath. His sister makes ugh-ugh sounds; their parents look apologetic. The lesbians look as relieved as only childless couples can look under the circumstances. Eric watches the teenager spit and spit trying to get rid of the bitter taste. "Take a lesson from that," he says. "You can't go rushing into anything out here in the rain forest." I begin to like Eric and think I can forgive him for his Perth roots. The kid starts whining; his sister takes up the chorus. Eric keeps walking, but after my ordeal with Rosie, I've had enough. I take a fork in the road; one of the Swedish women follows me.

We don't say much, the Swedish woman and I—just a grunt or two to indicate a tree or flower that has taken our fancy. Besides, when we are quiet, we can hear the others plodding along on a trail not far from where we are. Maybe it's our need to be quiet that offers us an extraordinary experience. We have been examining a flowering bush, a thorny sort with stay-a-while leaves that threaten to take pieces of your clothes, or your skin, if you brush against it. Suddenly, there is a thumping sound. We both look up. My life may have been bound to the city, but I'm savvy enough to know that thumping sounds in the woods are bad omens. But I also know not to run until I'm sure of the direction of the sound. You don't want to run toward the bear, my ex-husband had warned me when we were in Alaska. The Swedish woman obviously has not been warned. She takes off like a rabbit. I go torpid and freeze. There's more thumping. Then I realize I can't move. That damn stay-a-while is threatening to keep a piece of my index finger with it. That finger starts to sweat—I think the rest of me is too scared to do anything—but the moisture on my skin lets me pull my finger away from the plant, and that act may be what saves me. The next thing I know, a big bird breaks through the bush. I mean a big big bird—at least my height with a bright blue head and a big fat brown behind. I look at it; it looks at me; we both squawk and do a runner in opposite directions. I don't know how fast the bird's going, but I reach the group only seconds after the woman from Sweden. "Blue bird! Big blue bird!" I announce in what little voice I have left. Eric turns calmly. "Was it blue all over?" he asks. "Just the head," I pant. "Just the head." The Swedish woman nods in agreement. "A cassowary," Eric says. "First cousin to the ostrich. They are on the endangered list. Did you get a photo?" Maybe he doesn't understand the word *Big*, I think. "It's sort of hard to take a photo when you're running," I say. The teenagers giggle. "Pity," Eric says. "I think you missed a great opportunity." I look behind me. The leaves rustle a bit, then still to their usual gentle sway. "Just call me Missed Opportunity," I say. The seventeen year-old breaks her composure and laughs out loud.

If you think you missed the sixties and the hippies, go to Cairns. Outside of San Francisco's Haight and the Village in New York, you probably won't find so many flower children in one place. Old ones and new ones, dyed-in-the-wool and corporate escapees, all there and all using hair as a signal of their break with middle-class tradition. The difference is that this generation decorates itself in Rastafarian natty dreads, or the Dreaded Dreads, as my father calls them. Of course, Rasta hair doesn't have much to do with traditional Rastafarian religious beliefs. Now it's all surface: music and the latest mind-altering drugs, the haute couture of whatever marks the wearer's rebellion. Rebellion was the keyword in Cairns, where everyone seemed to be rebelling against something, if nothing more than being in Cairns. I saw more dirty blond dreadlocks in Cairns than I had in the States, except at some folklife festivals where everybody goes ethnic, meaning non-Anglo-Saxon mainstream. In Cairns, the hippies offered the usual market items: tie-dyed T-shirts, homemade candles, leather vests and bead necklaces, and of course, their version of Aboriginal art. I resisted. After all, I owned a dish full of witchetty grubs.

Cairns was a stopping off place, a divided town, crosshatched, really, where one group sometimes fell all over the other to gain right-of-way: tourists and Aussies, hippies and reef divers, Aborigines and shopkeepers, deep sea fishermen and opal miners. Visitors "go native" along the esplanade or head for one of the offshore resorts on Green or Fitzroy islands at the edge of the Great Barrier Reef, where room rates per night averaged more than the annual income of Aboriginals in the outback. Those places are done up like any time, resort time, any beach in the world. Still, if you could afford it, the reef was worth it. I resorted to day trips from Cairns.

I'd promised myself before I left for Australia that I'd see Ayers Rock, dive the Great Barrier Reef, and put my toes in the Tasman Sea. By the time I arrived in Brisbane, I'd added to my must-see list Botany Bay, the Daintree Rain Forest and River, the Kuranda Railroad, and all places leading to Darwin. I made it as far as the Tasman Sea, even stuck my feet in the water, although the wind was wickedly cold that day and the waves were full of raging froth. ("The deep breathing sea of Tasman," Seine Finay had called it in her journal entry.) My attraction to the Tasman Sea probably started when I was a child watching Saturday matinees where the image of Tasmanian devils had been abducted by Disney for cartoons. But the only Tasmanian devils I saw were in the zoo in Sydney, mean looking motor scooters, certainly closer to the mythical spirit chasers of folk stories than they were to the cute little cartoon creatures in Disney's world. So after Ayers Rock, all I had left on my original wish list was the Great Barrier Reef.

I dropped my swag at the luggage lockup in my hotel and headed for the reef. Ten minutes out, and I was beginning to think the barrier wasn't so much the reef as it was all those folks who'd come to see it: the swimmers and boaters and surfers and divers, and on the edge of the horizon and beyond, commercial fishing boats hauling in great nets of fish. The Great Barrier Reef might have been bountiful, but it was never quiet. There was as much activity on the surface of the water as there was below it. I booked a regular tour on one of the eight or so dive ships out of Cairns that gathered each morning at designated spots along the reef, each ship carrying more than one hundred passengers. Not all of them would dive, but most went into the water—some, like me, only once. I went down with a group of Japanese divers, powerful swimmers who seemed more graceful in the water than they had been on deck.

"You did what?" my doctor asked me when I returned home. "You're asthmatic. You're aquaphobic. You've got no business diving."

"I couldn't pass up the opportunity," I told him. "And it was only for twenty minutes." "Too long," he said. "Make that your last dive," he said.

"Ok," I said. "But if you could only see what these eyes have seen," I said, paraphrasing a line from *Do Androids Dream of Electric Sheep?*

My doctor wasn't impressed. You had to be there, I thought, underwater where the world turns upside down and you are foreign to your own planet. The reef was alive, a living, amorphous form that stretched for miles, blue water covering it like a veil. Above the coral, I'd seen fish that looked like tigers, like leopards, like zebras, twisting among rows of pink lace fan coral. Beautiful jellyfish, delicate as veils, undulating with their poisonous invitations. When I turned to get my bearings, I was surrounded by rainbows of fish: red stripes, cornflower blues, and yellow chevrons. I could not remember ever seeing so many fish in one place: butterfly and goat fish, eel fish and fish with bug eyes or those with seemingly no eyes. The water was clotted with divers, but the fish swam by as if they were simply avoiding traffic jams. I even saw fish that looked like hippies, their colors patterned like a tie-dyed shirt. Somewhere in that mob scene, I'd spotted a giant wrasse, or rather, it had spotted me. It came up slowly, its look intense, its face almost too human, one of those "smart-ass" kind of looks, rude and unbending. No wonder I later thought of the wrasse when I met Rosie from Perth. But while I could endure the bus trip, being captive underwater was another matter altogether, at least for an aquaphobic. It was sort of strange to be stared down by a fish, but that's what happened. I followed the bubbles of my own breath to the surface and quit his kingdom, making my ascent through the gaudily dressed crowd of parrot fish, angel fish, and coral trout. Below me, the wrasse flicked its tail and disappeared into the darkness of deep coral waters where it had been spawned.

As splendid as my visit was, I felt my trip to Australia had been cut short because I never reached Darwin. Too many places; too little time. The lack of time is a frequent complaint for most travelers. "I don't have time to go there," they'll say. "I'm running out of time," they'll say. But in Australia, I constantly had the feeling that as I moved forward toward some beginning, my sense of time had fallen into a holding pattern. I'm sure that was partly caused by the landscape. When I was on the desert, time seemed to have slipped into some sort of primordial pattern. From shield shrimp that looked like fossils to the way in which the sun cast the desert in primary colors, I felt as if time had shifted to the dawn of the land itself, the past rearing its head like a frilled lizard basking in an eternal sun. Scraggly opal miners from Coober Pedy and Bush Aboriginals both seemed to have stepped out of the same time warp. The sense of timelessness was trapped on the desert. In an Aboriginal arts and crafts shop, I saw a T-shirt that read: *Three thousand years of dreamtime/Three hundred years of colonialism/*

Thirty years of T-shirts! Time, alas, that final measure. But it was not just on the desert that time seemed to warp back upon itself. In the mangrove forests along the Daintree River, crocodiles with faces full of that "spooky, dreadful-ancient-knowledge look," as Elizabeth Gilbert termed it, floated like logs. In the trees, kookaburras laughed at my amazement.

It doesn't take much to amaze me; my vision is steeped in American sensibilities. Even the sight of kangaroos grazing like cattle in pastures near the Cook Highway made me think I'd found a place where time stood still. Hadn't those kangaroos been there long before the intrusion of the highway? This didn't happen in the city. The mystery of time seemed to fade in the tangle of cars, buses, and high-rises. In places like Sydney, Brisbane, and Melborne, everything was in present tense and urgent. Urban landscapes seemed to be outside of the notion that time was fluid. (Anyway, I've always held to the idea that office buildings are intolerant of history.) But outside of the city, I felt as if I could see where I'd been while I was moving away from that place. Like traveling on the train between Cairns and Kuranda: when I leaned out of the window to take a picture, the end of the train, still snaking across the three-mile trestle, was curving away from me while the front section where I was seated plunged into a tunnel. For one dizzying moment, it was as if I had turned away from myself, as if I had glimpsed a place of spirituality that I couldn't give a name to—as if I was moving forward while parts of me still lived in the past. That was as near as I came to understanding anything about dreamtime, the sense of coming out of myself to understand what moved me forward. Of course, it was my own naive view of dreamtime, and perhaps as close as I would get, being outside of Aboriginal culture. "Do you think these blokes really have visions?" a man seated next to me asked at the end of a Tjapukai Dance Theatre performance depicting dreamtime stories. "I mean, what do they know that we don't know?" he asked. "I don't have enough time to explain it," I told him.

I've done a lot of traveling alone. Sometimes on purpose, sometimes inadvertently. For a black woman, traveling alone can be awakening, a way of defining myself that is not dependent on the American system of color coding. I know the traps are out there, the biases set for race, religion, and gender, but skin color is no longer an absolute measure on that thin line between black and white. There are shades of difference dependent on history, ancestry, and boundaries of land. Perhaps I am the traveler G. K. Chesterton referred to when he wrote: "The more I see of the world . . . the more I come back with increased conviction to those places where I was born . . . narrowing my circles like a bird going back to a nest." In Australia on the Red Desert, I started to believe that was what I was looking for—the daughter come home, the evolution of me. These memoirs are filled with the detours, the half steps and circuitous routes I've taken, where strangers became neighbors, where towns blended into maps of ruins, and fellow travelers remained surly in every language. A world of enchanted shores that beckoned me with its forests full of primal wonder, its seas connecting continents from the South Pole to the equator, its languages singing of vowels, its songs filled with the warnings of a hundred ancestors.

On my flight home from Egypt two years before my trip to Australia, I received the usual customs declaration slip asking me to list my purchases. I made my check-and-balance listing and was ready to complete the declaration when I noticed the directive above the signature line. *Sing on the reverse side after you read warning.* I rang for the cabin attendant. "What song shall I try?" I asked, pointing to the customs form. She frowned. "There must be some mistake," she said, and handed me another one. There was no mistake. They both held the same command: *Sing,* they ordered. *Sing.* "Perhaps it is a new trend," I told her, and kept the extra slip. Why not sing on your way home, I thought. That's what the folks from Fiji had done, and the ones from Yugoslavia. As the planes neared home, they indeed began to sing. Home was the heart, the place of birth, the starting point. Home, where I learn how to survive. Where I dream of trips I've yet to take and identify outgoing airplanes by the insignias on their tailfins. I return home to replenish my friendships, to touch base with my family and snuggle down in my own bed, but the sound of jets streaking overhead fills me with longing. There's something out there beckoning me—I don't know what; I don't know where. But I can hardly wait for my ticket to get there. And I don't plan to stop until I find it.

BIBLIOGRAPHY

Alexander, Ziggi, and Audrey Dewjee. "Editor's Introduction." *Wonderful Adventures of Mrs. Seacole in Many Lands.* Bristol: Falling Wall Press, 1984.

Andrews, William L. *Sisters of the Spirit: Three Black Women's Autobiographies of the Nineteenth Century.* Bloomington: Indiana University Press, 1986.

———. "Annotated Bibliography." In *To Tell a Free Story.* Chicago: University of Chicago Press, 1986.

Andrews, William L., Frances Smith Foster, and Trudier Harris, eds. *Oxford Companion to African American Literature.* New York: Oxford University Press, 1997.

Baldwin, James. "Encounter on the Seine." In *Notes of a Native Son.* Boston: Beacon Press, 1955.

Bambara, Toni Cade, ed. *The Black Woman.* New York: New American Library, 1970.

———. *Gorilla My Love.* New York: Vintage, 1972.

———. *The Salt-Eaters.* New York: Vintage, 1980.

———. *The Sea Birds Are Still Alive.* New York: Vintage, 1982.

———. *Deep Sightings and Rescue Missions: Fiction, Essays, and Conversations.* Edited and with a preface by Toni Morrison. New York: Pantheon, 1996.

———. "How She Got Her Name." In *Deep Sightings and Rescue Missions.* New York: Random House, 1996.

Barr, Alwyn. *Black Texans: A History of African Americans in Texas.* Norman: University of Oklahoma Press, 1996.

Bell, Howard H. "Introduction." In *Search for a Place: Black Separatism and Africa, 1860.* M. R. Delany and Robert Campbell. Ann Arbor: University of Michigan Press, 1969.

Bennett, Gwendolyn. Unpublished travel diary of 1925. Manuscripts, Archives and Rare Books Division, Schomburg Center for Research in Black Culture, The New York Public Library.

Berghahn, Marion. *Images of Africa in Black American Literature.* Totowa, N.J.: Rowman & Littlefield, 1977.

Blakely, Allison. *Russia and the Negro: Blacks in Russian History and Thought.* Washington, D.C.: Howard University Press, 1986.

Blyden, Edward Wilmot. *From West Africa to Palestine.* Freetown, Sierra Leone: T. J. Sawyer, 1873.

Bolster, W. Jeffrey. "Every Inch a Man: Gender in the Lives of African American Seamen, 1800–1860." In *Iron Men, Wooden Women: Gender and Seafaring in the Atlantic World, 1700–1920.* Edited by Margaret S. Creighton and Lisa Norling. Baltimore, Md.: Johns Hopkins University Press, 1996.

———. *Black Jacks: African American Seamen in the Age of Sail*. Cambridge: Harvard University Press, 1997.

Bonner, T. D., ed. *The Life and Adventures of James P. Beckwourth* New York: Harper & Bros, 1856.

Boone, Sylvia Ardyn. *Radiance From the Waters: Ideals of Feminine Beauty in Mende Art*. New Haven, Conn.: Yale University Press, 1986.

———. *West African Travels*. New York: Random House, 1972.

Brooks, Gwendolyn. *Report from Part One*. Detroit: Broadside Press, 1972.

Brown, Sharon Rogers. *American Travel Narratives as a Literary Genre from 1542–1832: The Art of A Perpetual Journey*. Lewiston, N.Y.: Edwin Mellen Press, 1993.

Brown, William Wells. *The American Fugitive in Europe: Sketches of Places and People Abroad*. Boston: John P. Jewett, 1855.

Bunche, Ralph. *An African American in South Africa: The Travel Notes of Ralph J. Bunche, 28 September 1937–1 January 1938*. Edited by Robert R. Edgar. Athens: Ohio University Press, 1992.

Campbell, James. *Talking at the Gates: A Life of James Baldwin*. New York: Viking, 1991.

Campbell, Robert. *A Pilgrimage to My Motherland: An Account of a Journey among the Egbas and Yorubas of Central Africa, 1855–60*. New York: Thomas Hamilton, 1861.

Carter, Vincent. *The Bern Book: A Record of a Voyage of the Mind*. New York: John Day, 1970.

Cohn, Michael, and Michael K. Platz. *Black Men of the Sea*. New York: Dodd, Mead, 1978.

Coppin, Fanny Jackson. *Reminiscences of School Life, and Hints on Teaching*. Philadelphia: AME Books, 1913.

Crowder, Michael. *A Short History of Nigeria*. New York: Frederick A. Prager, 1962.

Crummell, Alexander. "The Relations and Duties of Free Colored Men in America to Africa." In *The Future of Africa, Being Addresses, Sermons, etc. Delivered in the Republic of Liberia by Rev. Alexander Crummell*. New York: Negro University Press, 1969.

Cuffe, Paul. *A Brief Account of the Settlement and Present Situation of the Colony of Sierra Leone*. New York: Samuel Wood, 1812.

Cullen, Countee. "Countee Cullen on French Courtesy." *The Crisis* 36, no. 6 (June 1929): 193–94.

Davis, Angela. *Angela Davis: An Autobiography*. New York: Random House, 1974.

Davis, Arthur P. et al., eds. *Selected African American Writing from 1760 to 1910*. New York: Bantam Books, 1991.

Dean, Harry. *The Pedro Gorino: The Adventures of a Negro Sea Captain in Africa, and on the Seven Seas in His Attempts to Found an Ethiopian Empire*. Boston and New York: Houghton Mifflin, 1929.

Dean, Harry, with Sterling North. *Umbala: The Adventures of a Negro Sea Captain*. London: Pluto Press, 1989.

Delany, Martin R. *Official Report of the Niger Valley Exploring Party*. New York: Thomas Hamilton, 1861.

Detter, Thomas. *Nellie Brown, or The Jealous Wife with Other Sketches*. Lincoln and London: University of Nebraska Press, 1996.

Dodson, Jualynne E. "Introduction." In *An Autobiography: The Story of the Lord's Dealings with Mrs. Amanda Smith, the Colored Evangelist.* New York: Oxford/Schomburg Edition Library, 1988.

Du Bois, W. E. B. "Pan African Portugal." *The Crisis* 27, no. 4 (February 1924): 170.

————. "Sketches from Abroad: Le Grand Voyage." *The Crisis* 27, no. 5 (March 1924): 203–5.

————. "Little Portraits of Africa." *The Crisis* 27, no. 6 (1924): 273–74.

Dunham, Katherine. *Island Possessed.* New York: Doubleday, 1969.

Elaw, Zilpha. *Memoirs of the Life, Religious Experience, Ministerial Travels and Labours of Mrs. Zilpha Elaw.* London, 1846.

Ehrenreich, Barbara, and Deidre English. *Witches, Midwives and Nurses: A History of Women Healers.* Old Westbury, N.Y.: Feminist Press, 1973.

Fabre, Michel. *Black American Writing in France, 1840–1980 from Harlem to Paris.* Urbana and Chicago: University of Illinois Press, 1991.

Fauset, Jessie. "Dark Algiers the White." *The Crisis* 29–30, nos. 6–7 (April–May 1925): 16–22, 255–58.

————. "Yarrow Revisited." *The Crisis* (January 1925).

Fish, Cheryl J. "Voices of Restless (Dis)Continuity: The Significance of Travel for Black Women in the Ante-bellum Americas." *Women's Studies* 26, no. 5 (summer 1997): 475–95.

————. "Going Mobile: The Body at Work in Black and White Women's Travel Narratives, 1841–1857." Ph.D. diss., The Graduate School, City University of New York, 1996.

Foner, Philip S. *History of Black Americans from Africa to the Emergence of the Cotton Kingdom.* Westport, Conn.: Greenwood Press, 1975.

Foster, Frances Smith. Introduction to *Nellie Brown, or the Jealous Wife with Other Sketches,* by Thomas Detter. Lincoln and London: University of Nebraska Press, 1996.

Fryer, Peter. *Staying Power: The History of Black People in Britain.* London: Pluto Press, 1984.

Gibbs, C. R. *Black Explorers.* Silver Spring, Md.: Three Dimensional Publishing, 1992.

Gilroy, Paul. *The Black Atlantic: Modernity and Double Consciousness.* Cambridge: Harvard University Press, 1993.

Grant, Jacquelyn. "Black Women and the Church." In *All the Women Are White, All the Blacks Are Men, but Some of Us Were Brave.* Edited by Gloria T. Hull et al. Old Westbury, N.Y.: The Feminist Press, 1982.

Griffin, Farah Jasmine. *"Who Set You Flowin'?": The African American Migration Narrative.* New York: Oxford University Press, 1995.

Gruesser, John C. "Afro-American Travel Literature and Africanist Discourse." *Black American Literature Forum* 24, no. 1 (spring 1990): 5–20.

Haley, Shelley P. "Introduction." In *Fanny Jackson Coppin: Reminiscences of School Life, and Hints on Teaching.* New York: G. K. Hall, 1995.

Harris, Eddy L. *Native Stranger: A Black American's Journey into the Heart of Africa.* New York: Simon & Schuster, 1992.

Harris, Sheldon H. *Paul Cuffe: Black American and the African Return.* New York: Simon & Schuster, 1972.

Haywood, Harry. *Black Bolshevik: An Autobiography of an Afro-American Communist.* Chicago: Liberator Press, 1978.

Henson, Matthew A. *A Negro Explorer at the North Pole.* New York: Frederick A. Stokes, 1912.

Hine, Darlene Clark, ed. *Black Women in America: An Historical Encyclopedia.* New York: Carlson Publishing, 1993.

Hughes, Langston. "Going South in Russia." *The Crisis* 41, no. 6 (June 1934): 162–163.

————. "Love in Mexico." *Opportunity* 18, no. 4 (April 1940): 107.

Isichei, Elizabeth. *A History of Nigeria.* New York: Frederick A. Praeger, 1962.

Jacobs, Sylvia. "The Historical Role of Afro-Americans in American Missionary Efforts in Africa." In *Black Americans and The Missionary Movement in Africa.* Edited by Sylvia M. Jacobs. Westport, Conn.: Greenwood Press, 1982.

Jefferson, Paul, ed. *The Travels of William Wells Brown including Narrative of William Wells Brown, a Fugitive Slave and the American Fugitive in Europe: Sketches of Places and People Abroad.* New York: Markus Wiener, 1991.

Jordan, June. "Report from the Bahamas." In *Moving Towards Home: Political Essays.* London: Virago Press, 1989.

Katz, William Loren. Introduction to *The Life and Adventures of Nat Love, Better Known in Cattle Country as "Deadwood Dick,"* by Nat Love. New York: Arno Press and New York Times, 1968.

King, Martin Luther, Jr. "My Trip to the Land of Gandhi." *Ebony.* July 1959, 84–92.

Lacy, Leslie Alexander. *The Rise and Fall of the Proper Negro.* New York: Simon & Schuster, 1970.

Ladd, Florence Cawthorne. "Excerpts from a Dakar Diary." *Sage* 2, no. 1 (spring 1985): 55–56.

Lee, Andrea. *Russian Journals.* New York: Random House, 1981.

Lee, Elaine, ed. *Go Girl: The Black Woman's Book of Travel and Adventure.* Portland, Ore.: The Eighth Mountain Press, 1997.

Leed, Eric J. *The Mind of the Traveller from Gilgamesh to Global Tourism.* New York: Basic Books, 1991.

Logan, Rayford, and Michael R. Winston, eds. *Dictionary of American Negro Biography.* New York: Norton, 1982.

Lorde, Audre. "Grenada Revisited" and "Notes from a Trip to Russia." In *Sister Outsider: Essays and Speeches.* Trumansburg, N.Y.: The Crossing Press, 1984.

Love, Nat. *The Life and Adventures of Nat Love, Better Known in Cattle Country as "Deadwood Dick."* New York: Arno Press, 1907.

Lynch, Hollis R., ed. "Introduction." In *Selected Letters of Edward Wilmot Blyden.* Millwood, N.Y.: KTO Press.

Matthews, John, ed. *The World Atlas of Divination.* London: Headline, 1992.

McElroy, Colleen. "No Stops until Darwin." In *A Long Way from St. Louie.* Minneapolis: Coffee House Press, 1997.

McKay, Claude. "Soviet Russia and the Negro." Parts 1 and 2. *The Crisis* 27, no. 2 (June 1923); 27, no. 3 (January 1924): 61–65, 114–18.

Morris, Mary, with Larry O'Connor. *The Virago Book of Women Travellers.* London: Virago, 1996.

Paul, Thomas. "Letter to the Editor." *Columbian Sentinel*, 3 July 1824. In *Early Negro Writings, 1760–1837*. Edited by Dorothy Porter. Boston: Beacon Press, 1971.

Peterson, Carla L. *"Doers of the Word": African American Women Speakers and Writers in the North, 1830–1880*. New York: Oxford University Press, 1995.

Peterson, Daniel H. *The Looking Glass: Being a True Report and Narrative of the Life, Travels and Labors of the Rev. Daniel H. Peterson*. New York: Wright, 1854.

Porter, Dorothy. *Early Negro Writings, 1760–1837*. Boston: Beacon Press, 1971.

Pratt, Mary Louise. *Imperial Eyes: Travel Writing and Transculturation*. New York: Routledge, 1992.

Prince, Nancy. *A Narrative of the Life and Travels of Mrs. Nancy Prince*. 1853. Reprint, New York: Oxford/Schomburg Library, 1988.

Raboteau, Albert J. *A Fire in the Bones: Reflections of African-American Religious History*. Boston: Beacon Press, 1995.

Rigsby, Gregory. *Alexander Crummell: Pioneer in Nineteenth Century Pan-African Thought*. Westport, Conn.: Greenwood Press, 1987.

Robinson, Aubrie. "Letter to Hometown: A Request from East Indies." *Opportunity* 23, no. 1 (winter 1945): 48–49.

Rowan, Carl T. *The Pitiful and the Proud*. New York: Random House, 1956.

Salem, Dorothy C., ed. *African American Women: A Biographical Dictionary*. New York: Garland Press, 1993.

Saltzman, Jack et al. *Encyclopedia of African American Culture and History*. New York: McMillan Library Reference, 1996.

Schomburg, Arthur. "My Trip to Cuba in Quest of Negro Books." *Opportunity* 11, no. 2 (February 1933): 48.

Scott, Hazel. "What Paris Means to Me." *Negro Digest*, November 1961.

Seacole, Mary. *Wonderful Adventures of Mrs. Seacole in Many Lands*. 1857. Reprint, New York: Oxford/Schomburg Library, 1988.

Shange, Ntozake. *If I Can Cook/You Know God Can*. Boston: Beacon Press, 1998.

Singh, Amrit. Unpaged introduction to Richard Wright, *Black Power: A Record of Reactions in a Land of Pathos*. New York: Harper & Bros, 1954.

Shick, Tom W. *Behold the Promised Land: A History of African American Settler Society in Nineteenth Century Liberia*. Baltimore, Md.: Johns Hopkins University Press, 1977.

Smith, Amanda Berry. *An Autobiography: The Story of the Lord's Dealings with Mrs. Amanda Smith, the Colored Evangelist*. 1893. Reprint, New York: Oxford/Schomburg Library, 1988.

Stovall, Tyler. *Paris Noir: African Americans in the City of Lights*. Boston: Houghton Mifflin, 1996.

Stowe, William W. *Going Abroad: European Travel in Nineteenth Century American Culture*. Princeton, N.J.: Princeton University Press.

Talalay, Kathryn. *Composition in Black and White: The Life of Phillippa Schuyler*. New York: Oxford University Press, 1995.

Thurman, Sue Bailey. "How Far from Here to Mexico?" *The Crisis* 42, no. 9 (September 1935): 267–74.

Ullman, Victor. *Martin R. Delany: The Beginnings of Black Nationalism*. Boston: Beacon Press, 1971.

Wall, Cheryl. *Women of the Harlem Renaissance.* Bloomington: Indiana University Press, 1995.

Washington, Booker T. *The Man Farthest Down.* New York: Doubleday, 1912.

Williams, Cheryl. "Conceived in Transit, Delivered in Passage: Travel and Identity in African American Women's Literature." Ph.D. diss., University of Pennsylvania.

Williams, Walter L. *Black Americans and the Evangelization of Africa, 1877–1900.* Madison: University of Wisconsin Press, 1982.

Woodson, Carter G., ed. *Negro Orators and Their Orations.* New York: Russell & Russell, 1969.

Wright, Richard. *Black Power: A Record of Reactions in a Land of Pathos.* New York: Harper & Bros, 1954.

ACKNOWLEDGMENTS

The editors would like to thank the following people and acknowledge the assistance we received from librarians and staff at a number of institutions:

Deborah Chasman and Tisha Hooks at Beacon Press for their patience; Carla Peterson for suggesting the idea for this collection; the librarians and curators of the Photographs and Prints Division of the Schomburg Center for Research in Black Culture; the New York Public Library, and the Library Company of Philadelphia, The University of Pennsylvania; the interlibrary loan staff at Nassau Community College; and student research assistants Salamisha Tillet, Patricia Hopkins, Felicia Gordon, and Nicole Childers.

We also wish to thank all the friends and colleagues who offered us valuable suggestions. Among these, Jerry Watts, Paula Giddings, Robin Kelley, and Florence Ladd were especially helpful.

CREDITS

Gwendolyn Bennett. Selections from an unpublished Travel Diary of 1925. Manuscripts, Archives, and Rare Books Division, Schomburg Center for Research in Black Culture, The New York Public Library, Astor, Lenox and Tilden Foundation.

Sylvia Ardyn Boone, "Alpha," from *West African Travels*, copyright 1974 by Sylvia Ardyn Boone. Reprinted by permission of Random House, Inc.

Excerpts from Gwendolyn Brooks, *Report From Part One*, reprinted with permission from Broadside Press, Detroit, MI.

Excerpt from Toni Cade Bambara, reprinted with permission from The Hatch-Billops Collection, New York, NY 10012.

Excerpts from Ralph Bunche. *An African American in South Africa: The Travel Notes of Ralph Bunche*, reprinted by permission from University of Ohio Press, Athens, Ohio.

Paul Cuffe. *A Brief Account of the Settlement and Present Situation of the Colony of Sierra Leone*, Boston: Beacon Press, 1971.

Countee Cullen. "Countee Cullen on French Courtesy," p. 193 Vol. 36, No. 6 June 1929, reprinted by permission of The Crisis Publishing Company.

Thomas Detter. *Nellie Brown, or The Jealous Wife With Other Sketches*. Lincoln and London: University of Nebraska Press, 1996.

W. E. B. Du Bois. Excerpts from: "Pan Africa Portugal," p. 170 Vol. 27, No. 4 Feb. 1924; "Sketches from Abroad: Le Grand Voyage," 203 Vol. 27, No. 5 March 1924; "Little Portraits of Africa," 273 Vol. 27, No. 6 1924, reprinted by permission of The Crisis Publishing Company.

From *Island Possessed* by Katherine Dunham. Copyright © 1969 by Katherine Dunham. Used by permission of Doubleday, a division of Bantam Doubleday Dell Publishing Group, Inc.

Jessie Redmon Fauset. "Dark Algiers on the White," p. 255, Vol. 29, No. 6., April 1925. Cont. pg. 16 Vol. 30, No. 1, May 1925; Yarrow Revisited, reprinted by permission of The Crisis Publishing Company.

Excerpts from Harry Haywood. *Black Bolshevik*. Reprinted by permission of Lake View Press: Chicago.

Langston Hughes. "Going South in Russia," p. 157, Vol. 41, No. 6 June 1934, reprinted by permission of The Crisis Publishing Company.

Langston Hughes. "Love in Mexico" from *Opportunity* Vol. 18, no. 4, pg. 107, April 1940, reprinted by permission of The National Urban League.

Martin Luther King, Jr. "My Trip to the Land of Gandhi," reprinted by arrangement with The Heirs to the Estate of Martin Luther King, Jr., c/o Writers House, Inc. as agent for the proprietor.

Alexander Lacy. Excerpt from *The Rise and Fall of the Proper Negro*, copyright 1970 Leslie Alexander Lacy, reprinted by permission of Simon & Schuster.

Florence Cawthorne Ladd. "Excerpts from a Dakar Diary" *Sage* Vol. II, No. 1 Spring, 1985, reprinted by permission of Sage Women's Educational Press, Inc.

Audre Lorde. "Notes from a Trip to Russia" from *Sister Outsider: Essays and Speeches by Audre Lorde*, copyright 1984, reprinted by permission of The Crossing Press, Inc.

Audre Lorde. "Grenada Revisited" from *Sister Outsider: Essays and Speeches by Audre Lorde*, copyright 1984, reprinted by permission of The Crossing Press, Inc.

Colleen McElroy. Excerpt from "No Stops Until Darwin," from *A Long Way From St. Louis*, reprinted by permission of Coffee House Press, 1997.

Claude McKay. Soviet Russia and the Negro, p. 61. The Crisis Vol. 27, no. 2, June 1923; Cont. page 114 Vol. 27 No. 3, January 1924, reprinted by permission of The Crisis Publishing Company.

Sterling North and Harry Dean. *Umbala: The Adventures of a Negro Sea Captain.*

Thomas Paul. "Letter," *Columbian Sentinel*, July 3, 1824. In Dorothy Porter, *Early Negro Writings, 1760–1837*. Boston: Beacon Press, 1971.

Aubrie Robinson. "Letter to Hometown: A Request from East Indies," from *Opportunity* Vol. 23, no. 1, p. 48, Winter 1945, reprinted by permission of the National Urban League.

Arthur Schomburg. "My Trip to Cuba in Quest of Negro Books" from *Opportunity* Vol. 11 no. 2, p. 48, Feb. 1933, reprinted by permission of The National Urban League.

Mary Seacole. *Wonderful Adventures or Mrs. Seacole in Many Lands*, New York: Oxford/Schomburg edition, 1988. [reprint of 1893 edition]

Sue Bailey Thurman. "How Far from Here to Mexico," Vol. 42, No. 9, Sept. 1935, reprinted by permission of The Crisis Publishing Company.

Richard Wright. Excerpts from *Black Power*, copyright 1954 by Harper & Brothers. Reprinted by permission of John Hawkins and Associates, Inc.

Printed in the United States
By Bookmasters